The Gospel

and

Frontier Peoples

PUBLISHER'S NOTE: In a sense the production of this book involved a bit of the pioneering and crossing of frontiers with which the conference itself was concerned.

In the first place you would not have a compact, printed report in your hands at all if the rather drastic decision had not been made to sidestep many of the usual decencies and niceties of modern publishing.

Once over that hurdle the people asked to prepare papers were sent the specifications for a format which could economically be photographed without further typing or modification. This is thus a case where not the publisher but the various authors themselves are solely responsible for what you see on these pages! This also explains the variety of type faces throughout the book. This does not apply to the long section provided by David Barrett--the format of his report required complete recasting which he did not have a chance to proof-read.

But it only takes one thing to hold up the schedule of a book. The unexpected delay resulted from the ticklish task of converting the beautiful, multicolored original map of Africa--in the same report mentioned--so that its colored distinctions could be communicated in black and white. We lost more than a month with this problem.

The novelty of production reflects the novelty of the conference. More than that: it is altogether fitting that this book should appear at a very low price, produced quite willingly under abnormal limitations. How else could it appropriately represent the tragic limitations of interest and support which characterize the cause with which the Consultation was concerned?

THE GOSPEL
AND
FRONTIER PEOPLES

A Report of a Consultation
December 1972

Edited by R. PIERCE BEAVER

William Carey Library

533 HERMOSA STREET • SOUTH PASADENA, CALIF. 91030 •

International Standard Book Number   0-87808-124-0
Library of Congress Catalog Number   73-78228

Published by the William Carey Library
533 Hermosa Street
South Pasadena, Calif. 91030
Telephone 213-799-4559

PRINTED IN THE UNITED STATES OF AMERICA

CONTENTS

INTRODUCTION: THE ORIGIN, DEVELOPMENT, PROGRAM, CHARACTER, AND RESULT OF THE CONSULTATION

R. Pierce Beaver

ORIGIN AND DEVELOPMENT

The overseas missionary enterprise of the North American boards and societies gradually moved in general from an evangelistic and church-nurturing endeavor to support of, and cooperation with, national indigenous churches which are the fruit of earlier mission action. National churches have been recognized as autonomous and responsible in their own areas, and they have progressively been rising to the fulfillment of that responsibility. Churches in Asia, Africa, and other "third world" areas have tended to claim, and American and European churches to agree, that all evangelistic efforts anywhere within their national boundaries should be launched and controlled by them, regardless of initiative and resources. The result of following such a policy for the last twenty years has been assignment of Western personnel to institutional and denominational administrative and service agencies. Increasingly the national churches now provide their own personnel, and the financial stringency in America causes the boards further to reduce their overseas representatives. The lack of visible evangelistic action and the diminution of the missionary force have been factors which are responsible for the decline of interest in, and support of, world mission, including mission to America.

However, the North American mission boards have not been excluded from primary evangelism to the degree that pastors and laymen believe, and many agencies are eager to find opportunities for new ventures in communication of the faith. A surprising number are still engaged in evangelism and church nurture among tribal peoples in remote places. The Consultation on Frontier Missions emerged rather spontaneously out of genuine existing concern.

The executive secretary of one of the oldest Protestant mission agencies, the Rt. Rev. Edwin W. Kortz of the Board of Foreign Missions of the Moravian Church in America, suggested to Dr. Randolph Nugent, then associate general secretary of the National Council of Churches of Christ in the U. S. A. and chief executive officer of the Division of Overseas Ministries, that some attention be given to frontier missions among tribal peoples. The Bishop commented that much attention was regularly given to problems of church and evangelism and other ministries with respect to urban industrial situations but very little about frontier missions. Help with problems

1

in that category of mission work, beginning with the sharing of experience, was highly desirable. Dr. Nugent, believing that this concern
touched the central function of the church and the chief business of
the D. O. M., requested that a survey be made by R. Pierce Beaver,
then serving as a research consultant to the D. O. M. and being the
professor emertius of Missions in the Divinity School of the University of Chicago.

A canvass was made of all American mission boards and societies, not
just of participants in the Division of Overseas Ministries, excepting those confined to work in Europe, since information and illumina-
tion were needed from all quarters. Questions asked were: the
present extent of involvement in frontier missions, any interest in
new ventures in primary evangelism, and whether a consultation on the
subject would be welcome. Agencies defined or interpreted the term
"frontier missions" in various ways, and none of the varients were
challenged. There was a response of more than 90%. Only one board
disclaimed any interest and concern. A number reported that they had
currently no such involvement and under present conditions did not
expect to undertake new ventures. But there was across the board
participation beyond all expectation. Extensive activity in frontier
missions was, as anticipated, reported by those agencies which had
long given high priority to remote and tribal peoples, such as the
New Tribes Mission, the Christian and Missionary Alliance, the Sudan
Interior Mission, and the Lutheran Church -- Missouri Synod with its
large mission in Papua/New Guinea. What was surprising to many who
had been sceptical about the project was the extent of current commitment by many old boards aligned with the D. O. M., including the
boards of the American Lutheran Church, the Lutheran Church in
America, the United Methodist Church, and the United Presbyterian
Church in the U. S. A.   Even the oldest of all American agencies,
the United Church Board for World Ministries (formerly the A. B. C.
F. M.) assigns personnel to primary evangelism through national
churches. There was evident a desire for pooling of experience and
common sharing of insights.

Even more surprising to some persons drawn into the discussion was
the avowal of concern by administrators of boards to find new opportunities for engagement in primary evangelism and their readiness to
consider the possibility of a frontier mission. A consultation was
a particularly welcome proposal to such agencies.

Dr. Nugent authorized Mr. Beaver to initiate planning.

                                PLANNING

A small *ad hoc* committee was gathered. It was enlarged and made the
Planning Committee, and when the Consultation was held it became the

Steering Committee. The membership at the time of the planning session was: the Rt. Rev. Edwin W. Kortz (Moravian), Dr. Rodney A. Sundberg (Commission on Ecumenical Mission and Relations, the United Presbyterian Church in the U. S. A.), the Rev. Alfred C. Krass (United Church Board for World Ministries), Dr. G. Linwood Barney (Jaffray School of Missions, Nyack, and Christian and Missionary Alliance), Dr. John E. Buteyn (Reformed Church in America), Dr. Alan R. Tippett (School of World Mission, Fuller Theological Seminary), Mrs. Elizabeth S. Muldrow (missionary to Ethiopia, COEMAR, UPCUSA), the Rev. Thomas Tunney, C. S. Sp. (Holy Ghost Fathers, Tanzania), the Rev. Karl A. Stotik (Papua/New Guinea, Lutheran Church--Missouri Synod), the Rev. Milton Robinson (Bolivia, United Methodist), Dr. Isaac Bivens (United Methodist), Dr. Charles R. Taber (United Bible Societies, Ghana, and editor, *Practical Anthropology*), Dr. George M. Cowan (president, Wycliffe Bible Translators), Dr. Eugene L. Smith (World Council of Churches), the Rev. Robert J. Flinn, S. V. D. (Chicago Cluster of Theological Schools), and R. Pierce Beaver, who was designated chairman. Dr. Cowan could not continue as he went abroad, and Dr. Smith could not attend further meetings. Two missionaries returned to their posts: Rev. Karl Stotik to Papua and Father Tunney to Tanzania, but Dr. Eugene Hillman, C. S. Sp., who had earlier been engaged on the West Coast was able to enter into the activities of the Committee by the end of the summer. Six or eight of the societies most heavily engaged in frontier missions were asked to send representatives, but did not, and the loss of their knowledge and experience is still regreted.

Support of the consultation has proved to be excellent, but much of it was slow in coming, and the chairman/executive secretary could not make some decisions with regard to invitations until it was too late to bring persons from a distance. The large amount of financial contributions demonstrates the degree of interest and commitment among the boards. Contributions to the end of December amounted to $21,275 and pledges to be paid early in 1973 amount to an additional $1,500. The agencies which made gifts are: United Church Board for World Ministries, Medical Mission Sisters, COEMAR - United Presbyterian Church, U. S. A., World Division of the United Methodist Church, Passionist Missionaries, Society of the Divine Word, American Lutheran Church, Church of the Brethren, Lutheran Church in America, Christian Church, Moravian Church, Reformed Church in America, Evangelical Covenant Church, Mennonite Board of Missions (Elkhart), American Baptist Foreign Mission Society, Presbyterian Church in the U. S., and the Lutheran Church -- Missouri Synod. The Chicago Cluster of Theological Schools gave the services of the Coordinator, Father Flinn, who devoted the larger part of his time for many weeks. The Wycliffe Bible Translators, Inc., and the Association for the Final Advance of Scripture Translation (F. A. S. T.) gave much expert and valuable service. World Vision International and the Organizing Committee for the coming World Congress of Evangelism (Bishop

Jack Dain, chairman) paid the expenses of three overseas graduate
students in the School of World Mission at Fuller Theological Seminary. Father Flinn and his associates carried through the preparation
of material, distribution, registration, and all local matters of
logistics at a minimum cost. Moreover, it was arranged to hold the
Consultation at the Shoreland Hotel on the doorstep of the Cluster in
adequate, but modest circumstance and at the lowest possible cost to
the participants and their boards and societies. The management of
the Hotel was most courteous and helpful.

MISSIONARY FRONTIERS AND FRONTIER MISSIONS

All sorts of frontiers of mission -- most of them of urgent importance -- began to clamor for attention as soon as discussion began,
and there was some fear that the planners might be thought to be
unaware of these and to think of far places and tribal peoples as
the only frontiers. There is the frontier of the encounter with
other faiths and that of witness to the seemingly impervious Muslim
and Buddhist societies. There is the realm of encounter with the
independent, separatist churches in Africa and elsewhere. There are
peoples of subcultures in every land around the world to whom little
witness and ministry are being offered. By-passed peoples, the
hordes of displaced political refugees, war victims in many lands,
the depersonalized masses of the great cities all demand attention
as genuine frontiers where new principles, strategy, and tactics are
demanded for effective communication of the faith. One consultation
can deal in a limited way with only one subject, and it is desirable
that other study projects and conferences deal with those subjects
just mentioned. It was definite concern about tribal peoples most
often in remote places that called forth this project, and it was
resolved to restrict concern to such frontier missions.

Frontier tribal societies are in most places under tremendous pressure from encroaching, land-grabbing settlers, economic aggression,
and governmental policies of assimilation. Isolation is ending, and
alien forces are causing disintegration of cultures. Change is
inevitable, but a people should be permitted to determine the direction and extent of change. Even where there is a policy of "protection" and "self-determination," it seldom happens that the
integrity of an ethnic minority's genius is honored in more than
words.

Expansion of Christianity since the fifteenth century has been
chiefly out of Europe, North America, and the Commonwealth countries
which have a predominantly British population. Mission action during this period has been involved in political and cultural imperialism and ecclesiastical colonialism. This was sometimes true in
the long earlier history of missions, but more often peoples found

in the Christian faith a power that effected cohesion and unity,
transformation without destruction of culture, and strength to endure
in adversity. There is now a general understanding that the gospel
may not be identified with any nation or culture, although it must be
given indigenous cultural expression. It is recognized that the
church must be THE CHURCH as soon as formed and that it should have
freedom under the Holy Spirit to develop in its own way under the
judgment of the gospel. Extreme sensitivity to these issues is a
prime requirement of all Christians who would enter upon primary
evangelism.

However, just when there is penitence for past mistakes and a resolve
to proceed according to the new light, anthropologists and national
politicians increase their attacks on missionaries for daring to
interfere in the life of tribal peoples. The so-called "Barbados
Declaration" is evidence. (See this document in the Appendix.) Some
national governments exclude not only expatriate missionaries but
also national evangelists and service ministers from "sensitive
areas." They want to seal them off from foreign influences and to
keep them as preserves for future activity by the dominant religion
of the country. Christian concern for justice, compassion for people
forced to painful change, and the constant compulsion to introduce
the Lord Jesus Christ to all men makes responsible action by churches
towards frontier tribal societies a genuine and urgent challenge and
a ministry of high priority. How can primary evangelism and church
development be fostered without falling into the old errors and with
the goodwill, or at least the neutrality, of government?

                          QUESTIONS FOR DISCUSSION

Questions which emerged for discussion are:

Who and where are the presently unevangelized peoples? How can
accurate, thoroughly reliable information be secured?

What light is to be found from missionary experience, both of a
positive and a negative kind, from present and past evangelistic
endeavors among tribal peoples?

Circumstances demand changes in old methods of discharging the missionary mandate. Many Christians even think it to be outmoded and
no longer binding. How is the missionary mandate to be understood
in the twentieth century, especially with respect to frontier
tribal peoples?

How is the integrity of a people's genius to be honored and con-
served, on the one hand, and on the other effectively employed (and
not exploited) in evangelism and church development? Are there

fundamental principles governing the interrelation and interaction of faith and culture?

How do evangelistic agents who first communicate the faith set free a new Christian community to be led by the Holy Spirit? How then do they impart the essential gospel and the fellowship of the universal church? Is tension between the two inevitable? Can it be avoided? If tension develops, how is it resolved?

Who shoul. take responsibility for primary evangelism? What can be done actually in view of government policies, the sensitivity of national churches, international relations, rapidly changing social and economic conditions, and other current factors? How do we do what can be done? How share experiences henceforth.

PROGRAM AND GOALS

The Committee determined that the Consultation would be truly a consultation, -- a time of sharing of information supported by exper- ience, knowledge, and insights of the participants. It would be unofficial, sponsored by an *ad hoc* consortium of interested mission boards and societies and the Chicago Cluster of Theological Schools. It was understood that the Consultation would have no authority other than the experience and wisdom of its collective membership and the guidance of the Holy Spirit. Findings would be understood to be advisory and not binding on any participant or organization. The Consultation would be characterized by informality, spontaneity, and fluidity, the participants being allowed to change the agenda as might be necessary. There would be no set papers read nor addres- ses made. Preparatory papers would be sent out and studied in advance. The time at the Consultation would be entirely free for discussion. The program schedule would not be crowded and exhausting. There would be ample time for worship and intercession.

Preparatory Material

The preparatory material sent out for study in advance of the Consul- tation is of three kinds: First, surveys of unevangelized peoples and existing frontier churches. Second, case studies of evangeliza- tion and church development. Four papers intended to provoke thought about the missionary task and factors in contemporary encounter with tribal peoples and three papers on the specific themes of each day were prepared by recognized authorities in missiology and all but one were sent to participants in advance of the consultation. This is the third category. Fourthly, there were also some miscellaneous items.

The major failure was in the area of surveys and case studies. Dr.
David B. Barrett and his colleagues provided a magnificant survey of
the Africa scene, and the Wycliffe Bible Translators and F. A. S. T.
provided detailed information on western hemisphere peoples. Further
comment will be made on these surveys. The able scholar who had
previously done considerable study of the tribal groups in India was
unable in the time allowed, despite some travel and searching, to
produce the desired information. Sickness, absence, and failure of
the mails prevented attempts in other areas. The same reasons kept
some case studies from being written, and in one instance the paper
was written and presented to church leaders in the region and they
requested that it not be used and published in America for fear of
the reaction of the political and religious leaders of the dominant
element in the country.

All of the preparatory papers are included in this report, excepting
the large surveys. There is a summary of the Africa Report in this
volume and F. A. S. T. has provided a sample of *The Scripture Translation Information Bank*, which is included as an appendix. The
entire *Bank* can be purchased from F. A. S. T. at the price of $3.00.
Address: Westminster Drive, Denton, Texas 76201. There are still a
few hundred copies of the entire Africa Report, *Frontier Situations
for Evangelization in Africa, 1972*, available from either:[1]

Rev. Jobert J. Flinn, Coordinator   Rev. Alfred C. Krass
Chicago Cluster of Theological   United Church Board for World
   Schools   Ministries
1100 East 55th Street   475 Riverside Drive
Chicago, Illinois 60637   New York, New York 10027

Program

The Consultation began with worship at 5:00 P. M. on Sunday, December
10, and each day's sessions began and ended with worship and intercession. Arrangements were left to Father Flinn and his associates
and were carried out through utilizing the personnel resources of the
Chicago Cluster of Theological Schools. There was much variety. The
contributions of all who led the services are highly appreciated.

Sunday night was devoted to a dinner at which participants introduced
themselves, the welcome of the Cluster was extended by Father Flinn,
and an explanation of the Consultation made, and to a session on
"Frontier Situations." Dr. David B. Barrett of Nairobi presented the
survey on *Frontier Situations for Evangelisation in Africa*. Mr. Alan
W. Bergstedt of F. A. S. T. and Dr. Benjamin F. Elson, executive vice
president of the Wycliffe Bible Translators, presented the data developed by their organizations on the ethnic and linguistic groups of
Latin America and what this reveals about peoples still unevangelized.
Dr. Nirmal Minz spoke about India and frontiers in general. Program

[1]See note p.12

and methodology were discussed and a consensus reached. Dr. Rodney
A. Sundberg presided.

The adopted plan was to devote each day to a theme: Monday to "Gospel
and Culture," Tuesday to "The Indigenous Church Under the Holy
Spirit -- Freedom and the Transmission of the Faith," and Wednesday
to "Guidelines and Practical Measures." The writer of the paper on
each theme introduced the day's topic with a brief statement. Thus
the discussion on Monday was begun by Professor John Mbiti, head of
the Department of Religious Studies at Makerere University, Kampala,
Uganda, and a noted author. On Tuesday the topic was introduced by
Dr. Nirmal Minz, until a few weeks ago the principal of the Lutheran
Theological College at Ranchi, Bihar, India, and now a bishop of the
Gossner Evangelical Lutheran Church, a large tribal church.   Dr.
Charles R. Taber, editor of *Practical Anthropology* and translations
expert of the United Bible Societies at Accra, Ghana, opened Wednes-
day's discussions. There was each morning plenary discussion and
debate until the coffee break.

Small groups permitted more intimate and intense exchange of opinion.
Six of these met in general discussion of the theme during the last
two hours of the morning. In the afternoon there were six other
groups on specialized subjects but relating to the day's topic.
These were: 1) Initial Contact, 2) Total Effect of Relations, 3)
Church/Mission and Government Relations, 4) The Catechumenate, 5)
Bible Translation, and 6) Development of Leadership. These afternoon groups each had the help of an expert resource person, -- Alan
Tippett, Gene Hillman, Linwood Barney, Donald C. Flatt, John Boberg,
men from the Bible organizations (American Bible Society, Wycliffe,
F. A. S. T.), and Alfred Krass. Each group had a recorder. The
viewpoints and insights of each group were fed into the general discussion at the night sessions.

The Findings Committee members are Dr. Jose Farjado, chairman,
Colombia; Mrs. Louise Paw, Burma; Mr. Musembe Kasiera, Kenya; Dr.
Rodney A. Sundberg; Dr. John T. Boberg; Dr. Eugene Hillman.

Bishop Edwin W. Kortz presided on Monday morning, Rev. Alfred C.
Krass on Monday night, Dr. John E. Buteyn on Tuesday morning, Rev.
Fr. Edward F. Mann, S. J., on Tuesday night, Mrs. William F. Muldrow
on Wednesday morning, and Pierce Beaver at the final session.

Goals

The goals set for the Consultation were: First, effecting acquaintance among persons concerned about frontier missions. Second, the
exchange of experience and knowledge. Third, stimulation of renewed
concern for witness to the Lord Jesus Christ to all men and especially to frontier peoples, by national churches and American mission

agencies. Fourth, the gaining of some perspective on the dimensions of the task and discovery of how to secure full and accurate information. Fifth, attain some insights regarding faith and culture, particularly with tribal peoples in view. Sixth, to be open to the prompting and leading of the Holy Spirit in the sessions and to learn something about the Spirit's role in evangelization and church development. Seventh, to arrive at some practical guidelines which may be helpful to missions and boards.

NO NEO-IMPERIALISM

It was made clear from the outset -- or at least the effort was made -- that the Consultation is not intended to launch a nineteenth century type adventure in cultural imperialism and ecclesiastical colonialism. It was announced that there would be genuine concern for protecting the cultural integrity of any society, to avoid any and all kinds of exploitation of tribal peoples, to evangelize in ways that would leave the new Christian community free to develop under the leading of the Holy Spirit, and to avoid recognized errors of the past. Yet again and again one met scepticism and disbelief that there can be any mission to tribal peoples which is not imperialistic and exploitative. The desire of the participants was the opposite, and members of overseas churches were alert and watchful with regard to this possibility. Moreover, although this was a conference in the United States and North Americans were most numerous, the challenge to study and action was addressed to churches, societies, and Christians in every country. The responsibility for frontier missions rests on all, but first of all on the Christians in any country where there are still aborigines unevangelized. May their members who participated in the Consultation help stimulate them to action.

Nevertheless, American agencies may hope to enter into partnership with national churches in frontier evangelism, and there are certainly some opportunities for direct action. Given the mutual antagonism and mistrust between aboriginal communities and the dominant society in many nations, contact, witness, and assistance may sometimes initially be made more easily by a foreigner than by a national belonging to the ruling ethnic body. Tribal missions are really foreign missions -- certainly transcultural missions -- in the eyes of aborigines. The national representative may appear to them even more imperialistic than a person from overseas.

PARTICIPATION

Seventy was deemed the optimum number of participants and 90 the topmost limit. Actually 97 persons registered, and about ten or a dozen others came to the opening dinner and some of the sessions

without registering, -- wives, students, professors, and mission
executives in the Chicago area. They are persons whose devotion to
Christ and his mission transcend labels, but it is noteworthy that
they divided one-third each as Conservative Evangelicals, Conciliar
Protestant churchmen, and Roman Catholics.

Highest priority was given to a search for members of emerging frontier churches, but none could be found in North America. They are
seldom highly educated adacemically and rarely come to America for
visits and study. The consultation could not afford the cost of
bringing any from their homes. But there were participants who were
of tribal stock, themselves perhaps one step away from the frontier
or their churches one or two generations removed from the pioneer
state, -- Toba and Karo Bataks from Sumatra, others from India,
Kenya, Bolivia, and elsewhere. Some were members of national
churches which vigorously promote frontier missions, such as the
Gossner Evangelical Lutheran Church of India and the Huria Kristen
Batak Protestant of Sumatra. There were numerous "Third World"
Christians who could speak from the perspectives of Asia, Africa,
and Latin America. They comprised about 21% of the participants.
Missionaries engaged in work with tribal peoples were numerous along
with mission executives responsible for tribal areas. There were a
few professors of missions. Among the missionaries, professors, and
executives there were anthropologists, sociologists, historians of
religion, demographers, linguists, Africianists, and others competent in a variety of disciplines. Here was assembled a group whose
knowledge and competence matched their commitment.

The boards and societies did not send enough women. There were about
ten only. It was hoped to have present some North American Indians
who might speak to the issues out of three centuries of terrible
experience. There was only one who could speak for them, a Canadian
priest. The Black church mission boards did not respond to the invitation, and the one Black member of the Steering Committee was
abroad when the Consultation was held. No others were enlisted.

                               WHAT WAS DONE

The Consultation was above all a rare experience in Christian unity.
The whole spectrum of mission theology, theory, and organization and
the entire range of ecclesiastical polity were represented by persons equally devoted and obedient to our Lord Jesus Christ and his
mission. Devotion to mission produces spiritual unity, and unity is
essential to making witness to Christ. Dialogue, discussion, sharing
of experience, worship, prayer, and fellowship nurtured friendship
and understanding. Mutual concern for the evangelization and disci-
pling of the nations bound together Christians holding to many
different views and practices.

Indications during and since the Consultation are that it has stimulated new zeal for world mission and awakened a sense of responsibility for frontier tribal peoples. The complexities of such evangelism have been more clearly recognized and will be taken into account. Some guidelines have been offered to "Third World" churches and American mission boards and societies. Thought-provoking and illuminating literature has been offered for study.

The dimensions of the task have been dimly discerned in general, but very clearly and definitely with regard to Africa. The *Scripture Translation Information Bank* reveals that there are 202 ethnic groups in Latin America among whom no missionaries of national or foreign churches are at work. Concretely and emphatically the members of the Consultation have called for the provision of area demographic reports modeled after the Africa survey.

The Consultation's work did not end with adjournment on December 13. The Steering Committee has been charged with creating a Continuation Committee, and the Steering Committee will have acted before this report has been published. The Continuation Committee will enable the churches, boards, and societies to take further steps in frontier missions.

FRONTIER SITUATIONS FOR EVANGELISATION IN AFRICA, 1972

This survey, produced by Dr. David B. Barrett with the assistance of Dr. Malcolm J. McVeigh, Mary Linda Hronek, George K. Mambo, and Professor John S. Mbiti, is summarized in this volume and is available in full as indicated above. The survey is a remarkable demographic and missiological achievement. It was possible for the Consultation to receive this document only because Dr. Barrett and his associates, building on his earlier studies, devoted all their time and efforts to it for many months and because the United Church Board for World Ministries made a large grant for the project without waiting to see whether other boards and societies would financially support the Consultation. The members of the Consultation expressed profound gratitude to Dr. Barrett and his associates for this magnificent survey.[1] Read the summary, especially read the entire survey, for detailed information on the distribution of tribal religions, Islam, and Christianity and on the 263 "unevangelised and resistant tribes," which includes the categories "evangelised but resistant," "half evangelised," "partially evangelised," and "sparsely evangelised" (0-10%, 68 tribes). The members of the Consultation regard this document as a model for other areas.

Dr. David B. Barrett, a missionary of the Church Missionary Society, based in Nairobi, is now the recognized expert on church/mission

[1]See note p.12

statistics and demography. He is an editor of the *World Christian Handbook* and author of the important book, *Schism and Renewal* on the African independent churches.

REPORT OF THE FINDINGS COMMITTEE AND INTERPRETATION

It was originally expected to include in the Report in addition to papers a transcript of tape-recorded discussions as well as the report of the Findings Committee. Some investigation affirmed the chairman/executive secretary's impression that little attention is later paid to printed transcripts of tapes. The great expense in time and money is not justified. Further reflection brought conviction that the report of the Findings Committee would genuinely be an effective report on the whole course of the Consultation since the members attended the plenary sessions and each meeting of all the subgroups. They have given expression to the thinking of the assembly. Adoption of their report, after discussion and amendment, by the whole body makes it the report of the Consultation.

It is not often that conference reports are readily intelligible to laymen and pastors. It is helpful for professionals to undergo the criticism of an observer from without the initiated circle. Dr. Holly Arpan, an active Presbyterian laywoman and a member of the Department of Journalism of the University of Indiana, was requested to record her observations for these purposes, and graciously consented. Two comments by an administrator and a teacher are included.

Warm thanks are extended to Dr. Ralph D. Winter and the William Carey Library for publishing the report promptly, for producing it inexpensively, and for making it widely available.

                                        R. Pierce Beaver
                                        Chairman and Executive Secretary

---

[1]Due to a later decision the entire Africa Report is contained in this present volume (pages 233-310). The original report, the availability of which is mentioned on page seven, is still of value however, since its very large pages (9½ x 12½) make the tables easier to read and the maps are presented in a large fold-out which is printed in five colors.

PART I

The Preparatory Papers

Section A

MISSION TODAY

THE MISSIONARY MANDATE IN THE TWENTIETH CENTURY
John T. Boberg, S.V.D.

2

The operative words in the title of this paper are surely "in the twentieth century." The missionary mandate, understood as the love of God revealed in Christ Jesus which draws all men to himself and which consequently places a "burden" on all who believe in Him to share with others that faith and love which they have received, has not changed. St. Paul's "Woe to me if I do not preach the Gospel" is as valid today for every Christian as it was in his day for Paul.

For some, perhaps, this statement is adequate in itself and there is no need to explore the "twentieth century." For them what is lacking in the twentieth century is simply our own deep, fresh faith-experience in the Risen Christ and in the Spirit which He poured forth on Pentecost. There is probably some truth in this. Certainly without a deep living faith, without some experience of Christ and His Spirit and of the love of fellowship in the community of believers, there is no realization, no desire to share that faith and love with others.

As important as this might be, I think there are other factors that condition the missionary mandate " in the twentieth century," negatively and/or positively, that need to be considered: new problematics that demand new understandings, new situations that demand new approaches, and new insights which may respond more or less to the new problematics and situations but which at least give some new orientation to the continuing duty and privilege of preaching the Gospel.

The twentieth century does confront us with profound changes both in the world and in the Church.1 Without claiming to be exhaustive, the following are at least among the most significant.

Changes in the World

I. Secularization

Any re-examination of the missionary mandate has to begin with an examination of Christianity itself and its relevance in the modern world. The process of secularization, understood as the loss of function of religion and Church in daily living, raises far-reaching questions. Even though this process can perhaps be considered the result of Christianity itself in liberating man from the forces of nature, it can take on a dynamic of its own and lead to pure secularism: at the least it demands a new understanding and expression of the continuing function and relevance of Christianity for "man come of age."

II. Modern Cultures

A far more general change that has affected the missionary mandate is the shift from what might be called classicist culture to modern cultures. Classicist culture was conceived normatively. Apart from it there was only barbarism (or primitiveness of some sort). Others might participate in it to a greater or lesser extent and, in the measure that they did so, they ceased to be barbarians. It took its stand on the way things ought to be, on the unchanging essence of human living. Since classicist culture conceived itself normatively and universally, it also had to think of itself as the one and only culture of all times. The modern notion of culture, by contrast, is empirical. Culture denotes something found in every people, for in every people there is some apprehension of meaning and value in their way of live. The modern notion recognizes all cultures as relative, as man-made and, as such, able to change. No culture then is normative. Each culture has its strengths and weaknesses, its richness and blindness. While the modern notion undercuts the presumption of cultural superiority and is far more open, better informed, more discerning than classicist culture, it lacks the convictions of its predecessor: its clear-cut norms, its elemental strength. The genuine meeting of cultures in our day, then, is an occurrence requiring much sensitivity, openness, willingness to dialogue and the necessity of change on both sides.

III. Future Orientation

In modern society, science and technological planning are playing a more and more important part in the building up of the world and the promotion of the well-being of all peoples, and in this process man's earlier pre-scientific and pre-industrial attitude towards the world is radically changing. The two concepts of building up the world and promoting the well-being of all mankind are especially representative of historically new realities, since they have become possibilities only through the advances in science and the technological planning which has resulted. Formerly, man was orientated primarily towards the past, but now he looks resolutely towards the future. Whether we like it or not, the ever increasing importance in modern life of the natural sciences, technology, and the behavioral sciences is thrusting man towards the future. Man's religious experience today is therefore having to assimilate something entirely new -- an industrial, urbanized world which, under the guidance of science and technological planning, is intent on creating a better future for mankind.[2]

IV. Technology

While the accomplishments of technology are almost unbelievable
and the opportunities technology present are un-dreamed of, its
dangers can strangle the humanity of those who create it: mass
pollution, large-scale organizational control, secularism, and
the amplification of the inequalities among peoples. The challenges
that it brings to modern man include the harmony of man and nature
(ecology), the necessary choices of controlling one's destiny in a
way that does not destroy what is deeply human, the need for long-
range planning, the transition to technology without the loss of
previous values, justice to all in the use of technology, a critical
stance to the creeping values of consumerism.

V. Global Unity

At no time has man become so conscious of being a world citizen,
of living in a "global village." While the history of any
particular people would always eventually have some effect on
others, that influence may not have been felt for hundreds of
years. Today the action of any nation has immediate reverbera-
tions around the world. Communication is instant and mobility is
rapid and large scale. Immigrants and refugees are a phenomenon in
many countries. A vast wealth of world information is immediately
available to all, even the poorest and most illiterate, at least by
radio.

Man is living in a period of transition from his history -- the
origin and development of his own particular people, culture,
religion -- to world history, which necessitates the passing-over
to other peoples' lives, cultures, religions. Two world wars
and the precarious balancing of world military might are the most
obvious signs that the transition to world history has taken place
in this century, and they attest to the real failure to pass over.
That the failure to pass over should be so deadly, though, seems
to show that the time for passing over is ripe and over-ripe. It
is the task of our times.

VI. Nationalism

Many new independent states have arisen since the end of colonialism.
Self-determination has become an urgent goal for all who have not
yet achieved it. This struggle for identity and self-determination
is occurring on at least three levels -- political, cultural and
economic. Although Western political domination has by and large

come to an end, its cultural and economic domination is only
beginning to face a challenge. The struggle for independence
and a proportionate voice in international affairs can take the
form of an outright rejection of the West or of some kind of
national absolutism.

VII. World Justice

Instant communication and mass mobility in transportation has
locked the development of every country into a vast structure of
world interdependence. Beyond the justice or injustice of the
acts of individuals or even nations, there is the justice or injustice of structures and systems that are truly international and
reach beyond the ability of individuals to change or be responsible
for. In fact they often seem to be beyond the control or care of
anyone. In this sense not only individuals and nations can be
exploitive but also the structures that relate nations to nations
such as international trade and aid systems. As recently as
September 17, 1972, the World Bank reported that despite billions
of dollars of foreign aid and "impressive" economic growth in the
poor countries, "it is probably true that the world's burden of
poverty is increasing rather than declining." Also, it is a well-
known fact that an industrialized country as the U.S. with less
than six percent of the world's population consumes about forty
percent of the world's resources. And in an age of mass information, such facts cannot be hidden but are known by all. A world
in which there is such an imbalance of rich and poor, of dominance
and dependence, is intolerable. The relationship between nations
then is a whole new area of activity open to today's world.

VIII. Violence and War

Also closely allied with the above is a violence that is either
open or immediately below the surface. Though war and violence
have always been a part of human history, it takes on new dimension
in today's world. a) War is more expansive due to the greater
interdependency and alignment of nations. Even local struggles
can soon mushroom into an involvement of many nations. The threat
of total war is a constant danger. b) War is more deadly due to
the greater destructive power of modern weapons. Even the total
annihilation of a people or of all peoples is no longer just an
idle fantasy. c) Occasions for war are more frequent. Nations
have much more contact with one another and are more dependent on
one another. The inequalities of rich and poor nations, rich elite
and poor masses, are much more consciously known due to modern
communication. In addition there is often a deep sense of powerles
ness and frustration due to the anonymity and impersonality of the
structures that determine individual's lives. Peace, then, in

today's world is not just a sporadic concern of a few and occasional historical moments of crisis, but an area of constant concern for all.

IX. Deeper Awareness of the Dignity and Freedom of the Person

Underlying and running through all of the above is a greater sensitivity to the fundamental value of the dignity and freedom of each person. This is not to deny that counter-movements are not also present: subjection of individual lives to vast organizational structures, rejection of people who are not "producers" -- the aged, the poor, war victims, the unborn. However, the new sensitivity does shift questions from how to more effectively employ development projects to what is human development in itself, from how to increase foreign aid to what is necessary for genuine self-help, from how to get more men into the field to what does effective presence in another land, culture and religion really mean.

Changes in Understanding the Church

I. Grace and Salvation

There are two very definite shifts in understanding that have a profound influence on the missionary mandate.

a) The role of the Church in relation to grace and salvation. Without trying to make a caricature of previous understanding, grace and salvation were often considered to be, if not the exclusive domain of the Church, at least its principle possession. Much missionary motivation was enkindled by the thought of so many pagans who would be lost without the Church. An emphasis on numbers with respect to baptism, confessions, and communions can also be at least partially attributed to this understanding.

The understanding of grace and salvation in the Second Vatican Council, especially in Lumen Gentium (9, 14-16), is more nuanced. It states that God and His grace is accessible to every human being, in every age and in every race. Further, it suggests various ways that grace is mediated, e.g., in the life of the individual through his conscience, in the life of a people through its religion and culture. Therefore even the Christian Church must approach others " in dialogue" with their conscience, religion and culture to discover how God and his grace are already operative.

This missionary urgency, then, is not built on the notion of salvation and damnation, but on helping the divine initiative to come to its full fruition -- the concrete unity of man with God and man with man.

b) Relation of the Individual and the Community to Salvation. Again, previous missionary activity placed a strong emphasis on the salvation of individual souls. Vatican II, however, states, "God does not make men holy and save them merely as individuals, without bond or link between one another" (L.G., 9). The Christian concern for salvation can never be just "care for souls" but must always be care for all men and their world. Only in the context of a people, and of all people, does an individual come to salvation. The Church must be the sign of this new community. In this sense the Church is necessary for salvation, not so much of the individual, but of the world. The Church mediates the outcome of what in fact is going on in the heart of each man and gives concrete expression to the consummation of the world in Jesus Christ. For if in fact salvation means that all men are my brothers, then anyone who lives out of God's grace will by that fact be drawn into the task of working for and giving expression to the unity of all men.

II. Local Churches

At one time it was rather simple to speak of the missionary mandate in terms of "home country" where money and personnel were gathered and "mission country" where missionary work was carried out. A number of factors have called that clear dichotomy into question.

a) Practically every country has its own established church to some degree, including hierarchy. The young local churches have won a certain independence and are responsible for bearing the main burden of the missionary activity in their area.

b) At the same time churches in the "home countries" are finding themselves in crisis or becoming minorities. Or, these churches may in fact be very much identified with exploitative or unjust structures and relations to the very countries they seek to serve.

c) The understanding of the nature of the local church has developed A local church is not the smallest administrative unit through which the whole church (or Rome) looks after the salvation of the individual (something on the model of General Motors and its distributors around the world). Rather, as Lumen Gentium says, "This Church of Christ is truly present in all legitimate local congregations of the faithful which, united with their pastors, are themselves called Church in the New Testament"(L.G., 26).

Thus all local churches, whether young or old, have equal status within the universal Church. One church is not more church than another. Catholicity, then, means not one monolithic structure but the Catholic (universal) communion of local churches with one another and with all. "Giving" and "receiving" are mutually inter-related activities.

d) The radical nature of this change is briefly expressed in the new slogan, "mission in six continents," which is highly popular today. This slogan may be criticized as blurring outlines and overlooking differences of which account still has to be taken. Mission in the run-down areas of Philadelphia and Chicago may be even more difficult than in Cairo or Bangkok; but the problem of approaching with the Gospel those who have been conditioned all their lives by a non-Christian culture and religion is not the same as that of making the Gospel real to those who live on the margins of a civilization that bears a profound Christian impress. It is misleading when such differences are overlooked. But what the slogan does effectively make clear is that mission is not something that allegedly Christian countries can impose on an unhappy heathen world. Mission is something that all churches are engaged in all the time. Every church, for the sake of its own health, must be both a sending and a receiving church. Wherever a church exists, older or younger, strongers or weaker, richer or poorer, there is the potential center of mission.

e) It should occasion no surprise that leaders in some younger churches, flushed with their new sense of spiritual freedom, resentful of the patronizing and domineering attitude of some missionaries in the past, and unwilling to risk any encroachments on their hard-won independence, say frankly that now the current should flow in the other direction. The younger churches, with their greater vigor and the freshness of their faith, are now called to help the older churches to recover the vision that they have so largely lost and to become again living members in the body of Christ.

III. Service and Development of the World

Genuine missionaries have always worked for the growth and development of mankind. So long as this effort was expended within the limits of a parish or a diocese, no special problem presented itself. But today the organization of development has become a much more complex affair; it has assumed the dimensions of whole nations, of entire continents, of the wide world itself. It has become a task for specialists, and the ordinary missionaries run the danger of no longer seeing and understanding the role they

are called on to play in the task of development. At the same
time, though they have traditionally concerned themselves with
the poor, concern for the poor is not necessarily the same as
"concern for the development of the world."

It is possible to feed the hungry, clothe the naked, heal the sick,
shelter the homeless while leaving untouched the economic, social
and political structures that cause hunger, nakedness, disease
and homelessness. Traditionally Christian concern has been
content to deal with the effects of social injustice rather
than with the cause, to succor the miserable rather than to
root out misery.

Concern for the development of the world directs itself toward
the building of a humane society ruled by justice.

The theology of mission and development should help missionaries
to bring into practice a fidelity to their missionary vocation
of evangelization and of the fostering of the full growth of man
within this new framework of development. But often enough
missionaries have the impression that the mission of Christ has
been drowned, submerged in a great technical or human enterprise,
instead of being its soul and its force.

IV. Ecumenism

One of the most positive changes that has resulted since the
Second Vatican Council is the spirit of ecumenism which has
grown. The Council clearly removed other Christians from being
objects of mission and called for cooperation among agencies.
Heretofore, the image of the missionary had been that of a fierce
partisan, be he Roman Catholic or Protestant, hostile to and
aggressive towards the other party, competitive and imperialistic.
Now friendship has to a great degree replaced hostility, and there
are going forward scores of cooperative projects from Bible
translation to development schemes. A new image is being fashioned
and its maintenance requires that new appointees be prepared for
mutual acceptance, friendship and joint action.

Self-Transcendence as Authentic Existence

Given all these changes in the world and in the Church, how does
one express an understanding of the missionary mandate of the
Church that while faithful to the Scriptures has meaning and
relevance to the changed conditions of the twentieth century.
Evidently within the limited framework of an article, one cannot

give a presentation that touches explicitly all the shifts in
thought listed above. Rather I will offer simply an approach,
based on the thought of Bernard Lonergan, that, I believe, provides
a fundamental perspective and orientation for answering many of
the questions being raised.

In his major works, Insight[3] and Method in Theology,[4] as well as
in several articles,[5] Bernard Lonergan, S.J., has developed his
understanding of man as one who is called to a level of existence
that transcends man himself. In the present order for a man to be
simply a man is what he cannot be; to be fully a man is to go
beyond the merely human to a life open to Transcendent Being, to
a life lived out of values that transcend his own capacity. Only
such self-transcendence is authentic existence for man.

The basis for Lonergan's position is the structure of human knowing,
which he presents most completely in Insight. Human knowing does
not consist in one single act that is analogous to looking and
seeing; it is rather a dynamic self-structuring process involving
several distinct operations, none of which is sufficient in itself
but which together and interdependently form one act of human
knowing:

> "Human knowing involves many distinct and irreducible
> activities: seeing, hearing, smelling, touching, tasting,
> inquiring, imagining, understanding, conceiving, reflecting,
> weighing the evidence, judging.
>
> "No one of these activities, alone and by itself, may be
> named human knowing. An act of ocular vision may be
> perfect as ocular vision; yet if it occurs without any
> accompanying glimmer of understanding, it is mere gaping;
> and mere gaping, so far from being the beau ideal of human
> knowing, is just stupidity. As merely seeing is not human
> knowing, so for the same reason merely hearing, merely
> smelling, merely touching, merely tasting may be parts,
> potential components of human knowing, but they are not
> human knowing itself.
>
> "What is true of sense, is no less true of understanding.
> Without the prior presentations of sense, there is nothing
> for a man to understand; and when there is nothing to be
> understood, there is no occurrence of understanding.
> Moreover, the combination of the operations of sense and
> of understanding does not suffice for human knowing.
> There must be added judging. To omit judgment is quite
> literally silly: it is only by judgment that there

emerges a distinction between fact and fiction, logic
and sophistry, philosophy and myth, history and legend,
astronomy and astrology, chemistry and alchemy.

"Nor can one place human knowing in judging to the
exclusion of experience and understanding. To pass judgment on what one does not understand is, not human knowing,
but human arrogance. To pass judgment independently of
all experience is to set fact aside.

"Human knowing, then, is not experience alone, not
understanding alone, not judgment alone; it is not a
combination of only experience and understanding, or of
only experience and judgment, or of only understanding
and judgment: finally, it is not something totally apart
from experience, understanding, and judgment. Inevitably,
one has to regard an instance of human knowing, not as
this or that operation, but as a whole whose parts are
operations. It is a structure and, indeed, a materially
dynamic structure.

"But human knowing is also formally dynamic. It is self-
assemblying, self-constituting. It puts itself together,
one part summoning forth the next, till the whole is
reached. And this occurs, not with the blindness of
natural process, but consciously, intelligently, rationally.
Experience stimulates inquiry, and inquiry is intelligence
bringing itself to act; it leads from experience through
imagination to insight, and from insight to the concepts
that combine in single objects both what has been grasped
by insight and what in experience or imagination is relevant
to the insight. In turn, concepts stimulate reflection,
and reflection is the conscious exigence of rationality;
it marshalls the evidence and weighes it either to judge
or else to doubt and so renew inquiry.

"This dynamic, self-structuring process, then, culminates
in a judgment of fact. The subject affirms that something
really and truly is so and thereby has gone beyond himself,
has got hold of what is independent of himself, has somehow transcended himself."6

This epistemological proposition is central to Lonergan's thought
and is treated especially in Chapter 11 of Insight. Briefly:
human knowledge in the proper sense is knowledge of reality or
knowledge is intrinsically objective. This objectivity of human
knowing rests upon an unrestricted intention and an unconditioned

result. "For the objectivity of human knowing is a triple cord;
'there is an experiential component that resides in a givenness of
relevant data; there is a normative component that resides in
the exegencies of intelligence and rationality guiding the
process of knowing from data to judging; there finally is an
absolute component that is reached when reflective understanding
combines the normative and the experiential elements into a
virtually unconditioned, i.e., a conditioned whose conditions
are fulfilled."[7] Since the intentionality of human cognitional
activity is unrestricted, it follows that human knowing "intends
the transcendent and (is) a process of self-transcendence that
reaches it."[8]

With judgment, then, self-transcendence, insofar as it is
cognitional, is complete. But human self-transcendence is not
only cognitional, it may also be real. In fact, by virtue of
its total dynamism, it <u>must</u> be real. What has cognitionally
been judged to be true and good becomes value, and value calls
for deliberation, action, responsibility. Thus the dynamism
of cognitional self-transcendence leads to the dynamism of
personal, existential self-transcendence where a person is
called upon to structure his life and his person according to
the values which confront and beckon him. On the top most level
of human consciousness, then, the subject deliberates, evaluates,
decides, controls, acts. He is a rationally conscious, free,
responsible subject that by his choices makes himself what he
is to be and his world what it is to be. In the measure that
one's living, one's aims, one's achievements are such a response
to values, in that measure a real, or moral self-transcendence
is effected. One has got beyond mere selfishness. One has
become a principle of benevolence and beneficence, capable of
genuine collaboration and of true love.

Man's capacity for self-transcendence, therefore, is based on
the dynamic, self-structuring process of human knowing and
loving. It is effected by being faithful to what Longergan
calls the transcendental imperatives: be attentive (experience),
be intelligent (understanding), be reasonable (judgment), be
responsible (decision). Because these imperatives, which
correspond to the operations of human knowing and loving, are
unrestricted, open-ended, man's capacity for self-transcendence
is also unrestricted and unlimited. Thus human authenticity
consists in being faithful to the pure, unrestricted desire to
know and love.

Does this capacity find fulfillment? To answer this question,
Lonergan's approach proceeds in two ways. In <u>Insight</u>, he

argues that if man is faithful to the open-ended structure of human
knowing he will arrive at a conception and an affirmation of God,
as well as at the realization that God grants him the means to
overcome sin and evil through His gift of supernatural faith, hope
and love.[9]

In his later articles and in Method in Theology, he takes both
the reality of God and his communication to man for granted, and
proceeds from a sort of phenomenology of religious experience.

He places religious experience at the level of rational self-
consciousness, of responsible decision, the level of choosing to
live by values. At this level, he says, man finds his fullest
achievement when he falls in love. Falling in love, though
proceeding in some ways, as all decisions, from experience,
understanding and judgment, really is an exercise of vertical
freedom, it is like a conversion, in that it goes beyond its
antecedents of knowing. The dynamic state of being-in-love
itself becomes a source or drive for further knowing.

This is true of the human love of intimacy between man and
woman, parents and children. It is also true, but in a quite
different sense, of being in love with God. Being in love with
God, though it is the fulfillment of man's unrestricted capacity
for knowing and loving, is not the product of man's own knowledge and choice. It is God's gift. As such it does not abrogate
human knowing and loving, but raises them to a new level, a
level at which man's knowing and loving are informed and guided
by faith and absolutely transcendent values.

Man is aware or conscious of God's love and experiences it in
such ways as deep-set joy and a radical peace that bear fruit in
a love of neighbor, but it is not known as such. Ordinarily it
remains within subjectivity as a dynamic vector, a mysterious
undertow, a fateful call to a dreaded holiness. Because the
dynamic state of being in love with God is conscious without
being known, it is an experience of mystery.

This religious experience, Lonergan maintains, is the basic
component in all the world religions. Similar religious
experiences, however, become objectified differently at different
stages of human development. There is moreover a still further
source of difference. Religious experience has been conceived
in terms of self-transcendence, and human self-transcendence is
ever precarious. Self-transcendence is always involved in a
tension between the self as transcending and the self as not
fully transcended, between the pure, unrestricted desire to know

and the various biases to which man is subject. It follows that human authenticity is never some pure and serene and secure possession. It is ever a withdrawal from inauthenticity, and every successful withdrawal only brings to light the need for still further withdrawals. Our advance in understanding is also the need for further elimination of oversights and misunderstandings. Our advance in truth also demands the continuing correction of mistakes and errors. Our moral development is through repeated repentance for our sins. Genuine religion is discovered and realized by redemption from the many traps of religious aberration.

This dialectical character of self-transcendence explains why almost any genuine characteristic of religion can be matched in the history of religions by its opposite. It also leads one to ask whether in addition to communicating His love to man in the depths of his consciousness, God has not also communicated His love in another way.

On an analogy with human love, in fact, we would expect such a communication. If a man or woman were to love each other, yet never articulate their love, there would be lacking to their love an interpersonal component, a mutal presence of self-donation. Without that interpersonal component, their love would not have the opportunity to grow. There would not be the steady increase in knowledge of each other. There would not be the constant flow of favors given and received that would make love conscious of its reality, its strength, its durability, aware it could always be counted on.

Now if there is this interpersonal element to human love, if that element is a distinct and important factor in its emergence and its growth, something somehow similar could also be thought of a religious love. But, then, we should not solely have the gift of God's love flooding our hearts. We should not solely believe what results from the objectifications of that love. Besides completing our personal self-transcendence in the secrecy of our hearts, God would also address us as a people, announce to us his intentions, send to us his prophets, his Messiah, his Apostles. In that case religious beliefs would be objectifications not only of internal experience but also of the externally uttered word of God.

Self-Transcendence and the Christian Message

Our Christian belief is precisely that God has so spoken, that especially in His Son Jesus he has revealed his love and explicitly

called men to share in his life. He has revealed that union with
Him is the goal of human existence and is the fulfillment of man's
desire and thrust towards unlimited knowing and loving. In Christ
this fulfillment is actually achieved, and is achieved precisely
through a process of self-transcendence. It is through his total
giving of himself to God as a ransom for the many that Jesus is
established as the Lord in his resurrection and exaltation. He
is at one and the same time the fullest expression of God's self-
communication to man and the fullest response of man to God. "He
who is the 'image of the invisible God' (Col. 1:15) is Himself the
perfect man." In him we see that the value of self-sacrificing
love is the "basic law of human perfection and hence of the world's
transformation." 10

To believe in Christ, to accept Him as Lord and Saviour, therefore,
is to accept the reality that human authenticity is achieved throug'
self-transcendence; to believe in Christ is to seek after authenticity by attempting to live out of the values that He incorporated
especially total self-sacrificing love.

To believe in Christ is to accept His role as "representative,"
as mediator, as the New Adam in and through whom all men in
principle have achieved the fullness of human existence in the
union with God and all men.

To preach Christ, then, is not to bring something completely new
or extraneous, but to respond to the search and struggle for human
authenticity that is already operative in all men. To preach
Christ is to give an explicitness to the goal towards which men
are striving, and by the concrete example of Christ's achievement
to provide not only a model that can be followed, but also the
assurance that it can be achieved.

To preach Christ is to affirm that efforts to realize genuine
human values are not apart from but are basic to that perfection
which He exemplifies and towards which He draws all men.

To preach Christ is to introduce men into a community of believers
who consciously live out of the values of faith, hope and self-
sacrificing love; who together seek the further meaning and implica
tions of these values; and who through common prayer and worship
find the support to be faithful to these values in their daily
living.

To preach Christ is to work for the unity of all men not on the
basis of economic, political or cultural ties, but on the deepest
value level of their brotherly relationship to each other in their
relationship to God.

Such an understanding of Christ and His message, related to self-transcendence as authentic existence, gives to the missionary mandate, I believe, a continuing relevance and meaning -- even amid the changed conditions in the world and in the Church of the twentieth century.

FOOTNOTES

1. Much of the two sections on changes in the world and in the Church was worked out jointly with Eugene Ahner, S.V.D., in a paper for the Tenth General Chapter of the Divine Word Missionaries.

2. Cf. E. Schillebeeckx, God the Future of Man. New York: Sheed and Ward, 1968, p. 169-207.

3. Lonergan, Bernard. Insight. New York: Philosophical Library, 1967 [1957].

4. Lonergan, Bernard. Method in Theology. New York: Herder and Herder, 1972.

5. Lonergan, Bernard. "Cognitional Structure," "Existenz and Aggiornamento," in Collection, ed. F. E. Crowe. New York: Herder and Herder, 1967; "Faith and Beliefs," unpublished article, much of which is subsumed in the chapter on "Religion" in Method in Theology.

6. "Cognitional Structure," Collection, p. 222-23.

7. Ibid., p. 230.

8. Cf. Method in Theology, p. 105.

9. Cf. Lonergan's own summation in Insight, p. 731.

10. Second Vatican Council, "Pastoral Constitution on the Church in the Modern World," #22 and 38.

3

PLURIFORMITY IN ETHICS:
A MODERN MISSIONARY PROBLEM
Eugene Hillman, C.S.Sp.

It is widely recognized these days that missionaries have been notoriously obtuse in their approaches to non-Western cultures.[1] Thanks to the modern social sciences, however, and to the present mood of the post-colonial period, there is today a new openness to the ways and values of non-Western peoples. The fact of mankind's necessary cultural pluriformity is now accepted and taken seriously.[2] But the implications of this fact have not yet been fully thought out.

How is Western Christendom's traditional understanding and practice of the faith to be reconciled harmoniously with an entirely new awareness of the intrinsic necessity, validity, and value of the myriad human cultures through which Christianity is supposed to become incarnate, contemporary, relevant, and catholic? As cultural creations, the art forms and thought patterns of non-Western peoples may easily enough find their rightful place in the life of the church in the days ahead. But what about the

---

[1]See Stephen Neill, Call to Mission (Philadelphia: Fortress Press, 1970), pp. 22, 28, 31; Helmut Thielicke, The Ethics of Sex, trans. by John W. Doberstein (New York: Harper and Row, 1964), p. 181; Bernard Haring, A Theology of Protest (New York: Farrar, Straus and Giroux, 1970), pp. 140-141; Bolaji Idowu, Towards and Indigenous Church (Oxford University Press, 1965), p. 5; Poikail John George, "Racist Assumptions in the 10th Century Missionary Movement," International Review of Mission, LIX (July 1970), pp. 271-284; Israel K. Katoke, "Encounter of the Gospel and Cultures," Lutheran World, XIX, No. 1 (1972), pp. 24-41.

[2]On the need for theologians to abandon the classicist notion that only one culture (their own) is truly human and universally normative, and to take seriously the modern empirical understanding of culture as essentially pluriform, historical, and changing, see Bernard Lonergan, Method in Theology (New York: Herder and Herder, 1972), especially pp. 49-51, 78-81, 123-124, 300-302, 326-329.

diverse ethical systems, the moral values and behavior patterns, of the different peoples of the world? These also are cultural creations. Can we accept pluriformity in ethics? If so, why and to what extent are the different ethical systems and behavior patterns compatible with Christianity?

Without pretending to be anything like a definitive statement, or even a comprehensive treatment, the following reflections are offered merely as a basis for discussing this substantive issue.

A Recurring Question

Here again is the perennial question of Christianity's cultural catholicity or universality. This issue was first raised, and settled in principle, at the Jerusalem meeting of the apostles and elders in the year 49 A. D. (cf. Acts 15: 1-30; Gal. 2:1-10). Just as peoples of the world need the sign of a servant savior who does not quench the wick already burning among them (cf. Isa. 42:3; Matt. 5:17), so also the church, for the fulfillment of her own catholic vocation, needs the cultural "riches of the nations," and the "hidden wealth of the peoples" (cf. Isa. 10:13-14; 45:3, 14; 60:3-16; Ps. 2:8; 71:10; Rev. 21:24). This "wonderful exchange," as the fathers of Vatican II expressed it, is to be accomplished "in imitation of the plan of the In-carnation."[3] Hence the church is not constitutionally bound to the limited world view, the ephemeral forms and ethnic conventions, the local laws, customs, and practices of any particular segment of humanity. Indeed, the new life of Christian faith is to be expressed in the socio-cultural context of each people, in the terms of their respective historical times and places, "according to their own national traditions."[4]

Nevertheless, as every missionary knows, it is one thing for theologians and church leaders to verbalize the principle of cultural catholicity, but it is quite another thing to see this

---

[3]Vatican Council II, "Decree on the Missionary Activity of the Church," in The Documents of Vatican II, ed, by Walter M. Abbott and Joseph Gallagher (New York: Guild Press, America Press, Association Press, 1966), no. 22, p. 612.

[4]Ibid., no. 21, p. 611.

principle actually applied in the real world. The practical
application of this principle has been a matter for debate
ever since that day in Antioch when Paul withstood Cephas to
his face (cf. Gal. 2:11). As a result of the church's missionary encounter with one new people after another during the
past nineteen hundred years, the same debate, in countless
different historical contexts, has been an ever recurring source
of tension, of anguish, of schism, and also of renewal. But
each generation of Christians must face in their own time and
place the same central question: How are we to harmonize culture and Christianity?

Are missionaries and local church leaders in our time really
prepared to go along with the implications of this principle,
as it relates to a diversity of moral values and behavior
patterns among the peoples of the non-Western world? How far
can they go? How far should they go? These are questions
which can no longer be avoided by those who are concerned about
the continuing validity of the church's missionary ministry.

No Christian Culture As Such

The fact that Christianity has become an integral part of all
Western cultures does not mean that these have become Christian
cultures. Although Christianity and particular cultures have
had far reaching influences upon one another, no single culture
stands over and above all the others as _the_ Christian culture.
No particular set of cultural patterns and social structures is
in itself specifically Christian. Aside from a short-lived
experiment in radical communalism, the earliest Christians generally continued to follow the basic patterns and structures of
the societies in which they lived prior to their acceptance of
the Christian "way". Even "the ethical teaching of the early
Church," says C. H. Dodd, "falls into a scheme of practical
precepts for everyday living, a scheme based upon a realistic
recognition of the structure as it then was, and following in
general outline the patterns of ethical teaching which were
being set forth by the teachers of other schools."[5]

---

[5]C. H. Dodd, _Gospel and Law_ (New York: Columbia University Press,
1951), p. 25. For more on the extent to which the early Christians
as also those of the Middle Ages, borrowed their ethics from the
pre-Christian Graeco-Roman World, see Heinrich A. Rommen, _The_

Even if they had wished to do so, the first Christians could
not have created a whole new socio-cultural complex, with its
own new ethical system, to guide them in their new lives as
Christians. They could not have done this any more than they
could have invented a new language. It was expected, of course,
that the Christian gospel, acting after the manner of a leaven,
would profoundly influence all cultures.[6] Thus the unity of
mankind would be, hopefully, signified through the pluriform
manifestations of the same faith in the diverse cultures of
the tribes and peoples and nations who constitute the whole
of humanity in the extension of different historical times
and places.[7]

It was in keeping with the logic of the Incarnation that the
first Christians should have expressed their new faith in their
own indigenous cultural forms. These happened to be Judaic and
Graeco-Roman. Perhaps because he participated in both of these
cultures, St. Paul was better able than most men to achieve a
measure of cultural transcendence. He provided the theological
rationale for the cultural pluriformity of Christianity. Indeed,
the whole of his theology is best understood as a response to
those who imagined that the Judaic culture alone provided worthy

---

Natural Law, trans. by Thomas R. Hanley (St. Louis and London:
B. Herder, 1948), pp. 3-5, 21-22, 34-39; John Giles Milhaven,
Toward a New Catholic Morality (Garden City, New York: Doubleday,
1970), pp. 37-39, 145; Gerard Watson, "Pagan Philosophy and
Christian Ethics," in *Morals, Law and Authority*, ed. by J.P.
Mackey (Dublin: Gill and Macmillan, 1969), pp. 39-59; and
Hendrick Kraemer, *The Bible and Social Ethics* (Philadelphia:
Fortress Press, 1965), pp. 11-12.

[6]See Yves Congar, *This Church That I Love*, trans. by Lucien
Delafuente (Denville, New Jersey: Dimension Books, 1969), p. 60:
"...Where the tension between the Church and the world is keenly
felt, the Church is considered a leaven in the mass, carrier of
a message and a life meant for the benefit of the whole world."

[7]See C. H. Dodd, *Christ and the New Humanity* (Philadelphia:
Fortress Press, 1965), pp. 1-7; and Vatican II, "Decree on the
Missionary Activity of the Church," in *The Documents of Vatican
II*, no. 22, pp. 612-613.

patterns and structures for the expression and development
of their new faith.[8] This very question of culture and faith
provoked the first great theological crisis in the church:
The first of many similar crises that have since arisen from
the ethnocentrism of dedicated ecclesiastical functionaries.[9]
With the acceptance of Paul's views, however, the principle
was at least extablished that Christianity not only could,
but should, take on the cultural flesh of one new people after
another in the course of history.

It is not surprising therefore that elements which are recognizably Christian in their inspiration, if not always in their
actual functioning, should have developed in many societies
as a result of the church's missionary outreach. But no single
culture has become the Christian culture, just as no man has
become a perfect follower of Christ: none of us. We are all
"pagans" trying, sometimes, to become Christians. At the same
time, elements that are recognizably "pagan" in their inspiration were drawn into the service of the church: Platonism,
Stoicism, Roman Law, Aristotelianism, pontifical trappings,
Christmas trees, etc., etc. And such things as racism (tribal-
ism), found today in many Christian communities, owe nothing
to the spirit of the gospel, but everything to the cultural
attitudes of men who would become Christians. So also the
pernicious economic system through which nature is despoiled
and human relationships are reduced to naked self-interest.

The Relationship Between Culture and Christianity

The ambiguity of Christianity in its various historical manifestations, as well as the ambivalence of Christians in their
daily lives, may be seen as inevitable consequences of the
historical relationship between culture and Christianity. This
relationship is sometimes incarnational and sometimes merely
symbiotic; and, where culture and Christianity are both alive,
there is always tension.

---

[8]See John L. McKenzie, The Power and the Wisdom (Milwaukee: Bruce,
1965), p.202.

[9]See Eugene Hillman, The Wider Ecumenism (New York and London:
Herder and Herder, Burns and Oates, 1968), pp. 151-152.

These two notions, incarnation and symbiosis, may be used to describe the normal historical situation of Christianity in the world. The Lord himself fully accepted the Judaic culture into which he was born and which formed him as a human being. It was within the limited historical framework of this culture that Jesus accomplished his mission. His approach was incarnational. But, with many elements of his native culture, his relationship was merely symbiotic. Although his life contradicted many of the established religio-ethical patterns of Judaic culture, he nevertheless expressed himself through these very patterns, even manifesting an astonishing respect for religious and moral structure that were already obsolete and extensively tainted by the selfishness of men.[10] It was not every day the Jesus drove the money changers from the temple. And he firmly ordered the cured leper to make the legally prescribed offering to the priest. For the revolutionary vision of Jesus is more radical than that of utopian dreamers who imagine that institutions, rather than men, are the principal bearers of evil.[11]

The methodology of Christianity, to put it briefly, is to be present in the world as it is, and among all peoples, after the manner of a leaven. This is not at all the same thing as an extrinsic and legalistic "Christianization" of social structures, according to some latter day reconception of the ancient Corpus Christianum--as though new laws and foreign institutions were capable of renewing the hearts of men. Nor can we expect the leaven to function where Christians are not positively and creatively engaged in the dynamic processes of their own cultures. The reform of social structures and moral systems is a consequence, rather than a cause, of authentic changes within men and their cultures. This inner metanoia cannot be imposed

---

[10]See Randolf Schnackenberg, The Moral Teaching of the New Testament, trans. by J. Holland-Smith and W. J. O'Hara (New York and London: Herder and Herder, Burns and Oates, 1965), pp. 56-65.

[11]See Lonergan, op. cit., p. 49: "The same economic set up is compatible with prosperity and with recession. The same constitutional and legal arrangements admit wide differences in political life and in the administration of justice. Similar rules for marriage and the family in one case generate domestic bliss and in another misery."

from the outside. How many centuries passed before Western
Christians came fully to realize that their faith is essentially incompatible with the socio-economic institution of
slavery?

Moreover, Christianity's essential universalism, so manifest
at least in the pristine Pentecostal spirit of the earliest
Christians, precludes the total identification of Christianity
with any particular culture. The second century writer of the
Epistle to Diognetus took note of this in the following words:

> Christians are not to be distinguished from other men
> by country, language, or customs. They have no cities
> of their own, they use no peculiar dialect, and they
> practice no extraordinary way of life. Residing in
> cities of the Greek world and beyond it, as is the lot
> of each, they follow the local customs as in clothing,
> diet, and general manner of life.[12]

With this same sense of universalism and awareness of mankind's
cultural pluriformity, the fathers of Vatican II repeatedly urged
the church to move more generously toward the concrete realization of cultural catholicity in all forms of Christian life:

> Sent to all peoples in every time and place, the church
> is not bound exclusively and indissolubly to any race
> or nation, nor to any particular way of life or any
> customary pattern of living, ancient or recent. Faith-
> ful to her own tradition and at the same time conscious
> of her universal mission, she can enter into communion
> with various cultural modes, to her own enrichment and
> theirs too.[13]

---

[12]Epistle to Diognatus (second century), 5-6, abridged; as cited
by Dodd, Christ and the New Humanity, pp. 3-4. See also Edward
Schillebeeckx, Marriage: Secular Reality and Saving Mystery,
trans. by N. D. Smith (London and Melbourne: Sheed and Ward,
1965), II, p. 18.

[13]Vatican II, "Pastoral Constitution on the Church in the Modern
World," no. 58, p. 264. See also, in The Documents of Vatican
II, "Dogmatic Constitution on the Church," no. 13, p. 31;
"Decree on the Missionary Activity of the Church," nos. 21-22,

This ecumenical outlook, in the New Testament sense of the
world oikumene (cf. Matt. 24:14; Rom. 10:18), is based on the
belief that all men are equal before God. "There is no distinction: all have sinned," and "all have the same Lord"
(cf. Rom. 3:22f; 10:12). The salvation announced and accomplished in Christ is not the salvation of a favored elite, but
of humanity. Hence the same saving grace is universally available to all men, whenever and wherever they may experience
their brief participation in the history of redeemed mankind.[14]
All the works of men are therefore under the influence not only
of sin but also of grace. So the general unevenness of cultural
development is reflected also, and perhaps especially, in the
area of morality. The diverse ethical systems devised by men,
but not by them unaided, in the course of history reflect at
once the shame and the glory of man. No particular system,
just as no individual human being, is entirely bad or entirely
good. It is precisely on this assumption that the whole Christian ministry of reconciliation is based; not on the opposite
assumption that some peoples and their cultures are bad, while
others are good.[15]

Ethical Systems: Different and Changing

Anthropoligists have never encountered a people without an ethical
system: an interlocking set of judgments, norms and rules for
the guidance and evaluation of human conduct in relation to the
common good of the society which formed, and continuously reforms,
its own morality.[16] This cultural creation is a "social cement"

---

pp. 611-613; "Constitution on the Sacred Liturgy," no. 37, p. 151;
"Declaration on the Relationship of the Church to Non-Christian
Religions," no. 2, pp. 662-663.

[14]See Hillman, op. cit., pp. 34-59; Gregory Baum, Man Becoming: God
in Secular Experience (New York: Herder and Herder, 1970), pp.
28-36; and Bernard Lonergan, op. cit., pp. 282-283.

[15]See Dodd, Christ and the New Humanity, p. 14.

[16]See Raymond Firth, Elements of Social Organization (Boston: Beacon
Press, 1963), p. 213: Anthropology reveals "the existence of standards of right and wrong, and sensitive judgements in their terms,

which holds together in relative harmony the structures and institutions of each society. Without some such system dignified
human existence is not possible. Moral decisions have to be
made and structured for the purpose of guiding and controlling
human behavior which otherwise tends to become inhuman.

If family life, the elementary social unit upon which all larger
societies are based, is to be maintained, then obviously it is
necessary to have some socially accepted structures for re-
straining and regulating sexual activity. Every human society
has its own ways of controlling sex, by surrounding it with
checks and balances, taboos and permissions.[17] Even in the
hordes of primates "random promiscuity is rare and usually the
result of some kind of social breakdown."[18] Unregulated sexual
activity is, of course, not the only threat to social harmony.
The common good demands that such things as greed and violence
should also be systematically curbed. Thus a whole network of
interrelated and interacting norms, prohibitions and licenses
is developed together with, and as a dynamic element within,
each culture.

A culturally integrated ethical system represents a long sequence
of historically conditioned moral choices made by men who are at
the same time fallen and redeemed. No ethical system represents
the best of all possible choices. There must always be some
painful exceptions to the established rules of behavior, some
human compromises, adaptations and even radical changes of position. We have only to recall, for example, the ambivalence of
Christians in their moral attitude towards war and peace during
the course of Western history. After Constantine the theory of
the just war, borrowed from "pagan" antiquity, was baptized; and
this represented a new morality in contrast to the earlier position articulated by such persons as Justin, Athenagoras, Tertullian

---

in all human societies studied....Morality is a social cement
between individual means and social ends."

[17]See George P. Murdock, Social Structures (London: Collier-Mac-
millan, 1949; New York: The Free Press, 1965), p. 4.

[18]Robin Fox, Kinship and Marriage (Harmondsworth, Baltimore,
Victoria: Penguin Books, 1967), p. 29.

Cyprian, Origen, Minucius, and Arnobius.[19]

Men must live with the ethical system that happens to be available and intelligible to them where they are, at least until new
possibilities for change arise from within their own historico-
cultural situation. The presence of the church in each culture
is supposed to be a leaven; and Christian revelation provides
its believers with a norm for questioning, criticizing, evaluation, and reforming the content of their own indigenous ethical
system.[20] The community itself, enlightened by God's grace, is
alone competent to discern the values which protect and promote
its own well being; so it belongs properly to the community to
question, criticize, evaluate and reform its own patterns of
behavior; and to do this in relation to their understanding of
Christian revelation. It is only as persons experience life
together in the same historico-cultural world, as they reach out
together for what is good and true in their situation, that they
find the most appropriate ways of articulating verbally and in
their social structures the values which promote the life and
destiny of their community.[21]

What is suggested here is that the church cannot improve the
moral life of a people by issuing decrees from the outside, by
importing ready-made ethical rules, or by imposing extrinsic
modifications that have been borrowed from some foreign culture,
some profoundly different historico-cultural experience of life
together. Moral changes, if they are to be coherently integrated
and deeply influential in the normal functioning of existing cultures, must come from inside these cultures. For example, it is

---

[19]See Daniel Maguire, <u>Moral Absolutes and the Magisterium</u> (Washington and Cleveland: Corpus Papers, 1970), pp. 4-7.

[20]See Franz Böckle, "The Problem of Social Ethics," <u>American Ecclesiastical Review</u>, CLXIII (November 1970), p. 347; and Johannes B.
Metz, "Religion and Society in the Light of Political Theology,"
<u>Harvard Theological Review</u>, LXI (October 1968), p. 514.

[21]For this and the previous sentence, see Gregory Baum, "Does
Morality Need the Church?", <u>The Catholic Theological Society
of America: Proceedings of the 25th Annual Convention</u>, XXV
(June 1970), p. 163.

notorious that moral and social disintegration have been directly
consequent upon the imposition by missionaries, and by colonial
governments, of Western individualistic moral and legal codes.
This situation is, of course, exacerbated by the church's typically
Western experience of, and insistence upon, individuality in all
aspects of religion as well as morals, almost as though these
were private affairs, and not societal realities.[22]

A Specifically Christian Morality?

If all morality is culturally formed and historically conditioned,
always and only in the terms of some concrete society, then no
particular ethical system stands, in some kind of abstract Platonic
objectivity, over and above all human behavior. For this behavior,
and therefore all morality, is real only where men actually live,
in the diversity of their particular historico-cultural experiences.
The content of every ethical system, whether it is labelled "Christian" or not, exists as a functional element in some ephemeral cultural complex. In this sense, whatever comes under the heading
of Christian ethics is really pre-Christian, or secular. In the
words of John G. Milhaven:

> In short, any Christian ethics must rest on a secular
> base, man's experience in the world, his experience, for

------

[22]See Metz., op. cit., pp. 507, 509-510, 512-513; Stephen Neill,
Christian Faith and Other Faiths: The Christian Dialogue with
Other Religions, 2nd edition (London: Oxford University Press,
1970), pp. 148-149; Jomo Kenyatta, Facing Mount Kenya (London:
Secker and Warburg, 1938), pp. 115, 117-118, 188; and Bernard
Haring, op. cit., p. 144: "The moral theology of the last century sanctioned the individualistic concept of private property
as entertained by the ruling class and by an individualistic
European culture. Christian ethics....was for a long time uncritical with regard to this individualistic concept of property
with its many effects. The moralists were uncritical not only
because they have grown up in this climate and for the most
part came from the bourgeoisie, but also because they themselves
knew little about the missionary apostolate of the church to all
classes and all cultures.... Moreover, this individualistic concept of private property was utterly alien to most African and
Asian cultures."

example, in marriage. The secular experience is
irreducible; it cannot be altered by religious
faith or theological understanding. All the values,
responsibilities and obligations the Christian recog-
nizes--except those pertaining directly to God, such
as prayer--are forged first of all in this human experience.[23]

Fundamentally, therefore, it would seem that there is in reality
no specifically Christian ethics.[24] Nor is any ethical system
essentially inimical to the leaven of the Gospel. (Periodic
outbursts of savagery, as occurred for example in Germany under
Nazism, do not signify the presence of an evil ethical system,
but rather the breakdown of a good one.) For all positive
moral striving has the same source. All morality rests on
common ground; and this common ground is nothing other than
the historical nature of man, fallen and redeemed. Whether
they know about it consciously or not, there is only one final
destiny to which all men are summoned by the same saving grace
of God in Jesus Christ (cf. Jn. 1:3, 9; 4:42; 12:32; Acts 4:2;
10:36; Rom. 8:19-24; I Cor. 8:6; Eph. 1:9-11; Col. 1:15-20;
Heb. 1:3).[25] Unless we regard this as a kind of pious fiction,
we must accept the implication that the victorious and super-

---

[23]Milhaven, op. cit., p. 37.

[24]See Bockle, op. cit., p. 347: "The Bible does not wish to offer
a complete material ethic which would claim validity for all times
as the specifically Christian one....In this sense, there is no
specific Christian material ethics." See also John Macquarrie,
Three Issues in Ethics (New York, London, Evanston: Harper and
Row, 1970), pp. 82-110; Charles E. Curran, Contemporary Problems
in Moral Theology (Notre Dame, Indiana: Fides, 1970), pp. 233-
234, 236; Josef Fuchs, "Is There a Specifically Christian Morality?", Theology Digest, XIX (Spring 1971), pp. 39-45; Josef Fuchs,
Human Values and Christian Morality, trans. by M. H. Heelan,
Maeve McRedmond, Erika Young and Gerard Watson (Dublin and London:
Gill and Macmillan, 1970), pp. 112-147; and R. Simon, "Specificite
de l'ethique chretienne," Le Supplement, XXIII (February 1970),
pp. 74-104.

[25]See footnote 14, above.

abounding grace of God is universally operative among all men in
the terms of their respective historico-cultural experiences.
"If men do not reject this grace," says Josef Fuchs, "they
accept it."[26]

All upright moral behavior--and Christians certainly have no
monopoly on this--is therefore a manifestation of God's grace
at work among men of all times and places. This understanding
of grace prevents us from imagining, even without any convincing
evidence, that Christians are somehow morally better than the
rest of men--as though Christians experience a kind of love
which is not found among non-Christians.[27] "The work of Christ,"
according to Fuchs, "is not meant to proclaim a higher moral
standard, but rather salvation, which the love of the Father
grants us through Christ."[28] Is this just some novelty invented
by contemporary theologians? No. This very idea, that "Christian morality is in essence a true human morality," and that
"no new moral directives are given by Jesus Christ beyond those
dictated by human virtue,"[29] is found also in the teaching of

---

[26]Fuchs, Human Values and Christian Morality, p. 69.

[27]See George Crespy, "The Grace of Marriage," in George Crespy,
Paul Evdokimov and Christian Duquoc, Marriage and Christian
Tradition, trans. by Agnes Cunningham (Techny, Illinois: Divine
Word Publications, 1968), p. 50: "...Christians in no way enjoy
a monopoly by which they are secretly admitted to a kind of love
which unbelievers can never experience. They love as all men
love, with the ambiguity attendant upon love...."

[28]Fuchs, Human Values and Christian Morality, p. 76; see also p. 77:
"Joy in Christ and in his law sometimes encourages the Christian
to compare this law with the law of non-Christians, as if there
existed a twofold moral law, one for Christians and one for non-
Christians, for the latter maybe even a purely natural law. Yet
the conception which makes such a comparison is guilty of an
under-valuation of the law of Christ."

[29]Ibid., pp. 120-121. See also pp. 122-125, where Fuchs goes on to
explain how, and in what sense, it is possible to speak of a
specifically Christian morality.

Thomas Aquinas on the contents of the New Law.[30] What is new is that this idea, with its practical implications, is being taken more seriously these days than heretofore.

If the content of all morality is pre-Christian, and if the same grace of God inspires moral uprightness or holiness among non-Christians no less than among Christians, what then is the significance of the morality we call "Christian"? Fuchs gives this reply:

> ...We must call the morality of Christians the explicit and Church-societal form of this morality, which non-Christians, too, realize in an implicit manner.... The Christians are those who, in an explicit manner and in a Church-community, direct the moral formation and organization of their life and world towards the person of Christ.... The visibility of the morality founded on Christ's person has just this task: to help the non-Christian to a more explicit comprehension of not only the single elements, but also the deepest sense of the morality founded in Christ, which fundamentally constitutes their own morality.[31]

What Christian revelation adds, then, to this world of human values and to pre-Christian morality is not a new set of rules or norms, but a new perspective, a new understanding, a new consciousness, and consequently a new challenge to the blind

---

[30]See Thomas Aquinas, <u>Summa Theologiae</u> (Ottowa: Impensis Studii Generalis, O. Pr., 1941-1945), 5 volumes, I-II, q. 108, art. 2.

[31]Fuchs, <u>Human Values and Christian Morality</u>, p. 70; and see also p. 131: "When one speaks of <u>human</u> morality as such, one is really speaking of Christian morality, even if under a particular aspect, its human aspect." According to John Macquarrie, <u>op</u>. <u>cit</u>., p. 110, "...there is no conflict between the ideals of a Christian ethic and the moral ideals to be found in humanity at large.... Christianity does not establish a new or different morality, but makes concrete, clarifies, and, above all, focuses on a particular person, Jesus Christ, the deepest moral convictions of men. Christ declared he was fulfilling the law, not abolishing it."

selfishness that permeates the entire human condition. Christian faith, in other words, offers a new vantage point for a fresh approach to the meaning of all human values and moral systems, a new incentive for self-criticism and for continuous conversion, and a new hope in the possibility of realizing the potential for live that is in every man.

Some Conclusions

This is not a matter of saying that Christians should tolerate any ethical system. Rather, they must live with the operative system of the particular culture within which they find themselves. For it is only through this sort of incarnation or symbiosis that it will become possible for the gospel to lay its transcendent claims on all the works of men, and to act as a transforming leaven within each culture and among all peoples. Man's struggle with his own selfishness, blindness, prejudice, stupidity, and wickedness--as also his altruistic aspirations and transcendent desires--must be expressed, and can be realized, only within his own concrete historico-cultural context. So the best culture for the manifestation and development of each man's Christian faith is his own culture, because normally this is the only one available to him, and he can hardly find himself in some foreign culture. To say all this is simply to affirm the principle of incarnation.

At the same time it is recognized that some cultural elements can stand only in a tentatively symbiotic relationship to Christianity. We may recall, for example, the selfrighteous pharisaism that so marked God's revealed relgion in the time of Christ, and the vested-interests then associated with worship. Self-righteousness is still the major temptation, and sometimes even the outward sign, of those who see themselves as God's "chosen people." For centuries the Christian conscience was undisturbed by the socio-economic institution of slavery that was so well integrated into cultures which were regarded as Christian. And how many Christians in our own time are actively participating, for their own material advantage, in a system of economic imperialism which works for "the increasing enrichment of the rich, and the increasing impoverishment of the poor"?[32]

---

[32]Yves Congar, "The Place of Poverty in Christian Life in an Affluent Society," *Concilium*, XV (May 1966), pp. 34-35.

While working against all forms of individual and collective
egoism, we must realistically accept the well attested fact that
we will never fully succeed; for this same selfishness is quite
alive in all of us. While each culture preserves much that is
good, beautiful, unique, and irreplaceable, each one at the same
time has its own ways of institutionalizing human selfishness.
So the transformation of the world, in so far as this is to be
signified through the visible witness of Christianity amont all
peoples, is a task to be accomplished within, and in the terms
of, each culture. It cannot be done by transferring from one
culture to another various rules and institutions that seem to
be clean, and thus purely Christian. What looks clean to the
members of one culture might be, in some different historico-
cultural context, a bucket of worms.

4

THE SUPRACULTURAL AND THE CULTURAL: IMPLICATIONS FOR FRONTIER MISSIONS
G. Linwood Barney

INTRODUCTION

The concern of this paper is to consider the supracultural and the cultural (defined below) in the context of communicating the Gospel of Christ and planting the Christian Church in cross-cultural situations. While this has implications for the Church in all areas it has particular significance for the problems encountered in frontier missions. It will be necessary to consider both theoretical assumptions and practical procedures in relating the supracultural to the cultural in this context.

It should be noted that this problem is not entirely new in the history of the Church. In a brief study we cannot enjoy the luxury of a careful historical survey of the issues but we can gain an appreciative awareness that it is not a problem which suddenly appeared in the 20th century. Perhaps one of the most obvious case studies in a cross-cultural situation is found in the early church when many gentile peoples followed the Jews in receiving the Gospel, responding to it, and forming local churches. The book of Acts (especially chapters 10, 11 and 15) and many of the Epistles (especially Galatians) document the tensions which can develop when the Gospel is presented and obeyed in multicultural areas. The forms and structures by which Christians in different cultures express their Faith vary but, too frequently, this incites misunderstanding, suspicion and antagonism. A study of Church History from this perspective would show that the problem is usually repeated whenever a church which has become established in one culture shares its Faith across cultural borders. The tendency has been for the witnessing community to expect the new Christians in the different culture to express their faith in the cultural patterns of the witnessing community.

In the 20th century, especially in the last few decades, there has been an increasing interest and study given to this problem. Kenneth Scott Latourette[2] has given much attention to the inter-

action between the Church and the socio-cultural system in which
it finds itself. Niebuhr's writings[3] have provided helpful insights into some of the concepts involved. The different editors
and contributors in the journal, <u>PRACTICAL ANTHROPOLOGY</u>[4], have
produced a body of material, theoretical and practical, which
relates more specifically to this problem. Certain institutions
and a growing number of scholars[5] are struggling with the problems
from many perspectives. Inter-disciplinary studies involving
theology and anthropology,[6] as well as other behavioral and social
sciences, have been particularly helpful. All of these are providing new bases for evaluating missionary effort, for applying new
insights to missions problems, and in implementing new methods in
missionary practice. This paper reflects the writer's beneficial
contacts with many of these people and their writings.

The current stigma placed on missions often stems from criticism[7] which either ignores or is not informed of many new dimensions in the missionary enterprise. Much careful thought, study
and planning is being exercised in developing a strategy for crossing today's frontiers in missions. We must seek to understand the
practice of the past and evaluate it objectively and wholesomely.
We must be just as objective and wholesome in evaluating present
programs or in devising new ones.

With this in mind, then, this paper presents the general
concept of the supracultural in relation to the cultural as one of
the basic issues in the cross-cultural outreach of the Church in
its missionary task.

By the term <u>cultural</u>, we refer to those phenomena, material
and non-material, (ideas, values, etc.) which have been developed
by man. Each ethnic group has patterns, explicit and implicit, by
which its members relate to one another and to their environment.
When these patterns combine to form a total configuration it constitutes <u>a culture</u>. Each generation of a given society receives
its culture from the passing generation, modifies it, and passes
it on to the following generation. Thus a culture is really not
static but constantly undergoing change. There are over 3500
ethnic groups in the world and yet no two of them have identical
cultural configurations. Each of these societies has a culture
which is systemic and patterned in a series of layers. The first
layer consists basically of material artifacts and observable
human behavior. The second layer is composed of a culture's
institutions and then come layers with values, ideology, cosmology and worldview. Cultural traits in the first layer are easily
described and even borrowed. However, each ascending layer is
more complex and abstract. It is one thing to describe or share
artifacts and observable patterns of behavior. It is quite an-

other thing to discover the functions of these in the culture as
a whole and it is still more difficult and demanding to decode
their meaning at the levels of values, ideology, cosmology and
worldview. The culture of a specific society is an integrative,
functional, systemic whole which gives order to the life of that
particular people.

By the term supracultural, we refer to those phenomena
which have their source outside the sphere of culture. This
does not preclude its penetrating the cultural sphere and finding
a cultural expression there. This writer postulates two sources
for that which is supracultural: (1) That which stems from God;
the Gospel of Jesus Christ, Faith, the essential Nature of the
Church, the fruit of the Spirit, the gifts of the Spirit, etc.;
(2) That which stems from Satan; evil, sin, etc.[8] The supracultural can be universal in the sense that it is not limited to any
one culture. Furthermore no culture is impervious to penetration
by the supracultural.

I. THEORETICAL CONSIDERATIONS

It is not difficult to speak of a God-man relationship but
one encounters real problems in locating and identifying components in this relationship. How does one relate the Infinite to
the finite, the supracultural to the cultural?

Certain basic assumptions of this writer will be obvious. He
assumes that God is and that man becomes. (1) God is creator and
man is creature. This man, made a "person" in the image of God,
was intended to have fellowship with God and he is incomplete
without that fellowship. (2) Man is the maker of culture. Culture reflects man's needs and his concerns. Man, alienated from
God, produces culture which reflects this alienation in its man-
centered concerns and perspective. Hence, there develops a kind
of vicious circle in which man makes culture but, in turn, is
shaped by culture in each new generation. In summary, culture is
anthropocentric and man is self-centered. Each society has its
own peculiar patterns of man-oriented culture which tends to
alienate each generation from God and screen out any God-oriented
perspective and life style.

Reconciliation between God and man is initiated by God in His
redeeming acts in Jesus Christ and is effected in the experience
of a man through the dynamic activity of God, the Holy Spirit.
However, to distinguish between that which in essence is determined by God's activity (supracultural) and that which is man's
response (cultural) is difficult. Continual culture change which
is always in process only adds to the difficulty. A God-man rela-

tionship does not occur in a socio-cultural vacuum. Therefore, any separation between the supracultural and the cultural in a God-man relationship is in theory only. The crucial question would seem to be: "Can the supracultural find adequate and meaningful forms of expression in any culture?" If the answer is in the affirmative then we should encourage the Christian community in a "new" culture to develop its own cultural forms for a meaningful expression of the supracultural: its new Faith, the communication of the Gospel to others, its common life as people of God, etc. The essential nature of these supracultural components should neither be lost nor distorted but rather secured and interpreted clearly through the guidance of the Holy Spirit in "inculturating"[9] them into this new culture. If our designation of man as the source of culture is correct (see above) then man-oriented culture will have to be modified (transformed) and reoriented to reflect the supracultural with its divine source. However, such innovations should not be the imposed cultural forms of one society on another but rather relevant changes within a culture--changes which are consistent with the character of the supracultural.

In struggling to present clearly these concepts and to locate properly the components in the appropriate categories of the supracultural or the cultural, certain models may be useful. Some scholars (Charles Kraft, Eugene Nida, etc.) have associated the absolute with the supracultural and the relative with the cultural. By definition the absolute is that which is underived and unchanging. Conversely, the relative is derived (dependent) and changing. God is absolute, underived and unchanging. But consider the following implications. The Gospel is given of God. Therefore it is derived. It can not be absolute. Is it therefore relative? If so, it is changeable. Yet Paul (Galatians) speaks of the one Gospel. We need another conceptual category between absolute and relative. It would seem that the term "constant" might meet this need. Constant refers to that which, by nature, does not change though it may be derived. If we add "constant" between "absolute" and "relative" as conceptual categories in our consideration of the supracultural and the cultural it can be helpful. Then it follows, God is absolute. That which he initiates and affirms to man in his covenant and redeeming acts is constant; however, the forms in which man responds to God, expresses Faith, and lives out his relationship with God are tied to his culture and therefore are relative. The absolute and the constant are supracultural but man's response is relative and thus can vary from culture to culture as each society expresses the supracultural in forms peculiar to its own cultural configuration. Thus a relevant expression of the God-man relationship can preserve the integrity of a culture but in no way needs to compromise the essence and nature of the supracultural.

The Gospel, the good news of God's redeeming acts, is a constant. However, the linguistic forms which encode the Gospel should not be considered synonymous with the Gospel. Nor is the verbal encodement of the Gospel limited to one particular language.

Faith in Jesus Christ, that which establishes and maintains a relationship between God and a man is another constant. Again, the cultural forms employed to express one's faith in Christ are not synonymous with that Faith. Nor is the expression of Faith limited to the particular forms of any one culture. As the Gospel is not proclaimed in a linguistic vacuum so Faith in Christ is not experienced in a socio-cultural vacuum. Yet neither the Gospel nor Faith is dependent on the particular forms of any particular language or culture.

The essential nature of the Church is also a constant. Witness, worship, fellowship and service, functions inherent in the nature of the Church, issue through the dynamic of God, the Holy Spirit, but are expressed in forms and structures which are sociocultural in nature. Again the particular forms and structures practiced by the institutional church in any particular culture should not be considered synonymous with the essential nature of the Church.

The role of the Holy Spirit is quite apparent in considering the supracultural. He is the prime mover in effecting Faith and in forming the Church. He produces the Fruit of the Spirit (Galatians 5) and distributes the gifts of the Spirit (I Cor. 12 and Romans 12, etc.) all of which would be considered "constant" in the categories above. The teaching and power of the Holy Spirit brings the supracultural into the ethical behavior and life style of every believer and to every community of believers. The forms by which any community expresses this life of the Spirit will be peculiar to the culture of that community. Herein lies the basis for true unity--at the level of the supracultural; but also the basis for wholesome diversity--at the level of the cultural.

There are two theoretical implications which seem pertinent to draw at this point. (1) There is no such thing as indigenous Christian Faith or the indigenous Church. Christian Faith and the Church are not native to the soil of any particular culture. These have their source from God and come into existence by His divine initiative. These are indigenous in expression only. (2) Due to the continually changing nature of culture, this indigenous form of expression is always in process. In crossing cultural borders, geographically or chronologically, the supracultural seeks a relevant expression--one which is continually current.

II. PRACTICAL IMPLICATIONS

Theoretically, therefore, there is neither necessity nor justification for cultural "imperialism" by the missionary. If this supracultural-cultural dichotomy has theological and anthropological validity it provides basic principles which should be reflected in the Church's understanding of its missionary task and the methods it employs. The question is not what modification will the next culture have to make in its expression of the Christian Faith, (i.e. how will it differ from ours) but rather (without any necessary comparison with ours) how will the new Christians in that "new" culture encode the Gospel, express Faith in Christ, and structure their fellowship and ministry. The distinction between culture change induced from the outside and culture change induced by a people's new relationship with God and a God-oriented perspective must be understood by both missionary and national. The missionary in frontier missions should expect to observe new forms for expressing the supracultural and accept these without surprise or undue suspicion. The national should be concerned to live out his new relationship with God without making a meaningless copy of the missionary's forms nor fearing undue criticism from him. While the missionary may be a friend, a catalyst of ideas and even a source of alternatives (due to his knowledge of church history and the church in other cultures) he should not be the determiner of the cultural shape and forms which the supracultural acquires in the new Christian community. In the final analysis the national Christian community must decide how best to inculturate the supracultural elements in its relationship with God.

Perhaps a few illustrations will suggest the wide range of possibilities in a cross-cultural situation. The following are drawn from the writer's missionary experience among the Meo people of Laos.

In the language of the Meo the heart is simply one of the vital organs of the body. The center of emotions and the will is identified as the liver. Hence the Gospel of Christ appeals to the liver of man, the believer will love God with all his liver, and members in a Christian community make "one liver" (collective) to go the "Jesus Way." This is a rather obvious linguistic (and cultural) encodement which is relevant to the Meo. Most Missionaries and nationals accept this accommodation readily.

The cultural form of communicating new information among the Meo is narrative in style. Proclamation of the Gospel is more effective and efficient if presented as a narrative account of God's redemptive work rather than a sermonic argument or proposition. This generally requires a new kind of mindset for the

missionary and is offensive to that missionary who is locked into
a rigid system of homiletics.

Conversion among the Meo often comes about through a complex
series of communicative events concluding in group decisions made
by consensus. This can be very disturbing to a missionary who con-
siders individual decision as the only authentic manner of conversion. Time and space permit neither a full description of the
process which precedes a decision by consensus nor a discussion of
the pervasive character of this form of decision-making in Meo
culture.

Even as Jesus seemed to touch the "key-issue" in the lives of
those he encountered (Nicodemus, the woman of Samaria, Zacchaeus,
etc.) so different cultures may have particular emphases or concerns to which the message of the Gospel speaks most directly and
for which Christ is most earnestly embraced as Savior and Liberator.
The Meo are as conscious of Christ delivering them from oppressive
spiritual powers as from their sins. The Christian community is as
repulsed by Christians who engage in gossip as those involved in
extra-marital relations.

The priesthood of all believers fits well into the Meo social
patterns of equality and mutuality between persons. While they
readily recognize those whom God has gifted to be evangelists,
pastors, teachers, etc. they do not conceive of these in the full-
time specialist model of the more complex societies. Even the
village chief and others with special responsibilities plant their
own rice fields. The Christian leader should do as much.

The Meo church calendar tends to reflect a total Christian
"way of life." This will include a ritual which consecrates areas
to be cleared for planting and a series of similar rituals throughout the annual cycle of farming. The Meo Christian thus stands in
marked contrast to the non-Christian. However, it is a contrast
which is relevant to Meo life. The Christian Meo need not be
identified with an alien culture by his non-Christian Meo friends.
In fact, one might postulate: To the extent that the Christian Meo
is borrowing alien forms to express his Faith--to that extent he
has not yet internalized his Faith.

CONCLUSION

The writer has selected only a few situations in which the
Meo Christians seek to find relevant cultural forms to express
their relationship with God. There are many more and as these Meo
people encounter the mainstream of world society with its great
cultural complexities they will have more such struggles, many of

which may be even more difficult. Parallel situations could be described for all areas where the outreach of the Church is crossing cultural frontiers.

Despite the movement toward "one world", the popular notion of the world as a "global village" is a gross oversimplification. The demise of overt colonialism and the birth of nationalism are overshadowed by increasing segmentation and tensions related to the self-consciousness of some 3500 distinct ethnic groups (each with its own language) in the world.

There are many more frontiers to be crossed with the Gospel. The Church must be born in many "new" cultures. The insights of present disciplines as well as the lessons learned from the past should be reflected in today's missionary activity on these frontiers. Definite steps should be taken to:

(1) Gather sufficient data of cross-cultural missionary work to allow better elicitation of common principles which are applicable universally.

(2) Incorporate these and the concept of the supracultural into the training and orientation program of missionaries.

(3) Incorporate the concept of the supracultural and the cultural into the instructional program of the national church. It is important that they understand these principles in relating to missionaries, to minority ethnic groups in their own nations and in their missionary outreach across frontiers.

Missionary work is far from completed. It must be carried on. This kind of understanding in the philosophy and practice of missions does not compromise the supracultural but permits the Church to fulfill its Biblical mandate without offending those who are embarrassed by, or critical of, the "cultural imperialism" of past missionary activity.

NOTES

1. The <u>Supracultural</u> and the <u>Cultural</u>, so defined and used in this paper, is similar to the concept <u>Ethnotheology</u>, which has been discussed by Charles Kraft of the School of World Mission at Fuller Theological Seminary in a manuscript prepared earlier this year. Kraft is proposing this as a cross-discipline which will develop its own perspectives, concepts and methodology. This present paper anticipates some of these objectives in an incipient way but does not purport to have nearly attained the sophistication of a discipline.

2. In the introduction to <u>A History of the Expansion of Christianity</u> (7 volumes) Latourette sets forth seven basic questions relating to the relation of Christianity and the environment in which it takes hold.

3. <u>Christ and Culture</u>, <u>Misunderstanding the Church</u>, <u>Social Sources of Denominationalism</u>, etc.

4. Robert Taylor, E. A. Nida, W. A. Smalley, Charles Taber, William Reyburn, Jacob Loewen and William Wonderly among others.

5. The former Kennedy School of Missions, The School of World Mission at Fuller Seminary, The Jaffray School of Missions at Nyack, N. Y., departments at Wheaton College, Bethel College, etc.

6. This writer, an anthropologist, has been team teaching with theologians for 12 years in the preparation of missionaries.

7. A case in point would be the <u>Declaration of Barbados</u> produced jointly by the Programme to Combat Racism and the Churches Commission on International Affairs of the World Council of Churches, together with the Ethnology Department of the University of Bern (Switzerland). It is evaluated by another anthropologist, Alan R. Tippett, in <u>Evangelical Missions Quarterly</u>, Summer 1972.

8. This writer has employed the concept of supra-cultural for many years, but generally in the category related to God's activity among men. In the last two years he has posited the demonic activity among men as stemming from Satan. The implications of this are not developed in this paper but the existence of this category of the supra-cultural should not be overlooked.

9. Inculturate should not be confused with the term enculturate
   which is employed by social sciences to refer to a culture's
   process of orienting a person to that culture. "Inculturate"
   is coined here to refer to that process or state in which a
   new principle has been culturally "clothed" in meaningful
   forms in a culture.

5

SITUATIONAL GIVENS IN FRONTIER MISSIONS
Alan R. Tippett

In the past most missionary operations have gone ahead (often
blindly) on the simple presupposition that the Lord's parting
injunction to disciple the nations was an adequate generalization
for mission at any time or place and under any conditions. While it
is perfectly true that we need no other authority than our Lord's
word for emphasis on mission, nevertheless he left other utterances
which signify that he was well aware of the diversity of situations
in which his servants would be operating, and sometimes he gave them
quite specific instructions (Luke 9:1-6; 10:1-16).

"Givens": Mission Not Without Context

I have been assigned the task of writing about "The Givens" for the
Conference on Frontier Missions. What do we mean by "the givens?"
I think we mean that Christian mission(s), in which we are planning
specific programs or projects, cannot be undertaken blindly, merely
on a basis of theological abstractions or generalizations. We are
recognizing that every project with mission as its goal be seen as
something precise, with a concrete context. We are implying that
each project has its own peculiar context, and that these contextual
"givens" may either help or hinder the mission. Sometimes they will
have been set up by political leaders, especially to defeat our
purposes. In any case we may have no option but to accept these
limitations and operate within them. In as much as there are always
some "givens," every missionary situation is unique.

This may be demonstrated historically as nothing really new,
although it has to be pointed out to missionaries in every generation, lest they abstract or generalize their theology, and project
their own home situation and values into their missionary enterprises.

The Great Commission itself was not given in a vacuum, neither was
it meant to be applied in one. Our Lord came at a specific time in
history and in a multi-cultured society, as indicated for example by
the three languages used on the cross. In many ways it was "the
fulness of time" (Gal. 4:4). The Church began to spread in a world
of Roman roads, merchant caravans, and moving armies, and in a
period with more traveling than the world had known up to this time,
when the Greek language was widely known and used, when the Jews of
the Dispersion formed colonies as far away as Egypt, Mesopotamia and
Rome, and when they kept in touch at the annual festivals at
Jerusalem. In this kind of a specific world situation the Gospel
was first proclaimed with a missionary purpose.

One can pass down through the history of the expansion of
Christianity - reading books like Bede's Ecclesiastical History of
the English Nation, O'Farrell's Saint Patrick, Emerton's The Letters
of Saint Boniface, or Villari's Life and Times of Savonarola, to
name a few at random, which I can see from my desk as I write. In
each case the "givens" were quite different both from each other and
from the Graeco-Roman world in which the church expansion began. Or
one may come down to the technological developments of the eighteenth
century, the new navigational techniques, reports of Cook's Voyages,
and the discoveries of 'new' pagan races in Oceania, which so
inspired William Carey and began the then new age of Christian
missions, that phased later on into the period of colonial missions,
in which Christian mission became so caught up with western commercial expansion and inter-national rivalry. It is quite valid to
conceptualize the history of the expansion of Christianity in terms
of eras, if we see those eras as different contexts, and evaluate
the respective missionary enterprises in the light of their
different frames of reference.

If we consider the mission of God diachronically like this, then we
must admit that, at least in its imperialist form, the day of
colonialism is dead, and therefore the kinds of mission that
emerged to meet the colonialist situations are also dead. A post-
colonial era in social and political conditions must call for a
post-colonial approach to Christian mission. Each era, like each
locality, has its own peculiar set of "givens."

Let me illustrate. There was a day when a great expedition set out
from England for a West African river. One of the driving motives
behind it was the hope for better control of the slave trade, which
had been outlawed in Britain, but not effectively controlled on the
African coast. The expedition carried three leading characters,
white men with authority - one for an administrative post, one for a
commercial establishment and the third for a Christian mission.
Such a combination was a peculiarity, a given, of this period of
history. It is difficult to envisage it in any other. The
insecurity of the frontier situation for all foreigners -
administrators, traders and missionaries - threw them into each
others arms. This does not justify the colonial pattern or its
values. It is merely to recognize the peculiar givens that were
there. Regular supplies, initial expenditure and daily protection
were their common needs. The combination was not good. The misunderstandings that came from it injured the African view of the
Christian mission. Indeed, today, in another era and context, we
are embarrassed to have to defend it. Yet if we look back honestly
and see it in the historic sense, it is hard to nominate a substitute way for that historical context.

In every era of mission both obstructions and opportunities have
been conditioned by the "givens" - for better or worse. It seems
timely, therefore, to survey briefly some of the "givens" which confront us in this post-colonial era, when the Powers which once ruled
the colonies have surrendered their authority, and national governments and national churches have taken over. What shifts have taken
place in the "givens" within which Christian missions have to operate
today?

Before turning to the political, social, transitional and technological "givens" of the new age of mission, I think we might well look
at the theological dimension, and settle the question of whether or
not the theological "givens" are changing or abiding.

The Theological "Givens"

The doctrine of the mission of God has its roots in the divine act
of creation itself. Man, the greatest of God's creations, may be
distinguished from the other creatures in numerous ways, covered in
general by the scriptural notion of "being created in the image of
God" (Gen. 1:27). Man, is the one creature with the capacity to
commune with God and aspire unto holiness. According to the Law of
Moses, this aspiration unto holiness and the divine demand for holiness in the life of man, are based on the character of God (Lev. 12:2;
20:7), and these references from the Law are confirmed by Jesus when
speaking to his disciples (Matt. 5:48). The whole idea of the
mission of God springs from His creation of man with a spiritual
capacity from the very beginning (Eph. 1:4), man as unique among His
creatures and the special object of His grace. It is not the will
of God that man should perish (2 Pet. 3:9).

On the other hand man does share certain things with the other
creatures God has made. He is confined within the space-bound limitations of this earth, between his birth and death, like every other
creature. Yet the Lord set him over the other creatures (Psa. 8:4-8)
and made him the one dichotomous creature, born both for physical
limitation and spiritual aspiration; for imprisonment and for
freedom, as it were. Thus the physical world becomes the stage for
the divine-human encounter (Eph. 1:9-14; Phil. 2:5-11).

The theology of Christian mission as Jesus stated it to the disciples
while he was yet with them physically, was based on this view of
Creator and creation. For their ministry they were called "out of
this world" into an entity we have come to speak of as "the fellowship of believers (John 17), for it was Jesus' purpose to leave such
a fellowship company behind him (see J.W. Bowman: The Intention of
Jesus). This Christian fellowship became a self-disciplining

fraternity or community, growing in grace (II Pet. 3:11-18) unto holiness, for the very reason that He who calls men thus, is himself holy. Nevertheless the disciples thus called out of the world are, at the same time, sent back "into the world" (John 17:18; 20:21) to proclaim the Gospel as his ambassadors (II Cor. 5:18-20), to witness by their personal testimony to the power of his saving grace, and to incorporate new believers into the fellowship (I John 1:1-3), and to serve fellow man, not after the manner of the Pharisees, but in the name of Christ with "fruit worthy of repentance" (Luke 3:8). The Christian is thus a man of two worlds, with a ministry on earth, where he is a stranger and pilgrim (I Pet. 2:11), and his citizenship in heaven (Phil. 3:20). On earth he has no abiding city but seeks to come (Heb. 13:14).

Thus the Scriptures encourage us to recognize that He expects his servants to live in this state of creative tension between two worlds. Many of the tragedies of our past can be traced, on the one hand, to our trying to be so other-worldly that we have neglected the ministry in this world; or on the other hand, by being so overwhelmed by the needs of this world that we have neglected to draw aside and share fully the resources of the fellowship of believers, the entity which Jesus brought into being so that his followers might not forget their citizenship in heaven. The man of God is surely a dichotomous creature, not of this world, yet ministering in the world.

This is the way the Scriptures depict the human situation.

In His "act of creation" God had to take a risk with man, if man was to be in His image and likeness, a being capable of communion with Him and with a will of his own. When man abused his freedom, and sin entered, and his communion with God was thus injured, a mission of God to fallen man became inevitable - God being what He was (Rom. 5:12). Here one might make the distinction between the human situation and the human condition. The mission of God is to rectify the human condition, but the divine-human encounter takes place in the human situation.

The Holy Scriptures reveal how God spoke to the human condition through the prophets and psalmists, and later through His son (Heb. 1:1), but all these proclamations were made in specific human situations. Although these pronouncements all contained universal truth, nevertheless they were presented within the limitations of precise historical and cultural situations. Thus, for example, when Amos thundered, "Thus saith the Lord ...," or "Hear the word of the Lord ...," he did so within the context of extortion and injustice in the market at Bethel, and the expositor has to understand the

cultural complex of that human situation to expound the mind of God
on the human condition reflected in it.

> I despise your feasts, and take no delight in
> your solemn assemblies... I will not accept
> them, and the peace offerings of your fatted
> beasts I will not look upon ... to the
> melody of your harps I will not listen
> (Amos. 5:21-23).

This does not mean that God does not appreciate liturgical
offerings, but that in the light of the cultural context, these
offerings are spurious. The human situation reflects a human condition. "Let justice roll down like waters" (v. 24) is the message.

Even the death of our Lord, which on his own authority and that of
the apostles we interpret as a theological universal, was nevertheless a dramatic action, which took place in a Judao-Roman situation,
with a Roman and a Jewish trial, and a Roman mode of execution.
Even the theological terminology of redemption, based on these
events, is ethnolinguistically defined. There is one sense in which
the cross of Christ is timeless and involves all history. There is
another in which it is rooted firmly in the earth of Palestine and a
multi-cultural situation at a precise point of time in history.

Therefore, in our consideration of the mission of God, we need to
distinguish clearly between the human condition and the human situation. Unfortunately we do not always make this distinction clearly.
On the one hand it is possible for us to be philosophical theologians
'bogged down' in the notion of soteriology itself, and forget that
no theology (or worship) is worth its salt unless brought to bear on
precise human situations. Or on the other hand, it is of no abiding
value to spend ourselves in struggling with some temporary human
situation if we alienate this struggle from the theological under-
pinnings of the Christian mission itself. Thus I see the dichotomy
of the mission of God as directed to the human condition (i.e. man
as sinner in need of a Savior), but operating within a human situation which ought to be elevated by the mission (i.e. being socially
and culturally relevant and meaningful to those to whom the ministry
is rendered).

In these days between the colonial and post-colonial times, there
has been too much talk about the demise of Christian mission.
Neither the Scriptures nor the facts about mission in the world
support this notion. As the Vatican II "Decree on the Mission of
the Church" put it, "the time for missionary activity extends
between the first coming of the Lord and the second." Stephen Neill's
Call to Mission begins with these words:

> The missionary work of the Christian Church
> is a fact of the modern world. We may like
> the fact or we may dislike it. That makes
> no difference; whether we will or no, it is
> just there. Not only so; it is a large and
> ever expanding fact.

So we turn away from any thought of the demise of Christian mission,
and formulate the remainder of our discussion around the expectation
of a new era in mission, with new machinery, techniques and strategy
on the one hand, and new obstructions and problems on the other. We
may anticipate continued blessing from the Lord and continued
obstruction from Satan. Man is still the dichotomous creature, with
his hope in heaven and his encounter on earth. We are still concerned
with the human condition manifested in the human situation.
Christian mission is still the God of love reacting to the sin of man.

To recognize the human condition is to understand the basic theological need of man. To recognize the human situation is to understand that political, social and cultural diversity must be reflected
in the modes of communicating the Gospel. Without the former our
mission is invalid. Without the latter it is meaningless. Either
of these without the other is impotent.

Therefore the theological "given" for frontier missions in the
seventies is the re-assertion that there must be a Gospel which
comes to grips with human sin and offers salvation to sinners, in
terms which are spiritually meaningful to the hearers, and appropriate within the social situations in which they live.

"In simple and godly sincerity, not with fleshly wisdom, but by the
grace of God, we have had our conversation in the world" (II Cor.
1:12). John Wesley had a powerful sermon on that text, expounding
it in terms of total involvement in the secular world. The theological given is that mission should take place, not in the home
church, board or mission house on the hill-top, but in every local
situation. True there must be the Antiochs and Upper Rooms; but the
effectiveness of mission is registered in Capernaum and Caeser's
household.

The Political "Givens"

Among the most obstructive factors in frontier missions today are
the political "givens." Their variety may be regarded as a basic
feature of the post-colonial age. Their frustrative character cannot be fully described. Some of them are unpremeditated and arise
from governmental action with unrelated political movitation. Some

are deliberate and planned anti-missionary legislation and action.
Or it may be that a rising popular mood of response to Christian
evangelism, leads a non-Christian government (or even a strongly
entrenched Christian government) to react in a negative manner by
laying down regulations intended to thwart the mood of popular
response. In any case, today we live in the midst of such frustrations and have to give them consideration. The Christian mission
cannot ignore these political "givens" and can seldom resist them.
They are there like the "thorn in the flesh" and have to be endured.
But we are very foolish to plan new frontier missions without taking
a hard look at them.

When the Gospel first began to spread through the Graeco-Roman world
it latched itself to numerous cultural and political facts,
homogeneous groups and structures - communities of Jewish proselytes,
Greek and Roman households, village structures as at Lydda and
Saron, extended families and occupational groups, even a sub-group
in the royal palace. A net-work of churches sprang up along the
major roads and shipping routes. The notion of itineration was
built into the New Testament Church. The cultural givens of the
Graeco-Roman world were the seed-bed of the first church planting.
They made use of the freedom and stability of Roman peace and Roman
law, and operated within its regular patterns of communication,
relationships and social institutions - witness, the reflection of
the official mail cycle in the sequence of the seven churches of
Asia (Rev. 2-3). Paul respected the roles of master and servant and
knew when to rely on his Roman citizenship, Hebrew tradition or when
to speak Greek. Christians were urged to pray for their rulers and
to be good citizens. The New Testament letters depict churches
operating within the cultural and political "givens." This does not
mean they condoned everything Roman. Indeed many things they found
quite frustrating and had to suffer much persecution when their
spiritual motives were politically interpreted. This very misunderstanding was itself one of the "givens" they had to endure. However
both our Lord and the apostles showed that the faith and ministry of
the faithful had to be manifested within the secular world where
they found themselves. The Christian theology of persecution and
suffering developed out of encounter with political "givens." This
was so with the people of God in the Old Testament days; it was so
in the days of the earthly ministry of Jesus, and he warned the
apostles to expect this (Luke 11:49; 21:12) and that it would even
be a source of blessing to them (Matt. 5:10-12).

The main political difference between the world in which the New
Testament Church began and our own today, would be that ours is so
definitely fragmented. We are not united by the Greek language, by
Roman law and an imperial unity. The complexity of the post-colonial

age is brought home to us by the ever-increasing number of young
nations, each with autonomy for creating its own political "givens."
The problem facing Christian mission in foreign lands today is not
so much that doors are fast closed against missionaries but that
operations are hedged in by so many political "givens." And let it
be quite clear that "foreign missionary" here is not merely the
westerner. Research done recently at the School of World Mission in
Pasadena and continuing "in progress" has revealed over two hundred
third world Christian missionary agencies in lands foreign to them
(Pentecost, Wong & Larson: "Third World Missionary Agencies"). In
the next few pages I propose to list a number of these political
"givens," and perhaps because of their sensitive character I had
better do so ambiguously, though they could be documented with no
trouble.

The most common way of controlling the foreigner if a country is so
disposed is through the mechanism of the <u>visa</u>. This may be simply
held up indefinitely for no reason or for an imaginary one. This
often happens when a strongly entrenched national religion,
Christian or non-Christian, feels threatened by the growth of the
missionaries seeking the visa. Or it may be due to some unfortunate
aspect of past missionary activity that has identified Christianity
with colonialism, land alienation or commercialism in the minds of
the people. Sometimes officials of the visa-granting country will
discriminate between applicants from one country or another for
political reasons. For example, the denial of military aid by the
applicant's country to the visa-granting country, or giving aid to
their enemies, can operate against the issuing of missionary visas.

The visa is certainly a powerful tool. The length of the term for
residence granted the foreigner, or the kind of visa, or the
restrictions on its renewal, may force a mission body to use only
short term workers, who have insufficient time to learn the
vernacular language. Some countries will admit only the foreigner
whose skill is one which is in short supply in the visa-granting
country. Even a country sympathetic to Christianity may impose this
limitation. Thus a foreigner with a technical skill that is
undeveloped in the target country may be admitted for a limited
period of time during which he is expected to train a national to
take his place. This may happen in medicine, education, radio,
journalism, agriculture or accountancy, to name a few I have come
across. These "givens" do not always arise from a desire to
obstruct the spread of Christianity. They may spring from governmental priorities in the national development programs. They
recognize that these technological fields are themselves developing
and technical guidance from outside is continually required, but the
nations which follow this pattern are saying by this policy that

though they will accept help, they have no intention of returning to the paternalism of the colonial period. Such nations often prefer to take the initiative of sending select nationals overseas for special training rather than admit foreign experts with a visitor's visa.

The visa is only the first hurdle. Even after entry to a country one's visa can be withdrawn if one does not "play the game according to the rules." Quite often these rules are laid down to limit Christian work. Some countries, highly resistant to Christianity, have made the only opening for entry in medical work, even educationalists being denied entry. Certainly there is to be no church planting. There may be some specific "Medical Assistance Program" co-operating perhaps with the Missionary Aviation Fellowship, through which co-operation the medical assistance is alone possible. The two situations of this kind which I know of allow for no missionary witness save the fact that the recipients of medical aid know their servants are Christians. But usually, once the visa is granted some kind of witness is possible. Little can be done with a tourist visa, which may mean six months residence before departure, and then the hassle all over again if a return visit is required later. Leaving the country for furlough is another problem. Frequently the time of absence is limited by the adopted country or the visa is forfeited.

In some countries, although on the surface the control of the visa is in the hands of the government, nevertheless, it is really the local Church which calls the tune. Missionaries can be brought from overseas if and when the initiative comes from the national church. This has the advantage of saving the country from flooding by scores of rival and poorly trained missionaries, thoroughly western and many of whom make no attempt to learn the language. This happened in many places in the decade after the war. Many of these post-war, western invaders had little knowledge of the basic rules of cross-cultural contact and courtesies. They did far more cultural damage than the old much-criticized colonial missionaries of the last century. (Anthropologists in general are still critical, but when one is driven to nominate a specific 'Aunt Sally' he will almost certainly name one of this untrained type – as cynical about anthropology as the anthropologist is about his type of mission.) This situation is brought more under control when the initiative lies with the national church, which has the right of selection, can verify the missionary qualifications and select according to situational needs – evangelism, teaching, medicine or theological training as the case may be.

This permits continued co-operation between a home church and a
national church. Both the mission fields of the world and the
national churches need more theological seminaries, for example, and
this is one position where short-term missionaries can be used with
advantage. I know of one hospital where regular instructional help
is received by highly qualified medical experts, who fly in for short
programs of a week or so. This could surely be done for seminaries,
the invitation and initiative coming from the national churches and
the personnel and funds from a supporting church or board.

Many countries, which will not issue visas for evangelists or
general field missionaries, will open their doors readily to
educationalists, nurses, doctors, agriculturalists and other
technologists. In some cases these persons are forbidden to preach,
but often there are no restrictions as long as the primary time is
devoted to the skill for which they were admitted. In some places
there is no restriction whatever on the non-professional missionary -
e.g. a medical man admitted as a doctor, but who links up with a
church as an active layman. I know a number of these personally,
who perform a splendid service to the churches. In some cases
prayers and Christian worship are permitted in schools and hospitals
and in others they are not.

Where missionaries have been admitted to a country as educationalists
and medical workers these projects have usually a long-range
uncertainty. Sooner or later the government will take over education, health and medicine, and the mission may find itself left with
a huge and useless set of buildings and no church congregation. I
can document such a case in detail, even where the government was
not hostile to Christianity.

Or maybe you have another case, in which the government is run by a
minority community, wealthy and powerful, whose religion is a form
of syncretistic Christianity and sceptical of Evangelical missions.
The latter have been admitted for educational and medical purposes,
but also to serve as a bulwark against encroaching Islam. In this
case the areas for Christian mission have been designated, and
except for the capital city, these areas are mostly frontier
situations. There is to be no evangelization in areas considered to
be the domain of the syncretistic Christianity of the ruling people.
Yet despite the caution of the missionaries, who try to keep the
rules, many are converted, so that pressures and persecution are
brought to bear on the national evangelists, some of whom have a bad
time. In the last few years one Protestant mission has handed over
its converts for baptism by the ancient church. As yet it is too
early to know if the policy should be regarded as successful, but it

is mentioned here as an example of how one body of missionaries is
struggling to perform its ministry within the "givens" of a frontier
situation.

The question now arises for a mission body confronted with such a
situation: how can these "givens" best be utilized for the spread of
the Gospel? Take the medical institution, for example. I have in
mind a certain mission with several frontier situations not far
distant - quite animist, with no converts at all as yet. Their headquarters are in a city of half a million people - this too, by the
way, is a governmental demand. Their stated designated service is
medicine, but they have some freedom in how to go about it. Is it
better to build a large hospital complex in the city or to distri-
bute it over the rural area in clinics and mobile activity?
Obviously the former will impress the government more. Its promo-
tional score is high. If I could believe that in twenty years it
would have trained enough doctors and nurses to staff the hospital
and have it taken over as a national institution, I would give it
serious thought. But this has not been my experience in the past.
The bigger the hospital complex the more dependent they tend to
become. But a chain of clinics and mobile programs ramifying
through the frontier areas, will provide a better functional substitute for the medicine-man, and open the way for Christianity to enter
acceptably through the social structure. I am not speculating or
rationalizing here. I speak of cases I know.

There may also be "givens" which relate to the availability of land.
This arises sooner or later when a frontier mission begins to gather
a fellowship of believers who want a church building - or are
thought to want one. In the frontier missions of the new era the
missionary body should never attempt to buy land, unless forced to
do so by the "givens" laid down by the country itself. In the first
place, if it is a real frontier situation, the tribal people most
probably will not understand the notion of selling land at all, and
they will not appreciate it later on when they discover this meaning
when it is too late. Second it should be the church of the people,
not of the missionaries, whatever the pattern of tenure. If the
land is communally held and the 'trustees' are the council of the
tribal elders, then let this pattern be incorporated into the church
structures you plant. There are other places where the land, though
communally held, is allocated to individuals for personal use, or to
groups for public use, and so retained until the person dies or the
public function is to be terminated. It is not a bad pattern for
starting an indigenous church from the beginning.

It may well be that you do not really need a building at all - if
the people hold their village assemblies under a large tree on the

beach, on the village green, by the river or at the meeting of the
trails. In this event the foreign acquisition of land may even ruin
the possible capture of a social group for Christ. Why does every
frontier mission have to begin with negotiations, through imperfect
interpreters, for the purchase of land for the mission - even before
the language has been learned for making these negotiations
meaningful?

If a missionary lives beside his people he should obtain his land in
the same way as laid down by local custom and through the same
competent tribal authority. In some cases land is just not available
for foreigners, and there is no mechanism for so distributing it,
but there will be some way of making a place for him. This he
should understand before taking up residence.

This last issue of land so often ties up with the notion of <u>authority</u>.
It may well be that there are both national and tribal "givens"
which may not be in agreement. This is specially so in many frontier situations, where both the <u>tribe</u> and the <u>nation</u> claim ownership
of the land or authority about its use. The missionary may have to
come to terms with each separately. He may find himself fighting
all kinds of issues with the government in the interests of the
tribe to whom he ministers, and if he does so effectively he may
find himself without a visa. The amount of tension that can be
generated between the over-lords and frontier-men is considerable -
one controls your visa and the other lives on your doorstep.

One calls to mind a country, officially atheistic, which does not
allow the private ownership of churches, and where any church
buildings are, in point of fact, government property; where the law
prohibits street preaching, but permits the use of loud-speakers outside the churches; where any church planting or building has to be
initiated by nationals; and foreigners can only enter the place by
invitation, and even then not in leadership roles. We have several
significant "givens" in this situation. They are important because
the place is wide open for evangelism. Much migration is going on.
People are moving into the urban areas, which until recently have
been possessed by squatters. Now they are being accommodated in hugh
high-rise complexes, each internally complete with entertainment and
shopping facilities and the occupants in a common income bracket -
no-one among them a foreigner. Whatever kind of church is required
in that situation, there will be none at all unless some national
takes the initiative to inaugurate it. Even though this is an urban
situation, it is a foreigner initiating it, even though the door is
open. Here is a "given" which speaks loudly to the indigenous
church.

Although I have warned against the notion of missionary ownership of
land, there are indeed some situations where the "givens" actually
require it. I heard only this week of one country where the government, having learned to build into its public life and records a
slot for the mission station during the colonial days, now demands
that any new mission must purchase land and develop a compound.
They understand what this is and know how to deal with it. Many of
the institutions of the colonial period have been accepted as part
of the scene and legitimatized.

It is almost impossible to separate the matter of residence from
that of land ownership. Some countries insist that the headquarters
of a mission be in the city under the watchful eye of the central
government, even though all the work may be on the peripheral
frontier. In this case the government requirement means accessi-
bility and control.

Still another country permits missionaries to have a ten years
residence, during which time they cannot evangelize among the major
religious groups or regular inhabitants. Their evangelistic work
must be confined to the communities of resident aliens. This is an
interesting "given" which is bound to condition the character of the
emerging church by forcing upon it an ethnoreligious quality. This
is an Islmaic land with many animistic frontier tribes. These
however are classified as Moslem, although they are quite animistic -
a most obstructive "given" by definition.

The political "givens" of the frontier situations are extremely
diverse. Indeed each situation is quite unique, and needs to be
clearly understood before any frontier mission is inaugurated,
whether engaged in by an older or younger Church.

The Anthropological "Givens"

If the theological "givens" of the Christian mission continue to
demand spiritual dimensions that go back to New Testament times, the
practical outworkings of the Christian mission in the down-to-earth
situations of this world have changed out of all recognition. This
is due to more than the changing political scenes of history. We
have come into the new day of the social sciences. In the science
of anthropology, for example, we have developed techniques for
looking at human society that we never had before. We have new
methods for collecting and organizing facts about mankind. We have
learned to see man in his context, interrelating with his fellow man.
We have learned more how to respect people with value systems and
world views different from our own. We have reached out beyond
descriptive to applied anthropology, and we are better equipped to
take a new look at the world into which our Lord has sent us. All
this is new resource material at our disposal, and we should be

asking ourselves (as Carey did in his day of new navigational techniques, exploration and the discovery of pagan tribes and new languages) if these new resources give us a new angle of the meaning of the Great Commission for our day and generation. At least we can say that we have no longer any excuse for the old paternalism and ethnocentricity, or for sending out missionaries untrained in anthropology. The missionary of today and tomorrow must be thoroughly aware of both the potentials and the dangers of cross-cultural contact. This applies equally to the missionaries sent out by the Third World Churches. The first anthropological "given," therefore, is a new kind of missionary who understands the science of man as well as the purpose of God.

Closely related to anthropology is linguistics. In the last century when a missionary went to a frontier area he usually had to reduce the language of the people to writing and prepare an adequate vocabulary. After many years he might even have translated the Bible. For many men this was their life work, providing the tool for those who followed to use after them. Today the frontier areas sometimes have permissive or restrictive "givens." Governments have specific attitudes to linguistic work, and two of them may be diametrically opposite. For example, one government will desire the reduction of all the tribal languages to writing, and may even be ready to sponsor some of the basic work. Such a government may be said to have an enlightened attitude towards cultural heritage, and even though it may be atheistic in its religious orientation, will allow Scripture translation, to capitalize on the available resources for preserving the cultural heritage in a written form. At the opposite pole is the government with no desire at all to codify its dying languages, because it clashes with the political urgency of unifying the nation, which has to be done on the idea of one common language - English, or French, or the local language of the ruling elite. The eradication of the subordinate dialects is therefore acceptable.

If the former is a non-Christian country the linguists may not be missionaries in the true sense of the word, and cannot establish churches. However one does find many converts through the translation of the Bible, and they have to be channeled into some existing church or establish an indigenous one of their own. In the case of the second government, it may allow missionaries to reside and preach, but only in the national (ruling) language, so that the preachers become instruments for disseminating that language as the lingua franca. This may make them popular in the capital and unpopular in the frontier situation.

In my experience the former will be more anthropologically oriented and easier for a mission to co-operate with. When people have a pride in their heritage they will talk about it. The latter usually means that people are sensitive about being thought 'primitive' or

'tribal' and will strive for westernization, even though they might
hate the west. They tend to build establishments they cannot equip
or staff and manifest another kind of colonialism. This latter
pattern, where the national language is the enforced lingua franca,
can produce some disastrous side-effects, especially if political
events should some day remove that ruling minority. If the "givens"
relating to language obstruct teaching and preaching in the local
dialects, and their use in translation of both Scripture and
general church literature for the nuture of converts and the worship
of the congregation, this is a serious limitation. But any situation which permits the missionary use of local languages and
dialects is a great advantage to those engaged in spreading the
Gospel.

Among the aspects of the science of man studied by anthropologists
is the nature and dynamics of social change. This includes the
process of religious change. Perhaps the greatest change in our
life-time has been the passage from the control by the western
churches to the autonomy of the national churches. This means, not
only change in the old mission churches, but also changed thinking
about the nature of church planting and frontier mission. Furthermore we have not only lost the authority of the foreign mission
board and the sending church; but we have a new authority at the
other end of the process, the authority of the young church itself.
We have a new set of "givens" laid down by the indigenous or
national churches. We are now being confronted by the "givens" of
the indigenizing process.

We have already seen how in some countries the entrance of a western
missionary is determined by the national church. The initiative
lies there. The young church knows its need and only invites such
missionaries as it believes will fill the roles required. In
another pattern the national church decides in conference before a
missionary goes on furlough, whether they desire his return or not.
Many of the "givens" laid down by the national churches are beneficial to the work of God, but others are as obstructionist as the old
paternalism of colonialist missions. It is good for a national
church to be responsible for its own affairs. It should represent
the Body of Christ ministering the mind, the voice and heart of
Christ in its own local community. It has to see itself as His Body
there in the world. Some national churches do this greatly to the
glory of God; but others have merely substituted the national pastor
for the colonialist missionary. In preaching, teaching, organizing
and disciplining he is as much a foreign overlord of his congregation as the old missionary he remembers and imitates. In this kind
of situation the "givens" of the indigenizing process can be very
hard.

I remember in one country visiting a missionary who had great
personal resources and gifts to offer his national colleagues, and a
generous spirit to go with them. But he was completely discouraged
and wondered if he should even stay in the country. He spoke the
language superbly and answered all my questions about their culture.
As an anthropologist I can say he certainly understood the people.
He did not mind staying in the background and being a servant at
call; but he was deliberately shut up in the background by his
national superintendent, a small man, now with a big office, who
placed more weight on his own post as a 'bishop' than in channeling
the resources of his team to the situations where they were needed.
This missionary was not a "partner in obedience," or even a "servant
of the Church," but a prisoner in a national bishop's dungeon, with
virtually no freedom, save visiting a troop of boy scouts from time
to time. A fraternal worker should have some authority and initiative under God, and be held responsible for his stewardship. A good
steward, western or national, will see that the gifts of the servants
he supervises are fully used in the master's service. Some national
churches are gloriously alive to the potential of the new day.
Others are glorying in their independence. Where missionaries find
their ministry thwarted by such psychological 'hang-ups' - givens
that spring from the change-over from expatriate to the national
authority - the home church should consider the advisability of
missionary deployment to some region beyond. Deployment: not
withdrawal.

The process of indigenization or nationalization has also stimulated
some conceptual "givens" or rationalizations, that hold up Christian
evangelization by clouding the basic issues. Both missionaries and
nations are hindered thus in their presentation of truth. Take, for
example, the new nation, where the Christian Church is present, but
a minority. The Gospel is preached, often with power, but the cry
goes up from official quarters for "religious freedom." Of course,
it is a myth. Supposedly it means "freedom to choose your own
religion," including "freedom to change it." In reality it means
"freedom for the ancestral religions to remain unchanged," or their
"freedom from conversion." This is a good example of the semantic
"given" (a slogan if you like), which can be twisted to suit the
user. If such a slogan protects people from "strong arm conversion"
against their will, or prevents "conversion by bribery" that is one
thing; but to deny any right of persuasion, or personal freedom to
change one's religion, and to call it "religious freedom" is certainly
semantic distortion. Yet this kind of rationalization is a "given"
in many situations as soon as the Gospel is presented. Mostly this
happens in the older mission fields where the Christian apologetic
has been long and well presented. However they are still frontier
situations because the non-Christian population is very great. In

this kind of situation the Christian Gospel just has to be presented against this rationlization.

Another kind of situation which becomes confused by slogans and cliches is that which hosts a movement for unity or uniformity in which religious and political issues are difficult to distinguish. One country is currently much torn by such a debate with phrases like "united Church" and "federation of Churches" and "forced ecumenism" and "registration bureau" being heard on all sides. Shortly the movement becomes centered in a charismatic leader, and a missionary who desires to maintain denominational integrity is charged with being the "enemy of Christ," and one sending Church says to its daughter Church, "You are free to act within terms of your independence, but if you join in then we'll discontinue funds." How strange it is that few things have divided the Church more in our day than the fight for unity (uniformity)! But it does raise important issues which must be faced: "How important is the denomination any way?" for example. In this particular case, if the hidden base is "enforced ecumenism" for political ends that is one thing; but if it unites people under God, that is something quite different. We certainly live in changing times. The values we have taken to the mission field are being tested now as never before. But the situations are never simple, especially when charismatic figures enter the picture. Is it religious? Is it political? Politico-religious situations and charismatic figures are "givens" in the missionary world of our day. The basic fact that we need to remember is that a world ripe for a charismatic politico-religious movement is ripe for the Gospel.

One could write at length about cargo cults and nativistic movements away from Christianity, and people movements to Christianity. We certainly live in a day of dynamic movements. There is nothing secular about all this. The world is hungry and that hunger is essentially religious. Anyone who ties himself into mission-field frontier situations had better prepare himself for a world of power encounter with group movements, and understand the spiritual psychodynamics of these phenomena.

Conclusions

We began by pointing out that every frontier mission had a unique context of its own, a set of "givens," a concrete body of conditioning factors, "the world" into which we are sent. Thus we called for a relevant and meaningful witness in a particular situation.

Theologically we found our task in speaking to the human condition within the human situation.

Politically we found great diversity in the human situations open for frontier mission. We brought our focus to bear on the visa as a social mechanism for imposing certain "givens" on Christian missionaries, and we discussed the limitations put on the preaching of the Gospel in resistant and semi-resistant countries. (This concentration on obstructions should not be taken to mean that there are not many other places with doors wide open for the Gospel. There are, but talking of the "givens" we did not stress these.) We discussed the givens which go with medicine, education, land and residence.

Anthropologically we spoke of the potential and dangers of cross-cultural contact, linguistic "givens," the nature and dynamics of social change, especially as evidenced in the process of nationalization, the "givens" laid down by the national church, and charismatic movements.

This is merely a sweeping survey of things that came to mind as I thought about the subject of the "givens" - the hard, cold realities of the situations that lie before us in the world today. They have been strung together like a string of beads, during a very busy schedule, mainly to bring up a number of issues, so that participants may think about them before the Consultation on Frontier Missions.

I feel constrained to add one more thing for you to think about. Many of the political "givens" I have mentioned are obstructions set against the Christian Gospel by the countries concerned. Many of these nations want both to keep and eat the proverbial cake. They want medicine, education, agriculture and general technology without the Gospel. I think we need to ponder that fact. They want the aid without the commitment to Christ. During the last 200 years some of the non-Christian religions were much improved ethically as a result of Christian influence, but they did not accept the total Christ. They took the ethical teaching but not the religious authority or the Person.

This is a theological and not a political issue. The notion of the
Savior from sin has been rejected. Governments for various motives -
direct and indirect - have created these "givens," these regulated
situations within which we can operate. In most cases we accept
them or we get no visa. But I think we should keep our eyes open on
the matter. In many cases if we lead men to Christ it will mean
persecution, exile, imprisonment or maybe execution. This explains
the large number of <u>sympathisers</u> in some countries as over against
full members - people who will attend a Christian service but do not
come up for baptism. It may be that this is the only way of maintaining the cohesion of the fellowship. I merely raise the matter
for consideration and prayer.

It may be argued that the true Christian serves his fellow man
regardless of his response. Do we help the brother in need simply
because he is in need and it is the Christian thing to do?
Theoretically and theologically we would agree. But a troublesome
dimension arises when you know that you are being deliberately
exploited: when there is no intention on the part of the recipients
of medicine and education, even to listen to the Christian message
which goes with it, and when those who do so will be persecuted and
maybe killed, or as in one country, exiled into enforced prostitution. The gift accepted with the deliberate intention of rejecting
the giver, the repeated offer and the repeated rejection, especially
if there is another riper field nearby where the labourers are few,
raises a very difficult theological problem. One wonders if we are
not standing at the point of Luke 10:10-11. I am not arguing that
this is the answer. I am asking if it is. The words of the Master
leave one with the impression that there will be such situations.
Somewhere in this consultation I feel the question of missionary
deployment should be discussed. When it is, a clear distinction has
to be made between <u>deployment</u> and <u>withdrawal</u>. I see no biblical
instruction for withdrawal from mission "even unto the end of the
age" but as the Lord did lay down the principle of deployment I think
that at least we should discuss it as we consider the claims of
frontier missions. The Lord also lay down the principle of <u>watching</u>
and there may be situations where a small task force has to wait and
watch. We certainly need to pray for discernment about deploying
and watching. I hope this matter can be discussed in brotherly love,
because it speaks to the location of the harvesting force in
frontier missions. This is all part of the serious question of how
we bring ourselves into what has been called "the current of God's
will."

Section B

GOSPEL, CULTURE, HOLY SPIRIT

AFRICAN INDIGENOUS CULTURE
IN RELATION TO EVANGELISM AND CHURCH DEVELOPMENT
John Mbiti

6

Introduction

In this paper, culture will be used to mean a pattern of human life generated by man's response to his environment. This pattern is not static; it is always in a process of renewal, change, decay, interaction and modification. Part of it is inherited and part of it is created anew by each generation or group of society. Culture is manifested in both physical forms such as dress, arts, crafts, music, and so on, and abstract forms such as values, morals, aesthetics, and so on. "African indigenous culture" means, therefore, that pattern of life which, allowing for changes (as defined above) has been the norm for indigenous African peoples and which largely, still gives them points of reference as African peoples. It is in this cultural context that "evangelism and Church development" are to be viewed.

Evangelism cannot be carried out in a vacuum, neither can the Church be developed outside of particular societies; and these societies have a culture which constantly shapes them and in which, in turn, they help to shape in an ever continuing process. Evangelism, the Gospel, the Church and the Christian Faith itself, are 'strangers' to African culture, and African culture is largely a 'stranger' to them. Evangelism has to do with proclamation of the Gospel; Church development takes shape as a process of people's response to that proclamation. Between 'Evangelism' and 'Church development' stands the Gospel as a constant for all times and in all places. Both evangelism and Church development are subject to cultural differences, historical situations and human needs; but the Gospel is immuned to these human factors. Therefore, culture will and must affect both evangelism and Church development, whether we want it or not, since these two take place in time and space. Indeed, evangelism and Church development can only be carried out in a cultural (and historical) context. Because both evangelism and Church growth are strangers in the African cultural context (except in the ancient Churches of Egypt and Ethiopia, which for this essay will be left out of the discussion), the dialogue between the 'stranger' and the 'indigenous' (culture) must of necessity generate both conflicts and concord. The thesis of this paper is that Church development in Africa is taking place in the context of cultural conflicts and concords and that, in spite or

because of, this tension, the Gospel is heard and heeded by African
peoples. We shall first deal with the conflicts, and then attempt
a theological analysis of how the concords may be positively and
beneficially utilized in the work of evangelism and the process of
Church development.

Conflicts in Attitude

In her book, <u>An African People in the Twentieth Century</u> (London,
1934), Dr. Lucy Mair, a British anthropologist, observed that "Christian
missionaries have set their faces against all the patently 'uncivilized'
aspects of native culture, whether or not they were strictly forbidden
by the Scriptures: they have opposed polygamy, slavery . . . initiation
ceremonies, dancing, wailing at funerals . . . as all being repugnant
to a civilization in which mechanical warfare was a recognized institution" (p. 3). Mair was writing in particular about the Baganda, the
largest people in Uganda and the first to hear the Gospel. It was in
1877 that King Mutesa I of the Baganda welcomed the first missionaries,of
the Church Missionary Society having sent for them through the American
explorer Henry M. Stanley. Two years later came the first Roman
Catholic missionaries. Within less than ten years after the arrival of
the first missionaries, up to fifty Baganda Christians were executed
and many others persecuted for, among other things, their Christian
faith. The "Uganda Martyrs," as they are known today, are commemor-
ated in the Church every year on 3 June, and some were canonized by
the Roman Catholic Church in 1964.

In spite of the persecutions and executions of Baganda Christians,
so soon after the beginning of the evangelization of their country, by
the turn of the century, there was a thriving indigenous Church which
sent out African evangelists and missionaries to evangelize other parts
of their country and neighboring peoples. These are the people about
whom Mair was writing half a century after their first encounter with
missionaries and the beginning of their rapid and positive response to
Christianity. The Baganda had for many generations evolved their own
civilization, culture, traditions, and a long history (which included
a line of more than thirty successive kings). Theirs was an example of
one of the finest indigenous cultures in Africa. Yet, this was the
people against whose culture the foreign missionaries had "set their
faces."

We have isolated the Baganda more or less at random to illustrate, or rather to repeat, the well known pattern of attitude depicted towards indigenous cultures in the initial, and much of subsequent, process of evangelism in African societies. Terms like the
'heathen,' 'pagans,' 'primitives,' 'wretched,' 'savages,' 'children of
Ham,' 'the lost souls,' etc. were household words in the lips and pens
of western missionaries and some of the African converts, describing
African societies and their ways of life. One cannot swear that this

attitude is yet over, for as recently as 1959, a theologian as great
and 'ought-to-have-been-knowledgeable' as the late Dr. Paul Tillich
could advise, in his Theology of Culture (ed. R.C. Kimball, New York
1959), that "what we do with primitive peoples in the mission field"
should be the same as what he advises to be done with children, namely:
"We seek to answer their questions and in doing so we, at the same
time, slowly transform their existence so that they come to ask the
questions to which the Christian message gives the answer" (p. 206,
in the concluding chapter, my own underlining). Between Mair's and
Tillich's books lies a gap of one quarter of a century in time, the
second world war, the beginning of nationalism in Asia and Africa
and the crumbling of colonial empires plus a great deal more in human
history.

Twenty-five years do not seem to have brought about a radical
change in attitude. If anything, cultural superiority from older
and more powerful Christendom towards the "primitive peoples in the
mission field," is here given its theological imprimatur by one of the
theological giants of this century. If this is the tune that the
giants played, shall we not expect that the dwarfs danced and jubi-
lated in "the mission field"?

Evangelism percolating through this attitude has, nevertheless,
produced large numbers of converts. But these African converts have
become beggars of Christian spirituality, ideas, cash and personnel
from their "superior" overseas missionaries, Church boards and centers
of Church organizations. Even if it is not stated in so many words
today, basically African Christians still regard the missionary or his
home Church overseas, to be the 'omniscient' in all matters pertaining
to the Christian faith; as the 'omnipotent' in Church matters and
decisions and as 'omni-opulent' in money and wealth. And no doubt
some individuals and organizations have played these roles, consciously
or unconsciously. This attitude has pushed African Christians to the
opposite corners where they play the roles of being 'omni-ignorant,'
'omniweak' and 'omnipoor.'

Local talent has thus hardly begun to be exploited whether in
terms of cultural heritage or personnel. Evangelism has been carried
out under a false cultural superiority and the Church in African has
developed in the context of a false cultural inferiority. This is the
dilemma of the Church in Christian Africa. Indeed, it was not the
Gospel alone which has been proclaimed, but also a foreign culture as
far as Africans are concerned; and perhaps at one point in the past,
neither the missionaries nor the African converts, realized what was
happening. Indeed, nor did theologians such as Tillich cited above,
draw a distinction between the Gospel and the cultural content of
evangelism, both of which were jointly imported to "the mission field."

In many parts of Africa, the first Christians were called "readers"
-- a term which is still in use today in some areas. They were "readers" rather than 'Christians' because evangelism went hand in hand
with the art of reading and writing and school education. 'Reading
the Faith,' perhaps rather than 'accepting' the Faith, was the decisive

habit -- the former is a purely cultural transformation (as Tillich
would advocate), the latter would be more specifically 'evangelistic.'
The main negative result of using evangelism to put great stress upon
cultural transformation, was that African converts were drawn away
from their own cultural rooting. Hence, their conversion took place
largely outside of their cultural context; and the subsequent Church
growth and development occurred also largely outside of their cultural
grounding. This is the state of affairs which inevitably has led to
cultural conflicts within the framework of the Church in Africa. We
address ourselves now to this area of the conflicts.

Cultural Conflicts in the Process of Evangelism

Once the line was drawn between "the civilized" and the "savages,"
it was inevitable that one side saw itself as the apostles of a culture
falsely thought to be Christian -- and there are groups in Rhodesia
and South Africa who still regard themselves as the defenders of 'the
Christian civilization in Africa' -- and the other side was forced
to see itself as, or was regarded to be, the followers of a culture
which housed satan, the devil and the dragon. In this respect,
Christianity was like the child of one culture (though in effect it
was Christianity which had largely produced it even if it has since
moved away from Christianity and has even tried to destroy Christianity),
and to bring Christianity to Africa, the child had to be wrapped up
in that culture. There was nothing wrong with that provided that indigenous peoples could be 'allowed' to embrace Christianity without
cultural conditions. This, however, did not happen. Instead, everything Christian has had to be filtered through the missionary culture.

Missionary culture told Africa in effect that "unless you are
(culturally) circumcised, you cannot inherit the Kingdom of God." So,
unless they mutilated a large portion of their cultural foreskins,
unless they became culturally westernized, and then Lutheranized,
Methodistized, Anglicanized, Roman Catholicized, Presbyterianized,
Africans could not inherit one centimetre of the Christian Faith. We
were told that if we wanted Christianity (and this we had been persuad-
ed passionately to want), we had to pay the price: we had to lay down
our cultures, despise them as the missionaries did, condemn them as
the missionaries did, and run away from them since missionaries had
declared them to be dangerously demonic. A legion of sins suddenly
mushroomed around and from African cultures -- taking snuff, participating in traditional rituals or festivals, avoidance of one's in-
laws, remembering one's dead relatives, etc. etc. Almost everything
in African culture was tabooed in the course of evangelism. Sin,
rather than grace, became the central pass-word in evangelism and
Church development. Anyone who broke the many taboos imposed against
African cultural life, had 'sinned' and had to confess and be disciplined by the missionaries and Church elders or pastors.

This degenerated to a ridiculously low degree. For example,
upon travelling by bus and being shaken as they sat on their seats or
stood up, some Christians felt that they had used bodily movements

which were tabooed, and would go to confess the following Sunday in
Church that they had committed the sin of "dancing." There are
Christians in the East African Revival who hold strongly that it is
'sinful' for them (or other Christians) to keep dogs as that shows
lack of confidence in Jesus (to protect their homesteads against
thieves and robbers).

Not only were Christians made to despise their own cultures but
even their own selves or to regard themselves as second-class citizens
in the Church. For example, the present Archbishop of Kenya, the Most
Reverend Festo Olang', told me how, when he was a young man working in
Nairobi, and went to the services at the All Saints Cathedral, he
and other Africans were sprayed with an insecticide as they entered
the cathedral -- something which, of course, was never done to
European or missionary worshippers. There are missionaries today
(1972) in Rhodesia, for example, who would not enter an African home
let alone eat there (as I am told by one of them who was maligned by
others for breaking this tradition!)

Under these circumstances, the majority of African Christians developed a rejection of their cultural heritage, and a resistance
against its use in Church life. At a mild suggestion I made as recently
as August 1972 in a sermon in Uganda, that we should use some of our
musical heritage in Church worship, I received a letter from a leading
Christian questioning whether this "revolutionary" idea would not
bring back weeds into the Church. When the editor of a missionary
founded paper, Today in Africa, in Kenya, heard that a consultation
had been held at Makerere University, in the neighboring country of
Uganda in January 1972, on "African Theology and Church Life," at
which,among other things,the question of using some of our traditional
cultural heritage in Church life was discussed, he wrote an editorial
in the July 1972 issue of his paper that ". . . some of us would be
happy to continue with Christianity as we have received it from missionaries . . . Personally I must oppose the idea that Africans no longer
want to accept Christianity on terms dictated to them by the western
world. . . . If all they ((African theologians)) want to say is that
we need to praise the Lord while jumping up and down and full of emotions, singing our own tunes, or praying in the name of Jesus while we
sit under a mugumo ((wild fig)) tree . . . then I ask for permission
to remain as I am." But, what is he which he wants to remain?

These two cases are clear illustrations of the degree of transformation which has been reached through two, three or more generations
of Church development in Africa, with regard to indigenous culture
and its place in the Church. Many Christians have succumbed to this
cultural indoctrination in the process of evangelism and Church development. But some, and their numbers are on the rapid increase, began to
resist and protest, even at the risk of some individuals being thrown
out of missionary churches or being put under severe discipline and
embarrassment. Ample examples of this resistance to cultural annihilation, can be found in the so-called Independent Churches, on which

there is more literature than on any other aspect of Christianity
in Africa.

Africans who have shown at least partial resistance against the
process of cultural annihilation, are in effect saying that they want
to become Christian but unconditionally: they do not wish to pay the
price of becoming cultural puppets whatever attitudes and power may
still come from or through missionaries and their home Churches. They
want to say 'no' to cultural westernization, but 'yes' to Christianity.
This is a painful distinction: some people imagine that a rejection
of foreign culture in the Church is tantamount to rejecting Christianity altogether; and others imagine, like the editor of the paper cited
above, that to say 'yes' to African culture in the Church is a return
to or revival of concubinage with the devil and his demons (if ever
that was the case). In both, it is clear that Christianity and culture
(as far as missionary culture is concerned) have an inseparable
covenant. But as long as such an imaginary covenant exists, Christianity and African culture will remain in tension, in conflicts -- unnecessarily or, at least, on non-theological grounds. Until this
covenant is destroyed "in the mission field" (wherever that may be),
Christianity will not enjoy concord with indigenous cultures. Indeed,
this raises the question of whether or not such a covenant, wherever
it is established, is holy and mutually beneficial. Christianity
seems to lose in the long run whenever it becomes too intimately
linked with any given culture. Its very universality forbids it to
become too strongly allied to any local culture. We may legitimately
Christianize culture -- and that is what one hopes may be done in
Africa -- but we are moving in the wrong direction once we reverse the
order and begin to culturalize Christianity. The culturalization of
Christianity sets space and time boundaries to it, and thereafter it
becomes almost impossible to liberate it and set it afoot once more on
its universal outreach. Obviously Africa is not immune to the danger
of enslaving Christianity within its cultural boundaries.

Cultural conflicts have covered the areas of values and institutions as well. These include for example, marriage, position of women,
initiation rites, inheritance of wives, etc., about which much has been
debated. One classic example of these conflicts is that of missionaries'
attack on Gikuyu female circumcision rites in Kenya starting in 1906
and culminating in a crisis in 1929-1930. During that period of a
quarter century, missionary opposition to traditional female circumcision was mounted with growing success and support of some African
Christians among the Anglican and Protestant Churches. The Roman
Catholic Church quite rightly, took initiation to be a social event
and refused to interfere, though it expressed concern over the physical
and educational conditions of carrying it out. The then colonial
British government was involved in attempts to suppress the custom
when opposition (conflict) from some Africans began to emerge in 1923,
and the question eventually evolved into a political issue. (Further
account may be found in F.B. Welbourn, East African Rebels, London 1961,
pp. 135-143). This is a clear example of a purely cultural, and not
theological, issue being blown up enormously in the process of

evangelism and Church growth, and consequently developing into a political affair which, among other things, gave rise to resentment among missionaries and Africans and was used as an overt reason for the rise of independent Church and school movements among the Gikuyu people.

In contrast with the example of female initiation, at about the same time, Bishop W.V. Lucas in Masasi diocese of southern Tanzania, was carrying out experiments to Christianize local initiation customs. But he was ahead of his time in the eyes of other missionaries, their home Churches, and African converts. It was because of opposition to his experiments, from both missionaries and African Christians, that the attempts of Bishop Lucas failed -- they failed not because they could or did not succeed but because they had to be abandoned in the face of opposition. (See W.F. Lucas, "The Christian Approach to non-Christian Customs," in Christianity and Native Rites, Central Africa House Press, London, 1950, pp. 4-38). Thus a crucial theological attempt was not given room to germinate and bring some concord in the process of evangelism.

By and large, African converts to western type Christianity have become targets of cultural ridicule in all aspects of their pattern of life.

Conflict in the religious life of African peoples

A cheap, but fruitful technique used in evangelism has been to minimize traditional religion in order simultaneously to exalt the Christian Faith. Consequently it was repeatedly said that Africans had no religion, or that their religion was nothing more than magic, ancestor worship, devil worship, or nature worship. Even where it was clearly known that ideas about God were dominant in the religious outlook of African peoples, foreign writers and missionaries insisted on speaking about "the High God" of Africans, as if God were 'high' for them, but 'low' or 'medium' for other societies of the world. Evangelism was carried out officially as if African peoples were religiously illiterate and ignorant, and as if everything about or in Christianity was entirely new, unknown and even incomprehensible for African peoples. Where evidence pointed out to the reality of African religiosity, it was turned into or regarded as an enemy of Christianity which had to be uprooted first and cast into the lake which burns with fire and brimstone, to make room without opposition for Christianity.

Probably the most regrettable mistake made in evangelism was to regard African religiosity as an enemy to Christianity. More effort in evangelization seems to have been expended in fighting the supposed enemy than in actually depositing Christian truth. African peoples have reacted to this religious tension in various ways. Some refused point blank to abandon their traditional religiosity, thus upsetting

the hope of early missionaries to convert African peoples within a
few decades. Others accepted Christianity enthusiastically and
dramatized their rejection of traditional religiosity by renouncing
everything to do with it and with their culture, building houses in new
styles, adopting western types of dress, burning any religious objects
they may have had from traditional background, and obtaining new
names from the missionaries, western history or the Bible. The majority of African converts, however, accepted what missionaries taught
and expected of them, and publicly behaved accordingly, but secretly
retained their traditional religious world view and sometimes performed
some of the religious practices. Some of these eventually relapsed
into apostasy, though being reconverted later in some cases, while
others gave up most of their Christianity. The situation exists today
in which many people have "Christian names" that they once acquired
or which were given by their parents, but they themselves have little
or nothing to do with the basic tenets of the Christian Faith. They
still, however, hold onto something of their traditional world view,
sometimes modified by a Christian outlook, and use it whenever it is
convenient or whenever it gives them a meaningful point of reference
as they respond to various situations of life.

It is my contention that, even though officially Christianity
either disregarded African religion altogether, or treated it as an
enemy, it was in fact African religion more than anything else, which
laid down the foundation and prepared the ground for the eventual
rapid accommodation of Christianity in Africa, and for the present
rapid growth of the Church in our continent. Without African religiosity, whatever its defects might be, Christianity would have taken
much longer to be understood and accommodated by African peoples. It
is regrettable that no official attempts were made to find and establish a working dialogue between Christianity and African religion -- in
formulating guiding principles of evangelism, and in the development
of the Church. For example, African religion is deeply celebrational
of life, and this keynote of celebration could have been incorporated
into Church development thus making it unnecessary, ultimately, for
so many of African Christians to revert to traditional methods of
celebrating life. Indeed the Christian Faith is one of joy, and it is
a great pity that Christian joy is suppressed among peoples who otherwise approach life celebrationally. Another example where African
religiosity would have lent itself readily in Church development is
its communality and corporateness. African Religion and social life
lay great emphasis on communal welfare, values, concerns, and kinship,
both horizontally and vertically (to include the departed). On the
whole evangelism has presented Christianity on an individualist basis,
making individualistic appeals, and the development of the Church has
tended to ignore the communality dimensions of the Church's existence
and concerns. This aspect of Church development is, however, beginning
to be remedied in some countries of Africa, and is fairly evident in
the Independent Churches.

Misguided notions about African religion were responsible, initially,

for reacting too strongly against it and consequently missing the
possibilities of utilizing values, structures and institutions which
had been produced by, or which had themselves produced, African religion.

Christianity and Indigenous Cultures of Africa

In the early period of evangelism and Church development, nobody
tried to work out a theology of culture applicable, or directly relating to, the indigenous cultures of Africa. The whole question was
approached non-theologically by both missionaries and converts, thus
generating the kind of conflicts we have isolated in the preceding
pages. The intention in pointing them out was: (a) to show the dangers
of identifying one culture too closely with the Christian Faith; (b) to
indicate that in spite of Christianity being restricted to within the
boundaries of a given and foreign culture, African peoples did, nevertheless, accept Christianity partly on terms laid down by missionaries
(amounting to first giving up their own cultures and then becoming
'westernized' simultaneously as they accepted the Faith), and partly
(later) on their own terms with the result that they were cut off
from the missionary churches and had to form their own; (c) to argue
that just as missionary agents did not raise the question of the
theology of culture, in the process of evangelism, neither has the subsequent Church in Africa raised this question.

The situation today is that increasingly African peoples, whether
Christian or otherwise, are returning emotionally and in practice, to
their traditional or indigenous cultures. They are looking at them
for values which can be meaningful in giving them an identity and
sense of direction as peoples. Whether the Church wants it or not
(and in many quarters there is still more opposition to than acceptance
of the idea), it is increasingly being dragged into this traditional
cultural arena. Today, the majority of missionaries have suddenly
become more than ready to move along with the idea of bringing indigenous cultures into the life of the Church, and ironically it is often
the older generation of African Christians themselves who are more
opposed to this new thinking and openness, than are the missionaries.
This shows how successful temporary cultural uprooting in the hands
of missionaries was among the early converts. Indeed some missionaries
are so anxious to utilize forms of African culture in the Church that
they are almost obsessed with the idea. Similarly there are some
African Christians who are reacting so strongly against western ways
of Church life that they, too, are almost obsessed with reactionalism.
In both cases the Church may suffer if it is oversaturated with indigenous cultures at the expense of its universality, just as it did
earlier on when it was established in African societies exclusively
on western cultural terms. We need, therefore, to look at some of the
possible theological approaches which could guide the Church as it
enters a new phase of utilizing indigenous cultures. The use of
indigenous culture is and should be tried in all areas of Church life,
and its momentum will no doubt accelerate within this present decade.

These areas include: art forms, music, liturgy, dress (including that
of the clergy and other Church officers), Church structures, community
life, Church architecture, celebration of life, conducting of Church
rites and services, the use of traditional religious insights of
African peoples, etc. These and many other areas open up for the Church
enormous possibilities of making the Christian Faith relevant to the
traditional and modern situations in Africa.

The Church was careless and negligent about the question of
indigenous cultures by throwing out or rejecting traditional cultures
at one point in the past. The Church is equally careless as, in
reaction to one extreme, it is now admitting indigenous cultures so
readily back into its life. Both approaches are dangerous. The
warning of our Lord is appropriate here, namely: ". . . You traverse
sea and land to make a single proselyte, and when he becomes a proselyte,
you make him twice as much a child of hell as yourselves" (Matt. 23:15).
If this could be said, in some sense, to have happened at the earlier
period of evangelism and Church development, it is equally possible
to happen at the time when so much enthusiasm is in the air about
using African culture in Church life.

Christianity has always faced the danger of being so culturalized
that its universality would be lost. Starting as a religious movement
within an essentially Jewish culture, it had to break out into
Hellenistic modes of expression, and before long it encountered a
Roman culture which was comfortably backed up by Roman political power.
In the Greek environment it acquired an eastern and orthodox character;
while in the Roman environment it acquired Latin character in which it
spread to the rest of western Europe, the Americas and eventually
reached us in Africa. In a sense, therefore, wherever Christianity
crossed geographical boundaries, it also crossed cultural boundaries.
This is what happened when it came to Africa through the western
missionary endeavours. The trouble in this case was that it was not
allowed to settle down in the local cultural milieu being, instead,
transplanted in confusing if not conflicting cultural entities such
as those of German Lutherans, American Baptists, English Methodists,
Italian Roman Catholics, and so on.

As Christianity wandered from culture to culture, in its long
history, Christians addressed themselves to the question of the relationship between Christianity and cultures. A survey of these views
is discussed by H.R. Niebuhr, Christ and Culture (Faber and Faber,
London/New York 1952). Niebuhr discusses "culture" in the singular,
having in mind almost exclusively western culture. His otherwise penetrating views are not addressed to other cultures since they arise
from within a culture which has been created by Christianity and with
which, through the centuries, Christianity itself has had a long dialogue. Cultures into which Christianity comes suddenly and from the
outside, lack this basic familiarity with Christianity which western
culture has enjoyed and assumed for nearly two thousand years.

Niebuhr outlines four theological positions which have been held in regard to Christianity and (western) culture. One is that which totally rejects culture, in order to overstress the Lordship of Christ. This view tries to make Christians separate themselves completely from "the world" by which they mean their cultures. In various ways, we have seen this view put into practice in the course of evangelism, in which African Christians have been 'forbidden' to have anything to do with their own cultures, not in order to elevate the Lordship of Jesus -- but rather, in order to accommodate the culture of the local missionaries. In this respect, the theological force of this view is sacrificed since the 'separation' is only from indigenous cultures while simultaneously endeavouring to embrace another but foreign culture.

It is futile to try to put this view into full practice now, since no community of people can exist without a culture. The Church in Africa is made up of people who have often been converts from their traditional religion, and conversion for them cannot mean an abandoning of their cultural roots. The members of the East African Revival movement make attempts to condemn cultural expressions of both African and western cultures; but in taking this reactionary position they are in effect cultivating their own culture (the way they greet one another by embracing, singing their praise hymn to Jesus, holding fellowship meetings, disciplining one another, and so on), and are not, ultimately, throwing away culture as such. Biblical anthropology would seem to be against a total rejection of one's culture since God loves man within the cultural context. Therefore the Christian Faith cannot redeem indigenous peoples minus their cultures - a meaningful redemption of man presupposes the redemption of his culture as well.

Niebuhr discusses the second view which sees Christ as the fulfiller of culture so that in Him the hopes and aspirations of society are perfected. This view allows for a possible harmony between Christianity and culture, though Niebuhr himself criticizes it in favour of the transformation of culture. This view springs from the words of Jesus that He did not come to destroy but to fulfill. While in the Jewish context at the time of our Lord, there was the long chapter of religious history and eschatological expectations to which the words of Jesus had immediate and logical applicability, how would such a view find meaning in an entirely different cultural and historical context such as emerges when Christianity is taken to an indigenous culture separated in time by nineteen hundred years? The concept of Christ as the fulfiller of African culture, is gaining much popularity these days among the younger Christians. But we must search for the elements of fulfillment from our cultures, and the methods of reaching that fulfillment within Christianity. Furthermore, it should also be asked what in Christianity fulfills what in African indigenous cultures. Can we talk of fulfillment when we have largely 'foreign' modes of Christianity in our continent? How could a foreign Christianity be instrumental in fulfilling what in turn amounts to foreign (indigenous) cultures?

If the Church in Africa pursues this view seriously, and I feel
that it deserves such attention, it demands first that we isolate the
very essence of Christianity from its peripherals. What is it which,
in spite of cultural alienation, has found its way through and reached
African people who have embraced Christianity? How is the Gospel
understood as the very essence of Christianity? Secondly, we shall
have to isolate values within our traditional cultures, which are
fulfillable and need fulfillment from the Gospel which we establish as
the essence of the Christian Faith. Thirdly, it then becomes necessary
in practical terms, to work out the process and meaning of this fulfillment.

Perhaps fulfillment would have to be addressed initially to the
religious heritage of African peoples, and then working outwardly
from that towards other areas of indigenous cultures which, it would
seem, have largely been produced by traditional religion itself. This
approach would inevitably assume that God's revelation to mankind
has not been confined to the Hebrew people alone, and that God has
made Himself known to African peoples within their own history and
religious insights. Therefore, if that be valid, there is in African
heritage something which has, through the centuries, anticipated the
Gospel howbeit in terms largely different from those of Biblical
revelation. While this is not the place to identify what, in African
religiosity, has anticipated the Christian Gospel, we may reiterate
our earlier observation that, rather than being the enemy of the Gospel
(as was so often assumed in early types of evangelism), African
religious heritage has facilitated the fast accommodation of the
Christian Faith which we are witnessing in Africa today.

This line of approach has also to keep itself vigilantly awake
to the fact that the Gospel not only fulfills and thus redeems, but
also rejects and thus judges and destroys. Therefore, the Gospel
must be allowed complete freedom to judge African cultures almost
without mercy, so that only what is of value is redeemed and thus fulfilled. In the spirit of enthusiasm which is currently in the air to
utilize African cultures in the Church, the painful and pruning
slashes of the Gospel may be forgotten or kept out deliberately, for
fear, or for lack of the courage to face the full implications. But
the full liberation of the Gospel must also mean liberation from
cultural partiality and fear. Because culture is the pattern of life
of sinful man, every culture is, ipso facto, a transmitter of human
sinfulness from one generation to another and from one place to another. But, at the same time, this sinful man is the ultimate object
of God's redeeming love. Christ's own humanity was an act of self-
identification with a culture of man, but it was that incarnation
within the cultural limits of the Jewish people, which at the same
time brought about the redemption of man from his sinfulness and
that which transmits it. Christ sanctifies culture through the incarnation, and that sanctification is simultaneously an act of redemption and judgment.

If Christ identifies Himself with man's culture in order to redeem man within that culture, we have to develop a Christology which
makes it possible to interpret Christ in terms that are relevant to
the cultural expressions of our peoples. Yet, Jesus Christ resists
being made into a Jew, a Greek, an American, a Chinese or an African.
In another sense His being the expression of man, His being universal-
ized by the Ascension, makes it possible for Christians of all places,
cultures and times, to 'localize' Him within their meaningful terms.
Only because He is universal in this sense, can He redeem vertically
the peoples of every generation and culture. His universality re-
affirms our different cultures, and calls for a kind of cultural plur-
ality as we march into the Church. It is for this reason that no one
culture can have the exclusive monopoly of containing the Christian
Faith.

We have to Africanize Christology but keep the balance or
paradox of Christ's universality and vertical availability at any time
and place. This does not mean that we draw Christology into our
cultures: rather, we surrender our cultures to Christ and they surrender us to Him. It is not Christ's intention to abandon or surrender
any of His followers to a given culture. Culture is for man, and man
is for Christ. Therefore, culture should ultimately point us to
Christ, and if culture fails to or cannot do so, it becomes demonic.

The third view considered by Niebuhr holds that "in Christ all
things have become new, and yet everything remains as it was from the
beginning. God has revealed Himself in Christ, but hidden Himself in
His revelation; the believer knows the One in Whom he has believed,
yet walks by faith, not sight" (p. 161). This dualism or dilemma
does not seem to pose itself (yet) in the development of the Church
in Africa -- at least not at this stage of its history. The dilemma
arises out of the deeper concern that the world of culture is sick and
yet God lets it go on or sustains it and the Christian must live in
it all the same. If there is 'impatience' in African Christians, it
is in their expectations of an immediate parousia to thrust them out
of this world of suffering and pain and death. Such impatience would
seem to arise, not so much out of a theological conern as such, as
out of the traditional concepts of time which accommodate only a myopic
dimension of the future but a dynamic present and a deep past in time.

The fourth view is one which regards Christ as the transformer
of culture, converting rather than replacing culture with a new earth.
According to this view, history is the story of God's mighty deeds
and man's responses to them. All things are destined to transformation
so that they yield glory to God. This view is theologically more
plausible than perhaps the other views, particularly when projected
onto a world scene. But when applied to particular cultures, it
probably raises more problems than it solves. One would see the use-
fulness of this view when it is considered in conjunction with the
idea of Christ being the fulfiller of cultures. The two views are
ultimately complementary, since fulfillment means completing,

perfecting, transforming, changing, adding final meaning, crowning
with that which is perfect and ideal. Every culture would clearly
need the saving, the comforting and the uplifting powers of Faith such
as Christianity offers.

A combination of these two views would involve presenting
Christianity as a movement towards changing not just individuals (as
evangelism so often has tried to do), but the structures of society,
the social environment and cultural expressions. It would mean that
conversion must be aimed at the whole cultural milieu of African
peoples, to produce a Christian orientation and to employ the whole
cultural momentum in the expression of the Christian Faith. The
traditional poet, medicine man, musician, artist, story teller, priest,
diviner, initiation specialist, and other experts, together with
their modern counterparts, would need to be allowed to make their
contributions in the life of the Church -- contributions which,
however, would be subject to the transforming power of the Gospel.
But precisely how this will be done, I do not know.

The main problem in pursuing this view of cultural fulfillment
and transformation comes from considering the criteria of judging
when a culture is or is not transformed or fulfilled. What is the
authority for formulating and applying these criteria of judgment?
Furthermore, there is the great danger of 'culturalizing' Christianity
instead of Christianizing culture. To culturalize Christianity means
to use culture as the final point of reference around or from which
we interpret, understand, apply and propagate Christianity. To
Christianize culture means that the final point of reference lies
within Christianity, and it is from there that we transform culture,
judge culture, utilize culture, fulfill culture, change culture and
add to or subtract from culture.

Conclusion

In their indigenous setting, African cultures have been all-
sufficient and self-sufficient. They have exercised complete monopoly
over the whole life of the individual and his community, in terms of
values, beliefs, social and political structures and creative activities. The presence of Christianity in this type of cultural self-
sufficiency must challenge and force that self-sufficiency to be
surrendered as imperfect, deficient and wanting. In its true essence,
Christianity is deeply jealous, always ready to employ other systems
and achievements of man but unwilling to accept any of them as its
master. For that reason Christianity is supra-culture, it is grounded
in given cultural situations but it is simultaneously beyond culture,
it transcends all cultures. Unless our cultures see this beyondness
of Christianity, it will fail to command sufficient authority and
allegiance over our peoples to enable them to yield unreservedly to
its transforming grace.

The beyondness of Christianity over cultures must be and mean Christ. Therefore traditional cultural lordship must yield to the Lordship of Christ, if Christianity has to produce lasting and deep meaning for any peoples. Yet, it is culture which accommodates the Gospel, and the Gospel it is that accommodates or contains Christ. We need culture, therefore, to be the interpretive medium for the Gospel to find its own place among our peoples. Evangelism brings into close proximity the Gospel on the one hand, and culture on the other. Without evangelism, the Gospel cannot encounter culture; and without culture the Gospel cannot make Christ known and accepted.

Culture interprets Christianity as it accommodates it and as Christianity progressively transforms it. But as culture is not static, there cannot be anything like a fully Christian culture. No culture in its entirety can be fitted into a Christian framework. Therefore, while we may expect eventually to see Christianity finding a home within African cultures, this process cannot be reciprocated in full -- we cannot expect African cultures in their entirety to find a home within Christianity. Even if both Christianity and culture are compatible to within certain degrees, this compatibility does not mean interchangeability. No culture can become wholly Christian; and Christianity refuses to be totally identified with a given culture.

The accommodation of Christianity within African cultures is quietly going on in areas of belief, values, view of the world, rituals and rites, and through our nearly one thousand languages into 561 of which portions of the Bible have been translated. Attempts are being made to give Christian worship local meaning, in different parts of the continent such as, for example, the use of traditional African tunes with Christian words sung as hymns in Church services, works of art depicting African scenes of biblical themes for use as visual aids, the use of folklore materials as illustrations for Christian truths, the staging of drama plays based on biblical stories but in local African setting, and so on. Increasingly we are getting Christian story tellers, artists, wood carvers, musicians, poets, and writers, employing their talents to give Christianity a measure of African character within our cultures. But these men and women need the theological direction without which their talents may not be fully exploited and some of their efforts may come short of Christian orientation. In turn, too, theologians have to listen to the artists and interpret their message as Christians speaking in the African milieu. Only through Christian men of culture can we expect to find the most explicit mediation of our traditional and modern cultures to Christianity, just as it is only through theologians and Church leaders that we may expect Christianity to be mediated to African cultures.

African Christianity is emerging, wearing an imprint of our cultures and simultaneously its universal dimension is uplifting what otherwise have been local values. Indigenous cultures are localizing, indigenizing and temporalizing the universality of Christianity. In

turn the universality of Christianity summons and promises to admit
all types of peoples and their cultures within its umbrella, tolerating
their weaknesses and imperfections, and fulfilling, activating,
transforming their hopes and aspirations.

With the tools of our cultures we are both defenders and traitors
of Christianity, and this is a paradox which belongs to the whole
relationship between Christianity and cultures. We live between the
polarities of Christian ethics and cultural boundaries. Yet, the
process of transformation means, ultimately that we become more and
more Christian and less and less African (or Japanese, American, or
Swiss). The only identity that counts and has full meaning, is
identity with Christ and not with any given cultures. Cultural
identitues are temporary, serving to yield us as Christians to the
fulness of our identity with Christ. Paradoxically, culture snatches
us away from Christ, it denies that we are His; yet, when it is best
understood, at its meeting with Christianity, culture drives us to
Christ and surrenders us to Him, affirming us to be permanently,
totally and unconditionally His own. This is in keeping with the
eschatological paradox of our Faith which declares on the one hand
that we are pilgrims and aliens without an abiding city, and yet on
the other hand we have arrived in Zion, the city of the living God.
Perhaps what we need most in the relationship between indigenous (or
other) cultures, evangelism and Church development, is the eschatology
of culture rather than the theology of culture as such.

                        Some Reading Suggestions
            (none particularly useful for this essay)

D.B. Barrett, Schism and Renewal in Africa, Oxford University Press,
       Nairobi/London 1968.

Christianity and Culture, report of conference held in Accra, Ghana
       in May 1955, under the same title, published by the Christian
       Council of Gold Coast, Accra 1955.

H.G. Cox, The Feast of Fools, Harvard University Press, Cambridge 1969.

V. Deloria, Custer died for your sins, Macmillan Company, New York 1969.

E.B. Idowu, Towards an Indigenous Church, Oxford University Press,
       London 1965.

R. Kroner, Culture and Faith, University of Chicago Press, Chicago 1951.

W.V. Lucas, The Christian Approach to non-Christian Customs in Christi-
       anity and Native Rites, Central Africa House Press, London 1950.

H.R. Niebuhr, <u>Christ and Culture</u>, Faber & Faber, London/New York 1952.

J.V. Taylor, <u>The Primal Vision</u>, Student Christian Movement Press (SCM), London 1963.

P. Tillich, <u>Theology of Culture</u>, (ed. R.C. Kimball), Oxford University Press, New York 1959.

F.B. Welbourn, <u>East African Rebels</u>, Student Christian Movement Press (SCM), London 1961.

7

THE FREEDOM OF THE INDIGENOUS CHURCH UNDER THE HOLY SPIRIT AND COMMUNICATION OF THE COMMON CHRISTIAN HERITAGE IN THE CONTEXT OF THIS FREEDOM

Nirmal Minz

Introduction

The title of this paper is long and complicated, but the problem to be discussed is quite clear. The problem is to find out the way by which the Churches in Asia and Africa no longer remain in bondage but they become free under the Holy Spirit and that the Christian heritage may be communicated most effectively from one generation to another and from one cultural situation to another.

The nature of the church - the divine and the human in her - itself implies the problem of the relationship between the human and the extra-human. The indigenous church, as a concept and reality poses many theological and practical problems for us in our generation. As the extra-human dimension of the church relates itself to the human in terms of peoples, cultures and religions, problems of freedom are bound to arise. As the freedom of the church is based on the Holy Spirit the problem is still more complicated as the church moves from one nation to another nation. St. John's Gospel Chapter Three describes the freedom of the Holy Spirit which can not be detected and determined by any rational planning and programs. This stance of freedom of the indigenous church and her attempt to be meaingful to the local, regional and national situations creates a tension which can not be understood and resolved in a simple manner. Therefore, our approach to the problem at hand has been along the following line. There are four basic parts in our paper.

(1) Biblical Perspective - Here an attempt is made to describe the church in the context of our problem. (2) Historical Guide- lines - this part traces the trends that developed as the church tried to deal with the problem of freedom in her history. (3) Systematic Approach - In light of the previous two parts, systematic questions are raised and an attempt is made to answer these ques- tions in the life context of Churches in Asia and Africa in the second half of the twentieth century. (4) And finally in the last part we have discussed the problem of communication of the common Christian heritage under the freedom of the Holy Spirit.

There are many pressing problems facing the church in Asia and Africa. But the question of freedom of the indigenous church is

one of the most crucial problems for us today. The self-under-
standing of churches in these continents will, in many respects,
determine her relevant witness to her Lord till He comes. The
Biblical, historical, systematic and missiological materials have
been brought to bear upon the subject at hand.

PART I

Biblical Perspective

The purpose of this section is not to give an exposition of a
Biblical or New Testament doctrine of the church. Rather, the
major concern here is to present a picture of the church that
emerges as a result of confrontation of the people with the
Evangel Himself. It is an attempt to explore the inner working
of the Gospel of God in Jesus Christ and its consequence upon life
under the dynamic power of the Holy Spirit. This perspective
provides us with a better chance of dealing with our problem of
freedom of the Indigenous church under the Holy Spirit.

The Lord Jesus Christ, His disciples, and other followers gradually
formed a fellowship; and finally the dynamic power of the Holy
Spirit made them the pilgrim people of God. Jesus Christ is the
power and wisdom of God (I Cor. 1:24).[1] This provides the basic
structure of the church. She has her own dynamic and form which are
given her in the source of her life, even Jesus Christ. '...the
Church is part of the Gospel, an essential manifestation of the power
of the Gospel, to redeem men in society.'[2] The Gospel challenged
men and women to repent and believe in the Lord Jesus Christ. It
led them to change their minds and their ownselves and to become
new. They were converted and were given a new status in relation
to God and their fellowmen because of the Gospel. But the Holy
Spirit working in the total process led the converted into a two-
fold communion - the communion with the agent of conversion and
communion with other converted people. Here lies the process of
creation of the Church according to Biblical perspectives. Conversion and communion are the basic structure of the Christian
church which is not found in any other religious communities in
the world. This can be described as "to be" and "to belong", as
the two foci that make the church of Jesus Christ a unique fact
on this earth. Freedom and dependence are basic to the nature,
task and purpose of the church. The church has her height in her
relatedness to Jesus Christ; she has her depth in the inner
communion of the brethren through the word and sacrament; and she
has breadth in her relation to the world under the guidance of
the Holy Spirit.[3]

On this basic level the selfhood of the church (content and
expression or dynamic and form, power and wisdom) is determined
by the Lord of the Church. D. T. Niles has defined the Church as
follows. He says, "We are speaking about a church and its selfhood and we are saying that the selfhood of a church is rooted in
its experience of address. The essence of this experience will
naturally lie in the way in which a church hears itself addressed
by its Lord, and knows itself as speaking to Him."[4] The meaning
behind Niles' statement is that hearing the word and participating
in the word through the sacraments are constitutive of the church.
Therefore, freedom and autonomy of the church are always relative.
It is freedom and autonomy only from the external human or
environmental control. It can not be an absolute autonomy
because her existence is determined by listening and obeying the
word of God, which is communicated in the living Christ. In this
sense the Biblical perpsective informs us that freedom in Christ
is the freedom of the Church under the Holy Spirit.

From the primordial mode of existence the church by its very
nature moves into a secondary stage. Only to facilitate our
description and discussion we differentiate these stages.
Otherwise these stages are found simultaneously from the very
inception of the church. The secondary stage brings in the problem
of the indigenous nature of the church. As we have already said,
this problem is ingrained in the nature, task, and purpose of the
church to be the people of God. As the church is addressed by
her Lord, She listens to the living word in terms of human words,
and her life is expressed in the form of the human. There are
three basic forms in which the church began to express itself
during the Biblical period. The church appeared as a worshipping
community (Rom. 16:5). She was found at a place in a given span
of time being determined by geography and history (I Cor. 1:2),
and finally this church manifested herself as the body whose members
shared a common life (common occupation) (Philipians 4:22). This
meant that the self-hood of the church was formed by her confrontation with God face to face, in a specific given situation, and in
its penetration into it by secular engagements.[5]

Even before the church moved out of the Jewish environment She
had to face the problem of indigenization. The Lord of the
Church was the son of man, and son of God, descending from the
family of David and by the power of the Holy Spirit. And the
same principle continues to determine that a church to be the
church must be created by the power of the Holy Spirit through
the word and sacrament out of a people with a given history and
culture that negates or opposes this power of new creation.
According to St. James, the church as a people of God is the

first specimen of His new creation (James 1:18). Therefore,
even at the very beginning of the church was in the world, but
not of the world. But the problem became acute when the church
began to fulfill its purpose in the Greco-Roman world chiefly
through the mission work of St. Paul. The first council of
Jerusalem was the test case for the church. Here the problem of
indigenization was raised in an acute form. The Jewish Christian
believers wanted to kill the dynamics of the church which permits
indigenization and preserves the extra-cultural elements that make
a church the Church. The human in the church permits indigenization, and the Divine keeps her above and beyond a given national
and cultural situation. The first council of Jerusalem (Acts 15:6)
was guided by the Holy Spirit to frame the policy that would meet
the kind of preparation among the gentiles which He had already
affected.[6] This means that the Jerusalem Conference did decide
that there was an unchanging element in the church which must
continue no matter what cultural boundary is broken in the dynamic
movement of the church and there are the changing aspects which
must take the form of each given national and cultural situation.
Therefore, freedom under the Holy Spirit is basic both for creation
of the church and for being indigenous to the geography and history
which limit and compel her to take a definite form.

The church has both movement and order. The movement is primarily
the movement of the Holy Spirit through the word and sacrament.
The order also is primarily the work of the Spirit using the
environmental material to give shape to the church in a given
situation. St. Paul struggles with the problem of movement and
order in the church in all his epistles in different forms. The
Epistles to the Corinthians, to Galatians, and Romans are classic
examples of his struggles to help the Christians see that the church
must have both movement and order. But we should be quite clear
how these two dimensions of the church are related to one another -
which is primary and which one is secondary. Speaking of this
problem, Peter Beyerhaus and Henry Lefever make the following
remarks. They say, "Both movement and order are related to Christ
and his rule. A religious movement which is separated from
Christ's rule destroys the church's unity and weakens the very
vitality which it thinks it is promoting. Obedience separated
from Christ becomes a cold and lifeless code. Thus Spiritual
liberty and church order presuppose one another and remind each
other that both are directed towards the living Christ."[7]

As the church continues to carry her Lord's mission from one
place to another, and one people to other peoples and from one
nation and culture to other nations and cultures, she is con-

stantly tempted either to be purely dynamic and to be ineffective,
or to accept a form that gives stability leading to stagnation.
Yielding to either of the two temptations makes the church less
than what her Lord intends her to be. D. T. Miles has described
the nature of the church as over against a society in the following
words. He says, "This mission of the church is to be the people
of God. It is to be the people of God everywhere. It is also to
be the people of God on a journey. . . .A pilgrim people is bound
to have a set of values which are different from those held by
people who have settled down."8 This shows that the pilgrim people
must have a firm root in the Lord and, at the same time, they must
be related to the environment through which they are commanded to
pass in their mission.

PART II

Historical Guidelines

The concluding paragraph of the previous section has indicated
that the church as a pilgrim people under the guidance of the Holy
Spirit began to break through cultural and national boundaries in
early centuries. Here we would like to note some basic trends
in the solution of the problem of freedom of the church in a given
situation which developed in the course of the history of the
church from early times up to about the eighteenth century.

For our purpose the history of the church can be divided into the
following periods: The indigenous church in the Greco-Roman world;
The church in Northern Europe; Expansion connected with European
discoveries of Africa, Asia and Latin America, and finally the
renewed expansion of European people and the modern missionary
movements from the West.9 Latourette has defined our problem in
the following say. He says, "the problem, today 'is'. . . to be
one of adjusting Christianity to different cultural backgrounds
and making the accommodation in such a way that the Gospel as
presented shall retain its essential characteristics and vigor and
to become permanently an integral and transforming part of the
national life, and in time win the entire people to a vital
Christian faith in fellowship with the church universal."10
There are three major items of adjustments: doctrine, organization,
and leadership: in the process of indigenization of the church.
It is quite natural that different cultures related to the message
of the Gospel in different ways at different periods of history.
But for us it is important to note the consequences of one kind
of adjustment over against the other. Even during the same period
two kinds of adjustments of Christianity to the same culture do

offer to us good lessons. "In the first century," Latourette remarks, "Mission church development among those Christians who adhered to the Jewish customs rapidly sank into the position of a smaller and uninfluential minority and were frowned upon by the majority of Christians as heretics."[11] This statement is amply supported by historical evidences in the first three centuries. The major controversies that arose in this period which was finally settled in the form of the three ecumenical creeds are the indications of the above kind of adjustments. The uncompromising stream won the race and the compromising group ended up in almost complete annihilation. Therefore, it is quite natural that the dynamic church will not compromise with the cultural forces although it will seek to relate itself creatively to the environment. The first attitude and adjustment is bound to create tensions. In an attempt to describe this situation the church historian says, 'At the very outset it must be noted that Christianity, if it is not hopelessly denatured, never becomes fully at home in any culture. Always, when it is true to its genius, it creates a tension."[12]

The problem of the indigenous church in the Mediterranean world (Greco-Roman culture) can be described in the following words. As we have noted above the Jews wanted to conserve their cultural tie even after accepting Jesus Christ and accepting the fellowship of believers. Such Christian communities as the Ebeonites and others dwindled and eventually died out. It could be said that a process of complete domestication of the Christian message led to the final destruction of the church as the dynamic fellowship of Christians under the Holy Spirit. Christianity in the Greco-Roman world took over the sacred rites and forms of priesthood of pre-Christian religion but it refused to acquiesce. Here lies the key to the successful expansion of Christianity among the Greeks and the Romans. Among the Greeks we have examples of the Gnostics who completely harmonized their Christian faith with the cultural environment. They flourished for a while but finally they also died out. Therefore, it becomes quite evident that neither complete separation from, nor full absorption into, any culture is healthy for the life and growth of a church. Latourette again remarks, "Indeed, intransigence was one of the chief reasons for the triumph of Christianity in the Greco-Roman world."[13] During this period of church history, he continues, "It was the current in Christianity which held firmly to the uniqueness and centrality of Christ and declined to water down that conviction to ease the tension with those who found the belief offensive which ultimately became the mainstream. Others dwindled and disappeared."[14]

The period from the 5th to the 16th century is the time when the

church moved into Northern Europe. The mass movement among the
culturally and religiously backward people made the church. One
could say generally that accommodation occurred but at the same
time the missionaries (the monks) fought against paganism.
Speaking of the indigenization in this cultural area Latourette
has made the following remarks, "If, as many have suggested, the
reformation was the product of the Teutonic Spirit under the
stimulus of Christianity, or in other words of Christianity becoming
indigenous among those of Teutonic-Stock, this consummation required many centuries."15 Here history provides us with a major
fact in the discussion of our problem. Whether or not the above
statement is true, that is not our primary concern. But the
important thing to note in this statement is the fact that the
indigenous church is not a traceable fact at a given point in
history. It is rather a process which can be discerned in a fairly
long span of history. The indigenous church in Northern Europe
took at least a thousand years to become discernible in the eyes
of scholars. Moreover, the argument that the New Testament message
creates the church in a given situtation is only partially true on
an experiential level. The churches in Northern Europe are witnesses
to this fact. "The reformers were unable to create a church
constitution based solely on the New Testament. Luther had to
borrow elements from the idea of medieval christendom, the one
Christian society; and the Calvinists tended to think of the church
in terms of a community of saints, separate from the world, a
doctrine which received its extremist expression in the sects."16
This quotation shows that even in the process of indigenization
there always remains the tension between the local and universal
elements in the church without which the church can not become a
true church.

During the period of discovery and the expansion of Europe (after
1498) and in the movement of the church into Asia, Africa, North
America and Latin America, conversion was largely a concommitant
of conquest. The non-Christian cultures and customs in the two
Americas were simply erased by the help of military and other
physical forces. An attempt was made to accommodate Christianity
so far as feasible to the customs and cultures of advanced
civilizations of India and China.

History provides us with some practical guidelines for understanding
and dealing with our problem. It can safely be said that the Holy
Spirit guided the church in different periods through varieties of
cultural environments. In the early period, in Greco-Roman socio-
cultural environment, the Holy Spirit led the believers to hold the
uniqueness of Jesus Christ in the midst of many onslaughts of
relativistic, humanistic ideologies. The church was enabled to

formulate her faith in terms of the canonical scriptures, the three
ecumenical creeds, teachings of the apostles, sacraments, and a
form of ministry that could safeguard the life of the church, and
give fresh impetus to the dynamic movement of the church. In
general these formed the basic property of the Christian heritage
as means of expressing and communicating the Gospel of God in Jesus
Christ. During the second period, when the church moved through
Northern Europe one could hardly discern any freedom of the indigenous
church under the Holy Spirit. Only as late as the 10th, 11th and
16th centuries freedom of the church became noticeable under the
guidance of the Holy Spirit. Finally the Reformation became the
major expression of this freedom of the Indigenous Church in Northern
Europe under the Holy Spirit. We venture to hold this view on the
basis of the fresh discovery of the word of God, both written word
and the living word by the reformers. The work of the Holy Spirit
is discernible primarily in the word and sacrament. Here the
Christian heritage was redefined in terms of the message, rather than
the instruments hearing this message, in contrast to the church in
the Greco-Roman world.

As the church moved from European countries and cultures to the
Americas, African countries, and Asia, the freedom under the Holy
Spirit became much more questionable. Because the spirit of man,
rather than the Spirit of God appeared to be more active in erasing
the religions and cultures of the indigenous people by the military
and other physical forces. There was no room left for the
indigenous church to grow under the guidance of the Holy Spirit
in the above mentioned cultural areas. The last and present period
faces an acute problem in this respect. For one thing the church,
although it came as an integral part of the Western expansion,
did not make an easy conquest since the higher cultures and
civilizations of India and China could not be erased by sheer
physical force. For another thing, human pride and weaknesses
were contributory to the inhibition of the working of the Holy
Spirit and would not permit the freedom of the Indigenous Church.
This does not at all mean the complete absence of the guidance of
the Holy Spirit during these periods. The church could not move
into these cultural areas and people would not have accepted the
Gospel without the work of the Holy Spirit. We are bound to
acknowledge that in the midst of all faults and follies of men
the Holy Spirit was active and the church in these cultural areas
of the world had been guided by the Spirit of God. The question
is: how much have they exercised their freedom under the Holy
Spirit? The situation prevailing in the churches today speak for
or against this question.

The problem of freedom of Indigenous Church has become acute in the period which is generally known as the time of modern missionary movements from the Western countries to the African and Asian countries. During this period the cultures and ideologies of European and American nations seem to have become an integral part of Christian missionary expansion. As the church has moved from the Greco-Roman world through Northern European and American cultures to Africa and Asia, the problem of the indigenous nature of the church as become much more complicated. We shall deal with this period.

PART III

A Systematic Approach to the Problem

The modern missionary movement of the 18th and 19th centuries presents a peculiar problem for us in the 20th century. After the Reformation the Protestant churches and the Roman Catholic church of the West carried on missionary activities in a variety of forms in different parts of the world. The missionary motives, attitudes, policies and theological orientations of Western churches were different in each major denominational stream of non-Roman churches and the Roman Catholic church. Therefore, as the immediate background of our problem we have to assess the motives, attitudes, and policies of missionary thinking of the above mentioned period.

I.   Immediate Background of Our Problem

One of the greatest shifts between the New Testament teaching and the missionary teaching in the modern period is that in the former church always refers to the local congregation and in the latter to an administrative organization. The shift is from local congregation to the administrative organization as the church. It is not surprising even now that at least in most mission-churches in Asia and Africa, the highest administrative body is accepted as the true church. The local congregations are for all practical purposes, not taken seriously as being the church. Such an attitude has developed in the minds of Christians due to the basic shift in the missionary teaching on the church as an institution and organization rather than the fellowship of believers.

An extreme criticism on this shift can be seen in the following statement. "Simple trust in Christ was replaced by the missionaries ideal of self-reliance. Faith in recreating power of the Gospel was replaced by educational requirements and the Biblical concept of sanctification was replaced by considerations of human qualifications of the native Christians."17 There is some truth in this quotation. The very nature of the situation under which the

missionaries and mission societies of various denominations worked
as an integral part of Western-expansion provided them with the
orientation mentioned in their statement. In Niger (West Africa)
the then united Church of England and Ireland introduced episcopacy
by consecrating Bishop Crowther as the first Bishop among the African
people. But by this action of the church her own authority was being
extended directly to West Africa. In many mission fields, white
man s superiority and not the conviction of the people in Christian
faith gave the foothold for the missionary activities. The spread
of the Gospel in Africa and Asia by Western church was definitely
accompanied or undergirded by the ideological expansion of Europe
and America. The above mentioned attitudes, motives and policies
of missions in the early stage of the modern missionary movement
made it harder for the newly-born church to be really free even
under the Holy Spirit. Having said that, we should also be reminded
of the fact that there are at least some signs of the work of the
Holy Spirit among the mission society secretaries and missionaries
in the field. It is reported that Henry Venn of England wrote once
to Anderson (the secretary of mission board in America) that he
(Venn) had learnt more and more to follow divine guidance instead
of his own principles in missionary policies.[18] It is also recorded
regarding missionary Nommenson of the Batak Church (Indonesia)
writing the following words in 1890: ". . . At any rate we proceed
under God's guidance. The victory of the kingdom of God is
assured."[19] The above two statements show that the mission societies
and the missionaries of the West were not completely guided by their
own ideologies and superiorities. They did seek the guidance and
light of the Holy Spirit in the fulfillment of their task in the
countries of Asia and Africa. But it is safe to say that the dominant
trend was dependent upon the human resource more than upon the Holy
Spirit. This basic factor in the modern missionary movement has presented
many difficult problems in regard to the freedom of the indigenous
church under the Holy Spirit. With the above immediate background
in mind we should approach the problem from the point of view of
systematic theology.

II. The Indigenous Church

We have never questioned the meaning of the Indigenous Church so
far. We took for granted what an indigenous church was. But here
we must be clear what we mean by this concept. To begin with, it
will be helpful to confine our discussion to churches which are
established in Asia and Africa, as the result of modern missionary
movements. Let us summarize the different concepts used to
designate these churches in recent history. "Native Churches,"[20]
"The national church," and "the younger church" are some of the
major terms used to identify the churches whose problem of freedom

under the Holy Spirit we are discussing. These concepts by themselves do not convey any unpleasant ideas. But the historical,
cultural, ideological and theological backgrounds behind each one
of them are sufficient to distract us from the reality we want to
describe. Prejudices, superiorities, and paternalisms of one kind
or another undergird these concepts. The freedom of the Holy Spirit
has less chance in such situations to lead and guide these churches.
These concepts, moreover, are loaded with sociological meaning of
the word church. They are colored with racial, political and family
relations which make these churches not only different but in fact
below the rank of the churches in Europe and America.

One of the first definitions of Indigenous Church was given by the
Chinese delegates to the International Missionary Conference 1928
in Jerusalem. They observed, "An indigenous church is one that is
most adapted to the religious needs of the Chinese people, most
congenial to Chinese life and culture, and most effective in
arousing in Chinese Christians a sense of responsibility."21
Though the Chinese delegates seemed quite competent to present a
mature idea of the Indigenous Church in 1928, confused ideas about
the Indigenous Church appeared in the I.M.C. Tambaram (Madras)
Conference in 1939. The missiologists, churchmen, and theologians
in the West, out of their dissatisfaction discussed it in this
conference. The net result of this discussion was summarized by
(the late) Dr. Walter Freytag of Hamburg in 1940 as follows: An
indigenous church is: (a) the young church without foreign leader-
ship· (b) a church with national concommitants - changes in externals
like church buildings, and forms of worship, etc.; (c) a church
which incorporates the religious and cultural heritages of the
people· (d) an indigenous church is not to captivate the masses
but it should satisfy the Christians.22 In Dr. Freytag's opinion
there was a great danger of new paganism in the concern for the
indigenous church, and he suggested that keeping close to the Word
which is the basis of the creation of the church should be continued
to keep the church out of this danger.23

The outcome of the Madras Conference in 1939 as summarized by the
noted scholar suggests that basic concern about the indigenous
church was in the external adjustments and adaptations of the church
to its new environment. The discussion on "Indigenous Church" has
continued even up to the present time. The concept of "Devolution"
in Missions is another stage at which external change has been
stressed in order that the mission-church should become the truly
indigenous church in Asia and Africa. The principle of "Devolution"
and its execution led to the major idea of the self-governing,
self-supporting, and self-propagating church as the real indigenous
church. These three "selves" though important, are yet too

superficial, unrealistic, and un-biblical concepts of the indigenous
church. It is a simple change-over of the external things of the
mission into the hand of the local or national body of people. It
is not the kind of indigenous church we are looking for. Dr. S. L.
Parmar says, "Change-over from missionary leadership to that of the
nationals is described as indigenization. But this can be a
superficial change, unless our structures, attitudes, and thinking
are also indigenized, that is related more to our conditions."[24]
The above idea is unrealistic because the external change-over also
was taken as an event or a fact at a point of history. It was not
taken as a process. It is, moreover, un-biblical because the "self"
of the "church" is given so much prominence that the selfhood of the
church in Christ becomes completely identified with the externals.
It is not the self, but the "other" which has to be the foundation
of the indigenous church. The autonomy of the church has been taken
as its indigenous nature. Autonomy is purely a political and social
concept which is completely against the spirit of the church of
Christ, in which no autonomy but Christonomy and always relatedness
to all other Christians of the world are the basic structure of
existence for the indigenous church.

According to the old formula the church must be rooted in the soil
in order to be an indigenous church, but the new formula says that
the church must be relevantly related to the soil. "The church is
and must be relevantly related to every culture in which it finds
itself, but it is rooted and grounded only in Jesus Christ, so
that the identity of the church is the same as the identity of the
Lord.[25] This point of view challenges all the other views on
indigenous church because there is a fundamental shift of emphasis
here. Whereas the previous considerations focussed on the external
adjustments and complete adaptation as the final form of indigenity,
the present view keeps the foundation of this church in the Lord
of the church and calls for a meaningful relation to the socio-
economic, political, cultural and economic life of the people.
It is a constant process of tension between obedience to the Lord
of the church and willingness to be the people to whom the church
has been sent. Dr. M. M. Thomas describes the problem of indigenization as follows. He says, "The problems now associated with
indigenization is that of relevantly relating the church and its
word of judgment and redemption to the forces of cultural change
which are at work in the present and to the new cultural values
which are emerging in various situations."[26] The creative process
of an indigenous church in the making has been described by
Beyerhaus and Lefever as follows. They say, "The church becomes
indigenous by responding in obedience to God's call in the contemporary and local circumstances and by complete and truly
Christian identification with those to whom the church is commanded

to proclaim the Gospel."[27] A final statement is in order here.
The coming into being of the church is an act of God in Jesus Christ
among a people it is the power and work of the Holy Spirit to give
adequate shape to the indigenous church and regulate it to be the
church among them.

III. The Indigenous Church in Bondage

On principle we have defined and described the nature and form of
the indigenous church. The indigenous church as a process is found
in all mission-church situations as a result of the missionary work
in Asia and Africa. Our task here is to show the freedom of such
churches under the Holy Spirit. This statement presupposes that
the indigenous churches in many socio-cultural and politico-religious
situations are under bondage of one kind or another. The following
are some of these bondages.

(a) Historical legacy. The indigenous churches tend to fall back
on their past, historical legacies instead of moving forward in a
creative manner. The tendency to depend on the human resources is
found in many respects. Speaking of the Indian Church Bishop
Leslie Newbegin remarks, "One of our weaknesses is that there are
still many who are not ready to accept this [responsibility] and
want to retain an element of missionary control. This is shown
by the tendency to nominate missionaries to key positions."[28]
Without shouldering responsibility an indigenous church can not
grow. But responsibility emerges out of a firm foundation of the
church. If the indigenous church has its roots not deep enough
either in Christ and its relation to culture, then the church will
remain alienated and appear foreign. Still some churches are only
very superficially grounded. Prof. T. V. Philip has observed that
the churches and Christian institutions appear to be sales agents
of Western goods. This state of affairs can not strengthen the
self-identity of the church. He says, "When there is no freedom
and integrity there is no selfhood; because freedom to be oneself
in Christ is of the essence of selfhood."[29] The indigenous churches
lack freedom as well as integrity to relate themselves to the
immediate environment in which they are placed. It is quite natural
that such churches will be foreign to the people and places. "If
the church in India," declared the Catholic Bishops' Conference,
"today appears to be foreign it is because she has not realized and
appropriated the Indian heritage, India's treasures of culture and
religious values. The church has not fully shared the hopes and
aspirations, griefs and anxieties of the Indian people on their
march towards progress and development."[30] The above statements
hint at some of the deepest bondage under which the Indigenous
Churches live today. The superficiality of the indigenous church

is partly due to the misunderstanding between the Gospel and Western
cultural ideals. "Such a result was," says Dr. D. G. Moses, "that
we accepted the Gospel plus much besides - the politics, economics,
and the church administration. . . .Except for the land on which
our churches are built; everything else has been foreign and Western -
music, architecture, and ways of worship."[31] Such a condition of
the churches in Asia and Africa can be understood when we have the
following in our mind. K. S. Latourette says, "The foreign
missionary enterprise, both Roman Catholic and Protestant, is a
kind of ecclesiastical imperialism, and the churches found by it
are a form of the cultural invasion of the West."[32]

This leads us to consider the theological background of these churches.
A second-hand and derived theological thought can not take a church too
far in its life in a given environment. It must spring out of the
peoples' life situation. Until its theology is the struggle of the
church in a given situation in the proclamation of the Gospel, a
church will remain isolated from the situation with an alien vision
of Jesus Christ.

Missionary task of the church is dependent upon inspiration and
motivation for mission in the members of the church. By and large,
the indigenous churches in Asia and Africa draw their life for
missionary work from the overseas personnel and funds. There are
some national missionary societies also, but they appear so weak
and feeble that one begins to doubt the genuineness of such movements. The attempt for self-support in mission work is praiseworthy,
but money does not solve all the problems of a church to be the
church. Remarking on the pitiable conditions of the churches in
India, Dr. Chandran Devanesan, the Principal of Madras Christian
College says, 'This is not a bad thing and it is generally agreed
that the church in India should learn to stand on its own feet.
But the real tragedy is that no serious Indian missionary motivation
is taking the place of our overseas inspired movement. . . unless
there is an Indian, a truly Indian revival of the missionary spirit
within the church it will be a doomed church with a fossilized
existence."[33] The above statement shows that Christ, and the
Holy Spirit have not become the very source of life in the members
of the Indian church. Another Christian scholar of India again
says, 'There are ample evidences to show that as Christians move
up in the social and economic scale, they tend to court respect-
ability and social acceptance at the expense of their discipleship.
The sense of mission is blunted by a desire for social recognition."[34]

(b) Bondage to Environmental Factors and Forces

The indigenous churches in Asia and Africa are still in minority

over against the vast majority of men of other faiths - the Hindus,
the Moslems, the Buddhists, Shintoists, Confucianists, the Tribal
religious communities, etc. The minority consciousness and the over-
powering socio-economic and political pressure of the majority tend
to make the indigenous church only one of the many social groups in
a given situation. The Christian churches in the Middle East and
many other Moslem countries do take this form and lose the real
dynamism of the church of Jesus Christ, which moves under the dynamic
power of the Holy Spirit.

There is a very subtle kind of bondage in which the indigenous
church may live. Revival of national heritage and various forms
of neo-paganism might creep into the church and may dominate its
life and work. The Batak Church in Indonesia had almost succumbed
to this temptation and lived under the bondage of nationalism and
neo-paganism for a while after the repatriation of the missionaries.
Such environmental factors and forces always tend to rend the church
asunder. Separatist tendencies and personal or community autonomy
becomes the main interest of the peoples and groups with the result
that the church does not remain the church. Gossner Evangelical
Lutheran Church also suffers from this serious bondage to neo-
paganism. Such indigenous churches are false to the teaching and
Spirit of Jesus Christ.[35] Such churches, if they are not guided by
the Holy Spirit, might be destroyed by cultural accommodation and
doctrinal adjustments as it happened in the first century A.D.
with Ebeonites and the Gnostics respectively.

IV. Freedom of the Indigenous Church

"Freedom under the Holy Spirit has to be expressed in responsibility
before God and men. The church becomes free and responsible as the
Holy Spirit descends upon the church, calling it into communion with
God, to be ruled by His word, and the church responds through the
power of the same Spirit in worship and confession of faith."[36]
The work of the Holy Spirit is made manifest in and through the word
and sacrament in the church. Therefore, it is essential that the
indigenous church should have the inner freedom to be ruled by the
word of God. Lack of this freedom shows great immaturity in the
indigenous church.

A church must have the freedom to establish a relationship between
herself and another church, and not only with the mission societies,
because the same Holy Spirit leads and guides the churches. It
means a creative and new relationship with a hitherto unknown body
of people. Only the Holy Spirit guarantees the knowledge and understanding between one another. The church not only can work with
freedom under the Holy Spirit in relation to another church, but

also in relation to the world around her in a given situation. Dr.
T. Niles say, "He (Holy Spirit) works through ministry of the
church, which ministry He surrounds with his previousness and
impregnates with his presence."[37]

Freedom implies not only responsibility but obedience also. The
power to obey the Lord of the church and to fulfill His purpose is
directly related to the work of the Holy Spirit in the life of the
members of that church. This means not simple fulfillment of
religious rites and duties even in the most refined manner. It
rather means a creative response to the environment under the
inspiration and guidance of the Holy Spirit. "The fact is that the
possibility of Christian obedience is bound up with the experience
of the Holy Spirit. He directs the campaign in which the Christian
is participant so that without him the Christian life is simply
a religious exercise."[38] The freedom argued for here, is the freedom
to obey the Lord in a given socio-cultural and historical situation.
It is a freedom to be ruled by the word of God irrespective of the
political and social climate. This means that freedom of the
indigenous church is primarily to be "the church," i.e., the people
of God in relation to the given socio-economic, political, and
religious environments.

The freedom of the indigenous church under the Holy Spirit has a
direct result in the missionary activity of the church. The
mission is the impulse of the Holy Spirit who prompts the church
towards new fields of action. The early church's movement towards
new action among different countries and people can directly be
traced to the prompting of the Holy Spirit (Acts 1 and 2). The
missionary task of the church is not so much a finishing as the
beginning of the preaching of the good news of Jesus Christ to all
people. It is this beginning which is the unfinished task of the
church and to make a real beginning is the work of the Holy Spirit.
His strength and guidance are essential for the indigenous church.
Sometimes the indigenous churches are too panicky about dangers
in relation to the environment with the result that they may not
dare moving out of their four walls to proclaim the good news.
The church to be under the Holy Spirit must have the courage
to be what the Lord of the Church wants her to be. Dr. T. Niles
again says, "A Church must first find itself as the church for the
nation before it can warn itself of the dangers of its tasks. A
church must become a missionary church, its mission addressed to
that locus in the world where it has been set. . ."[39]

The free and responsible church in view of many scholars must be
in relation to other churches. These relationships are the
relationships of conversation, of belonging, and of oneness.

Such relationships finally mean the breaking down of the denominational barriers at every local, regional, and national level.
Until this is achieved, some would hold, that a truly responsible
and a free church has not been established under the Holy Spirit.

PART IV

Communication of the Christian Heritage Under this Freedom

This freedom under the Holy Spirit means that the indigenous church
is free (a) from the external forces and factors, (b) to be the
church of Jesus Christ in a given situation, and (c) it is freedom
for the fulfillment of the mission of God in Jesus Christ in this
world. The Christian heritage is an integral part of the origin
and development of the Christian history or history of the people
of God. The church has passed throughout at least five different
historical and cultural stages so that the common heritage is
difficult to be separated from the history of the divided churches.
These stages are the Jewish, Greco-Roman, the North European, the
Latin America, and the Asian and African cultural and national
contacts with the missionary movements of the Western churches.

Heritage, inheritance, and heir are words with similar meaning.
There are two different interpretations of the meaning of inheritance. In the legal sense, inheritance is the right to possess
the property of a deceased father or relative. But in the biblical
sense inheritance is a gift given by the gracious act of God in
Jesus Christ. Therefore, heritage is not anything that one
generation of Christians can claim from the previous generations,
or that which one claims by right of geneological lines. It is
rather, a gift from God, which is given to the Christian community
at a given place and point in history. The common Christian
heritage is not the body of materials primarily, but it is the
same God who has given and who still continues to give this
heritage to the believers.

In this primordial sense the common Christian heritage is Christ
Himself who has been given to the church at all times everywhere
by God the gracious father. But this common heritage has at
least two primary forms. They are the scriptures, traditions, and
the common ecumenical creeds - the Apostles', the Nicean, and the
Athnasian creeds. At the secondary level, the Christian heritage
expresses itself in the forms of ministry and sacraments which
are based on the doctrinal statements of particular churches and
traditions. In this secondary sense Christian heritage means
denominational teachings and practices in a particular church.

It is quite clear that the common Christian heritage is directly
related to or an integral part of the Christian Gospel itself.
The message of the Lord has a self-giving, adapting nature. Yet
in this process of adaptation and identification there is an
element of its true nature in the process of relating meaningfully
to a given situation. As the Evangel is the Son of God and Son
of man, so also the written word of God, the creed, and so on do
take the form of the given cultural environment, yet they retain
their original identity which can not be absorbed and lost at
any time and in any given situation. Hence the problem of communication of this common Christian heritage poses real difficulty in
the context of the indigenous church under the freedom of the Holy
Spirit.

Communication of anything is not without danger of its being lost
in the process of communication. It means that in order to be
communicated that which is communicated must have the freedom and
capacity of becoming a part of that to which it is communicated.
The common Christian heritage in order to be meaningfully communicated
in a given culture is bound to take the force of that culture. To
the extent it is able to take the shape of the other, Christian
heritage becomes meaningful to it. On the other hand, if it is
not able or not willing to identify itself with the cultural
environment, it remains isolated and finally becomes useless
for the given situation.

An element of syncretism is a necessary part of a meaningful
communication of the common Christian heritage. When I say
necessary, it does not mean that syncretism is a must for
communication. But it means that this risk of syncretism is
quite obvious and natural if the communication is meaningfully
related to the men and women of other faiths. The logical question is who determines and how one does set forth the limit in this
process of adaptation of the Christian Gospel to the non-Christian
world.

At this point, we have to remember that missionaries and many
scholars have played an adverse role in the matter of communication. They have helped the church to be more isolated than related
to the cultural environment of the people in Asia and Africa.
This is one of the basic reasons why the Christian Gospel has not
been made a real part of the heritages of countries and people
of Asia and Africa. Even though Christianity has been in India,
for instance, for the last 1900 years, yet the cultural life of
India and the Christian heritage as described above have not been
able to influence each other in any substantial manner. Here is
the necessity of the work of the Holy Spirit in the indigenous

church. The Lord Jesus has promised a deeper understanding of
Himself and of the secret of God's calling of His church. The
Holy Spirit is able to lead the indigenous church into deeper truths
of the common Christian heritage. This means that the churches in
Asia and Africa will express the message of the Gospel in their
basic thought pattern, the creeds, forms of worship, and forms of
ministry together with the sacraments will take the cultural forms
without losing their Christ-like character.

The communication of the common Christian heritage is again another
life pattern of the Christian individual and that of the Christian
community as a historical expression of the body of Christ. In
this basic sense, communication itself is a process in a given
cultural context. It will take many years for the church to convince
people that the Holy Spirit is the primary guide, power, and
strength, in making it relevantly related to the situation. The
church as the people of God, or as a community, understands itself
as but one of the many communities in Asian and African situations.
Therefore, all sorts of communications are blocked. The channels
for the work of the Holy Spirit are narrowed down to words and
worship, with the result that even these minimum of means become
ineffective. It is hoped that the above discussion of the indigenous
church will encourage the members of the churches in Asia and Africa
to be open to the leading and guidance of the Holy Spirit for the
efficient, effective, and meaningful communication of the common
Christian heritage in their rapidly changing religio-cultural and
political situations.

REFERENCES

1. R.S.V. Bible

2. Beyerhaus, P. and Lefever, H. The Responsible Church and
    the Mission of the Church. Grand Rapids, Mich.: William
    B. Eerdmans Publishing Co., 1964. P. 107.

3. Ibid., p. 112.

4. Niles, D. T. Upon the Earth. New York: McGraw Hill Book
    Co., Inc., 1962, p. 141.

5. Ibid., p. 142

6. Ibid., p. 64.

7. Beyerhaus and Lefever, Op. Cit., p. 129.

8. Niles, D. T., Op. Cit., p. 76.

9. Latourette, K. S. "History and the Indigenous Church,"
    International Review of Missions, Vol. XVII, 1928,
    pp. 101-118.

10. Ibid., p. 101.

11. Ibid., p. 101.

12. Latourette, K.S. "Indigenous Christianity in the Light
    of History," IRM, Vol. XXIX, October 1940, p. 431.

13. Ibid., p. 433.

14. Ibid., pp. 433-34.

15. Ibid. p. 436.

16. Beyerahus and Lefever, Op. Cit., p. 118.

17. Ibid, p. 121.

18. Ibid., p. 71.

19. Ibid., p. 74.

20. "Native Churches" - The word native is used throughout in all
     honor as designating the younger churches that have grown
     up amongst other than European races. The Jerusalem
     meeting accepted this word as the worthy and honorable
     appallation of such churches. IRM, Vol. XVII, 1928,
     p. 611 footnote.

21. Quoted by P. C. Hsu in "The Chinese Christian Church Coming
     of Age," IRM, Vol. XX, 1931, p. 260.

22. Freytag W. "The Critical Period in the Development of an
     Indigenous Church," IRM, Vol. XXIX, April 1940, p. 205.

23. Ibid. pp. 209 and 215.

24. Pamer, S. L. The Church in North India. Raipur, India:
     Christian Book Depot, 1969, p. 13.

25. Moses, D. G. "Identity of the Indian Church" in The Indian
     Church, Identity and Fulfillment. Zachariah M., ed.
     CLS, Madras 1971, p. 216.

26. Thomas, M. M. "Indigenization and the Renaissance of
     Traditional Cultures." IRM, Vol. 52, 1963, p. 191.

27. Beyerhaus and Lefever, Op. Cit., p. 143.

28. Newbegin, L., Bishop. "Twenty-five Years of CSI." NCC
     Review of India, Vol. XCII No. 4, April 1972, p. 143.

29. Philip, J. V. "Church History and Church's Selfhood," in
     NCC Review, Vol. XCII No. 2, February 1972, p. 66.

30. Philip, J.V. "The Church in India Today," NCC Review, Vol.
     LXXXIX Vol. 1, January 1969, p. 28.

31. Moses, D.G. Op. Cit., pp. 209-10.

32. Latourette, K. S. "History and Indigenous Church," p. 115.

33. Devanesan, C. "Wither Indian SCM?" in Footnotes, WSCF, Asia
     Office, Bulletin Vol. IV No. 3, June-July 1972, p. 28.

34. Pamer, S. L. Op. Cit., p. 5.

35. Beyerhaus and Lefever, Op. Cit., pp. 77 and 84.

36. Ibid., p. 114.

37. Niles, D. T. Op. Cit., p. 69.

38. Ibid., p. 64.

39. Ibid., p. 144.

8

EVANGELIZING THE UNREACHED PEOPLES: WHAT TO DO AND HOW TO DO IT
Charles R. Taber

This paper is concerned with the "how" of evangelism, especially the evangelization of the unreached peoples of the world.[1] It deals with questions of planning and methodology, though, for reasons which will emerge in the course of the paper, I will emphasize general principles rather than concrete techniques. In other words, I will in general answer the "how" of manner rather than the "how" of methods and means. Because of the pragmatic focus of the paper, and because of my own background and convictions, much of what I have to say arises from anthropological considerations. But I have found it impossible in the end to divorce these from more broadly ethical or even theological concerns; the two kinds of ideas turn out to be intertwined in a mutually supportive way.[2] Some of my points focus more on one aspect than on the other, but it will be apparent that there are close ties between them throughout.

I also want to emphasize that I claim no originality for these ideas; rather, I am restating themes which have been gradually developing within both the theory of missions and the social-behavioral sciences for many years. My reason for so doing is, first, that it is always good for us to remind ourselves of fundamental principles as we launch a major new effort, and second, that these principles have not invariably found their way from the lecture room to actual practice in the field. I think, in fact, that it will be found that grosso modo, successes in evangelism since the beginning have been related to conformity to these ideas, and failure to flouting them.

Though some of my discussion is explicitly, and some implicitly, addressed to the special problems of an evangelist who is a foreigner, I think the bulk of it is applicable also to the evangelist who is a national of the country in question. For we are talking about unreached groups, which means that by definition at least the initial contacts will be made by people who are not themselves members of the specific society, nor participants of that specific culture, even when they are citizens of the country. In not a few instances, they will be members of the majority and dominant national culture, and may therefore have to overcome in themselves negative attitudes towards the societies they are called upon to evangelize. This is at least as true, of course, in the

efforts of Western Christians to evangelize unreached sub-populations in their midst (e.g. hippies) as it is in the Third World.
The fact must also be faced that in most countries, but perhaps
even more in the Third World than in the West, the net effect of
theological education is to create a gulf between the minister
and his people, especially those who are not members of the
"establishment". So it is true that even my discussion of the
importance of anthropological training to overcome prejudices and
to give insight is applicable to the non-Western, national evangelist in many instances. Of course, it should be heavily underscored that from the first, converts on the local scene should
become in turn evangelists, and increasingly take over responsibility in their own area as they are able.

The Primacy of the Holy Spirit

Before going further, I would like to place on record my conviction that without the leading and enabling of the Holy Spirit,
there can be no effective evangelism; techniques can never replace
him. But I feel that the Holy Spirit leads through available information, and works through available skills to accomplish his
purposes. It is no sin to be involuntarily ignorant or incompetent, though it is no virtue either. But it *is* a sin, grave
enough to hinder the work of God, to be ignorant or incompetent
through laziness, indifference, or arrogance.

The Principle of Respect

Absolutely fundamental to effective evangelism is the principle of respect: respect for the Gospel, and respect for the hearer.

By respect for the Gospel, I mean trusting its own intrinsic
power to do its work, unsupported by any purely human power of the
evangelist over the hearer, for the use of such power demeans the
Gospel.

By respect for the hearer, I mean the unconditional recognition of every persons's and every society's right to listen or
not to listen, uncoerced, unmanipulated, and unbribed. This
emphatically does not mean that the evangelist should not be persuasive, quite the contrary. But it does mean that the persuasion must not be based on anything other than the wonder of the
Gospel itself, especially as manifested in the lives of its
bearers. It also means the recognition by the evangelist that
he has no divine commission to interfere with the lives and customs of his hearers, and that he works among them by their permission and at their sufference.

Lest the sharp point of this principle be missed, let me
spell it out in a bit more detail, though I will reserve treatment of some implications for later sections. The exploitation,
in support of the Gospel, of any area of relative weakness on
the part of the hearer or relative power on the part of the
evangelist, whether the discrepancy be the result of race, culture, level of education, difference of age, material resources,
disease, prestige, or any other human factor, is ethically wrong,
because it constitutes a more or less subtle form of coercion or
bribery.

A sensitive point which needs to be mentioned is the inherent
danger of manipulation in missions, just as in nation-to-nation
foreign aid, based on the power of money.

The principle of respect provides a helpful guideline in the
resolution of the question of participation by the evangelist in
the social and cultural patterns of the local people. As a good
guest, he ought to participate as fully and actively as the people
wish him to; but he must not do so to the point of compromising
his own moral and religious convictions, for both he and the people
would defect and condemn the dishonesty and artificiality involved.

The Vital Role of Third World Leaders

I said in my introduction that I would not primarily present
concrete techniques. One reason is that this would be premature
in the absence of Third World leaders in significant numbers.
Surely it is time to stop thinking and acting as if conferences in
the United States or Europe, attended largely by Westerners, can
provide a blueprint for world evangelization, when most of the
unreached peoples are in the Third World. It should be a matter
of principle that the wisdom and experience of Christian thinkers
from the Third World be called upon to play a fundamental and
even a determinative role in primary planning as well as in final
execution. I would hesitate to hold another conference such as
this one without a majority of Third World leaders, for fear of
doing more harm than good by perpetuating old paternalistic patterns.

In addition to being a basic principle, this is also a very
pragmatic matter: unless we obtain general participation by Third
World churches, it is doubtful that the evangelization of the world
can get far off the ground.

It is true that some of the existing churches, especially
those that have existed for two or more generations, have learned

all too well certain lessons taught them, consciously or unconsciously, by their founding missions; to do everything by the
book, just as in Europe or in America, right down to clerical
collars and the hour of worship; and to concentrate their efforts
and resources on maintaining themselves, leaving the evangelization of unreached areas to foreign missionaries. In this self-
centeredness they have too often been subtly encouraged by
missions which have failed to stress the evangelistic responsibilities of the churches they have founded and have in some cases
even discouraged local initiatives. The practices if not the
official teaching of missions has often induced in Third World
churches a strong, and often justified, feeling that they have
been kept in the background, in tutelage, and that their participation in a role of initiative and leadership would actually
not be welcomed by the older churches and their missions. To
overcome this feeling, it will be necessary to show to them by
our deep attitudes and our actions that this time it is really
different, that we expect them to take the initiative, that we
will actually defer to their ideas, that we will follow their lead
and that we will <u>not</u> snatch the program out of their hands if it
shows signs of developing in ways that are uncongenial to us.[3]
Unless we can convince them that we mean this, and that we will
<u>not</u> "rescue" the program as we have too often in the past, they
will have no reason to participate. I personally feel that if we
do convince them, and then follow through, they will participate
actively and fruitfully. They must be at the top, and not only
nominally and symbolically, from the state of initial plans to
that concrete implementation in individual activities. Westerners
who are involved must in all cases be in a genuinely and visibly
subordinate role. Those who would not find such an arrangement
congenial should by all means return to their home countries, as
they would do more harm than good.

<u>The Specificity of Evangelism</u>
       Because societies, cultures, and individuals vary so much,
the most effective evangelistic approach is the one which is most
specifically geared to the particular situation of the hearer.
The evangelist, before planning his approach, must discover what
assumptions the hearer holds about reality, truth, and value; and
more important, must be keenly aware of what problems deeply
trouble the hearer, so that he can maximize the fit of the Gospel
presentation to the hearer's needs. This is what Jacob A. Loewen
has called "scratching where it itches." This principle, as
shown by the example of our Lord himself, goes beyong a general
adaptation to each culture: it actually involves a specific
adaptation to each hearer (cf John 3 and 4). Such an adaptation

presupposes on the part of the evangelist more or less extended, more or less intimate contact with the hearer in a variety of social situations, and a keen sensitivity and awareness of what social scientists call the paramessage of the situation. True evangelism rarely flourishes in isolation from the whole of life, it rarely succeeds in reaching and transforming a man by operating in vacuo or at a distance.

This is a second reason why it would be premature to suggest highly specific techniques at this time, and why it will be in principle impossible ever to design a universally valid evangelistic technique. Rather, the approaches and techniques will have to be redesigned in each situation, using help from experiences elsewhere, and especially insights derived from anthropology (see following section).

It is also for this reason that mass approaches, though they do have their own important role to play, are not in themselves prime means of evangelism: they are too general, too imprecise, too unrelated to the real life of each person. Such approaches, it seems to me, are more suitable to pre-evangelism and to post-evangelism. By pre-evangelism, I mean the dissemination of a general understanding of the Gospel, with a view to establishing recognition and a favorable predisposition when evangelism proper is launched. By post-evangelism, I mean supplementing the efforts of churches to teach converts the basics of Christian faith and life, and to make them informed and active Christians. But I would emphasize that in order to achieve these important goals, the mass approaches will themselves have to prepare their materials with great attention to specific sociocultural situations, in order to be of maximum assistance. There should be an immediate halt to the indiscriminate broadcasting and publishing of materials suitable only for the Western world.

In the same vein, the new evangelism will divorce itself resolutely from all reliance on the huge mission compound, the ghetto in which missionaries have lived in isolation from the people they are trying to reach. The effective evangelist, now as in every age, will live and work among the people, in the strongest sense of the word.

The Role of the Social Sciences

The role of the social sciences, especially anthropology, needs now to be discussed, because we seem to find the temptation almost irresistible to see in anthropology an instrument of power

in evangelism rather than in instrument of sensitivity and insight.
I have already spoken about the existing imbalance in power along
human dimensions between evangelist and hearer, and of the danger
of exploiting these in order to induce the hearer to listen to the
Gospel. It is equally wrong, of course, to so use anthropological
resources. The proper role of anthropology is to change the evangelist, not the hearer; to make him more sensitive to his own
ethnocentrism, more understanding and appreciative of other people's
ways, gentler in dealing with persons. The difference in attitude
and approach between an evangelist who makes proper use of anthropology and one who misuses or ignores it can be as great as
that between a butcher and a skilled surgeon.

Anthropology and sociology will also provide a conceptual and
procedural framework for gathering, understanding, and applying the
masses of data of which we will be speaking next, and which are
vital to any effective planning in such a diverse world.

Background Information

Before anything else can be validly done, information must be
gathered on the givens of the situation. This may sound like a
truism, but too many efforts are still being launched without adequate use of easily obtainable data. I do not mean that we must
wait for years of costly fieldwork before doing anything at all,
still less that we should multiply conferences to pool our ignorance, but that we should make intelligent use of such abundant information as is readily at hand in libraries and in such resources
as the Human Relations Area Files, while waiting to supplement and
refine it through further studies. Much important information is
in libraries and files abroad, e.g. in universities. The crucial
thing is to find the information where it is, and get it to where
it is needed for immediate planning, both on a worldwide and on a
regional and local level. The kinds of questions which must be
asked and answered include the following:
1. What populations are today's unreached? These are not only
small, whole, homogeneous populations, such as remote jungle
tribes and bands, but definable sub-populations within otherwise
well evangelized societies, or groups which were evangelized in a
previous century or generation but not in this. This includes a
great many churchgoers, e.g. in the prosperous suburbs of Western
countries, who for all their churchianity have never come to grips
with a clear presentation of the Gospel. For such people, a real
obstacle is created by their illusion of knowing what the Gospel
is, and by their negative image of those who would present anything

different from what they comfortably practice. In some cases, there
is actual hostility to a presentation of the genuine Gospel; in others,
a total apathy. In either case, it can well be said that for all
practical purposes, these people are just as unreached as the jungle
tribes or as the masses of urban ghettos. We must therefore get
over thinking in terms of geographical areas, and start thinking in
terms of groups of people. A careful survey will not guarantee
that a sound strategy will prevail over piecemeal responses to
emotional appeals, but lack of it will certainly lead to the
opposite.
2. What factors have hitherto prevented effective evangelism of
these people? These may include such things as:
  (a) Geographical remoteness or difficulty of access
  (b) Political obstacles, e.g. doors closed by governments
  (c) Racial prejudice and hostility
  (d) Ideological resistance
  (e) Resistance by strong, resurgent traditional cultures
  (f) Indifference or lack of vision on the part of the church
  (g) Use of incompetent personnel, ineffective methods, etc.
3. What are the present characteristics of each unreached population?
  (a) Demography: numbers; spatial distribution (concentrated
      or dispersed, settled or mobile); sociological distri-
      bution (by age and sex, by social class or caste, by
      educational, occupational, and economic levels, etc.)
  (b) Traditional culture and social structure: historic char-
      acteristics, present state (stable, reactionary, in
      evolution, in revolution, in disintegration, etc.)
  (c) Patterns of leadership, dissemination and legitimation
      of new ideas, decision making
  (d) Options present as a result of contact with other cul-
      tures, e.g. Western materialism, Marxism, Islam, Bud-
      dhism; prognosis of relative success of each
  (e) Present political system, characteristics and prospects;
      relationship of the specific society to the government
4. What existing Christian agencies can be marshalled to meet the
new challenge? These include churches (both in the West and in
the Third World), mission boards, and specialized organizations.
In many cases, patterns of mutual ignorance, distrust, and indifference, or even hostility will have to be faced and overcome, as
well as a rigid and narrow focus on "the way we've always done it."

The above points are by no means exhaustive, only suggestive.
In most cases, data at least usefully close to accuracy are readily

available; what is needed is for the information to be dug out,
collated by highly competent people into sharply focused and di-
gestible reports, and fed into the planning process at all appropriate points. In some cases, it will need to be supplemented or
corrected by further field research or pilot projects. There will
need to be a constant flow of information back and forth at all
stages of the project, from preliminary planning to continual monitoring of ongoing programs.

One area of investigation needs especially to be entered in
depth. In addition to the "external" facts which need to be uncovered by research, such as population, political structure, and
so on, it is crucial that we come to a better understanding than
we have at present of what happens to a message in the process of
interpretation by the hearers. Random observation leads me to sup-
pose that there is a much greater difference than we like to admit
between what we think we are proclaiming and what our hearers understand us to be saying. This is, of course, not an original observation; we have all heard of, and perhaps participated in, debates on
"syncretism", "accommodation", and the like. But in spite of a
fairly extensive literature on the pros and cons of the issue at a
theoretical, theological level, we still know remarkably little, at
the empirical level, of what actually happens.

The discrepancy between the intention of the evangelist and the
understanding of his hearers stems, of course, from divergent cultural knowledge and assumptions at the outset. The evangelist's
assumptions as to what is clear, what is a priori probable or im-
probable, what is important, and so on, come in part from the text
on which his message is based, that is, the Bible. But to a much
greater extent than he is aware, they come from his own very human
culture. Especially as he enlarges upon the biblical text by way
of explanation, illustration, and application, he cannot avoid
drawing largely on his own cultural background and experience. And
crucially, he will tend to leave implicit such items of information
as appear _to_ _him_ to be self-evident.

The hearer, on the other hand, brings to the decoding of the
message quite different knowledge and assumptions; it would be surprising indeed if he did not fill in obvious gaps in the message in
ways that would astonish and dismay the evangelist, as when he makes
automatic indentifications between facts and concepts of the new
message and facts and concepts from his culture.

What we badly need is a dispassionate analysis, in a variety of
cultural settings, of what actually takes place. This will entail,
in large part, new fieldwork, because it focuses on issues which have

not been studied in quite this way before. But there is an extensive literature on acculturation to provide a starting point.

The hypothesis which I would propose for testing, and which I would expect to see confirmed, is (a) that any new message will be modified by its hearers in the process of interpretation in the direction of conforming to their cultural expectations, and (b) that there will therefore be a measure of homogenization when quite different messages are proclaimed, as by different religious groups, in a given cultural setting.

A good control situation is provided. by the United States, where such sociologists as Will Herberg (in Protestant--Catholic--Jew) have described empirically a kind of American folk religion which is remarkably similar regardless of the confessions to which various Americans officially belong.

Once the empirical findings begin to come in, we can look again at the principle involved, and ask about the legitimacy of accommodation, how far it should go, and what it may or may not involve if the gospel is to be preserved in its essentials.

In order to carry on and to promote research in all these areas, I am making the following concrete proposal: that a central, semi-independent research agency be established, to have the following characteristics:

1. Its central role will be to discover (both directly and by proxy, by stimulating others to dig), in the library and in the field, all relevant information, and to coordinate, focus, and test it, in order to make practical procedural recommendations solidly founded in facts and in relevant concepts from the social sciences. Its research would be both basic and applied, both long-term and short-term, both broadly and narrowly focused, and it would explore all the ramifications of the applications of the social sciences to evangelism in today's world.

2. Its permanent staff would be (a) very few in number, (b) highly competent by both training and experience in the social sciences and in missions, and (c) international.

3. It would give technical counsel and guidance to field research projects and pilot projects undertaken by others also involved in the total effort.

4. It would bring together in active participation on a temporary and rotating basis other qualified people not on the permanent staff for continual cross-fertilization.

5. It would call upon existing information and research agencies to assist in the areas of their special competencies.

6. It would formulate recommendations to planning agencies at all levels.

7. It would ensure a regular flow of information from all sources to all points of need.

8. It would coordinate the continuing monitoring and evaluating studies of the program.

It may be wiser, rather than establishing immediately a central research center at the world level, to begin at the local or regional level. Advantages of working through local research centers from the first would be: greater access to primary data, closer contact with specific problems, closer contacts with key people, greater impact upon theological training institutions (which are the key to future participation of the church), and the possibility of a less top-heavy organization. If it could be possible to place two professors well trained in the social sciences as well as in theology in each of the chief theological schools, this would go a long way toward improving church participation. A disadvantage with this approach would be that it would require multiple centers of primary initiative, which might be hard to set up.

The Coordination of Efforts
In speaking of the involvement of all Christian agencies, I must add that it is important to avoid both the proliferating of ad hoc agencies competing for the same resources to reach the same people, and a rigidly orchestrated effort under a single monolithic organization. The first leads to the present chaos, with its inexcusable overlappings and omissions, as well as to a caricature of the church which can only hurt its witness. The second leads to paralysis through excessive size and complexity, because too great a proportion of the resources are consumed by a top-heavy, unresponsive, and unimaginative bureaucracy; there would also be a tendency in this situation to try to devise those universal methods which we have seen to be a chimera. It would be much better to mobilize existing organizations, merging some when genuine gain can be foreseen, and establishing pragmatic links between them based on a minimum of machinery and a maximum of shared information and experience. I do not believe old-fashioned quasi-juridical comity arrangements are workable either, as both populations and circumstances are too fluid.

As was mentioned in an earlier section, leadership at all levels should be in the hands of Third World Christians rather than in those of Westerners.

The role of Westerners is thus in general an auxiliary one.
They should participate at the invitation of the churches in the
country of service, and in the capacities assigned to them. The
older churches in the West should for once exercise a measure of
Christian confidence in the integrity and abilities of the younger
churches and a measure of disinterestedness by providing funds
and other material and moral support without strings. After all,
"He who pays the piper calls the tune" is not in the Bible!
    There could well be in the context of locally controlled
programs, a two-way exchange of assisting personnel as well as an
exchange of ideas between older and younger churches.

Evangelism and Humanitarian Services
    Much controversy has surrounded the question of the relation-
ship of humanitarian services---medicine, education, etc.---to
evangelism. Some would include all of these efforts under an inclusive definition of evangelism; others would divorce them entirely, even to the point of denying the responsibility of the
church for human temporal needs. Both of these positions are extreme, and I believe untenable. Rather, concerns for a man's temporal and spiritual well-being are not identical, but they are
inseparable. I do not see how Christians could live and work in
areas of great human suffering and need and do nothing about it:
such unconcern is a negation of the compelling logic of the Gospel;
the Christian faced with human need is constrained by the love of
Christ to do what he can to relieve that need. If he has resources
and skill, he can act on a fairly large scale.

    But everything depends, it seems to me, on attitude and moti-
vation. To convey by one's attitude and actions, "I am helping
you because the Gospel has so transformed me that I care for you
with the love of Christ" is not only right, it is indispensable to
a valid presentation of the Gospel. But to convey, "I am helping
you because I want you to listen to what I have to say" or even "I
will help you if you listen to what I have to say" is wrong, because it is deceptive, and demeans both Gospel and hearer. To
offer one thing which the hearer desires, and then to substitute
or append something else which the presenter wants to "sell" (what
in American marketing jargon is called the "bait-and switch") is
ethically wrong in commerce, it is inexcusable in evangelism.

    How can one avoid giving the impression that services are of-
fered on condition that the hearer listen to the evangelist, or as
a reward for listening? This will not be easy, but the following
steps should help:
    (a) eliminate all such thinking from the mind of the evangel-
ist, and from the overt scheduling of his and his colleagues' programs (as when patients are treated only after they have attended
chapel);

(b) offer help first in areas which are of immediate conscious concern to the people ("the place where it itches"), without any condition, explicit or implicit, in relation to the Gospel (this was the invariable practice of Jesus Christ himself);

(c) place oneself as opportunity presents in a position of need in relation to the people, and solicit and accept their help with gratitude, so as to establish a pattern of reciprocity in the giving of service which will not only separate it from the presentation of the Gospel, but enhance the people's sense of worth (the principle of respect);

(d) avoid instituting any program for ministering to human need which does not have significant intelligent support within the leadership of the society, in the planning of which local people have not been involved from the start, and which does not fit in some way into the local pattern of things (this does not preclude gentle efforts at educating local leadership when they are not aware of real needs that the evangelist sees);

(e) turn over policy initiative and leadership to local people as soon as the program is underway.

Any program which cannot fit these specifications may well be too elaborate or too Western for the local situation.

This should not be interpreted as condemning all larger institutions; hospitals and major schools need at times to be established. But in most local situations, the above guidelines should if at all possible be followed, especially those about avoiding compromising the Gospel, reciprocity, and local involvement.

The Evangelist and Social Change
Evangelism will be carried out today in almost all cases in situations of more or less rapid social and cultural change. This would be so even if the Gospel were not a factor; it is a fortiori true, since the Gospel aims to bring very specific and fundamental changes into men's lives. Some of the change going on is intrinsically good, some intrinsically bad, some indifferent. But more important to the evangelist is the attitude of the people themselves to the change they are experiencing. The principle of respect demands that, unless there are compelling reasons to do otherwise, the evangelist should accept as normative the attitude of the people with whom he is working, and assist them in achieving goals they have chosen and defined for themselves. It should be pointed out, of course, that it will be rare that the people in such a situation will come immediately to a massive consensus. The more usual case is that there will be a range of views, all the way from the reactionary to the revolutionary. In such a case, the evangelist may well be called upon to play the role of broker,

helping these various views to find expression with a minimum of
conflict, and encouraging the development of the most constructive
consensus.

The Gospel itself, we have said, leads to change. But in the
past, insensitive and ethnocentric missionaries have too often
changed things that did not need to be changed, simply because they
disapproved of them; or they changed things too fast, with results
which were sometimes socially catastrophic. The new evangelism
must be gentle, following in the sociocultural sphere the
imperative of the Hippocratic Oath: "First of all, do no harm."
This is easier to state than to define; for in the sociocultural
area, it is even harder than in the area of physical health to
define what constitutes harm, and also to specify how one should
in every instance foresee the possible consequences of a given course
of action. But I ought at least to make an effort to explain the
concept lest my caveat become an empty phrase. "Harm", it seems to
me, must include anything that will weaken the wholesome integration
of a culture or of a personality. This includes the removal or the
denigration of customs and habits, values and beliefs, which have
in the past given the individual or the society its sense of direction, purpose, and meaning. Here the warning of Jesus in Matthew
12.43-45 against simply exorcising demons without a compensatory
"filling" of the "empty" life, should be taken very seriously. In
many a country, traditional patterns have been destroyed, at least
partly as a result of condemnation by missionaries; but the end
state of the society in question is worse than the first, because
even more unwholesome traits have replaced the old, in the absence
of viable and satisfying traits which ought to have been supplied
by the gospel. The changes introduced by the Gospel ought to be
in the direction of greater integration and well-being of society
and persons, rather than in the direction of disintegration and
anomie. In such a situation, the question must also be asked, Who
is judge of what is harmful? Missionaries have usually assumed this
role as by divine right; but it must be asserted that the principle
of respect demands that the society and the individual person be
judge of what he finds wholesome and satisfying. The evangelist
has the task of so presenting the gospel that it will make the most
appeal; but if people reject it, he cannot coerce them on the grounds
that the course they have chosen is harmful. Further, the evangelist must be very humble, realizing that both in the past and in
the present, many ministers of the gospel have in fact done more
harm than good by their approach to their task.

In assessing the most common attitude of missionaries in the past to change, it should be added that some missionaries took a reverse attitude and resisted certain aspects of socio-cultural change, even when it was evident that many people wanted them. Reasons included a sentimental and paternalistic desire to keep the culture intact in its pristine purity (in this, missionaires were in agreement with many anthropologists) and a negative view, on moral and theological grounds, of those aspects of their own culture which people wanted to adopt.

The role of a foreign evangelist in such a situation as ambiguous and even uncomfortable, and he must accept this ambiguity and live with it in humility. He has more responsibility than power, more duties than rights. If he introduces change too fast, he is properly criticized, and may even destroy his work. If he resists change desired by the people, even if he feels it is not good, he is damned as paternalistic.

In order to achieve a wholesome and measured impact, the evangelist must be versed in the relevant ideas and attitudes of anthropology; he must be genuinely humble in the biblical sense, and very gentle; he must operate totally in the open, discussing freely with local leaders everything he does or wants to do. In an atmosphere of sharing and mutual learning, the evangelist can be guided by local people, especially as key individuals are converted, into ways of maximizing the positive and minimizing the negative effects of his presence and work. And he must recognize that in the final analysis, the people themselves are the ones who have the right to decide what is too fast and what is too slow.

In a number of areas, the evangelist will find himself caught between the desires and aspirations of the immediately local population and conflicting national policies, especially when he is working with a racial, ethnic, or linguistic minority in a country where nationalism is strong in the majority society. In some cases, the national government actually oppresses the minorities. What is the role of the evangelist?

On the one hand, following the invariable practice of Jesus Christ, he will see it as his duty to identify openly and helpfully with the oppressed in all cases of manifest oppression or injustice. He will, using patience, firmness, a strong sense of justice, and the truth, speak out, trying to interpret and defend the legitimate interests of the people before the national government.

On the other hand, he will in fairness recognize those cases where the aims of the national government to implement national policies are right and proper, and attempt by moral suasion to help the local group come to terms with the government in its own interest.

In other words, he is a kind of broker, but not an impartial one: he in all cases tries to work in the best interests of the local people, primarily as they understand their best interests. He needs to keep in balance on the one hand his continued right to be there (especially if he is a foreigner), on the other the need to maintain his credibility with the local people.

The evangelist who is himself a member of the majority society experiences the dilemma at an even deeper personal level, as conflict between his own internalized values, which would identify with national policy, and his responsibility to his local friends. Even he, however, following the imperative to be all things to all men, should err, if at all, in the direction of identifying with the local people. However, even though he explicitly identifies with the oppressed peoples, he must at all times show love for both parties, i.e. the oppressed and the oppressors. He cannot (as I point out in my discussion of revolution) simply hate, denounce, and condemn. He must in love respect the oppressor, even when he has to speak out forcefully against his crime.

The Evangelist and Revolution

Revolution is, of course, the extreme case of sociocultural change, and as such could have been subsumed under the previous section. But it has become a topic of much concern in itself, and it does pose special problems to the evangelist, as to Christians in general.

The situation is that in a number of countries, sociocultural change is either already being carried on by revolutionary methods, or there is a strong feeling among responsible members of the society that revolution is the only available means of correcting oppressive and corrupt power structures.[4] Here again, certain principles seem to be basic.
1. The New Testament seems to establish a principle of non-violence for the Christian, especially as it relates to his own rights and to the presentation of the Gospel, but also in general. The Christian who wishes to follow his Lord, therefore, would not seem to be authorized to engage in or to encourage or condone violence, whatever the provocation.

2. Both the New Testament and human experience establish the point that virtually any government is better than no government. Human groups cannot function or even survive under chaos, they absolutely require some kind of working power structure. Therefore a Christian cannot enter into a program which has as its aim the overthrow of a government but which has no clear and plausible alternative ready to operate.

Some may feel that I am not fairly representing the ideology of anarchy; in its essence, it is quite true that anarchy is not the advocacy of lack of order and mutual respect. It is not a call for a return to the law of the jungle. In fact, as an ideal it is not far from the position of the Bible (cf. Heb. 10.16, quoting Jer. 31.33; and Gal. 5-6): the necessary constraints that make it possible for men to live in harmony should be internal, rather than external. My defense of my presentation is twofold: first, that in practice anarchy has been understood by most of those who have tried to espouse and practice it in the quite negative sense of absence of all restraint; and second, that the effective practice of ideal anarchy requires a new man, which only the power of God can produce. There is a sense in which the earliest church (before Acts 6) was anarchic; but even in this period, there quickly developed the need for organization and rules, simply because the saints had not been sufficiently perfected to practice anarchy. This is why, pragmatically though not ideally, almost any government is better than no government, a fortiori when we are dealing with societies in which the vast majority have not even been effectively exposed to the Gospel, let alone transformed by it. Parenthetically, orthodox Marxism is also based upon an idealized view of human nature, or at least upon the promise of creating a new humanity (through the new type of economy to be established); it has also stubbed its toe upon the sordid reality of human nature, and in practice is very far from its avowed ideals in part for that very reason.

3. These two considerations, however, do not constitute an excuse to identify complacently with oppressive establishments in the name of law and order, though they are sometimes misused in this way. For as we have seen, the clear duty of the Christian in an oppressive situation is to identify with the oppressed rather than the oppressor, and that openly and helpfully. The Christian in revolutionary times will dare to speak out against abuses of power and authority, whoever perpetrates them and whoever suffers from them. This may well entail such consequences as imprisonment, expulsion (for the foreigner), or even death. These are neither to be courted nor to be avoided from consideration of safety and convenience. One consideration which may lead a Christian to speak

less openly than he might otherwise is that this may bring an end
to his ministry; he may therefore weigh the possibility of doing
what good he can short of being expelled or shut up. This is not
an easy choice, and it ill behooves anyone who has not faced it
to pontificate or to criticize.

4. Nothing is helped, rather the contrary, when Christians get
carried away into making extreme, shrill, inaccurate, or slanderous
charges and manifestoes. "Speaking the truth in love" is the
absolute standard for the Christian. He will therefore boldly say
what is true, but refuse to go beyond this or lend his support to
pronouncements that go beyond it.

5. By every possible means, he will endeavor to bring about just
solutions to problems peacefully, to reconcile men, to heal society,
rather than to shout, condemn, and destroy.

6. Because of the special pressures and dilemmas involved, Christian agencies will need to avoid sending into revolutionary situations workers whose family or other personal responsibilities
would aggravate the problem for them. What I have in mind here
is the same kind of prudential counsel that Paul gives in I Cor.
7.26ff: "Considering the present distress" (TEV), or, in our
terms, the hazards of the revolutionary situation, it is better to
have evangelists who are unencumbered with family responsibilities,
so as to avoid unnecessary conflicts. I may generalize a bit, and
say that it seems to me that in our day as in Paul's, there are
certain tasks to be done in the Christian context that can be more
easily be accomplished by celibates than by married persons; though
of course the converse is equally true.

NOTES

[1]I am assuming that a more sophisticated definition of evangelism
will emerge through other papers; I am therefore using here as a
working definition "the presentation of the gospel to the not-yet-
believer"; similarly, I am using the term "evangelist" in its bare
etymological sense, rather than in its specialized modern sense,
and rather than the word "missionary", which automatically suggests
a foreigner.

[2]Significantly, this convergence of technical and ethical-philo-
sophical concerns is increasingly characteristic of the discipline
of anthropology, as scholars become aware of the implications of
studying and publishing information about societies and their
cultures.

[3]Taylor in <u>The Primal Vision</u> (fn on p. 22) tells of the preliminary planning of the first All Africa Churches' Conference (1958),
which was supposed to be run by Africans. "But when it appeared
that the African leaders intended to have no agenda but to allow
the findings to emerge from free, informal discussion, the
[Western] experts felt constrained to take a hand, and once again
Western methods prevailed!"

[4]By "revolution" I mean the violent bloody kind, of which the
French, Russian, and Chinese Revolutions are the paradigm; I do
not mean those programs of rapid change which in some countries
attempt to borrow extra impact by calling themselves revolutions.
I should perhaps justify this narrow definition by saying, first
that I am using this definition pragmatically, since it is in the
context of violent political revolutions that the question is
currently being debated in missionary circles; and second, that
the most fundamentally revolutionary ideology in the world is the
Christian Gospel, because it aims at the most basic changes in
society and values. So the Christian must be, in this latter
sense, a revolutionary; but, in my judgment, he may <u>not</u> be a
revolutionary in the political, violent sense, because it calls
for a negation of the principle of respect.

Section C

CASE STUDIES

AN ETHNOLOGICAL APPROACH TO MISSION: BRUNO GUTMANN IN KILIMANJARO

9

Donald C. Flatt

In the meeting of the World Council of Churches and the International Missionary Council at New Delhi in 1961, at which the two separate ecumenical bodies finally merged, occured another significant event. That was the re-discovery of the missiological importance of the doctrine of creation. There were, however, missionary societies and individual missionaries, influenced by the thought of such theologians as Nikolai Grundtvig and Gustav Warneck, who had never lost sight of this important factor in the winning of the peoples to Christ. Such a society was the Leipiz Missionary Society, which in the last decade of the nineteenth century took over the responsibility for the evangelization of the tribes in Northern Tanzania, then "German East Africa." And one of the most radical exponents of this type of approach was a now almost unkown missiologist, Bruno Gutmann.

There is little doubt that Gutmann was expressing a strong trend of thought and principle which shaped most of the work of the Leipzig mission in Kilimanjaro. However, since he pressed the theory in its most extreme form, and there was much controversy between him and his co-workers about some of his attitudes and statements, it will be well to admit that the policies he advocated were rigidly applied only in central Kilimanjaro around the mission station where he was located, at Kidia in Old Moshi. For lack of equal documentation for the other areas of Lutheran work on the mountain, and in light of the general pattern of development, the assumption is made that Gutmann's actual practice was not untypical, and that he does give some strong clues to the manner in which the now large and flourishing Lutheran Church in the area was established and developed.

In order to present the argument in a convenient and fairly logical form, the following arrangement will be adopted:

1. A very brief historical introduction.

2. An exposition of Gutmann's theory and practice, based on his own writings.

3. A brief description of the actual development of the church in Kilimanjaro, and central Kilimanjaro in particular.

4. A question as to validity of the argument, in the light of the lack of continuity of the Leipzig missionary personnel on the field for four or five years after World

War I, and for fourteen or fifteen years during and after
World War II.

5. A "control case" reinforcing the argument, derived from
   the neighboring Arusha area, where the same mission seems
   to have followed a different policy, with very different
   results.

Before proceeding to the issues, it may be well also to indicate
the credentials of the writer, since a number of statements will be
made with no other support than that deriving from intimate personal
knowledge of the area and the churches involved. The writer came to
Tanzania, then "Tanganyika Territory," in 1937 as a provincial administrative officer under the British trustee administration. He served
in that capacity for nearly twelve years, in the course of which he
was required to pass the higher standard examination in the Swahili
language, to guide local government ("native") administrations in the
discharge of their duties, and to review--and occasionally hear on
appeal--a very large number of cases from the local court system.
His previous training had included studies in social anthropology,
law, the history of East Africa, principles of administration and
other related matters. In May, 1949, he joined the Augustana Mission
of the U.S.A. on a call to serve as Education Secretary to the Lutheran Church of Northern Tanganyika, temporarily deprived by the war
of its Leipzig missionaries. He served in this capacity for eight
years, with periods during which he also had other special responsibilities. The first additional special responsibility was to give
any possible assistance to the pastor and church council of the Kidia
congregation in Old Moshi, where he was resident on the station for
eighteen months--the first missionary successor to Gutmann, though
at that time a layman. The next extra post which had to be carried
owing to staff shortage was that of acting headmaster of the Lutheran Secondary School in Arusha, a task which lasted for another
eighteen months. In September, 1957, after ordination in 1954, the
final role was that of president of the Church and Mission, involving a re-organization and the installation of the Rev. Stefano Moshi,
now Bishop Moshi, as the first African president, in February, 1959.

I. Historical Introduction:

The work of the Leipzig Evangelical Lutheran Mission in N.
Tanzania dates from 1892, when Leipzig took over work in the Old
Moshi area of Kilimanjaro started two years previously by two Church
Missionary Society missionaries. Bruno Gutmann arrived in 1903 and
was assigned to the Kidia station in the heart of central Kilimanjaro.
He continued to serve here until 1920, when political factors con-
cerned with the post-war situation were considered by the British to
necessitate the withdrawal of the German missionaries. He returned

in 1925, and continued to work in the area until shortly after the
outbreak of the second world war in September, 1939. In the interim
period, from 1921 to 1925, the Augustana Lutheran Church of the U.S.A.
supplied missionaries and supervision, at the request, and under the
auspices of, the National Lutheran Council.[1]

Augustana and the National Lutheran Council, U.S.A., again came
to the rescue during World War II, furnishing a considerable number
of missionaries and recruiting others from Scandinavia, as well as
giving supervision and funds.[2] It was 1954 before German missionaries were again given visas to enter Tanganyika. Gutmann was not
among those who were able to come into the country, and he never did
return. Nor did the Leipzig Society ever resume direction of its
work.

Meanwhile the church had in 1942 drawn up its first embryonic
constitution as "The Lutheran Church of Northern Tanganyika," to
avoid possible absorption by a non-Lutheran mission, and developed
it to a complete constitution by 1949. Although it was 1959, when
a major revision of the constitution had been carried out, before the
church was de facto self-governing, it was independent de jure from
1942.

Such are the bare historical facts of the institution of the
mission and the constitutional emergence of the church.

II. The Theory and Practice of Bruno Gutmann:[3]

Among the Chagga people Gutmann and his fellow missionaries
found a highly structured, tightly-knit and conservative society,
with criss-crossing lines of inter-relationship, in which there was
a place for everyone and everyone knew his place. The elaborate
system of greetings, which still exists today wherever the Chagga
language is used, has forms varying according to rank, age, sex,
degree of relationship, closeness of acquaintance and other factors.
Status played a big role, and was very well defined. Gutmann regarded society as an organism. No man is truly a man except as a
member of his society and a live part of that organic whole. As a
solitary individual he is lost. Life and salvation are impossible
without that community. Freedom is realized in the interdependence
of his social order, constituted by God and to which he is called by
God. His conscience is the organ which keeps him in harmony with his
fellows and ensures right relationships. The leading thought which
determines Gutmann's ethnology, ecclesiology and missionary practice
is described by Beyerhaus as "man in the community, through the community and for the community."

In Chaggaland there were three basic units of social structure, the clan, the age-group and the neighborhood. The first was based on kinship, real or assumed; the second was a horizontal classification right across the clan lines and embracing the entire tribe; the third depended on the guilds that controlled the water-furrows. These forms, Gutmann decided, blood, age-group and village community were basic to Chagga society. Of them the whole people was built-up as a body of different cells. Here in essence were the elements of the primitive church, for the social relationships are constituted by the will of the Creator.

The duty of the mission, therefore, was not to break but to strengthen and restore the primitive social order. It must not pull out individuals in order to form them into a new organization, the Church. It should not break up clans in an attempt to exalt the nuclear family. When God has created an organism, do not supplant it with an organization. When God has raised up sons for himself, do not bastardize them. Dissolution of the original forms of society is not just a matter of culture change; it is a thwarting of the life-giving spirit of God, which brings about spiritual death, for the divine purpose is wrapped up in the sociological package.

Gutmann as a good Protestant (and a good Lutheran) believed that the Church is constituted by the Word of God. However, that Word is <u>first</u> the Word of creation, when it entered the world as efficaciously as in the redemptive work of the Son, and it is still active in the constituting of human relationships. So the Church is first an <u>order of creation</u>, expressed in the primitive community, in and through which man both finds a degree of fulfillment, and senses also his need of a more complete fulfillment. Having tasted fellowship on the human level, he learns to desire perfect fellowship and gets a presentiment of the coming of Christ to dwell among his people. When primitive society and the Church of Christ have become one body, there is the fulness of the presence of God, the great sacrament, which is the congregation as the body of Christ, made visible by the sacraments of baptism and the Lord's Supper.

There are three relationships which Gutmann regarded as expressing the heart of the Gospel--those of son, citizen and neighbor. Human sonship points towards the true nature of sonship, revealed in Christ, into which all human relationships are to be taken up.[4] In the age-grade system, in which men are bound together across the ties of kinship, the kingdom of God is present (Luke 17:21, "in the midst"). In the responsibilities of neighborliness a man is confronted with his human neighbor in such a way that he cannot avoid a confrontation with God. What then is the difference between "Volk" and Church? Only the difference between "disposition" and "fulfill-ment." The new features in the Church are the gathering for the sacrament, insight into the sinfulness of the old life, Christian substitution as the basis of service to the neighbor, and the tendency to a wider integration beyond the existing clan and tribal structure.

How then is mission to be carried out?[5] It is definitely not proselytization; it is not proclamation for calling men out from where they are into a new fellowship; it springs from the instinct of the organism to strengthen itself and grow; it is the will-to-growth of Christ in his body. God's Word is one Word in creation and in redemption, in Old Testament and in New, and speaks with one voice. Mission is not the separation of individuals from their society but the calling of whole tribes and peoples. Early converts were claimed as first-fruits or fore-runners of the whole people. To keep the clans intact baptism must, if necessary, be delayed until a big enough nucleus of significant people should be ready and could be received as a group. The unities of tribal organization are to be grafted into the new body of Christ. The program is the "churching of primitive society." So evangelism must follow the natural lines of communication, kinsman to kinsman, brother to brother in the age-grade, neighbor to neighbor in the village community.

Leadership of the congregation should not come from a special class set up by the foreign mission, nor by the development of offices alien to the society. Leadership depends on the principle of representation, the congregation expressing itself as an organism. That must come by the conversion of leading men, with natural responsibility and authority, to become pillars of the Christian fellowship. Patience might be necessary, but it was the chiefs, headmen and elders who should become the bearers and ministers of the Gospel to their own people. Gutmann wanted to get all the natural orders of society into the Church. So the youth organization was patterned on the lines of the corresponding age-group in the tribe, confirmation included a rite analogous to the old ceremony of affirming blood-brotherhood, clan and tribal elders became church elders, and women assumed their place in the new society similar to that in the old. The priesthood of all believers was to be lived as a reality: the life of the congregation was not to depend on the ability of any individual, but to be borne and expressed by the whole body.

Is there then a place for an ordained ministry in such a church? Not indeed as an office independent from the congregation, but only insofar as the pastor should be a true representative of the whole church he served. Out of internal growth in Christ and a deep fertilizing of the soil would eventually come a true indigenous ministry. Nurture, pastoral care and teaching would be equally as important as preaching. Halthy and active families and clans would produce healthy

leadership. Premature ordination might cause a man to misunderstand
his role, so that the principle of representation would be lost.
(The obvious danger was that the indigenous pastor might model his
function and status on that of the missionary - though this is not
stated in those terms). Consistent with this theory, the first
ordinations did not take place until 1934, 42 years after Leipig
entered the field and 31 years after Gutmann's arrival. It is
possible they would not have taken place even then, except that both
the missionaries and the church were beginning to see the threat of
another world war just over the horizon.

One corollary of Gutmann's policy was the belief that western
civilization, vis a vis the tribal society, was an evil, the penetration of which should be avoided at all costs. It would mean uprooting, proletarianization, the supplanting of human by material values
and the replacing of ties of kin and neighborhood by greed and competition. So the indigenous culture and social structure must be
strengthened at all costs, to protect the church against the infil-
tration of false values. He went so far as to forbid the school-
children to speak the Swahili language in his presence, even though
this was the language of trade and business, and starting to become,
from the later 1920s on, under the trustee administration, the
language of the schools and of the country at large.

III. The Development of the Church in Kilimanjaro

The statistical facts of the growth of the church in
Kilimanjaro, with which the Central Kilimanjaro district kept pace,
are very striking. In 1919, just after the end of World War I,
there were about 12,000 baptized members. By 1939 the total was
nearly 40,000. In the following twenty years, from 1939 to 1959, it
had risen to 180,000. And this rapid development seems to have been
almost unaffected by the dislocations caused by the two world wars.
Growth continued until there were no more unchurched Chagga in
Kilimanjaro, except for some who had fallen away from either the
Lutheran or the Roman Catholic Church (the other main church in the
area) and resisted attempts to win them back.

What kind of a church was it? It was a church with a strongly
congregational polity, and in which laymen had, and still have a
strong voice. In fact, the 1958 constitution provides that elected
representation to church conventions shall be in the ratio of two to
one in favor of laymen as against ordained ministers. (The actual
delegate ratio is closer to parity, because of the number of ex
officio delegates, many of whom are pastors.) The ministry of the
laity is very much a reality. It is also a church which has been
very active in reaching out not only among the Chagga, but also

around and beyond the foot-hills of the mountain among the miscellaneous populations settling in the plains, or working for plantation
owners. True, the absorption of the original tribal people slowed
growth, but it has never stopped. The "will-to-growth" in the body
has continued. Wherever a Chagga Christian family has re-settled a
small congregation may be expected shortly to emerge, even if it is
no longer an ethnically homogenous group. There has seemed to be an
underlying Christonomy at work, and perhaps the absence of excessive
clericalization has helped.

It has also participated in the support of "foreign mission"
work among the Sonjo people in north-west Tanzania, and across the
Kenya border.

Chagga Christians are playing a leading part in the top councils
of the Church in Africa and in the world, in the All-Africa Conference
of Churches, in the Lutheran World Federation and in the World
Council of Churches. The ordained ministry of the church has always
been numerically small in relation to the size of the parishes, most
pastors having to serve well over 2,000 parishioners, with the help
of evangelists and other lay assistants. The educational level of
the ministry, in terms of formal schooling on the western model, has
been low in general, and distinctly so in Central Kilimanjaro. In
recent years the provision of overseas scholarships to a considerable
number of men has done much to change that picture. Predictably the
leadership strength of the pastorate has been directly related to
the degree to which the indigenous structures provided for strong
personal leadership roles. Thus the East and West Kilimanjaro
districts of the church, where there were strong chiefdoms, have
tended to have much stronger pastoral leadership than Central
Kilimanjaro, where authority was more fragmented.

Two real problems have troubled the Central Kilimanjaro district
in particular. One has been the proximity of Moshi town, the main
trade and administrative center for Kilimanjaro. Indigenous culture
and social structure have not been able to resist the powerful
influences of secularization and westernization which have radiated
from it, not to mention the destructive moral forces of a material-
istic philosophy of life. The church has suffered accordingly. The
devil got into the garden, and Adam and Eve were ill-prepared to
cope with him. Nowhere on the mountain has the church been weaker
than in this area, where the village life of the community has been
largely replaced by the dormitory mores of a commuting population.

The second problem has been the definite tendency of the nurture
and discipline of the church to legalism. Whether because that
emphasis was already deep-rooted in the tribal life, or because of
Gutmann's over-protectiveness of the traditional forms, the fact is

that nurture and discipline have too often resembled a trial in a
court of law rather than pastoral care and spiritual counseling.
The consequence has been the suspension and excommunication of large
numbers of men and women, many of whom have never returned to the
church, and who have formed a barrier, sometimes quite an active
barrier, against its mission and outreach.

Missiological criticism of Gutmann's theory and practice has
tended to zero in on what is considered a lack of individual conversion and individual responsibility in the new Christians. Slashing
attacks have been made on his concept of the tribe and clan as
"orders of creation" and on his understanding of the Christian
ministry. Kraemer speaks of the indigenous forms and structures as
"relative," "ambivalent," "demonic" as all human creations.[6]
Bavinck says: "Folk is not a constituent element of church: it can
be an exaggeration of the meaning of community...a threat to moral
and spiritual life, for it may blot out the personal relationship
and responsibility of man to God.[7] Beyerhaus says the ministry of
the Word must be present from the very beginning: "God has appointed
in the church first apostles" (I Cor. 12:28f.). The pastor's office
is fundamental, not the crowning climax of a process.

On the other hand Erik Nielsen, reviewing Beyerhaus's book,
defends Gutmann along with other German missiologists. They believe,
he says, in immanent divine working. "The Christonomy manifested at
the beginning must continually be realized and obeyed anew under
changing circumstances, in new struggles and growing tasks."[8]
Perhaps Gutmann's theory should be interpreted not as a complete
theology but rather as a footnote to, and an application of, article
VII of the Augsburg Confession, which states: "......The Church is
the congregations of the saints, in which the Gospel is rightly
taught and the sacraments are rightly administered. And to the true
unity of the Church it is enough to agree concerning the doctrine of
the Gospel and the administration of the sacraments......."[9]

Finally, for those who want to delve further into the underlying theoretical questions, Siegfried Knak has a quite elaborate
defense and apologetic for the German missiologists, Gutmann and
Keysser, claiming, in particular, that they did not neglect individual conversion. They just approached it a different way than those
who prefer to gather a church by isolated conversions and separation
from pagan society.[10] The church is God's Church from the start.
It does not exist because of definition by certain external criteria
of performance (e.g., the three "selfs"). It is constituted by the
Father's creative Word, redeemed by the Word incarnate, Jesus Christ,
the Son, and activated by the immanent Word, the Holy Spirit. If
there is an over-emphasis, it is in the right direction - of trust in
what God has done and can do.

IV. Is the Argument Justified by the Facts of History?

Granted there was remarkable numerical growth in the Lutheran
Church in Kilimanjaro, and that a significant Christian church has
continued and expanded its mission until to-day, surely at least two
other influences must have affected the course of events. Gutmann
and most of his co-workers were on the field for a period of only
about thirty years or a little more. There have been many other
missionaries, from societies and churches other than the Leipzig
Society, including the United States and Scandinavia, operating with
different policies based on different premises. Again what was the
effect of the big disruptions of the world wars, especially the
second one? How can you claim that the early theory and practice
were determinative of the church as it moved towards full autonomy
in the late fifties?

These questions are relatively easily answered. During the
period from 1920 to 1925, when the Augustana Church of the U.S.A.
was supervising and supplying the field, it is clear that nothing
more than a caretaker administration was carried on. "The mission
was saved for the Church and could be returned to its original
Society."[11] Two Estonian missionaries of the Leipiz Society had
been allowed to remain on the field. For the rest, the two other
European missionaries who arrived in 1923, and the nine Americans
who came at intervals, approximately three a year, between 1921 and
1924, simply could not have had time to introduce any radically new
policies, or to influence in any marked degree the general course of
development. After the return of Gutmann and Raum in 1925 it quickly
became apparent that Augustana would have to have a separate field of
work. So in 1926 the American Mission pulled out of Kilimanjaro to
take over the Iramba-Turu field, barely opened by the Germans before
the war broke out. This period was simply an unwelcome intermission
in the continuity of the Leipzig work.

The second period of non-Leipzig involvement in the Lutheran
Church in Kilimanjaro was potentially much more significant, since
it extended over 14 years, there was no expectation that Leipzig
would ever resume direction, and there was a much larger missionary
contingent employed. By 1954 there were 28 missionaries on the field,
nine of them pastors, all of whom were from the U.S.A. Only four of
the 28 were Leipzig personnel, and they were all laymen. However,
there are a number of facts which must be set off against this change
in missionary staff. By the late 1930s the young church had become
increasingly conscious of itself and independent-minded in its thinking. The Africans had pressed the Leipzig Society to turn over
responsibility and property to the indigenous church before world war
should break out once more, and were not a little bitter when a
second war caused the confiscation of mission and church properties

and assets all over again. On this occasion the department
missionaries had handed over responsibility to nationals in many
departments of work. In fact there was only one Leipzig missionary
who could remain, since he had Russian citizenship. Immediately it
became necessary to protect the identity and integrity of the
Lutheran Church, and in 1942 the first constitution was drafted. In
1949 it was printed in an enlarged form, and in 1952 it was amended
to permit the church to apply for membership in the Lutheran World
Federation.

In short, the "Lutheran Church of Northern Tanganyika," as it
was named, was determined never again to be dominated by any foreign
mission or missionary agency, and this determination appeared both
in its formal relationships and in the pattern of inter-personal
relations between nationals and missionaries. It was successful in
its effort. There can be little doubt that the basic character of
this church had been completely formed by the time the 1942 constitution was drafted. Subsequent events may have modified it: they
never fundamentally changed it. The church was the church planted
by Gutmann and his Leipzig Society co-workers.

One further piece of evidence has already been cited which, in
the main, supports this position. That is the growth rate of the
church over the years. From 1919 to 1939 the membership had grown
nearly 350% (12,000 to 40,000). In the next twenty years it increased
450%. Granted some of this increase may be ascribed to the new
feeling of self-confidence and initiative coming with the march to
autonomy, and I believe it was. Yet the general trend is the same
throughout the whole forty year period, and the acceleration in the
second half is comparatively slight. And indeed the very
"nationalistic" spirit which began to show itself could also be
ascribed, along with the growth rate, to the insistence of the early
missionary policy on the importance of the indigenous community.

To deal with lingering doubts as to the relationship of
missionary policy and evangelistic results in this Kilimanjaro
Lutheran Church, let us compare briefly policy and results in the
neighboring country of Arusha, also under the Leipzig Society
initially, but where theory, practice and development contrast
strongly with the Chaggaland story.

V.   A "Control Case" - the Work of the Leipzig Mission in Arusha.[12]

The social organization of the Arusha tribe, located in an area
some 50 miles to the west of Kilimanjaro, was in essentials almost
identical with that of the Chagga. They had well-knit clans, a
strong age-grade system, and village relationships conditioned by
the control of the water supplies. Like the Chagga they had a proud

and independent spirit and were not very open to culture change from outside the tribe. They too lived in a very compact area, with a population only a little less dense than that on Kilimanjaro. Relationship and neighborhood were ever present realities for them.[13] And their age-grade system had only just recently been tested in resistance to the forces of the German colonial government. One might have supposed a "Gutmann" type policy would have been applied there. It well might have been so, except for two factors - the strength of the pagan diviners and the personality of the chief architect of the missionary approach in Arusha. The man who was pitted against the diviners was missionary L. Blumer, who was in charge of the only mission station at Il Boru, Arusha, continuously from 1907 to 1930. Arusha Christians are unanimous that it was he who had the chief hand in determining the missionary approach. A clue to the problems he faced and to the policy which was developed may be found in an article written by him in 1927.[14] Following Blumer continuity was provided by the leadership of an African pastor, Lazarus Laiser, who was ordained in 1934 and in 1942 became president of the Arusha-Meru-Masai district, as well as vice-president of the whole Lutheran Church in Northern Tanganyika. A man of great force of character, he dominated the scene till his tragic death in a truck accident in 1958. Arusha Christians speak of him the "second Blumer."

From the start missionary strategy in Arusha aimed at as complete a separation as possible between the new Christian convert and his old pagan associations and environment. There was no effort at the transformation of the existing non-Christian community: individual converts were to be worn out of it and to become the nucleus of a new confessing Christian society, the church. New loyalties were to be formed to fresh values, based on a Christian world-view. One informant said: "There was a rigid separation of Christians from pagans, and constant denigration of pagan customs." Another stated that the young converts were told they should never attend any ceremonies or festivals involving any non-Christian religious practice. If they should meet their relatives and friends on the path, they should not linger, but move on after brief greetings. Since just about every family festival did have some pagan rituals connected with it, this effectively cut them off from any close contact with their relatives. One of the first converts vividly recollects the rejection by parents and relatives of the newly baptized young men, and their expulsion from home, to be brought up on the mission station. Long afterwards when they did attend a pagan celebration they were not accepted by their male relatives, but made to sit with the women and children. On one occasion, when a boy disregarded the separate arrangements made by the mission for the circumcision of the Christian young men, and joined his age-mates for the pagan ceremony, he was suspended from the church and made to do hard labor as a penance and an earnest of his desire to be re-instated.

What the mission had done was to take the young converts right out of their clans and age-sets, cutting the vertical and horizontal ties that made them integral members of families and quasi-military units. In fact for many years the Christians were forbidden to refer to themselves by the designation appropriate to the age-set of their non-Christian contemporaries. Eventually the restrictions became somewhat relaxed. A boy may now be circumcised together with his relatives and friends in the traditional ceremony, but with the warning not to take part in the preliminary or the ensuing ritual activities. The Achilles heel of the whole program seems to have been the girls' initiation. Like the Masai, the Arusha practice female circumcision, or clitorodectomy. No provision could be made in this case for the operation to be carried out under mission auspices. Sentiment among the expatriate missionary staff was too strongly against it for it to be given the status of an approved custom. Yet the parents were insistent it was essential. The uneasy solution was for the surgery to be done at home, apart from the non-Christians and without the traditional instruction, but by the women who normally performed the operation. It is not clear how long it was possible to keep the Christian girls from receiving traditional pagan instruction, together with the physical initiation. To-day in most cases Christian girls are circumcised together with their non-Christian relatives, and there can be little doubt they share in whatever formal instruction is given. The women have maintained the tribal integrity that the mission tried to destroy in the case of the men.

In one area of social life and organization the mission did attempt to adapt and duplicate traditional patterns.[15] This was in regard to Christian elders. Senior and junior elders were selected and appointed on similar lines to the tribal and clan elders, and performed similar duties in arbitrating family disputes, helping to settle land claims, adjudicating on points of legal procedure and so on. To-day, and for a good many years past, the Christian elders are admitted to the councils of the whole people on the same basis as the non-Christian elders. Here again is another link with tradition which has helped to keep the tribe together.

These comments are probably sufficient in the present context to indicate the main thrusts of mission policy in regard to Arusha culture and social structure. Two questions remain: (1) What induced Arusha parents to relinquish control of some of their children to the missionaries? (2) On what means did the mission rely to form the young converts into a new society?

It is a familiar story in the history of missions. In both cases the answer is the same - education on western lines. How

would that have been an inducement for parents to part with their
children, unless forced to do so? The answer seems to be threefold.
First, the Arusha had been compelled by overwhelming military force
to acknowledge the superior power of the white man. Naturally there
were some who wanted to discover the secret, if possible. Secondly,
the tribal leadership had little option but to try to collaborate
with the new rulers, and little distinction was made by them between
the secular authority and the mission, with the result that some
children of influential families were among those brought up on the
mission compound. Thirdly, one could always turn over a sickly, or
otherwise unwanted child, to the missionaries: that also happened in
some cases.

Education became in the course of time the main attraction of
the mission to the Arusha people. Especially during the years of
World War II and afterwards the increasing concern of the people to
get the advantages of literacy and modern technology, together with
the greater consciousness of the trustee administration of responsibility for moving the population more rapidly into the twentieth
century greatly accelerated the expansion of the school system and
accessions to the church by that route. Initial slow growth in
church membership was transformed into relatively rapid increase,
though many Arusha will tell you that for them the church means
education and social advancement, rather than speaking of any
distinctive biblical values. This tendency was aggravated by the
ever-increasing involvement of government in, and control of, the
nominally church-school system, - a situation of which the people
were well aware.

From the initiation of the mission in 1904 unti 1962 there was
only one parish in Arusha - a chronic example of the restrictions
imposed by an over-centralized control. A rough estimate gives a
baptized membership of the church of 400-500 in 1926, after twenty-
two years of work on the field. In 1950 the total was just under
3,000: by 1965 it was around 8,300.[16] The slow start, and the policies then begun, appear to have inhibited growth right along. Only
to-day, after eleven years of national government in Tanzania, does
it seem that the barriers between Christian and non-Christian Arusha
are disappearing in a common attempt to preserve some sorth of
ethnic identity within the larger community of the new nation. The
churching of about 10% of the tribe in only a little less time than
it has taken the whole Chagga people to be christianized is an
interesting contrast.

Notes:

1. S. H. Swanson: Foundation for To-morrow. (Rock Island,
    Augusta Book Concern, 1960) pp. 182f.

2. Gustav Bernander: Lutheran Wartime Association to Tanzanian
    Churches, 1940-1945. (Uppsala, Gleerup, 1968) pp. 25-27.

3. The following account leans heavily on Peter Beyerhaus: Die
    Selbständigkeit der jungen Kirchen als Missionarisches Problem
    (Wuppertal-Barmen, Rhenisch Mission, 1956) pp. 89f.
    "Volksorganischer Geneindeaufbau."

    The primary source is Gutmann's own writings, especially
    Gemeindeaufbau aus dem Evangelium (Leipzig, 1925), with which
    the writer has wrestled. However Gutmann's style is
    notoriously difficult even for those whose mother-tongue is
    German.

    See also articles by Otto Raum and C. Wagner under the heading
    Gutmann's Work in Kilimanjaro: Critical Studies, in the
    Internationational Review of Missions, Vol. XXVI (1937)
    pp. 500-513.

4. "Gemeindeaufbau..." pp. 87 and 146.

5. Ibid., pp. 114f.

6. Hendrik Kraemer: The Christian Message to the Non-Christian
    World (Grand Rapids, 1956) p. 340.

7. J. H. Bavinck: Introduction to the Science of Missions.
    (Philadelphia, 1960) pp. 162-163, 168.

8. An authentic quote, but source not immediately to hand - probably
    the International Review of Missions or the Lutheran World.

9. Quoted from W. J. Kukkonen: Faith of Our Fathers. (New York,
    The American Press, 1957) p. 191.

10. IMC Madras Series, Vol. III, Ch. 14, pp. 314-326. See also, by
    the same author, Zwischen Nil und Tafelbei. (Berlin, 1931)
    pp. 143-174.

11. See note 1 above.

12. This account is based on a field study by the writer February
    to July, 1967, sponsored by the American Association of Theological
    Schools as part of a research project on Arusha religion and

values. No access to Leipzig Mission Society records was possible in the time available.

13. P. H. Gulliver: <u>Social</u> <u>Control</u> <u>in</u> <u>an</u> <u>African</u> <u>Society</u> (London, Routledge & Kegan Paul, 1963) Introduction and chs. 2-6.

14. L. Blumer: <u>Streiflichter</u> <u>auf</u> <u>Religion</u> <u>und</u> <u>religiosches</u> <u>Leben</u> <u>der</u> <u>Aruschaleute</u> in the Evangelisch-Lutherisches Missionsblatt, 1927, pp. 81-82.

15. EAF CORY in the University College Library, Dar-es-Salaam, Tanzania, Append. IV.

16. Figures are from official church records of the Evangelical Lutheran Church in Tanzania.

THE MISSION OF THE
EVANGELICAL PRESBYTERIAN CHURCH OF GHANA
TO THE CHOKOSI PEOPLE

Alfred C. Krass

10

In 1957, when the north of Ghana was for the first time completely open to the work of Christian mission, the Evangelical Presbyterian Church of Ghana (formerly the EWE Presbyterian Church) had already been autonomous for twenty-nine years. Orphaned in World War I because most of the missionaries working with that church were Germans of the North German Mission Society, the Church never again could count on large numbers of missionaries from Western churches. It flourished, however, and was a sèlf-supporting, self-governing, and self-propagating church. At various times in its history and even up to the present, the Church has received fraternal workers from the Church of Scotland, the United Church Board for World Ministries, and - most recently again - from the North German Mission Society.

When the news came that the north of Ghana had been opened to mission work, there was a spontaneous response on the part of the Church to this announcement. The teachers' union volunteered to have five percent of its monthly salaries deducted at source for the establishment of a Northern Mission Fund. A pastor volunteered to become the first missionary to the north. Four teacher-catechists volunteered to leave the EP Church school system in the south and serve in government schools in the north in order to assist in the evangelization of the northern peoples.

Prior to 1964 all the mission work was centered at Yendi. Yendi was the pastor's station, and the pastor was supported by between one and three evangelists, who were of northern extraction, and by an agriculturalist provided by the United Church Board for World Ministries. In 1964 the work expanded. A second EP Church pastor was assigned to Bimbilla and the author was assigned as district pastor to Chereponi and Saboba. Another United Church of Christ missionary served for a while as pastor at Yendi in order to make the tripartite division possible. He was, shortly thereafter, replaced by a Ghanaian pastor.

The author was assigned to an area of approximately 2,400 square miles, inhabited by approximately 48,000 people. These people belonged to the Chokosi, Komba, and Konkomba tribes. Very little work was done among the Kombas, and the majority of the work came to be that among the Konkomba and Chokosi tribes. Because of the pastor's residence at Chereponi, and because of the greater receptiveness to the Gospel on the part of the Chokosis, the work in Chokosiland developed more extensively than that among Konkombas. After the initial three years, the Church established Chereponi as a district in its own right, and the author stopped working in the Saboba district. He was able to concentrate on work among the Chokosis and with those Konkombas and Kombas located in Chereponi District.

        At first the author worked alone with one Chokosi evangelist,
a lad who, upon completion of middle school at Yendi, had attended
the EP Church's seminary in Peki for a two year Bible training program.
As the work developed, additional staff were made available: a southern
Ghanaian evangelist, and up to five "untrained evangelists", products
of the literacy and leadership training program which was held each
year.

        The approach which was taken was to preach the Gospel in
selected villages on a regular weekly basis, excepting only those
villages in which we could commit ourselves to be present for an
evangelistic service at least once a week. The lectionary of the
Church of South India was used as the basic scheme for the Gospel
proclamation. Preaching was, as often as possible, done in dialogical
style, rather than as a monologue. Songs of the Church in Malawi
were introduced at an early stage, translated into Chokosi, in order
not to introduce non-African elements to the worship. Meetings took
place either in the chief's compound, or under shade trees, or in
the entrance huts to the compounds of headmen.

        Invitations to baptism were never extended before such
preaching had been going on for one year. At that point after the
completion of the first year's preaching when it seemed that there
had been a good response in a given village, the sacrament of
baptism was explained, and an invitation was given to the people to
ratify their commitment to the faith and their desire to enter into
discipleship by being baptised. If the people accepted the invitation,
catechetical instruction was begun at once, taking place twice a
week, usually for a period of four to six months. At first the
catechism of the EP Church (a modified version of a 19th Century
German catechism) was used, but after initial frustrations with the
impossibility of translation of European, rationalistic thought
forms into Chokosi, a local catechism was developed, incorporating
questions which the peoples themselves had been asking about the
Gospel rather than questions asked about it in European culture.
At whatever point at which the pastor and evangelists were convinced
the people had understood the faith sufficiently to make a mature
decision about their commitment to Christ, the baptism would take place.

        Right from the beginning we recognized that the people tended,
on their own, to make group decisions for or against the Gospel. Over-
coming our initial European squeamishness about such group decisions
after a while, we accepted them and concentrated on methods of ensuring
that each member of the group personally ratified the decision by his
own personal decision and commitment to life in Christian discipleship.

        Permission was obtained from the Presbytery of the EP Church
before the first village baptism took place for polygamists to be
baptised, with all their wives. This had not been the practice of
the EP Church for the past one hundred years (it had been its practice
initially) but the southern Ghanaian pastors readily admitted that the

prohibition of baptism of polygamists and their wives had not achieved
its desired effect in southern Ghana. Permission was granted for an
"initial period" (which some imagined would be ten to twenty years).
It was demanded of those ministering in Chereponi and other parts of
the north that such permission would be coupled with strict teaching of
the nature of Christian marriage as the life-long partnership of one
man and one woman, and the warning that those who, subsequent to their
baptism, entered into polygamous or further polygamous unions would be
disciplined by exclusion from the Lord's supper.

        The response to the Gospel by the Chokosis was great. One
factor helping this was the absence of other denominations (for the
main part of the years of the author's work there) who acted in direct
competition with the mission of the EP Church. The Assemblies of God
decided, upon learning of our work there, not to pursue their earlier
plans to open work in Chereponi. After an initial period of competition
with the Roman Catholics, they too tended to leave the work to the
Presbyterian Church, while maintaining a small work there of their own,
but without opening a pastoral station for the permanent residence
of a priest. Both the Assemblies of God and the Roman Catholics agreed
that a district of this size, with only 25,000 inhabitants, would best
be served by only one denomination. No formal comity arrangements were
entered into, however.

        The Chokosis reside in only one town - a town of 2,300 people -
in Ghana. The rest of the Chokosis live, along with the Konkombas
and Kombas, in one hundred and eleven different villages. There was
no attempt made to establish the Chereponi Town Congregation (a congregation of about forty people, including southern Ghanaians resident
in the town as well as educated Chokosis) as the "Cathedral Congregation".
It was understood from the beginning that whatever work was done in
the villages would aim at the establishment of a Congregation in each
of those villages. It would have been too much to expect that the
very divergent life styles and languages of the people in the town and
the villages could easily be included in one form of church life. The
author, having had no formal training in anthropology, was not able
to chose the villages in any scientific fashion. The Lord seemed to
do the leading, however, for, as it turned out, among the initial six
villages chosen, all the three main clans of the Chokosi tribe were
included! The clan organization of the Chokosis served as an important bridge for the Gospel. Early on we witnessed that, when a village
became interested in the Gospel, they spread the news of our work to
their fellow clansmen in other villages, and invitations would quickly
come for us to open up work there as well. After the initial four years,
we never had to invite ourselves to begin work in any village. Rather
we always had a waiting list of villages which had requested work. Our
rationale for chosing villages during the early stages was often that
of size. Most of the Chokosi villages we chose had populations of at
least 180 people. As an economy measure, we decided not to choose
villages which had considerably fewer people. Later on, when we had
more workers, we were able to work in a number of the small villages.

Over the period from 1964 to 1970, when the author left
Chereponi, congregations were established in twenty-two villages, in
addition to the original town congregation. Preaching stations for
regular weekly visitation were also established at thirty-five places.
Yet, even by 1970, we had only two pastors and five paid evangelists
to carry out the work. How were so many villages served?

The answer lies in the leadership training program which
was developed beginning as early as March 1965, only one year after
the formal inauguration of the work. Each village which had demonstrated
a response to the Gospel was invited to send two young men to a
training program in literacy, Bible teaching, Christian ethics, and
worship. Literacy materials had to be devised, for the language had
never theretofore been written down. Progress was slow, largely because
of the primitive nature of the first literacy materials, and only
seven people finished the initial one year course (a one month residential
course followed by weekly market-day classes for the rest of the year).
But, using some of those who had finished that first course as aids in
the second year, we were able to have two courses and, in the third
year, three courses in different regional centers. In those three years
between fifty and sixty people were trained as Christian leaders. Many
of them went on to conduct services on a regular basis in their own
villages, some of them were able to preach in other villages as well,
and four of them were employed as paid "untrained evangelists".

By 1969 the literacy program had advanced to the stage that
most of those who came for leadership training courses had already
progressed very rapidly in their reading before coming for leadership
training courses. Such leadership training courses as were offered
from 1968 on were able to accomplish much more than the earlier
courses, because either those who came had already learned to read
or they were coming to a second residential course, having completed
the first one in one of the earlier years. Many of these village
leaders became highly competent. A simple liturgy was developed to
guide them in their leadership of worship. Weekly Bible translations
from the Church of South India Almanac were mimeographed and given
to them, and finally bound together in a "Chokosi Bible" from which
they could read the appropriate lesson for each Sunday. But at the
center of the work of the district was the weekly meeting at which
the pastors, evangelists, "untrained evangelists", and as many
voluntary workers as were free to participate did exegesis together
of the next week's scripture lesson and considered how to apply this
to the situation of the people to whom they were going to preach.
Voluntary workers were never paid, and were discouraged from seeking
employment, but they did receive some benefits which they valued
highly: 1. They were helped with English lessons if they desired to
learn English. 2. Some of them were given help in repairing their
bicycles so that they could preach in distant villages. 3. Occasionally
old clothing from the U.S.A. was made available to them. 4. Of
more importance than any of these, a real sense of community developed -

new, deep friendships were formed, and these workers came to know their selfhood as part of an in-group, an <u>ecclesiola</u> <u>in</u> <u>ecclesia</u>.

As part of the ministry of the church, community development projects and distribution of U.S. surplus food was carried out. An effort was made from the very start to see that no connection would be drawn between the willingness of a village to respond to the Gospel and their reception of such gifts or help. It was often frustrating to the Christian villages to find that they were not treated in any better way than were the non-Christian villages. The problems which arose often caused us to wonder whether it was worthwhile to carry out such programs, but the demands of the Lord's people and their needs in this situation of extreme poverty were such that we could not say we would not help. What we did find, however, was that when a village became Christian a new power for community development was to be found in their midst. The Christian villages far outstripped the non-Christian villages in coming together to work on self-help projects, such as wells, roads, and latrines.

Another important feature to be noted is that the entire budget for this work was borne by the Church in southern Ghana. The only contribution of the United Church Board for World Ministries for the work of the Church was the provision of its fraternal worker's salary, housing, and transportation expenses. Though the Board offered to do more, such requests were always refused. Only such a program as could in time be borne by the people themselves would be undertaken. Where gifts came from outside sources for the work, such gifts were never used for expenses which would be recurring expenses. The only help given to villages which wished to construct chapels was a grant which would pay for two-thirds of the cost of the roof of such chapels. The people would have to do the work on their own and raise their own funds for the remainder. With regard to the agricultural program and the public health program which later developed, an attempt was again made to keep external funds to a minimum though, in these cases, a basic support from overseas was necessary, in as much as the EP Church did not have the resources to fund such programs. The entire budget for the church program, before the district was divided in two, was eight hundred dollars. It was reasoned that the local people could themselves come to support this program in time.

An attempt was made from the beginning to develop stewardship. A pledge system was introduced in 1966 and, even if people would only pledge to give a penny a week for the support of the church's work, such pledges were received gladly. They grew from year to year until, by 1970, the people were supporting one fourth of the budget themselves. A fifteen year plan was developed for their taking over complete support of the work.

In addition to the specialized training given to the leaders, congregations were nurtured regularly through Bible instruction in their villages. Such instruction was by a group discussion method, and special discussion starters were published to aid the leaders of those discussions.

Each congregation chose presbyters and what the EP Church calls "church mothers" in the ratio of two for the first twenty communicants and one each for each additional twenty communicants. The governance of the local congregation was in the hands of these presbyters and church mothers. They also formed, together with the staff workers, the district session, which met quarterly and was the supreme governing body of the distruct. The presbyters and church mothers were given special training at regular semi-annual retreats of two or three days. Attempts were made to build up and reinforce their leadership rather than to take leadership away from them and put it in the hands of paid workers.

This was, in summary, a grassroots approach to the planting of village churches. Every effort was made to indiginize the work and the reward for all the efforts made was to see that people came to understand Jesus Christ not as a foreigner, but as their elder brother, as one who had come to new incarnation through His Spirit in their lives as people of Ghana in the twentieth century. The name the people most liked to give to Christ was "restorer" or "establisher of community". They found in the Gospel new power for new communal life.

11

THE PLANTING OF THE CHURCH AMONG THE DAMALS OF WEST IRIAN
John D. Ellenberger

It is now sixteen years since the first witnesses to the Christian gospel settled in the Ilaga, a valley of mixed Damal and Western Dani population. In these intervening years the church has not only taken root in these two tribes but has accomplished what McGavran calls a "clean sweep" of both groups.

How this was done has been recorded in Russell Hitt's gripping narrative, <u>Cannibal Valley</u> (N.Y.; Harper & Row, 1962). Some brief analyses of the factors involved have been made available to the public, one from a Church Growth viewpoint (J. Sunda, <u>Church Growth in the Central Highlands of West Irian</u>, Lucknow, India, 1963[1]). Unpublished papers dealing with background and causal factors have been presented to an Anthropological Conference on Interior Highlands people held in 1963, but unfortunately these are not available to the public.

This account will not recapitulate much of the information available in other sources. Rather it is presented as an analysis of the planting and development of the church from a communications point of view. All of the information here is from my personal involvement in the development of the Damal Church as a missionary-translator under The Christian and Missionary Alliance. The viewpoints and analyses represent my own appraisal of the situation and not an official viewpoint of the C&MA mission.

The Cultural Setting

Among the almost 350 tribes and 800,000 total population of the western half of New Guinea (called West Irian as a province of Indonesia), the largest tribes are located in the interior highlands. The Ekari (Kapauku) tribe of some 85,000 people, centers around the Wissel Lakes in the Western highlands. Some 65,000 Western Danis begin on the western edge of the large Baliem (Grand) Valley and extend over 100 miles to the west. Between these two large groups are several small tribes, one of them the Damal of some 12,000 people. This tribe is neolithic in their stone technology and extremely simple in their material culture. Principally sweet potato horticulturalists, they supplement their diet of sweet potatoes, taro and vegetables with a limited amount of domesticated pork and marsupials from the forest. No specialists exist in this unstratified society, although individuals do pro-

vide such services to the community as shaman. Wealth is distri-
buted rather than accumulated and its distribution is a key factor
in the development of political leadership as well as economic
exchange. Leadership of the kin group is informal in nature and
produces a head man who may be said to be first among equals!
Decisions are made by consensus involving all in the conclusion.
A pair of contiguous communities (one from each of the two moie-
ties) bound together by preferential marriage ties form the basic
socio-political unit. These kinship groups cut across tribal
boundaries resulting in much intermarriage and often the pairing
of clans from different tribes.

As animists, the appeasement of ancestral spirits is central
to their religion. However, Damals perform **tel** **kalok**, "devil
appeasement" which involves the placation of spirit beings whose
malevolence can be harnessed for the good of the particular kin
group. Moreover, legends of millenial expectancy pervade their
folklore, depicting man's fall from an immortal state and the
possibilities of restoration.

The Mystique of the Message

Given the context of expectancy amongst the Damals the appeal
of the "living message" (or "message of life") as it immediately
came to be known, was not completely surprising.

a) This expectancy was developed to a high degree amongst the
Damals. Largely due to the pre-contact "inner sources" mentioned
by Kamma[2] the Damals had experienced a series of small messianic
movements in the period between 1920 and 1955. I have catalogued
10 such movements which flowered then died in disillusionment.

b) The Damals are a small tribe being heavily colonized by the
large Western Dani tribe. Rather than withdraw, Damals have been
receptive to the many areas of culture change this has brought--
and perhaps thus been prepared in receptivity to further changes
the Christian message would introduce.

c) The conclusion that the particular circumstances surrounding the first enunciation of the Message in 1956 were divinely
directed is unavoidable. The first missionary moved into the
village of Kunga in the Ilaga Valley where lived a very influential Damal headman, Deen. Deen's grandfather had been an active
seeker after the elusive immortality sought by all Damals. He
himself was married to the daughter of the outstanding Western
Dani political figure in the valley, and had recently returned
from a far-ranging trip searching for the cause of his nephew's
untimely death. This fruitless search had disillusioned him

with the native concepts of the supernatural and opened him to the entrance of the new "words of life."

Here the problem of approach came into full focus. Should the gospel of eternal life be presented as the fulfillment of their millenial dreams of immortality? Could the pattern used by the Master be instructive, who amongst a people looking for a political kingdom preached "the Good News of the Kingdom" (Matt. 4:23) -- then went on to teach them that He meant a spiritual kingdom (John 18:36; John 6:26-58) when He saw them about to misinterpret His message (John 6:15) and crown Him as their political leader. This disillusioned many (John 6:60) and caused many to change their minds (John 6:66). However, some caught on to what He meant and elected to stay on because they believed in His spiritual message (John 6:67-68). This then was the approach used: Secure their attention by associating the gospel message with this expected immortality which was such a focus of their society, then work to teach the spiritual nature of the message. This is not to say that this was a clear policy decision in view of the cultural focus on immortality, for the extent to which this was developed amongst the Damals was not that clear at the time. However, there was a conscious relationship drawn here to secure a "point of attention."

Two questions naturally follow: Did this secure their attention? How successful has the Church been in teaching the spiritual nature of the Kingdom? The "message of life" has captivated the attention of the tribe! Of some 12,000 Damals, some 8,000 are KINGMI (Indonesian Alliance) adherents and some 3,500 are Roman Catholic adherents. Of the KINGMI adherents almost 4,000 are baptized members. Perhaps more important, from the Damals the message of life has travelled across the kinship bridge (first across Deen's kinship ties to his Western Dani father-in-law) for what McGavran calls a "clean sweep" of the 65,000 Western Danis.

On the effectiveness of communicating the spiritual nature of the message, it may be too early to assess. Pastors, leaders and laymen alike seem to understand and accept the "other-worldliness" of the message, while applying its moral aspects to today's rapidly changing world. At the same time a small messianic movement rocked four of the churches in a remote, poorly-instructed area. While true Christian experience and teaching should prove a strong deterrent to abberative messianic movements, time will give the final verdict on how effective this instruction has been. In the meantime, teaching of this nature goes on on all levels -- Bible school, witness schools, and village churches.

The importance of the attitudes of the missionary introducing

the message must not be overlooked here. In this case it involved
missionaries who understood the decision-making structure of a
kinship-oriented society. Social, political and religious activity
includes the whole community and decisions are made by the whole
kin group. Thus the Helato Tagam-Magai linked lineage (Deen's
group) was faced by the claims of the Gospel and a decision was
reached by the kin group as a whole to follow Christ. Such a
"decision" was not only encouraged, but the appeal was directed to
their decision-making unit. In addition, other problems, such as
the problems of polygynous families, was wisely not confused at
this stage with the basic issues of commitment to Jesus Christ.

"Witness Schools"and "Camp Meetings"

Because of the volume of people who had decided to leave the
old way and follow Christ, it became urgent to find a means of
mass instruction which would bring Christian truth and growth to
people in scores of villages -- first in one area (the Ilaga
Valley), then as the movement spread, in numerous valleys. The
means developed was dubbed the "witness school" because it trained
selected men and women from each area who then returned to their
home villages each week-end to share what they had learned with
their own community. They were part-time students, part-time
witnesses. In the early stages, instruction was given Monday
through Thursday, then the witnesses went home to instruct the
believers in their own villages on the long week-end and preach
at home on Sunday morning. When they finished a certain period
of instruction, these families then returned to their homes (or
some newly responsive area) to reside and start the process all
over again. They gathered around them selected families whom
they now taught and sent out in the same fashion. The witness
school became the backbone of the grass-roots education of newly
professed believers. Their classes at home turned into pre-bap-
tismal classes which then moved into the essential early sorting
out by the Church as to who had evidenced Christian testimony (and
should be baptized) and who had not. Witness schools are still
carried on today in all areas of the movement -- only now they are
operated completely by qualified national teachers.

"Witness men" too became the missionaries into new areas, not
only for instruction of new believers in these areas, but also for
preliminary evangelism. When people responded to the mystique of
the gospel, the witness man would stay and start the witness
school cycle (this being the only instruction he himself had had)
into operation with selected "witness men" in the new area.

Something which developed spontaneously was the "night of
telling the gospel legends." Adapting the pattern of the all-

night courtship sing-sing (now banned by the Church over our
efforts to sanctify it), the whole community would spend all night
sitting around the men's house fire swapping Bible stories and
gospel songs until the sun broke over the morning mountains.

Another technique which was used for grass-roots instruction of
whole villages of new believers was the "camp meeting." In this a
series of classes was held for the whole population of an area,
carried on for a week, two weeks, or even longer. The instructors
were the missionary and the witness man from that area. This practice, used widely for every-member instruction has not indigenized
as easily as the witness school, but has been revived recently by
two local pastors after a seminar in which this was encouraged.

The important thing here was that instruction covered two
levels simultaneously -- the instruction of every believer, and
the training of the leaders.

Struggling to be a Truly Damal Church in a Changing Society

In many aspects the Damal Church was never anything less than
an indigenous movement, handling their own affairs, supporting
their own witness men, expressing their faith in their own forms,
such as prayer forms, native chant hymns, and their ways of telling the "gospel legends." At the same time there is the inevitable mark of foreign missionary teaching and practice on their
expression. Hopefully much of it is Biblical (like the appointment of "elders" -- the "deacons" didn't serve a meaningful role
in Damal society and were eliminated by the Damals). Some forms
are unmistakably Western (like closing their eyes when they pray
which, they say, makes them sleepy!). However, the form of their
worship service, customarily held outside as they have no pattern
of indoor public gathering, is so different as to be dubbed "primitive Christianity" by outsiders. Local Church leaders arrange all
their own affairs and discipline offenders on a local group and
valley-wide basis. These are the two political levels which are
meaningful to them. Higher levels of relationship and organization (on an inter-area, provincial and national level), necessary
for formal government recognition, are completely foreign to the
Damals. Efforts at this pushed by the Indonesian KINGMI Church
and the C&MA mission in an effort to establish the Church as a
legal body, are having difficulty at the financial and organizational levels because it fills no real need to most of the tribal
believers and therefore is not understood. On the other hand,
financial and organizational responsibilities are assumed with
understanding on the socio-political levels which are meaningful
to them. Pastors, true to the pattern of non-specialists, support
themselves by farming, assisted by limited offerings from the

congregation, which is usually composed of the pastor's kin-group.

The responsibility that one feels for his relatives has become
a natural bridge on which the expansion of the Church has travelled
with explosive power. This has developed into a concern for the
unevangelized who are unrelated, and Damal witness men have been on
the forefront of evangelism in unrelated but adjoining tribes. The
ultimate extension came when Damals and Western Danis moved into the
lowlands to evangelize tribes historically considered by them to be
less than human (partly because they don't wear the penis sheath).
Along with each party of witness men go donations of penis sheaths
from the Damal and Dani churches to clothe the poor naked savages
their witnesses have gone to!!

To measure the "purity" of the Church against this backdrop of
freedom to express their faith, one must take into consideration
the factors involved: 1) the Scriptures in their language; 2)
instruction of all believers in the meaning and interpretation of
the Scriptures; 3) the development of Biblical and vital training
for Church leaders; 4) the development of well-instructed, spiritually vital leadership. These four factors are completely inter-
related. Only 85% of the Scriptures of the New Testament are
available to the Damal Church at this time. After some 15 years,
leaders trained in indigenous language and Indonesian language
Bible Schools, whose experience and training are warmly evangelical,
are in the positions of leadership in the Church (and potentially
the Bible Schools as the mission turns more and more of this
responsibility over to the nationals). Of course this control is
on the same basis of consensus as in their social and political
life, even though government regulations require a pyramid-struc-
tured church government on the books!

Doctrinal purity has been only minimally tested by association
with Roman Catholics. More sorting will come when the Seventh Day
Adventists and Jehovah's Witnesses -- both in the province now --
find their way into the Highlands. Few close to constant instruction have returned to spirit appeasement.

Biblical standards of practical purity have been upheld by
Church discipline. Some areas of tension are developing between
the Highlands churches' concepts and the Indonesian KINGMI Church's
concepts of practical purity. For example, in terms of polygyny:
Specifically, can polygamists be baptized without divorcing all but
one of their wives? Under what terms if any can a believer taking
a second wife be admitted into fellowship with the Church? Is
divorce of the plural wife desirable? Biblical? This is an urgent
issue amongst the Damals for whom the levirate continues to be a
responsibility -- even for a Christian! The Church faces an

unresolved problem with the monogamous Christian society in relation to widows and their necessity that they be married.

In many ways the Church is in a period of adjusting its native
modes of expression to a rapidly changing society. Education,
increased outside contact, governmental control and increased
economic opportunities are all making their impact on the traditional patterns, and the Church is seeking to establish Her identity
in it. I will list two as examples only:

1) Bride price. Part of the Damal (and also the Western Dani)
Churches feel that Christians should dispense with the bride price.
The others permit it, making intermarriage between the groups impossible and resulting in a very divisive issue. Missionaries have
maintained this is a problem the Church will have to settle -- or
agree to differ on!

2) The political role of the pastor or witness man. In a
society where social, political and religious life are welded into
an integrated whole, the political role of a newly established
position of prestige brings with it jockeying and re-adjustment.
Because decisions are arrived at by consensus rather than decree,
in most areas where the leading political figure is a believer,
both pastor and headman will sit in on the councils of both Church
and community.

What Lies Ahead?

The only certain prediction for the future is: CHANGE! There
has been more change amongst the Damals in these 16 years than in
the unknown millenia preceding. And change will accelerate in the
days to come. With three government posts, numerous schools, a
multi-million dollar copper mine, and oil exploration all going on
in Damal territory, new opportunities and pressures are inevitable.
How the Church will meet this change is crucial to her continued
virility amongst a changing people. How other groups move in certain key areas will also be critical:

1) Government policy: The government's policy in primary and
secondary education will be especially important. If the government withdraws support (as seems imminent) neither the people nor
the Protestant mission will be able to foot the bill, and other
groups could capitalize on this opportunity.

2) Mission involvement: Related to this are the plans of the
mission for continued involvement with the Church in teaching,
translating and other advisory ministries. Especially will this
be true in terms of mission help in advanced theological education,

and the mission's continued support of grass-roots training -- say on an extension education basis.

3) Control by the Indonesian KINGMI Church: Another issue is how much freedom from domination by the national KINGMI Church is going to be permitted, or, how much involvement is desirable to realize national identity.

These issues are difficult to predict with any certainty because they involve funds as well as attitudes. However, much more important to the future of the Church than any of the above outside influences will be an inside issue: the evangelism of the second and third generations. The tendency will be to nominalism in the succeeding generations who have never been animists. What the Church does to win the youth and call the nominal to repentance will be critical. Perhaps the day of the witness school will soon be over and give way to the day of the "revivalist" -- the Damal evangelist, not for new areas, but for the unsaved in the churches. If She fails here, the Church amongst the Damals is doomed.

A related concern is the potential for revivalistic movements amongst the Damals when nominalism turns into disillusionment. With the history of messiahs in her background, the urgent need for Damals is for a continuing vital experience of Christ as Saviour and Lord expressed in meaningful and indigenous forms. We have made a fair start on this. Tippett observes that "a mission that fails to produce an indigenous church within three or four decades from its large accessions from paganism is almost certain to experience this kind of movement (messianic movement)."[3] We are sixteen years on the way, and we may not have that many more to go, given the Damal's propensity and the rapidity of contact.

Other problems for the Church loom in the future: A surplus of marriagable women over men in a society where every woman must marry; the levirate and Christians who take a second wife; rising costs of Church administration to be supported by peasants in an economically depressed area; the stagnation resulting from a church having evangelized everything reachable and having no new fields for outreach.

These are only a few. But all of these pale beside the major concern of the Church to organize the revival and instruction of those now within the fold of the Church for vital commitment to Christ and continued growth into maturity. If the Damals are thus committed to their Master and are thus growing, the other issues are the problems of a vital Church and we have the promise of the Indwelling Spirit for their solution. We pray that this may indeed

be the situation of the Damal and Western Dani Churches in the
years to come.

*   *   *   *

FOOTNOTES

[1]See also Ellenberger, Multi-individual Conversions in W. Irian,
EMG Vol.1, No.1, 1964. and Ellenberger, "The Beginnings of
Hymnology in a New Guinea Church", Practical Anthropology, Vol.9,
No. 6 (Nov-Dec. 1962).

[2]F. C. Kamma, "Messianic Movements in Western New Guinea" International Review of Missions, Vol. 41 (1952), pp. 156-158.

[3]Tippett, A. Solomon Islands Christianity (London: Lutterworth
Press) 1967; page 215.

FRONTIER MISSIONS NEEDED FOR BRAZIL'S
FRONTIER ROAD SYSTEM
William R. Read

12

Geographers call Latin America the "hollow" continent. Mountains found close to the coastlines form geographic barriers that protect the inland plains. By holding a scale model of the South American continent in our hands, and by looking at it from the side we would see that it is generally high on the outside and low on the inside. The inland plains have a hot climate and a lush tropical jungle covers the great core or middle sector. Because of the hollow nature of the continent and its climate the greater part of the population is found along the coastline. Today, more needs to be known about the middle sectors of this concave continent, for as it is now, this hollow South American continent is in the process of radical change in the decade of the 1970's. Brazil, a country with 100 million people that occupies 47% of the entire land area of South America, two years ago decided to cut a road through the center of the vast Amazonian jungle to open up the "hollow" continent as never before and create a whole new era of frontier mission. Eventually this third class road through the jungle will develop into a frontier road system that will provide access into all parts of the "hollow" continent.

At the present time the effort to cut this road through the hollow sector is in progress. When finished, another great continental land rush to settle this area will have begun. The magnitude of this land area is so vast that it is equal in size to all of the land in the United States west of the Mississippi River. Compare this Amazon basin watershed with the total land area of the United States. See Figure I below. When the complete river system of the Amazon River is superimposed over a surface map of the United States the tributaries in the west almost reach the Pacific, the tributaries in the north are in Canadian territory, those in the south are found below the border and extend into the Guld of Mexico, and the mouth of the Amazon protrudes beyond the Great Lakes out into the Valley of the St. Lawrence in Canada! When geographers attempt to explain the hollow characteristic of the continent, many feel that a tremendous fresh water lake existed here in the ages past. When it disappeared it left the geographical basin that is now dominated by this mightiest of rivers.

FIGURE I

Taken from *National Geographic* — October, 1972

In 1965, I was a passenger on flight #516 of Pan Am from
Brasilia to Panama. This was a 2,800 mile flight over one of the
largest unsettled land frontier areas found in the world. It
took me directly over the Xingo National Park, an 8,500 square
mile refuge for Brazilian Indians. Seven years ago, no roads
cut across this "green inferno." An occasional landing strip
could be seen beside some isolated ranch houses. Rich, enterprising cattlemen were the first to purchase vast tracts of land
for their herds of Indu-Brasil hybrid cattle that could take
the humid tropical climate.

In 1972, taking the same flight, I saw something new being
carved upon the floor of this "green inferno." Flying at 37,000
feet in altitude, gaping scars had been left on the jungle floor,
and were visible as a series of roads was being hacked through
the dense carpet of trees and jungle. The Amazon basin was being
criss-crossed by a frontier road system. It staggers the imagination to ponder what the results will be. What will the same
flight show in 1980?

It boggles the Brazilian mind too. Magazines or newspapers
appear with pictures and articles about this dramatic, strategic
road. Immediately the issues are sold out at all the new stands!
This is one of the hottest items Brazilian journalists have
written about in years!

What does it really mean? It is the road of the century
that will connect the Atlantic to the Pacific. It is being cut
through the thickest jungle in the world. This long straight
cut through the heart of the mysterious Brazilian jungles will
connect with the Trans-Andean road in Peru, and the continent
will be linked from coast to coast, and join its widest expanse
of land from East to West. It will be a road 4,000 kilometers
in length beginning at Estreito, in the State of Maranhão, and
will make its way to the last jungle village in Brazil called
Boqueirão da Esperanca (Valley of Hope) on the border between
Brazil (Acre) and Peru. See Figure II. Within three years the
Trans-Amazonia road will connect with the Peruvian road that
will begin in Lima and cross the tortuous Andes mountains.
(Note the gap in Figure II that has to be connected.) Already
2,000 kilometers of the Brazilian part of this road is laid
open in the fierce jungle. The work continues uninterrupted
in spite of the rainy season. Modern machinery now avilable to
men must face the primeval enemies of mankind in this formidable
jungle vastness, regardless of the rain that falls almost daily
from November to May!

On some parts of this road, the soil has little consistency.

FIGURE II

It doesn't hold together
and the ground is like
mercury shifting with no
firm base. In such areas,
the earth literally dis-
solves in the rain and
defies construction work
in the squish of mud! In
this quagmire, powerful
tractors bog down but the
work continues with no
slackening.

All along this road,
a series of landing strips
has been provided and is
the means whereby the supply
lines from civilization
are maintained - food,
gasoline, oil, and repair
parts needed for the
different types of earth
moving machines and tractors.
In the dense jungle areas
tress that are more than
220 feet high and seventy-five feet thick at the base must be cut!
These mighty bastions triangular in shape, would look peculiar
placed beside the giant Sequoias of California, yet each would
contain the same amount of wood in square feet and volume.

As the road advances, the responsibility of bringing colonists
and settlers in has been given to the governmental agency called
INCRA (The National Institute of Colonization and Agrarian Reform).
Their plan is to have an agricultural village, called Agrovila,
set up beside the highway at twenty kilometer intervals. Assistance of all types is given to such settlers who come in to live
in these villages and work on this new land. They come from
different parts of Brazil. There are many problems involved in
learning to cultivate these humid lands, and eventually a whole
new life style will result. Already seven of these villages
have been established. Lessons learned already are being
utilized by those who settle in the next villages further up
the road as it opens up.

In five years the goal is to have 500,000 people settled in
these different villages along this 4,000 kilometer road. This
is only a small part of the larger number of people who will be

moving into these new lands, but it is a good start.

Frontier missions among settlers

What does such a road system mean for the rapidly growing
Protestant Churches in Brazil? In April and May of 1972, while
in Brazil, this question was put to me by different missionary
leaders and frankly discussed by leaders of some of the larger,
independent denominations.

If part of the answer is to be found in what has happened
along the road that was built from Brasilia to Belem - the
famous BR-14, then there is reason for Evangelical Protestant
leaders to be highly motivated by this new opportunity.

In 1962, the Belem-Brasilia highway was finished. See
Figure III. In a decade this highway has attracted large numbers
of people from all parts of Brazil. In 1962 this road had only
10 inhabited towns, but in 1972 there were more than 120 towns.
New centers emerged from one day to the other as conditions
became favorable for such fantastic growth.

The population along this road, not counting the large
cities of Brasilia and Anapolis, now exceeds two million people.
By the end of 1973, this road will be a first class hard surfaced road with asphalt and will be a primary all seasonal road.
Already this road has attracted people from every part of Brazil.
They come by bus, car, and truck from the overcrowded, depressed
areas. New arrivals will be settling along the feeder roads
that are now pushing out from the main road to the connector
roads that will move into the new lands that are adjacent and
adjoining. Such roads will provide rapid access to markets,
to trade, and to commerce.

In ten years, the Protestant churches that now exist along
this highway have grown to about 35,000 communicant members.
This is only a start. The next decade could triple this number
of communicant members that are found in the different Evangelical
churches that are here because of this highway and its growing
tributaries.

We have no recent statistical records of the growth of
Evangelical denominations on this road. Such a study needs to
be made as soon as possible. A study of this nature would be
of great value to missionary and national church leaders who

FIGURE III

are contemplating different ministries along this road system.

However, we do have the record of what the Southern Presbyterian Mission in Brazil did during this period. They gave high priority to church planting along this road. Now they have more than 15 churches that have been firmly established in key centers from Brasilia to Belem. Each major church has its own network of congregations and preaching points in the surrounding region, but this is only the beginning.

In my recent flight over the Amazon basin, I happened to be on the same plane with the gentleman who was then the Moderator of the Southern Presbyterian Church. He had just finished his exciting visit to Brazil. He had visited Southern Presbyterian evangelistic work along the Brasilia-Belem highway and mentioned his visit with Paul Long, a Southern Presbyterian missionary responsible for the Porangatu field. This is one of the important centers on this highway, see the map, Figure III. He spoke of other churches growing in a similar way along the highway. He was anxious to recommend that his church in the U.S.A. amplify and expand this exciting church planting activity along the newest roads that are being added to this growing frontier road system.

I had been present at a meeting in Brasilia when he spoke to a number of Presbyterian Church leaders. He emphasized with vigor and enthusiasm the desire that his church would dedicate additional resources to this pioneer evangelistic task of planting churches along this developing road system. He was convinced that this is one of the essential ways a North American church can make a vital contribution to the evangelization of Brazil at this important time in history. He was concerned that his field mission organization be given the freedom they need to work out a suitable plan by which the Southern Presbyterian missionary enterprise in Brazil can work with the Igreja Presbiteriana do Brazil in a satisfactory partnership arrangement.

The magnitude of the church planting task among the new settlers and the problems that such an effort along this road will face in the next two decades is breath taking. Many of the foreign missions that are now working in Brazil are pursuing the policy, from a distance, of watchful waiting, taking time to examine carefully this highly fluid opportunity. At the same time, some mission leaders are making definite plans for exploratory survey trips into the Amazon Basin areas. These surveys will become the means by which these missions will be able to gather the information they need that will permit them to formulate a strategy for their church planting effort in this vast hinterland area. National church leaders are anxiously following the latest reports that come out of this advancing road system. Some of these leaders are trying to determine what resources should be set aside for some adequate type of evangelistic endeavor that their churches can initiate in some of the more strategic centers. It takes time for many of the fast growing centers to be spotted in time for favorable consideration as "strategic" locations. Familiarity with the entire road system in all of its extension and vastness is a necessity in order to make many of these important decisions.

Leaders of Pentecostal churches in Brazil generally feel that it is too early for them to think about any highly concentrated work in this Amazon region. When the cities along the road are larger, teaming with people, then they intend to make their move into these frontier areas and consolidate their people who were some of the first to go in as settlers. However, many Pentecostal leaders remember how difficult it is to acquire suitable property for their large churches in urban centers, and might well be apprehensive about waiting too long before moving into these new lands. Because of the type of membership they have, Pentecostals must move into large populations that have a substantial money economy or they cannot survive and acquire the momentum and large number of members they need to build their churches. Their strategy for the present might be to enlarge the mother churches already established in the larger centers of Brasilia, Anapolis, and Belem. From such centers eventually will come the pastors and evangelists for the building up of their many churches. Twice or three times a year an enterprising Pentecostal pastor will take a trip up or down the Brasilia-Belem highway to visit the many small Pentecostal congregations that have sprung up with the arrival of Pentecostal people in the initial waves of internal migration. Pentecostal leaders, divided as they are about this, nevertheless are careful to keep abreast of developments. The Assembly of God church has decided to place evangelists in each Agrovila. More will follow. There is a Pentecostal communication system all up and down these roads that keeps them informed and provides a pretty good feel for what is happening in their churches.

One town Pentecostals have been active in is Imperatriz. This town is closer to Belem than it is to Brasilia. In 1953 the first automobile was taken in by boat. In 1958, when the road arrived, the municipio (county) of Imperatriz had a population of 6,000 people. In two years this number had doubled. In 1970, this same county had a population of almost 100,000, and 36,000 of these inhabitants were found in the city itself.

The following table shows a decade of growth for six Protestant churches in Imperatriz. Note what happens in 1958 and 1959, (See Figure IV) four years before the road opened.

FIGURE IV

GROWTH OF PROTESTANT CHURCHES IN IMPERATRIZ 1955-1966.

Denomination	1955	1956	1957	1958	1959	1960	1961	1962	1963	1964	1965	1966
Adventist												
Assembly of God	200	201	228	573	1220	1941	2193	641	765	879	1114	1235
Congregacao Crista								22	145	157		
Baptist				28	45	62	69	51	65	111	155	182
Presbyterian									316	333	351	371
Evan. Cristian	17	16	31	44	69	92	110	124			80	88
TOTALS	217	217	259	645	1334	2095	2372	838	1291	1480	1700	1876

This information was taken from the Religious Census the Brazilian Census Bureau takes every year for the Protestant Churches (I.B.G.E. 1955 to 1965). Total Evangelical growth for the period has doubled in each three year period. This represents a total Evangelical communicant membership growth

that is close to 1,000% for the decade. If the Assembly of
God Church had been able to grow without the schism that is
registered between 1961 and 1962, this percentage index of
growth could have been much higher.

Projecting this rate of growth out for a decade, there will
be close to 5,000 Evangelicals in the city by 1980. This does
not include communicant membership in the embryonic congregations
and churches already established in different districts of the
county and connected with the larger churches in the city. A
total membership in the county of Imperatriz could soar to
10,000 by 1980. This is only one of the 120 centers on this
particular road! A series of church growth studies should be
made to show the growth of all Evangelical churches that have
been planted along this road since 1962. A careful analysis of
such a study would provide many helpful insights, lessons, and
suggest growth patterns that Mission and National Church leaders
need at this particular time.

Everyone in Imperatriz is encouraged to believe that this
is one of the cities that will continue to accelerate in its
growth and development. There is much inexpensive land available for the new arrivals. Rich reserves of lumber are close
by. It is a good agricultural region and cattle have done well
here. It is the largest city near the intersecting point of
the Brasilia-Belem and the Trans-Amazonia highways. These two
roads come together at Estreito. Imperatriz will serve as the
major trading center that will be close to the new iron discoveries at Marabã. A road is now under construction to this
region, 200 kilometers away. Those from the Northeast call
Imperatriz their "Canaan" for they can get a new start here
and it is possible for them to purchase good land for about
one-fifth of that being paid for the old land where they come
from. INCRA provides loans and other helpful services for
serious people who will work hard on land that one day they
can call their own. This is the "promise land" that is attract-
ing thousands, and more are on the way!

Multiply the story of this town twenty or more times in
the next decade. This will probably not adequately describe
the unusual boom towns composed of settlers that will spurt in
their growth in the next decade for one reason or another.
This is the story of the road system that is yet to stretch
across the length and breadth of this vast area that was
recently described in these words:

"Having defied occupation for hundreds of years,

> the Amazon has its own special mystique. Its
> description runs all in superlatives - the
> area is a massive five million square km.,
> equal to half the surface of the moon.
> Alone it would be the eighth largest country
> in the world. It has 1/20 of the world's
> area, one fifth of its fresh water, one
> third of its forests and probably one half
> of its oxygen supply. The Amazon River is
> the longest navigable river in the world -
> 6,477 km. Its potential wealth includes the
> barely scratched but already fantastic mineral
> deposits, huge lumber reserves, and probably
> the world's largest oil bed. (Thayer,1972:8)

This system is more than the main arteries of the Brasilia-Belem
and the Trans-Amazonia roads that are rapidly being rushed to
completion. It is much more. It is a series of growing connector roads that will bring together all the roads that are
now in use in the area. It will provide the major connecting
roads that will crisscross this last remaining, unsettled land
area in the world. Below is a map of the projected highway
network that appeared in a recent article in <u>Americas</u>. See
Figure V. This map includes the projected Northern Perimeter
Highway and the Northeast Radial Highway. (Henriques,72:9)
These roads will eventually push into the Guainas, into
Venezuela, and into Colombia. (McIntyre,1973:473) All of
these roads could be in operation by the end of this decade.

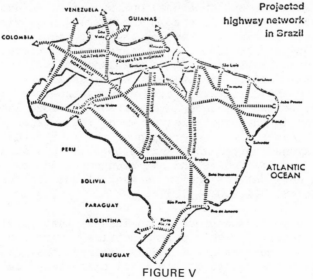

FIGURE V

These different segments, even though built in a fast, apparently
disorganized way, with few full blown plans for a full utiliza-
tion for the lands adjacent--will produce a miracle for their
respective regions. These roads act as magnets to attract new
settlers. In a short time villages, towns and major cities will
be planted in the better locations that will be found along the
roadway. Herds of cattle will graze on adjoining lands, and
eventually subsistence farming of the region will give way to
an intensive cultivation of corn, beans, rice and cotton.

This is happening now on the Brasilia-Belem highway. Study
this highway as a preview of what could happen on a system that
ultimately will be ten times larger!

Frontier missions among the Brazilian Indians

The experience of settling the North American frontier was
very cruel to the Indian. He was depicted as the villian to the
settlers who were part of the different waves of migrating
pioneers who courageously pushed into new lands. Between 1784
and 1819 the movement of people to settle new lands had begun.
These people formed a wedge of settlement whose point, by 1820,
had gone into the area where the Ohio River empties into the
Mississippi. This land wedge includes all of the area now found
in the state of Kentucky. By 1840, the westward movement had
pushed beyond the Mississippi, extending itself into the states
of Missouri, Arkansas, Oklahoma, eastern Texas, and Louisiana.
This westward settlement continued unabated for two decades and
the midwestern states of Kansas, Missouri, Indiana, Wisconsin,
and the eastern part of the Dakotas begin to receive large
numbers of people. In 1880 the pioneers who had traveled west
by covered wagon had laid claim to the lands of California,
Oregon, and the Pacific Northwest. The seasonal traffic of
settlers along the different trails used by the covered wagons
eventually dispersed settlers into most of the good land that
could be found in the great plains, among the Rockies, and
along the valleys and the watersheds of the rivers that drained
such vast regions. After 1880 and up to 1972 this westward
movement had run its course and had been consolidated decade
after decade until all of the lands west of the Mississippi
had been settled. (A.A.G. 1972)

In this unfortunate process the Indians that survived this
century and a half of ruthless land settlment were shuttled off
into smaller and more isolated Indian Reservations. Indian
Reservations in the United States still exist today as the last

vestige of diverse Indian culture and civilization.

In the North American frontier experience the Indian had suffered the losing part of the westward movement. He was given the image of the noble villain by novelists, by the productions in the motion picture industry, by T.V. writers, and others caught up in the modern communication media. All had depicted the Indian in these 15 decades of history as the enemy. This mood began to change in the 1960's. A new concern for minorities began to be reinforced by court decisions. People began to review and recognize the injustices of the past. A nation where its cities burned, its races shouted defiance, and its minorities adopted protest as a way of life was forced to a re-evaluation of its history, and began to take a new, sober look at its national sins. National misdealings and mistreatment of Indians eventually came up for this type of review.

Only a remnant of Indians exist today in the United States. These who survive, descendants of former occupants of a continent and in much larger numbers, are now confined to small islands of land, living out their lives under a canopy of dependency, virtual wards of a country that had struggled with the Indian problem but was forced to give in to the persistent demands for land. An insatiable lust and hunger for land was destined to confine Indians to smaller and smaller reserves while their remaining lands were opened for white settlement.

A recent series of maps entitled "Indian Land Cessions," designed by Sam B. Hilliard, were published by the Association of American Geographers. These maps geographically portray the story of a nation's growth at the expense of the American Indian. A look at these different maps in their sequence gives an overview of the spacial land devouring process of frontier settlement. This is a map tour of the North American experience of the frontier and is a somber, disquieting experience.

Not only in the United States, but in other parts of the world a strong consensus has been formed in the past decade about these acts of man's inhumanity to man. Certain groups are incensed, and are making strong statements about racism and the present and future treatment of indigenous peoples. One such statement is the "Declaration of Barbados." (W.C.C. 1971) It came out of the Symposium on Inter-Ethnic Conflict in South America that was held in Barbados on January 25 to 30 of 1971. This statement represents the voice of some Latin American anthropologists trying to fit the Indians into Latin American

political structures. This declaration is an extreme position
that is being discussed pro and con in the July, 1972 issue of
the International Review of Missions.

The discussion and debate that the Barbados Declaration has
engendered so far point up a strong need felt by Latin Americans.
They would see a common mind among Christian groups and missions
engaged in some of the different ministries seeking to evangelize
Indians in the multi-varied linguistic and ethnic pockets throughout the length and breadth of Latin America. (I.R.M. 1973:253-254)
This discussion of the issues involved in missionary work is
bound to point up many problems and clarify some of the solutions
needed.

The road systems described in the first part of this paper
will constitute the ultimate threat to the 50,000 to 90,000
Indians that still survive within this vast Amazon Basin. The
survival of the Indian culture, their civilization, their
habitat--all is now threatened. In the sixth Congress of the
World Federation of Road Builders, held in October of 1971 in
Montreal, Canada, the Brazilian Ministry of Transportation prepared a 23-page book explaining the international character of
the Trans-Amazonia road. Not a single word can be found in this
report to describe how this road would touch the lives of the
Indian population. Much was said about the political and social
benefits, the importance of a connection between the Amazon and
the Northeast of Brazil, the mineral riches that had been discovered in the area, and the possibilities of land settlement
for the Brazilians who would migrate from other parts of
extinction of certain Indian tribes in the period from 1900 to
1957:

> "Military action and posts established along
> frontiers; building of railroads and telegraph
> lines; ethno-graphic and geographic expedi-
> tions; rubber gathering in the Amazon and matē
> gathering in Parana and Souther Mato Grosso;
> the westward march of coffee in the state of Sao
> Paulo; cattle growing in Mato Grosso and Goias;
> mining and prospecting; and the highly
> individualistic activities of bugreiros (pro-
> fessional Indian hunters), grileiros (land
> manipulators), cangaceiros (bandits), and
> mascates (itenerant merchants)." (Kietzman,
> 1972:72)

Many of the factors listed above still threaten the Indian's existence in Brazil and form certain "faces of civilization" that continue to press in upon the Indian. The way these "faces" of civilization touch the Indian cultures in the Amazon in the next decade will determine their extinction or survival.

With the present plans for the Trans-Amazonian Road and the future connective links to be added in the entire frontier road system, these "faces of civilization" will accelerate their relentless confrontation and encroachment upon the Indians that still survive in Brazil. So far, most of the Indians that have been spotted along the route of the Trans-Amazonian highway have been friendly. Francisco Meirelles of the FUNAI (National Indian Foundation) discounts some of the early reports that there had been Indian uprisings along the upper Roosevelt River where some Cross Amazon surveyors had penetrated. He said in an interview in Porto Velho, Rondonia that members of the Wide Belt's (Cintras Largas) had killed a FUNAI representative, but this was because he had been confused with land grabbers who had been in the area. After careful negotiations by Meirelles with the "Wide Belts" they were reported to be "cautiously cordial." FUNAI succeeded in chasing the land grabbers out of the area. (Brazilian Bulletin, 1972:7). The Nhambequara tribe who speaks a language that is completely unrelated to any other Indian languages in Brazil had been frightening the inhabitants in their neighboring towns and thought that they were on the warpath. Meirelles said, "They just wanted to talk over their problems." (Brazilian Bulletin, 1972:7)

A preliminary study of Indians along the Trans-Amazonian Highway made by the Foundation (FUNAI - Fundaçao do Indio) indicates that approximately 5,000 Indians will have to be moved. These particular Indians are found in 29 tribes. Twelve of these tribes live completely isolated from civilization. Nine of them maintain some kind of "intermittent" contract with civilization. Eight of these tribes are considered to be some-what "integrated." Some, most notably the Aranas, Cararoes, Caiapas and the Haranas, are said to be "aggressive." (Veja 1970:18)

In the 1970's FUNAI was given the job of making peaceful contacts with all of the Indians between the Tocantins and Tapajo Rivers and in a diplomatic way to arrange for all transfers necessary in order to safeguard the Indians and maintain peace along this section of the highway. Two centers for this part of the road were selected. The Indian Post at

Pucurui was taken over by the Villas Boas brothers, Orlando and
Claudio. The Indian Post at Cararão was placed under the direction of Francisco Meirelles.

From the very beginning, there was an implied understanding
between FUNAI and responsible governmental officials, that the
course of the road could be altered if necessary in order to
cooperate with the policy adopted by FUNAI towards the Indians.
The guidelines set down by General Bandeira de Mello, president
of FUNAI indicates that all important decisions made about the
destiny of the Indian population along the road will be made on
the basis of each particular situation.

The next challenge of FUNAI comes with the "pacification" of
the Indians along the second half of the great Amazonia road from
Itaituba to Curzeiro do Sul and then along the route of the road
that Engineers of the Brazilian Army have begun to cut from Cuiaba
to Santarem. Along these two sectors of the growing frontier road
system are found the largest number of isolated Indian tribes, or
those who have only an occasional contact with FUNAI. These
tribes are the Apinajes, Surius, Paracanas, Acurunis, Aravas,
Acocoa-tis, Xicrens, Jores, Cararoes, Caiapos, Jurunas and the
Araras Caraibas. In total number of people, they represent less
than 3,500 Indians, but contact must be made with them using
great courage and diplomacy. FUNAI personnel engaged in this
work follow the motto of the heroic founder of FUNAI, Marshal
Candido Mariano da Silva Rondon, "Die if necessary, but never
kill."

In the August 1970 issue of Veja a map was published based
on a preliminary study by FUNAI. Later this map was published in
the Brazilian Bulletin and is reproduced on the following page
(See Figure VI).

In two 16mm movies of the Trans-Amazonia highway construction that were shown by Dr. Milton Machado Mourao at the Latin
American Center at U.C.L.A. in July of 1972, the cameraman
occasionally catches Indians peering from behind tress to watch
earth movers, Caterpillar tractors, and other machinery smoothly
fashion a road bed for a highway in the jungle. In one scene an
Indian accustomed to contact with Brazilians was shown playing
inside a tree used on the giant earth moving machines, primitive
man making the products of modern man his playthings!

Most Brazilian Indians are nomadic by nature. Instinctively
they will move out of the way of the road; but hundreds and,

FIGURE VI
CROSS-AMAZON ROUTE

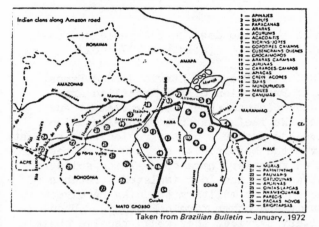

Taken from *Brazilian Bulletin* — January, 1972

perhaps thousands, of Indians will be moved by FUNAI into the Xingo National Park established by the Villas Boas brothers in 1961. Some of these parks are much bigger than most European countires and reserved exclusively for Indians. An article in The National Geographic magazine (Sept.1968), described how FUNAI was setting aside and beginning to use these Indian parks. In the recent October 1972 issue of the same journal, the lead article written by Loren McIntyre records the answer of General Jose Costa Cavalcanti, Brazil's Interior Minister, when asked about "article 198 of the Brazilian Constitution, which guarantees forest dwelling aborigines permanent possession of their lands and exclusive rights of its resources." His answer was:

> "Senhor, if all of us were hunters and gatherers, the entire world couldn't support ten million people. We will need room for 200 million Brazilians by the end of this century. Nevertheless, FUNAI is surveying Indian lands and setting aside parks and reserves there that will allow as much as 12 square miles per Indian." (McIntyre 1973:481)

FUNAI's President, General Oscar Jeronymo Bandeira de Mello was also interviewed by McIntyre and when asked about Brazil's Indian problem replied:

> "It seems that anyone - whether he's an anthropologist, evangelist, or newsman - thinks he has a better Indian solution than FUNAI's.

At this point in the interview he picked up a big of rice labeled KARAJA INDIANS - BANANAL ISLAND and said:

"The Indians must not be sidelined....They
must enter the mainstream of Brazilian national
life. To do so with dignity they must learn
how to work!"

     With this, he slammed the rice down on the table and said,
"This rice is proof that they can." (McIntyre 1972:481)

     Another Brazilian General, Rodgrigo Otavio Jordao Ramos,
chief of the Department of Production of the Brazilian Army
gave some of his views and opinions about the settlement and
occupation of the Amazon. He feels that the Trans-Amazonian
Road alone cannot resolve the problems of the region. He suggests
that male Indians be given the opportunity of joining a special
service in the Army called Frontier Commandos---These soliders
will be trained to scout some of the long isolated stretches of
the Brazilian Border and in their military training receive
special classes in Agronomy and other farming methods. Upon
completion of their military service, they would receive their
honorable discharge and the deed for a large parcel of land
upon which they could live using their newly acquired agricultural
skills. (Jornal da Tarde 1970:23)

     Some Indians now work on the road. Some become businessmen
who set up open-air "vendas" (stalls) in the jungle clearings
where they sell fruits, vegetables, pets and certain types of
meat to the highway workers. If an Indian wants to become
"Brazilian," he has only to put on a shirt and pair of pants
and "mix" with the crowd. This is rare, however, because these
Indians of the Amazon are noted for their rugged individualism.
They will push further back into the forests to sleep on their
leaf beds in the jungle rather than make the change to the
"patente" camas (beds) that the new civilization is bringing
up the highway by truck from Sao Paulo.

     There are more than 160 foreign missionary organizations
working in Brazil, but only seven listed in the directory of
"Protestant Missions in Brazil" actually work with Indians.
(MIB 1968:4,10,13,14) However, in a Missionary Information
Bureau survey, 15% of all missionaries in Brazil were found to
be located in the North, that part of Brazil that is called
Amazonia where the majority of all Indian tribes are located.
By far, the greatest number of missionaries in this 15% are
from the Wycliffe Translators who are engaged in linguistic
work in different Indian tribes and not directly working with
the establishment of churches. Not enough is known about this

15% that work in the Amazon. Some kind of survey is needed to supply this important information at this particular time.

Wycliffe Translators have headquarters for their linguistic work in Brasilia, and work very closely with FUNAI whenever they locate a couple in a tribal region. Several independent missions working exclusively with Indians in Brazil have their headquarters in Belem, and some in Manaus. The New Tribes Mission has a Bible Institute in the state of Minas Gerais whose goal has been the preparation of Brazilians for the work of evangelization with Indians in Amazonia. Very few Brazilians are motiviated for this difficult, exacting, and isolated type of frontier mission work.

Only one Brazilian couple has had notable success that has been publicized throughout Brazil with Indian work. Their work for the past 20 years has been among the Cayuas in Southern Mato Grosso south of Dourados. From time to time some reports come from Tom and Betty Young of the South American Indian Missions, whose headquarters are in Cuiaba, Mato Grosso where they have been working sice the late 1940's, but no substantial advance has come from this mission. Generally there is much frustration and discouragement, and a high rate of loss for first term missionaries who begin their missionary careers working with Indians.

At this important time in the history of the Evangelical Church in Brazil, a solid study of frontier missionary work among the Indians would be a substantial contribution to all mission and national church groups. Information is sorely needed for Evangelical leaders who must make important decisions in these areas.

This is a logical time for missionary and national church leaders to initiate a series of survey trips throughout the entire area that is being turned upside down. All of the significant literature in English and Portuguese must be made available, read, digested and carefully considered. All of this firsthand information and data is available for use in preparing courageous plans, both long and short term, for planting churches among the thousands of new settlers and remaining Indians in this largest of all remaining frontier land areas of the world. A vigorous, new form of frontier missions among settlers as well as Indians seems to be the challenge coming from this new activity in the hollow continent.

For those who desire to participate in such a bold venture, the time has come. Whatever a person, or a church or a mission, has to give to such an undertaking will be small indeed to the needs that exist and will be insignificant when compared to the harvest that is now in the stages of preparation. Needed, an army of volunteers for these frontier mission assignments along Brazil's frontier road system!

BIBLIOGRAPHY

A.A.G (ASSOCIATION OF AMERICAN GEOGRAPHERS)
    1973 "Indian Land Cessions" - Map Supplement Number 16, from
          Annals of the A.A.G., Volume 62, Number 2 (June 1972).

BRAZILIAN BULLETIN
    1969 (March) "Indians Preserve Tribal Way of Life in National
          Park."
    1969 (December) "Should Indians Be Museum Pieces? Experts
          Say No."
    1970 (April) "Background: Brazil's Tribal Indians."
    1970 (March) "Indians Learn Needed Skills Fast."
    1972 (January) "Finds Indians Friendly."

HENRIQUES, Affonso
    1972 "The Awakening Amazon Giant" in Americas, Volume 24,
          No. 2, pp. 4-11.

HILLIARD, Sam B.
    1972 "Indian Land Cessions" in Annals of the Association of
          American Geographers, Volume 62, No. 2 (June 1972),
          pp. 374.

I.B.G.E.
    1955 Culto Protestante, Rio de Janeiro, Instituto Brasileira
    1957 de Geografia e Estastica.
    1959
    1961
    1963
    1965

I.R.M. (INTERNATIONAL REVIEW OF MISSIONS)
    1972 "The Church and its Mission Among the Indians of Latin
          America," from I.R.M. (July 1972), pp. 252-256.

JORNAL DA TARDE
    1972 "A Amazonia, Um Problema" from Journal da Tarde, Sao
          Paulo (24-4-70), pp. 23.

KIETZMAN, Dale Walter
    1972 "Indian Survival in Brazil" (an unpublished Ph.D. thesis),
          Los Angeles, California, University of Southern California.

McINTYRE, Loren
    1972 "The Amazon, Untamed Titan of the World's Rivers, Flows
          Rich in Mystery and Legend Across 4,000 Miles of South

America," in National Geographic, Volume 142, No. 4 (October 1972), pp. 445-495.

MINISTERIO DE TRANSPORTES
  1970 "Carreteras Transamazonicas," Rio de Janeiro, a publication by the Brazilian Government for the VI Congreso Mundial de la Federacion Internacional de Carreteras.

MISSIONARY INFORMATION BUREAU
  1968 "Protestant Missions in Brazil," Sao Paulo, Brazil.

O.E. de S.P. (O ESTADO DE SAO PAULO)
  1972 "Hostilidade dos Indios" from O Estado de Sao Paulo (January 23, 1972), pp. 14.

THAYER, Yvonne
  1972 "The Amazon Catches Up With the 20th Century," from Brazilian Business (July 1972), pp. 8-15.

U.S. NEWS & WORLD REPORT
  1972 "Unlocking a Rich Frontier: Report from the Amazon Basin," in U.S. News & World Report (May 8, 1972), pp. 92-95.

VEJA
  1970 "Indios no Caminho" from VEJA (August 1970), pp. 18.

VILLAS BOAS, Orlando and Claudio
  1968 "Saving Grazil's Stone Age Tribes from Extinction," in National Geographic, Volume 134, No. 3 (September 1968), pp. 425-444.

W.C.C. (WORLD COUNCIL OF CHURCHES)
  1971 "Declaration of Barbados" from the Barbados Symposium, Program to Combat Racism, P.C.R. (1/71), W.C.C.

THE GOSPEL AMONG THE KARO BATAKS
A. Ginting-Suka

13

I. THE SPREADING OF THE GOSPEL BETWEEN 1890 AND 1942

In the earlier part of the 19th century, the major part of Sumatra was under the Dutch sovereignty except the Batak and Acheh regions which were subdued only between 1904 and 1907, at the end of the so-called Pacification War.

As soon as the Dutch got hold of the fertile coastal areas of Sumatra early in the 19th century, they invested in the land for producing raw materials such as tobacco, palm, rubber, coffee and tea. This land was made available by the Sultans in leasing it for a 75-year period. By the inroad of these investments, Sumatra was no longer isolated from the outside. It was now visited and resided in by both occidental and oriental peoples, mainly Dutch, British, Chinese and Indian. In order to secure common labor, the stricken poor people emigrated from Java for life-long contracts in the plantations. The new situation was resented by the native, especially the Karo Bataks of Deli and Serdang, who frequently made efforts to impede the plantations.[1]

Mr. J. Th. Cremer was a planter who made a proposal to the Government to educate the natives under the conviction that the situation would be better if they had Western education. It was for this purpose that the proposal for evangelizing was forwarded to the Netherlands Missionary Society (NZG) and the appropriate person in Holland. By the time the government granted permission for mission work in those areas, an amount of F30,000 was provided by the plantations. The reason is not known why the proposal was not forwarded to the Rheinishe Mission which had made tremendous progress in the Toba Bataks areas since 1861. It may have been that since the Rheinishe Mission was of the German Mission Association, it was thought that it would be a hindrance to the plantations' interests.

The Rev. H. C. Kruyt was the first missionary of the NZG to come to those areas, and he took residence at Buluhawar. He came

on the 18th of April, 1890, which was later considered as the
birthday of the Gereja Batak Karo (GBKP). It was a village of
200 couples adjacent to the tobacco plantations. He was assisted
by four Minahssa evangelists who were his former students at the
lower teachers' school of Tomohon, Minahasa. Besides direct evangelism, they also engaged in education and medical treatment. On
August 20, 1893, the Rev. J. K. Wijngaarden performed the first
baptism of six persons at Buluhawar. Another two persons were
baptized in 1894. The Third baptism took place in that year for
13 people. In 1900 there were 27 baptized members, which indicated that only 2.7 persons each year were added to the church while
there were five schools with 39 pupils.

In 1905 mission work was extended to the Karo Highland. However by 1910, that is after another decade's work, the membership
showed little growth, as seen by the following figures:

Karo Highland - 101 baptised members, 8 schools, 708 pupils.
Deli and Serdang - 331 baptised members, 17 schools, 113 pupils.

This reveals that there were 336 baptised members in a 20 year
period, which also indicates that there was an average of only 2.3
persons converted per year.

The progress of the Gospel was far greater in the Toba Bataks
areas since its inception in 1861 and up to the mass movement which
took place after 1883. In 1871 the converts numbered 1,250 and
after two decades' work the membership reached 4,958. This indicates that each year 20 persons were added to the church. The
actual mass movement began in 1901 and by 1911 the total membership
of the Bataks church was 103,528.

What was the reason for the slowness of the church growth in
Karo areas? As we look at the social situation of the Toba Bataks
prior to 1800 as described by William Marsden in the History of
Sumatra[2] there was evidently a similarity between the Karo social
condition and structure and that of the Toba Bataks. However the
latter had been merged into a solid structure under the Si
Singamangaraja dynasty. He was able to preserve his dynasty
through the 12th generation. They have the same type of community
organization, villages and architecture, even though Karo houses
are normally bigger than the Tobas.[3]

The clue to the mission success in Toba areas was not found
in the intellectual ability of that group to absorb Christian
teaching and values but rather in the political problems confronting the entire society at that time. A couple of decades before
the arrival of the missionary, the Sisingamangraja's dynasty had

been in a weak position, and the Selindung Rejas tried to loosen
their ties with Si Singamangaraja the 12th. At this time the process of Islamization in the Southern part of Toba Bataks areas had
been in progress. It actually began during the 1920's and at the
same time the Dutch colonial power had put the entire territory,
though nominally, under her sovereignty. Therefore by this time
the Bataks were confronting both the Dutch and the devoted Muslims
of Minagngkabau, who continually forced the Bataks to become
Muslim.

Ludwig Nommensen, a missionary from the Rheinishe Mission who
arrived in that area in 1861 had chosen Selindung district as his
mission post. This choice was right as far as the political situation was concerned. By this time Selindung could be considered
as a buffer state between the Singamangaraja areas and the Bataks
Muslim converts to the south. Nommensen was thoughtful in laying
out his strategy. In addition, Nommensen's personality as a
catalyst was a factor in the success. By his resoluteness, elo-
quence, sincerity and persuasive manner he was described as "the
possessor of sahala" or in the Biblical terms, he was a man of God.
He was able to make friends and was regarded as a figure on whom
one could depend.

Another evidence to support this thesis is that the actual
progress and growth of the church began in 1883, when Si Singamangaraja was undergoing diminishing power until he later succumbed
to the Dutch in 1902. People had to decide between 1883 and 1911
whether to cling to their tribal society or to be open to Western
influence.

The Karo did not have such a political background nor ever
had any devastating enemy from the outside; therefore when the
Dutch tried to occupy the land, it was the first experience of the
Karo in waging war against the outsider. It was evident that
although a part of the Delik, Serdang and Langkat areas was under
the Sultans' jurisdiction, there had been no religious war launched
against them. Islam had been brought to this country by the Sufis
from Acheh[4] who were more interested in religion than politics. The
Karo enjoyed their liberty in practicing their culture and religious system and there was no forceful interference from without.
The presence of the Dutch, therefore, was regarded as a threat to
their political and cultural heritage as well.

From the missionary resources, it is evident that they confused the missionaries with the Dutch officials. Hence it is
understandable that the parocial schools, hospitals and other
social programs had failed to attract them. They confused the
good that lies in them with the evil that was brought by the

by the colonial power, and they also failed to distinguish between the Christian Gospel and Western culture. "The Agama Belanda" -- the Dutch religion was the label given the Christian religion.

It was also felt that the mission school establishment was a part of the colonial structure. There was small enrollment and few sincerely desired to finish their schooling. School had been associated with the preparation of the future Dutch soldier. This at least let to the closing of the parochial schools in 1919. On the other hand, the literate people who had been enrolled in the parochial schools became more interested in politics than in joining the church. The situation among the Toba Bataks was different, where politics began to spread among the Christians rather than the pagans as it had made a great impact in those areas after the mass movement to Christianity reached its peak. Dr. Muller Kruger was right in his remark that the Gospel was too late arriving in the Karo areas.[5]

The natives in Deli and Serdang had been primarily concerned with their rights and the injustice of the plantations. This was the main reason why the nationalism-religious movement of the Parhudamdam had influence in these areas between 1918-1918 and had weakened the mission work during this period.[6] This might be the reason for the closing of the parochial schools in 1919. From the missionary point of view, this was the most desperate situation they ever had in those areas. Another event which proved that the Karo had been primarily concerned with politics, was the overwhelming of the Indonesian Peasants' Association a few years before the Second World War broke out. It was the passage to the insurrection against the native chieftains during the Japanese occupation which later on accomplished its goals in the Social Revolution. The Karo people were waiting for the liberation, but they could not recognize the liberator since he was disguised in a capatalistic suit.

The church has made a proportionately greater advance in the Karo Highland where resistance was not as great as it was in Deli and Serdang. The membership statistics of 1914 show that after 10 years' work in that part, 488 persons were converted. There were only 511 baptised in Deli and Serdang as the result of 20 years' labor. However the result was not determined by political factors only but also by the growth of the towns in the Highland. The people gradually moved into these towns, and this proved a stimulus to the church's advancement.

The second reason for the slow growth was the rigidity of the church's ordinances originating from the pietistic theological point of view, which failed to discern the truth and distinguish

it from the evil in the cultural religion. Since the church was
overwhelmingly ruled by fear, its method of reaching people was
negative and hence the converts were fenced by rigid laws. They
were not led to a living experience of the actual presence of God's
redemptive act. They were well-nurtured in a systematic understanding of God and Christ but had a lack of religious sensitivity. In
this sense the animists have more religious sensitivity than the
Christian. Because of this attitude the converts were not encouraged to become involved in any traditional rites nor allowed to
attend any traditional festivals.

On these grounds the Christians isolated themselves from the
community and became more individualistic. Because of this their
function as "Kalibubu anak beru senina" had been diminished to some
extent.[8] The Christian was a self styled minority in his own
community. The inability of the Christian church to confront the
cultural heritage limited the church's influence in the process of
reforming the culture's content and expression.

Despite all this, the missionaries sought to approach people
in groups. On several occasions such as the inauguration of the
missionary house and the church building at Buluhawar there were
200 and 300 people respectively that attended. Christmas celebra-
tions and open meetings were usually attended by large numbers but
they turned in no visible results.

As we again ponder the failures, it seems to me that the
method for approaching the people was not in a cultural context.
People were regarded as a crowd rather than a group of individuals.
They would respond more sympathetically if they are treated not as
an outsider in each mission program. They prefer to be included as
recognized persons in accordance with their lineage system. Therefore, they reacted negatively toward any program as long as they
were not included in it. The Missionary was concerned with goals
to be achieved while the people stressed solidarity, communion within the community, leaving the goals as secondary. No one denies the
fact that the missionaries had a deep concern for spreading the
Gospel. They had risked their lives by passing through the jungles
and meeting the resistent peoples. The last word expressed by the
Rev. J. K. Wijngaarden during his last hour in the hospital in 1894
and the expectation that was envisaged by the Rev. Guillaume after
he met the desperate situation in 1905, convinced us of the strong
biblical motivation that they had in bringing the Gospel to those
areas.[9] Nevertheless, as citizens of the ruling class they had not
been totally freed from the inherent status, privileges and pride
that was revealed in their manner in which they themselves related
to the native evangelists and the local christians. They never
made themselves real friends and were reluctant to hear any

opposition. The native evangelists, being treated in this way, copied it and unknowingly promoted themselves as the elite of the Karo society. This again created another chasm between the Gospel and the people. Therefore, the real confrontation between the Gospel and the people did not take place prior to the Second World War.

II. THE INDEPENDENT CHURCH AND THE MOVEMENT OF THE PEOPLE

As nationalism gained its influence in the entire island after 1908, the same fervour entered the ecclesiastical setting of the church. This brought about a division in the Toba Bataks Church in 1926 and in the Minahas church in 1934. It is wrong to say that these divisions would be looked on as merely political results. To some extent personal ambition had been involved. However, in general both the national leaders and the progressive missionaries saw that paternalism would no longer fit the new situation; besides it was unbiblical and would ruin the future leadership of the Church. The Mission Boards granted independence to several churches in Indonesia only after the people had struggled for it. This happened in the 1930's.

When the late Dr. H. Kraemer made his last visit to Sumatra in 1939, he was confronted with bitter criticism against the missionaries for their self-perpetuated paternalism. It was evident that after his visit the missionaries took new steps to share the leadership and the idea of Independence was on the way to be fully realized. Later on this was followed up by the sending of two candidated to the Pastor's School (Sekolah Pendeta) in Sipoholon in 1939 at the Toba Bataks' church establishment.

The formation of the Karo Bataks Protestant Church actually took place on July 21, 1941 in its first Synod meeting at Sibolangit during which two candidates were ordained to be full pastors. In the Karoao Bataks Church constitution it was stated that "the Missionary Association is 'teman meriah' of the Karo Bataks Church," which literally means "friend of." This laid the idea that both groups should work together in the Karo areas. It was also followed by the cutting of the budget. The Karo from this time would bear 50% of the total budget for the payment of the Karo Pastors and evangelists. Theoretically the Karo people had been responsible for their own church administration, but practically during the time that the Rev. J. H. Neumann was chairman of the church there was no opportunity for the Karo to lead the church by themselves.

Therefore the Karo were not prepared mentally or technically when they were forced to take up the church's administration during the Japanese occupation. The missionaries left the church without verifying any administrative matters, nor did they give directions as to how the church should function during their absence.

After almost one and one-half years without leadership the synod's Executive Body resumed its annual Synod's meeting. This was done only after the resolution of internal disagreements. The first meeting was in September 1943. At this time the members of the new Executive Body were appointed and led by the two ordained Karo Pastors. The fact would have been different if the chairman of the Karo Batak Church at its inception had been nominated from the Karo People, at least as the Vice Chairman.

Despite the suspicious attitude of the Japanese and some Indonesian politicians against Christianity in general, the church could keep its integrity and managed its witness. This was made possible only by the pledge given by faithful pastors, evangelists and christians. The social and political ordeal created by the war facilitated the church's maturity during which it was able to integrate itself within the society while retaining its uncompromised allegiance to the Lord. The real encounter of the church with the society in which it lives began when the church became indigenous as Christ took the form of mankind. Since then, the people began to understand that the real reason of the church's presence in those areas as a religious body was because it had a unique message. By the indigenization of the church, the christians were able to accept and to participate in the Indonesian Revolution of 1945. And being relatively more educated than others, some Christian youth had been responsible for its leadership. However that acquired status and the rapid growth was possible due to some spiritual development in the later days:

1. The Proclamation of the Indonesian Independence was followed by the Social Revolution in North Sumatra during which hundreds of people had been killed or executed with due legal process.

2. The formation of political parties which were eligible to have their own armed forces, led to a series of civil wars which later on were used by the Dutch as the main reason for launching war or so-called "police action" in 1947 and 1949.

3. Since the Karo Highland was made the stronghold for the Republic's guerilla war system, the Karo people had an opportunity for encountering an inter-religious context, and this later on opened their horizon beyond themselves.

4.   Political doctrine and organization introduced new ideas and
     brought about new values.

5.   After independence was secured, hundreds of Karos were accepted
     as members of the National Army and governmental service. The
     opportunity opened up for the Karo to live in urban areas. This
     led to renewed fervor in seeking the land left by the planta-
     tions around the towns, and this process continues up to the
     present time. Evidently those who live in the urban areas made
     great progress in the financial realm and therefore they have
     more access to mass communication than people in the remote
     areas. Being in the process of transition, however, they are
     in the dual position of being influenced by the former type of
     life while seeking for the new. In this process, the urban
     people are still very much the villager, but in terms of ambi-
     tion they are very much urbanized. They have lost some appre-
     ciation for the former faith and need a reinterpretation of
     their cultural heritage. This could not be provided by animism
     since it lacks the universal God.

When all these factors came together, the Karo were led to
look for something new. It was among this people that the church
made tremendous strides between 1950 and 1963, preceded by the
baptism of one Batalion of the National Army in the devoted Muslim
areas in 1953. In a 15-year period, the church grew from 5,000
35,000 or 2,000 per year. However another 60,000 were baptized
between 1966 and 1970, during which period the whole society was
shaken by the vague rule of the Central Government and its effort
to maintain order following the abortive coup of September, 1965.
The Karo people had been faithful adherents of the National Party
which ruled the country since its inception. But because they were
suspected of being in favor of the coup, actually led by the Commu-
nists, they were replaced and lost their confidence in any political
organization. They became skeptical and were unable to see any
future for the nation, and the pride of being fighters for the
Revolution was lost.

The church extended its service to this people intelligently,
not merely for the purpose of multiplication, but to present them
with Christ's Gospel in the context of their deep-seated problem.
Moreover, feedback was possible due to their long association with
Christianity through their relatives and the Bible lesson background they had had during their former schooling, which brought
fruit only after they were confronted with problems too hard for
them to solve on their own.

III. MISSION OBLIGATION OF THE CHURCH

As it has been described, the church had gained some respect after Indonesian Independence which later on opened new opportunities for its mission. The great obstacle of the past, that the Christian religion had been labelled as the Dutch religion, had gradually been removed, and hence the people accepted Christianity for what it is.

The Indonesian Constitution which put "the belief in the Supreme God" as the basis of the new nation, facilitates religious tolerance. Frequently it is thought of an an indirect encouragement to choose one of the existing organized religions -- Muslim, Christianity and Hindu-Buddhism.

The Karo people in general, after having a direct association with people of other faiths both during the Revolution and in their urban life, have been put in the crossroads to find a new direction. The urgency of choosing among these religions is greater in the urban areas than in the villages.

The question is, what religion is favorable and suitable for them? If they choose Islam, they will have greater opportunity in the future, since Islam outnumbers other faiths in the entire island. Though the Government is theoretically neutral in religion, the political and social structure make it possible for Muslims to have more opportunity in Government, trade and other fields.

However, the Karo people do not choose Islam despite the opportunity it offers, simply because Islam is too rigid against the cultural heritage. Islam, as it has been understood by the people, is totally different from them. To become Muslim is to lose one's identity.

The church was aware of the new trend and it has been able to cope with the new opportunity, though it was very weak in terms of personnel and financial resources. At this time there were only five ordained pastors and 40 evangelists, and most of them became school teachers.

The Dutch Missionary Consultative Body, which took over the former Dutch Missionary Association's responsibility, had little intereat in the Karo Church and no intention from its side of rehabilitating the former program. The church was left without parsonages as the result of the Second World War and the Revolution. Up to 1966 the total subsidy for the mission's outreach was only $600 to $750 per year. This does not include the Theological scholarships for Karo Candidates, which normally go directoy to the schools.

Since the church was so small and the members had not recovered from the damage made by the war and the Revolution, a strategy for mission had been laid out which made urban areas the first priority, with mobility of laymen for Christian mission, and the indigenization of the church.

1. In former times, the mission chose its station on the basis of preference for the plantations which provided the money on recommendation by the government for its own political purposes. In this respect, there had not been much freedom in laying out the mission's program when secular interest had to be taken into account in any policy to be made. However as time elapsed, the missionary had much freedom, and since then the mission had also been directed to the urban areas in North Sumatra. This indicated that the former ties between mission and the plantations had been loosened.

    It would have had a great impact if their work had not been interrupted by the War. A new era with a more promising future opened as moving into cities and towns became the trend. It will not stop so long as the villages cannot provide the same opportunities that the town and cities do.

    Despite some danger in this trend, the urban areas are more open to Christianity than the villages. In the urban situation, people feel that their religion no longer is adequate. They are seeking for something which is meaningful for the new situation.

    However, since they are also the children of the past, they cannot see themselves merely as Indonesians; therefore they are still looking back to the cohesiveness of life in the past. They are limited in their ability to identify themselves with the urban community. Therefore, whenever they go and take residence, they submerge themselves in the "in-group" community where they can nurture and practice their former social system.

    It is only the Karo church which has been able to express itself within the Karo social system. In this respect, the Karo church, which has made the towns its priority, could cope with the spiritual situation in these areas. Then if we examine the records of baptisms during the period between 1950 and 1965, it will reveal that the church was growing from the center of towns into the surrounding areas and to the villages.

    The process of becoming Christian is also facilitated by the lineage system of the Bataks; that is, by the endogamic

maternal marriages, the entire community is inter-related in
the family system. Therefore if one of the family, preferably the most respected, became Christian, then the rest would
follow. As they are coming from an animistic background where
the problem of religious truth is not argued, the group decision is possible.

Since the urban areas are relatively better educated and
wealthier and respected by their relatives, it was evident
that these people would be useful for the mission of the
church to the villages. Also the urban churches became the
source of financial support for the entire church.

2.   However, the opportunity would have been lost if the local
     congregation had not been able to understand the situation
     intelligently. Due to the limitation of church personnel and
     financial resources, the work could not be carried out if the
     churches did not feel their calling to express their faith
     openly. Stress on the mobility of the entire membership of
     the church and obligation of the Christian mission has been
     made. At least one must carry his witness to his family and
     friends. This trend has hammered down the self-styled super-
     church attitude of the constituted body of the local churches
     that used to dominate all the activities and program of the
     church.

3.   Despite the growth of the church, the issue of church and
     cultural heritage is constantly argued bitterly. The older
     generation of Christians refused the usage of tradition in
     the Christian context and believe that all religious rites
     and customs of animism belong to the satanic spirit.

     The new converts, who outnumbered the older generation by
     1960, believe that these practices have been secularized, and
     that therefore they will no longer do any harm to Christianity.

     Of course there was misevaluation by both those who favor and
     those who are against the usuage of the cultural heritage. It
     was not right to say that the usage of Karo musical instruments
     in funerals, weddings and the inauguration of houses is without
     any danger. However it is the task of the church to expel the
     satanic aspect from these practices so that they can be used as
     the means for conveying God's message. They will remain as
     they were if the church does not use them.

     It needs to be taken into account that some of this heritage,
     such as Karo dances and music, are related to the whole

cultural structure, without which the people will be empty
and lose their identity.

Finally after much bitter dispute, the Synod's meeting in 1966
accepted the usage of Karo music and dance both in church
feasts and outside the church service in weddings, funerals
and other ceremonies. The decision was accepted with great
joy both by the Christians and the society. Since then, the
common people no longer regard Christianity as a threat to the
cultural heritage.

However in recent years there has been a resurgence of animistic people who call themselves "The Merga Silima", which means
literally "The Five Clans", derived from the five main groups
or clans of the Karo. The movement is dedicated to reawakening the sense of belonging of the people by practicing the
traditional social system and beliefs. This reawakening is a
part of the reaction to the progress of Christianity after
the church became indigenous. What the Merga si Lima would
tend to provide is the pure customary law and orthodox beliefs.

This organized animistic religion adopted modern organizational system with primitive content, which stand in contrast
to one another. Moreover, they don't have a relevant message
such as the Christians have -- the living Word to be proclaimed
and to live by. They will break down by themselves from within
and become Christian if the church can have a broad-minded
attitude toward them.

The church is not concerned only with the application of the
cultural heritage to the church's institutions by which the
rate of the indigenization is generally measured, nor with
relating its program primarily by self-reliance as such, but
seeks its maturity in the form of Christ's Incarnation. This
suggests that the church could only mature and indigenize if
it could identify itself with the community wherever it might
live and to which its program is directed not because of its
generosity, but because it has to do so in order not to deny
its own nature as the body of Christ.

This would also indicate that identification is not necessary
for reasons of cultural adaptation, but in order that the
church live for and with the society as the instrument of
God's redemptive act. And if Christ's incarnation is the
basis of the church program of self-reliance, the church will
also be released from cultural and moral arrogance irrespective of how much of a particular cultural heritage has been
taken into it. This last statement nullified also the

church's conformity to the world. On the other hand it reveals that the church would not evade the social perdicament
but rather stand for it, because it has a great deal to say
and to offer.

Having recovered from the former mistake of not being able to
identify itself with the community need, the Karo Batak church
had extended its service to people in the chaotic period from
1966-1968, not necessarily in material help, but by self-
emptied concern for them. This was another difference between
the Christian mission and others who used to persuade people
by wealth and political power.

IV.   CONCLUSION

The church has made a remarkable growth since 1950, that is
after Indonesian independance. It was by the guidance of the Holy
Spirit that the church was able to cope with the opportunity that
was being presented. As has been described, the openness of the
formerly resistent people is due to the search for new meaning, as
the former values are no longer valid for the new Indonesian society. It is in this context that the mass conversion has taken
place.

Traditionally, the church has opposed any motive other than
spiritual as the reason for becoming Christian. Anyone who seeks
to be Christian on a selfish basis will be turned down by the local
pastor. Mass conversion has been denied as the ideal concept in
the traditional understanding of conversion. If the decision is
made in the spirit of the whole, it is thought it will lessen personal responsibility. The method of teaching and evangelism is
built on this concept and stresses the ability of the candidate to
memorize the creed and Bible verses before baptism takes place. In
mass conversion, this requirement is less taken into account.

It is undeniable that such requirements are worthwhile as
they brought about the right understanding of religious matters.
But too much reliance upon intellectual capability will lead to
the convert's lack of personal experience with God to whom he is
converted.

We also tend to underestimate the complexity of mankind. We
think by giving enough understanding of requirements, a person can
become a genuine Christian. However, the convert may cease to
practice paganistic customs outwardly but inwardly still be tied to
former values. The persistence of the former is due to the deep-

rootedness of the cultural heritage which began to be absorbed at a very early age.

Since conversion is a radical change in one's total value system,[10] it presupposes a lifelong process. Therefore neither individual conversion nor mass conversion will guarantee the quality of faith that one might have before and after baptism takes place. The bearing of fruit only takes place if one continually abides in Him. (John:15).

The second concern is how to nurture the converts who have left the former life in a search for meaning. The process of secularization will be continuing and will bring about further change. It is a challenge for the church to re-examine its message, so that it can adequately nourish the Christian for his own health in order that he be a strong and creative child of God.

If the message does not become indigenous, relevant to the needs of the people, then the church will die.

The third concern, as the church has a missionary zeal by which it has put all resources into the evangelistic outreach with remarkable success, the Karo church should be asked, what is its expectation for its future mission? Since the church has taken root among its own people, it is natural that such a church was able to invest its strength into its own people. Does the Karo church have an expectation and sense of obligation for communities of other social backgrounds? This would be another challenge to the churches in North Sumatra.

FOOTNOTES

1. M. Joustra Batakspiegel, Uitgaven van Bataks Institute no. 21, S. C. van Doesburgh, Leiden, 1926.

2. William Marsden, *The History of Sumatra*, J. M. Creery, 1811, p. 301.

3. M. Joustra, *op. cit.*, p. 124, 128.

4. P. Tambun, Adat Istiadat Karo, Balai Pustaka, Djakarta, 1952, p. 60. In an account of Teuke Syech in Karo Highland who was killed without making any effort to resist.

5. Muller Kruger, *Sedjarah Geredja Indonesia*, BPK 1959, p. 201.

6. E. J. van den Berg, De Parhudamdam beweging, Mededelingen van wege het Nederlandsche Zendeling Genootschap, 1920, no pp. 32-38.

7. My personal collections, unpublished.

8. An account of Anak Beru, senina and Kalimbubu in P. Tambun, *op. cit.*, p. 75.

9. Missionary letters, published later on in the Mededelingen van wege het Nederlandsche Zendeling Genootschap.

10. Eugene A. Nida, *Religion Across Culture*, Harper and McGraw, p. 85.

BIBLIOGRAPHY

1. Peter Bayerhouse and Henry Lefever, *The Responsible Church and
    the Foreign Mission*, Grand Rapids: W. B. Eerdmans Publishing
    Co., 1964.

2. P. B. Pederson, *Batak Blood and the Protestant Soul*, Grand
    Rapids: W. B. Eerdmans Co., 1970.

3. Eugene A. Nida, *Religion Across Culture*, New York, 1968.

4. Muller Kruger, *The Sedjarah Geredja in Indonesia*, Djakerta:
    Badan Penerbit Kristen, 1959.

5. Ronald Friedman, *Principles of Sociology*, Indonesian Transla-
    tion by Trikarya Bhakti S.C.

6. Ebbie C. Smith, *God's Miracle, Indonesian Church Growth*, South
    Pasadena, California: William Carey Library, 1970.

THE REVIVAL IN TIMOR
Frank L. Cooley

14

Note: This important article is in form of an answer to
an enquiry. Dr. Cooley has offered it for use to the
Consultation and The Occasional Bulletin from the Missionary Research Library. Major concerns of the Consultation are the consequences of the kind of original
evangelistic impact made on a people, the effect of the
types of Christian nurture and pastoral care provided
by a mission, and how the presence and power of the Holy
Spirit may be known. This report on a church not more
than two generations removed from the pioneer stage
throws light on these subjects.

Dear Dr. Shortess,

     I have been back from Timor a little over a month
and want to start fulfilling my promise to write you in
detail about the "movement of the Spirit" in Timor, as
it is connomly referred to there. Since writing my
earlier letter to you I have learned a lot and thought
a lot about the spiritual phenomena you enquired about
and their meaning and implications for the growth of
the Church and of the faith in Timor.

You wrote, "...I believe in the Holy Spirit and I believe that God through His Holy Spirit can do mighty works. But I am also a scientist by profession, and so I feel impelled to seek some sort of confirmation that these things are really happening."

My belief and situation are similar to yours. I am biblically and theologically trained in one of America's most respected divinity schools, an ordained minister in one of America's respected main-line churches, a missionary who has worked in two of the most challenging places on earth since 1946, China and Indonesia, and a social scientist who is engaged full-time in research work in the sociology of religion in Indonesia. And I, too, am puzzled and challenged by reports of what is happening in Timor.

Thus my efforts to discover and evaluate what has happened in Timor since 1965 are both in response to your question (and similar questions coming from increasing numbers of people outside and inside Indonesia) and to the demands of my own professional and private vocation. So I spent six weeks this summer in Timor, not just studying the spiritual movement but the whole condition of the Timorese Church (and other churches working there) and the environment or atmosphere in which it lives and works.

In the process I read all the books I have seen or heard of which deal with this question. They are:

1. The Revival in Indonesia, by Dr. Kurt Koch, a German Christian writer interested in the occult, who visited Timor twice and wrote his book in German from which it was translated into English (with some later writings added) and published by Kregel Publications, Grand Rapids, Michigan in late 1970. This book is the most detailed yet to appear and describes "the revival" in various parts of Indonesia, including Timor.

2. Dead, Yet...Live, by G. T. Bustin (Bustin's Books Publishers, Westfield, Indiana), no publication date, but also based on a trip to Timor at Christmas-time, 1968, only 44 pages, describing primarily the miraculous happenings in Timor.

3.   Like a Mighty Wind, by Mel Tari (as told to Cliff
      Dudley) published in 1971 by Creation House, Carol
      Stream, Illinois (of which Cliff Dudley is Executive
      Vice-President and General Manager). Mel Tari is a
      young Timorese Christian who was involved directly
      in many aspects of the spirtual movement.

4.   Miracles in Indonesia, by Don Crawford, Tyndale
      House Publishers, Wheaton, Illinois, 1972, 160
      pages, written on assignment and based on a brief
      visit to Indonesia including a week spent in Timor.

      Both Koch and Crawford relate the "revival" or
"miracle" phenomena for all of Indonesia, not just for
Timor, though the latter region figures prominently in
both.

      In addition to reading the books (significantly,
all written in English; there is nothing I know of this
nature and scope in the Indonesian language), I also
visited several of the places, including SoE where the
movement of the Spirit took place and talked with people
directly involved both as participants and observers.
In several cases these were persons I had known since
before the movement began. With these people, dozens
of them, holding all the varying opinions about the
movement, I discussed the matter fully using the
Indonesian language. This was the language of the
movement to a predominant degree. With only three or
four Western missionaries did I use English to talk
about what they thought had happened. Perhaps I should
point out here that Koch, Bustin and Crawford all
worked through interpreters. Mel Tari is Timorese and,
I was told, speaks English quite fluently, but the
writing of his book was done by another. Some of the
things they tell, about which you might like to ask
questions, but cannot, I was able to ask, though often
failing to get a clear or satisfying answer!

      There is one source of information, used almost
exclusively by Koch and considerably by Crawford, which
I did not have the opportunity to utilize. I refer to
the people of the Indonesia Evangelists' Institute at
Batu, Malang, East Java, whom it appears have been
connected with the movement from before its inception

up until now. The Batu people were not in Timor when
I visited, though they run a sort of Bible School or
Evangelists' Training School in SoE. I should mention
here that those who seem to think most highly of the
movement of the Spirit are those with a Batu-type
theological orientation, usually having some direct
contact with the Batu organization.

To summarize, I didn't go to Timor to study the
movement of the Spirit, but in the process of research
into the Timor Church I focussed fairly sharply at
times on the movement. Thus my observations may lack
in depth and sharpness of focus on the "revival" and
"miracles" aspect of that story, but they are probably
better rooted in the general and church situation in
Timor by virtue of my wider study, longer visit in
Timor than the others, except Mel Tari, of course.

What really happened in Timor? I should begin to
answer this question with a brief description of the
movement of the Spirit. I conclude that what is
generally meant by this term is a movement which took
place primarily between the latter part of September
1965 and the end of 1969. It took the form of groups
of Christians coming together in order to witness to,
and to experience, what they apprehended as "mighty
acts of God's Spirit". They also proclaimed the Word
of God for the confession of sins and the receiving of
liberation resulting from renewed faith in and
obedience to the guidance of the Holy Spirit. One of
the most distinctive features of the movement was the
formation of groups of Christians into "teams" which
went out to many of the villages and congregations in
the area served by the Evangelical Christian Church of
Timor. The teams were numbered and known only by their
number. They were led by one person who had been
"called" or instructed in some extraordinary fashion
which she or he always believed to be the guidance of
the Holy Spirit. The Spirit also revealed the names
or faces of those who were to be included in the
team as the leader's assistants or colleagues. Some
teams were small, only three or four persons; others
were quite large, possibly twenty or more. They were
composed largely of young people, many school teachers
and students of both sexes. Often they were led by
simple, uneducated folk, in many cases women, but

included elders, deacons and even pastors as members.
Where they went and what they did was wholly dependent
on the direct guidance of the Spirit, usually revealed
through prayer. The teams spent many hours each day in
prayer for guidance and for power.

The number of teams which went out is not easy to
determine. In the books and in conversations seventy
odd, perhaps as many as ninety teams were specifically
referred to by number. Koch's book on pg. 220, refers
to "150 evangelistic teams" (after his second visit in
1969); earlier, on pg. 159 he speaks of "the number of
teams having grown steadily and passing the 200 mark
already" (in July 1968). Such imprecision is natural
both because of the nature of the phenomenon and Koch's
distance from it.

Most of the teams originated in or near the town
of SoE, the district capital of South Central Timor
and went out initially to villages and congregations on
Timor, later spreading to the islands of Rote, Sabu,
Flores and Alor, all within the region of the Timor
Church. Some individuals and small groups went further
afield in Indonesia and even overseas.

What did the teams do? As indicated above, this
depended on the specific guidance of the Spirit in
each case. Usually before entering a village or house
they prayed together seeking guidance related to the
particular circumstances, problems or opportunities
they faced. However, there were several activities
generally undertaken. One universal phenomenon in
Timorese society, especially on the part of men, is
ownership of and reliance upon charms, fetishes,
amulets and weapons believed to embody magical powers
which help to achieve or maintain desired states.
Often illnesses are attributed to possession of and
belief in such fetishes, a kind of idolatry. Quite
generally, one or more members of the teams we are
referring to would have the gift of determing what
fetishes were being hidden, where and by whom.
Therefore, the first thing to be done in case of illness
was to have fetishes identified, confessed, revealed
and ultimately destroyed after prayer to erase their
power over the owner and his family. Countless healing
of illnesses caused by these fetishes were recounted.

Confession of sin was a second common feature of
the work of the teams. This was often related to
illness also, or to bad family relationships or relations between people, sometimes involving the leaders
of a congregation or village.

Preaching Jesus Christ to the people and witnessing to the power of God in their own lives and in their
experiences with other people, was a central activity
of the teams. Often meetings and services would last
for several hours, five or six hours not being uncommon,
because the teams, particularly the leader, clearly
manifested spiritual power and authority. Personal
"conversion" was sought directly of all, especially
those who had confessed sin, as well as personal
commitment to Christ and complete obedience to the
guidance of the Holy Spirit. This is the aspect of
their work which has led to its description as
"evangelism" or "revival". Most of the people in the
villages visited were nominal Christians; in certain
areas there were significant numbers of people
adhering to indigenous ("animistic" or "heathen")
beliefs and practices. In confronting the believers in
"animism" the teams would lead them to destroy the
shrines, temples, the objects and paraphenalia of their
indigenous religion. In all parts of Timor and the
surrounding islands, belief in spirits, demons, occult
powers, black and white magic are prevalent. This is
not uncommon even amongst those who call themselves
Christians and are baptised church members. The teams
therefore concentrated heavily on cleansing and
liberating individual Christians and the church from
these burdens.

I have mentioned the reliance on prayer. Singing
was also a prominent element in the activity of the
teams, especially in meetings in homes or church or
school. Also team members frequently engaged in
fasting, especially when facing difficult decisions or
problems.

In most cases team members travelled by foot,
except when going to cities and towns where they could
secure motor transport. They took little or nothing
with them, in keeping with New Testament injunctions.
Sometimes they took food, more often they relied on the
hospitality of their hosts for which Timorese people are

known. They lived very simply, relied on whatever was
provided for their needs. Thus there was no need for
a financial organization or fund-raising effort before
they went out. People of all kinds were moved to offer
assistance. It was a characteristically "faith mission".
Team members left their jobs temporarily and went in
obedience to the call. For several months the schools
in SoE could not function normally since many of the
teachers and students were away with the teams.

Thus the coming of a team to a village was
certain to cause a stir. In some it aroused expectations,
in other anxieties. To those who believed, the team
came as a blessing, they were healed and ministered to;
to others the team represented a threat, especially
perhaps to leaders of local congregations. The latter
was especially true when team leaders were very young,
uneducated people or women or both, people with no
formal status or recognition in the church. Yet they
demonstrated undeniable spiritual gifts and powers, even
though their knowledge of the Bible and the Christian
faith (in a formal, theological sense) was sketchy.
Some church leaders quite naturally saw them as danger
and threat to both their own position and to their
congregations. The fact that the teams were composed
of both males and females living in close communal
fellowship raised questions and eyebrows. In view of
the situation some leaders of congregations or presbyteries decided the best thing to do was to receive the
teams, let them witness and work but keep their activities under close supervision. Others decided that it
was best not to permit them to enter and work in their
area.

For the first several months after the movement
erupted, towards the end of September 1965, the teams
were very active and the movement was felt everywhere.
If there were as many as a hundred teams averaging six
or seven members each, then clearly this was a movement of wide scope and considerable manpower, which
could and apparently did make a substantial impact in
those regions where they were active.

Throughout the period when the movement was active
most of the miracles and mighty works recorded in the
New Testament were reported and were believed, by many,
to have occurred, especially healing of all kinds of

illnesses and physical suffering, by prayer and faith
alone. Both Koch (pg. 160) and Mel Tari (pg. 80)
state that more than 30,000 people were healed between
1965 and 1970. Voices, visions, dreams and
appearances provided guidance to team leaders. On
numerous occasions food was said to have been provided
in miraculous ways. In at least one instance it was
reported that team members walked on water to cross a
raging stream. They reported being given protection
from the rain, given shade from the hot sun, provided
with light for walking in the dark night, enabled to
brush the dirt out of their clothes when no laundry
facilities were available and no change of clothes
possible. Demons and spirits were overcome and cast
out. Several instances were recounted of persons being
brought back to life after being dead for hours or, in
a couple of cases, one or two days. Koch reports that
on eight consecutive occasions between 1965 and 1968
the SoE congregation was miraculously provided communion
wine from water drawn from a certain well or spring
after it was prayed over. Mel Tari states that this
miracle happened 60 times between October 1967 and 1971
(when the book was published).

Despite disclaimers and warnings by the writers of
the books, (Mel Tari; "...Don't put too much emphasis
on miracles. Instead put your eyes on Jesus. We want
Jesus to minister to our hearts and lives", pg. 91;
and Koch, "Miracles are not an end in themselves. They
are merely signposts designed to point us to the
Lord...", pg. 142), it is the very numerous and
lengthy reports of miracles performed during the Timor
"movement" which, together with spectacular reports of
"revival" and church growth, receives primary attention
and so raises many problems related to the events in
Timor.

I shall return to this subject again later when I
attempt an evaluation.

It is necessary in trying to understand such phenomena as these to know in some detail the environment and
atmosphere in which they occurred. This is particularly
true for Christians in the West where the environment
and atmosphere of the modern world are so different
from that of Indonesia in general and Timor in particular. The general conditions of life in Timor,

especially in villages off the main road, are much closer to conditions prevailing in New Testament times than they are to anything that can be found in the Western world today.

The atmosphere in Timor villages is almost wholly traditional, tribal, only half a century out of a completely indigenous ("animistic") religious sphere, and 94.36% of the people live in villages. In the indigenous situation belief in and practice of miracles, the visible, physical acts of the spirits and demons, the vivid manifestation of power in curse and blessing, the unquestioned authority of function-aries related to the world of the spirits and demons was practically universally held and experienced. This accounts, in one respect, for the continuing powerful hold of amulets, charms, taboos, curses, etc., on the Timorese.

The two major institutional structures in Timorese village life today are both non-indigenous: the govern-ment and the church (though many indigenous elements and to some extent an indigenous spirit characterize both). Both came to the interior of Timor (where most Timorese villages are) only after the turn of this century. Thus the Christian Church (both Protestant and Catholic) and modern government--and with them education and Western medicine--are quite shallowly rooted in Timorese village life. There are very large Christian communities in the Province (according to the Indonesian Ministry of Religion figures for 1969: 1,063,483 Catholics and 665,235 Protestants) but the level of Christian teaching and comprehension, and practice of the Christian faith in daily life are still very low, according to both Protestant and Catholic church authorities. The Protestant Church in Timor was almost wholly under the control, direction and financing of Europeans until as late as 1949, and the Catholic Church even more so.

This is one aspect of the background situation that must be kept in mind when talking about "revival," "miracles" and fantastic church growth", etc., in Timor in connection with the movement of the Spirit which began in 1965.

Another set of facts has to do with things already happening some time prior to the recent movement of the Spirit. For one thing, this is the third "movement of the Spirit" in the last 20 years, though surely the most far-reaching and spectacular. In 1943, during the time of suffering and trials under Japanese occupation, there was a movement similar to the recent one, lead by a Timorese minister and his wife, that originated in nearly the same place, aroused quite a stir, especially because of the healing miracles, lasted for two or three years during which time it spread to other regions of Timor, and finally ended in Kupang, the capital city of the region. A second movement, somewhat smaller than the first, surfaced in 1963-64 under the leadership of a layman, Ratu Alu, who with a group of followers went about preaching, performing healing and other miracles. But within a year or so the leader succumbed to the excesses of pride, women and money, against which he had been specifically warned by the Moderator of the Evangelical Church of Timor. Thus "movements of the Spirit" are not so unusual in Timor, nor are their accompanying features of miraculous events, especially healings. Indeed there are "healers" or medicine men (or women) in almost all Timorese villages who are believed to possess powers, knowledge and connections (spiritual relationships) which enable them to help under many sorts of circumstances of acute need. And it should be borne in mind that medical and healthy knowledge is very limited in the villages all over Indonesia, and medical personnel and facilities are even more scarce. Thus most people have nowhere else to turn but to "spiritual healers". In this respect, then, the situation was ripe for a third movement of the Spirit in 1965.

But there are still other interesting facts that may (though it would be very difficult to prove scientifically) be related to the 1965 movement. In two respects the people of Timor in particular, but also throughout the Province, experienced difficulty and anxiety-producing times prior to September 1965.

1963 and 1964 were reported to be difficult years for agricultural production due to extraordinary light rainfall. This caused acute food shortages and general economic malaise, particularly in the interior including the region of SoE.

In addition to the economic pressures, the population of Timor generally and South Central Timor district in particular (of which SoE is the capital) were under very severe political pressures. The strength of the Communist Party and the Indonesia Peasants Brigade (the C.P. subsidiary amongst farmers) was growing steadily and rapidly beginning in the early 1960's under Sukarno's "guided democracy" and by 1965 this political force was practically in control in many villages and districts. This placed both Protestants and Catholics in a very difficult position; many laymen had joined the Communist Party or organizations and in some places threatened to take over control of church organizations which caused not only deep anxiety but also much disburbance and conflict. Thus the period immediately preceding September 1965 was one of profound political, mental, spiritual and emotional disequilibrium. The movement of the Spirit broke out in SoE on September 26th, 1965, and the attempted coup (in which the Communist Party and its organizations were at least heavily implicated if not the sole perpetrators, as the Indonesia military courts have ruled) on September 30th in Jakarta and a few days later in the outer provinces. Anyone who knows these facts and the atmosphere surrounding both cannot help but ask whether there are common casual factors at work in relation to these two pheonema, or in the relation of the coup to the movement.

But there is no doubt among informed persons that events following the abortive coup--the positive attribution of it to the Communist Party by the Indonesian Army, the prompt rounding up, arrest, interrogation of all known and suspected communist activists and sympathizers and the continuous unobtrusive but widely known execution of communist leaders and those suspected of being such during November, December and January throughout the region, and finally the identification of a person's having no demonstrable religious affiliation (Islamic, Protestant, Catholic or Hindu-Buddhist) with being an atheist and thus a communist--proved to be strong motivation for thousands of people to establish or renew an affiliation with the Church. Thus Catholic and Protestant clergy and laymen in government positions, knowing full well the desperate plight of these people, accepted them into the church immediately, except in cases of known, pronounced

loyalty to the communist cause, leaving Christian
instruction until later. It was this, rather than the
movement of the Spirit that accounted for most of
whatever abnormal numerical growth took place in the
Christian Church in Timor between 1965 and 1969. This
is not to say that there was no effect of the witness
of the teams on statistical growth of the churches. I
am satisfied that there was. But I am also quite
certain that most of the "conversions" reported by
Mel Tari and Koch were from nominal or statistical
"Christians" to more serious and committed Christians,
which should surely be recorded as fruits of the
movement but not as striking numerical growth.

The final component in the contextual situation of
the "movement of the Spirit" is the unhappy state of
the Timor Evangelical Church (GMIT). Koch's description, derived via, if not directly from the Batu organization is as follows:

"The spiritual state of the churches was almost
catastrophic...Timor, therefore, had never been
evangelized, only Christianized. The former
atheistic beliefs, the magic and sorcery, the
promiscuity and alcoholism, all continued to
propser together...." (pg. 121).

While many serious students of and participants in the
Timor Church would question the accuracy and senstivity
of this unrelieved dark picture of G.M.I.T., they would
admit that there is more truth in it than they wish
were the case. Nor will anyone familiar with the
background situation set forth briefly in the early
paragraphs of this section be surprised at this.
Nevertheless, it is a fact that in 1964-65, prior to
Koch's not very accurately focussed snapshot of the
Timor Evangelical Church, evangelism was being undertaken both amongst and outside the membership of
G.M.I.T. by pastors, evangelists and laymen; converts
were coming, into the Church on confession of faith;
the Word was being preached, at least in some places;
the sacraments were being administered fairly regularly,
if not always with proper preparation, etc., etc.
However, at the same time it is true that there was much
spiritual and intellectual hunger that was not being
fed by relevant biblical preaching. There was much
lack of concern for the issues of social justice, human

suffering, intellectual and spiritual prostitution to
political ideologies and loyalties that was not checked
or challenged by the church. There was always a
decided tendency to spiritualize, futurize, moralize
the Gospel due to an inadequate and inaccurate understanding of a biblically based Christian theology on
the part of a large proportion of those with responsibility for preaching and teaching in the church.
Finally there was a generally uncritical stance, a too
easy acceptance of the "culture Christianity" which had
developed in this folk church. Thus the Timor
Evangelical Church was ripe for a corrective, was in
urgent need of renewal, was in a generally unsatisfactory spiritual state, and therefore was a proper
target for extraordinary activity and attention by the
Lord of the Church working through the power of the Holy
Spirit and through human instrumentalities such as the
Fellowship of Indonesian Evangelists in Batu, Malang,
East Java.

Such was the contextual situation out of which was
born the movement of the Spirit which started with
great vigor in late September 1965, grew in volume and
area covered, reaching its peak within a couple of
months. It continued unabated for some time and then
began to subside in volume and intensity by the end of
1966. However, the activity of the teams continued--
some of the earlier ones fading out and new ones
forming--until 1969. Since then there have been no
reports of new teams or new activities though the work
of some teams and individuals in some areas continued,
as it does today in a few places. Young people
continue in training both in the Bible School in SoE
and in Batu, Malang to be sent as evangelists to other
regions, but the movement in Timor is largely a matter
of recent and vivid memory.

What came of it all? How shall we assess its
fruits? What did it accomplish? I would attempt a
balance sheet in this way. First, what was the
influence of the movement on the Church in Timor? I
refer to the Evangelical Christian Church of Timor, but
do not doubt there were effects on other Protestant
groups, particularly those related to the Christian and
Missionary Alliance. As far as I could tell from
contacts with priests in various parts of Timor, the
movement did not spill over into the Catholic Church in

any noticeable way. In fact, I encountered in one or
two priests scepticism and even cynicism in regard to
the reported miracles. One asserted that the so-called
miracle of turning water into wine was simply deception,
adding potassium permanganate to the water to produce
the desired color and sections of the banana tree trunk
to get the taste of wine, the latter a quite common
practice.

What of the claim that the "revival on Timor" has
produced remarkable Church growth? Koch, Tari and
Crawford all affirm that 200,000 converts were won by
the movement between 1965 and 1970. What does a careful look at church statistics show?

Statistical analysis of church life and growth in
Indonesia is difficult and risky because of the
paucity of reliable data. Most churches do not keep
regular or reliable statistical records except on the
local level in some denominations. The Timor Church
can come up with two fairly reliable figures on overall
church membership: for 1953, 253, 501 and for 1972,
517, 779 baptized members. Thus in an interval of 19
years the Timor Church grew by 264,278 members. We
know that the rate of annual population increase for
Timor at present is 2.1% and it is safe to assume that
this figure has been fairly stable since the middle
fifties. On the 1953 base of 253,501 a 2.1% natural
growth for 19 years would yield an increase in membership of 100,147, assuming that all children of members
are baptized sooner or later. This would leave 164,151
new members to be accounted for in other ways. Since
there is little movement into the Timor Church from
other churches, it can be assumed that on the average
between 1953 and 1972, 8,642 persons each year joined
the church on confession of faith, from a background
of the indigenous religion. Thus it is clear that the
total growth of the church due to new accessions over
a period of 19 years is only 164,151, considerably
less than the increase claimed between 1965 and 1970
by the spokesmen for the "revival". Still a growth of
104% in 19 years is not insignificant. This means an
annual growth rate of 5.4% which if the % of growth
due to natural increase (excess of births over deaths)
be subtracted, leaves 3.3% increase per year due to
new converts.

It has proven impossible to secure any figures which would enable us to compare annual growth before and after 1965, when the movement began. It is reported that in 1954 the Timor Church was receiving around 10,000 new members each year from the indigenous religion. Obviously this volume of growth was not maintained for the entire 19 years, for if it had, adding to it the natural growth of 5,323 per year, would produce a total figure of 543,648 membership for 1972, 25,849 more than actual present membership. Indeed the Timor Church leadership reported a membership of 650,000 to the Council of Churches in 1967, but in light of the 1972 figure (517,779) and the undeniable fact that no reliable statistics were being kept, it can only be concluded that this was purely an estimate, probably based on very enthusiastic reports of conversions being registered by the revival movement.

It seems reasonable to assume that the rate of growth dipped substantially after 1955 when the Timor Church began to experience extreme financial difficulties. Again during the early 1960's, under the increasing pressures from the communist movement which was active and widespread in Timor, the rate of growth almost certainly dropped still further. And so it should be expected that the rate of growth would move up sharply under the twin influences of the aftermath of the abortive coup (which wiped out completely all communist pressures and influence on the Church) and the outbreak of the movement of the Spirit, coming as they did simultaneously as noted above. In several places in Timor I was told of mass accessions to local congregations immediately following the coup, and that these people were immediately accepted into most congregations in order to save them from being suspect of communist sympathies. After all, family and village ties are still very powerful in Timorese society. Thus, if it could be demonstrated that there was a marked acceleration in church growth after 1965 (which so far it cannot), it would still have to be shown that it was due more to the revival than to the radically changed political and religious situation following the coup.

Thus I am left with the conclusion that claims of extraordinary church growth (200,000 "conversions") resulting from the movement of the Spirit are greatly exaggerated, and that such increase as there was must

be explained at least equally as a result of the
radically altered political-religious atmosphere
following the abortive September 30 Movement.

To conclude this does not mean that the movement
of the Spirit had little or no effect on the growth of
the Timor Church; statistics can reflect little beyond
the quantitative dimension anyway. It does mean that
we must look in other directions for the influences of
the movement.

For instance, did the movement of the Spirit
affect the witness of the Church, the proclamation of
the Gospel? Here the answer must clearly be in the
affirmative. Both the range and intensity of
witnessing activities were heightened for those participating directly in the movement. If we assume that
there were around 100 teams going forth to "preach,
heal and cast out devils", and that the average team
had seven members, then at least 700 people were
directly involved in witness and ministry.

As suggested earlier these teams went out to
villages and cities close by and far away. They
covered not only most parts of the island of Timor but
crossed over into Portugese Timor and to the islands
of Alor, Flores, Sumba, Sabu and Rote. Some team
members even went as far as West Irian and Java where
not a few ended up in the Indonesian Evangelists'
Institute in Batu, Malang, East Java. Their work was
not only extensive but also intensive. They carried
the Gospel to areas and levels of Timorese life where
it had seldom been applied, thus deepening and
strengthening the faith of many. They demonstrated the
guiding influence of the Holy Spirit; they demonstrated
the sovereignty of Christ over "principalities, powers,
spirits and demons" which move freely and strongly in
the deeper levels of life and consciousness of many
Timorese. They helped many people of all ages and
classes to discover a personal relationship with God,
and to know his love and forgiveness in a personal way.

In another dimension their witness, preaching and
healing activities revealed, all too frequently, the
sad condition, the spiritual poverty, the formalism
and bureaucracy of the church organization as well as
the weakness, insecurity, pride and sense of preeminence

on the part of many Timorese ministers and congregational leaders. In some cases this witness had a
salutary effect, in others it resulted in rejection,
opposition and efforts to counteract the activities of
the teams.

Yet another effect on the witness of the Church
was the fact that perhaps for the first time,
certainly never before on such a scale, laymen, women,
young people and even children were actively and
devotedly participating in proclaiming the Gospel and
in serving the spiritual needs of people. This will
surely have long-term influence as well as immediate
effects in the life of the Timorese Church.

Another facet of the movement of the Spirit is its
effect on the unity of the church. What marks does it
get on this score in my judgment? Here the picture is
more complex and paradoxical. There are reports of the
reconciling ministries of certain team members who
seemed to be given special gifts and concerns for
unhealthy relationships in congregations and rivalries
and conflicts between church workers. In two areas,
south Belu on Timor and Thie on Rote, I sensed a strong
clear sense of unity in mission and church life amongst
the congregations. In the past both these regions have
been noted for their problems and difficulties.

However, on balance, I feel that the movement of
the Spirit has created a new division within the body
of the Timor Church. Several distinct factors or
forces can be seen operating. Perhaps the most obvious
and immediate, at least on the organizational dimension,
is the relationship of the revival movement to the
Indonesian Missionary Fellowship (JPPII) in Batu,
Malang. As has been made clear already the Batu organization has been an active participant in the movement.
It may legitimately be doubted whether the movement
would have occurred at all, or taken some of the forms
it did, but for the stimulus and direction of the
Batu people, especially P. Octavianus, president of
the Indonesia Missionary Fellowship and a well known
evangelist, and D. Scheunemann, principal of the
Indonesia Evangelistic Institute, both in Batu, a
mountain resort center near Malang in East Java. This
conscious and intentional identification of the movement with Batu, Malang both on the part of those

involved in the movement and those critical of it, has
definitely created tensions in the Timor Church. One
of the main reasons for this is that several ministers
of the Timor Church, and the presbyteries and congregations they lead, feel spiritually more loyalty to Batu
than they do to their own church and its leadership.
For example, two of the most prominent presbytery
moderators with close ties to Batu did not feel it
necessary to attend the last annual meeting of the
Synod Council which had to formulate policy on
important questions concerning church organization and
finance crucial to enhancing the unity of the Timor
Church. Thus for church leadership and many of the
ministers, this special relationship to Batu on the
one hand and the activities and influence of Batu on
the other have threatened to split the Timor Church.
Crawford, writing about this matter refers to "the
Indonesian Bible Institute at Batu, the school
credited with launching the disputed revival in the
now-divided Timorese church" (pg. 134). This can be
taken to reflect the judgment of the Batu people who
were Crawford's main informants. The Batu oriented
faction in the Timor Church has not formally split off
as yet, though at times the tensions have been intense.
In this a great deal depends on the attitude, spirit
and goals of the Batu organization. It is not a
promising development that since the beginning of 1972
they have established their own separate denomination,
the Evangelical Church of Indonesia.

A second factor contributing to the pro and contra
polarization in regard to the Timor revival movement
was a consequence of the preaching, healing,
exorcising activities of the teams. Experienced and
devoted ministers and elders of the church, together
with those not so experienced or devout, have never
been blessed with the spiritual gifts and power
demonstrated by some of the young team members. Thus
the work of the teams in the congregations often has
been seen as a criticism or challenge to church
leadership. When their authority was called into
question, one way of defending themselves was to refuse
to allow the teams access to their congregations.

Different theological emphases also lead to tensions
and division into factions. In general the theological
tradition of the Timor Church has been Reformed of the

staid Dutch variety, with little lively theological
interest or activity manifest. The coming of the
revival movement thrust into prominence several
emphases hiterto not in evidence: the dominance of
belief in the Holy Spirit, an emphasis on personal
salvation through a conversion or rebirth experience,
an emphasis on public confession of sin and repentance
manifest in changed life and habits and on absolute
reliance on prayer for guidance and power, to mention
the most prominent. Setting up such beliefs and
practices as essential to Christian faith and life
naturally tends to divide the sheep from the goats,
creating opposing factions within the church at all
levels.

Thus the revival movement has added yet another
source of tension and division within the Timor Church
whose unity is already made difficult to achieve
because of ethnic rivalries and loyalties, geographical
separations and historical forces. Until the
appearance of the movement of the Spirit, theological
and ecclesiastical differences were not important as
they seem now to be becoming. This is unfortunate,
unless it should lead to renewal of the church.

The revival movement has had no visible influence,
either positive or negative, on the service ministries
of the Church. This is surely due to the revival's
inward rather than outward orientation. This aspect of
the phenomenon is worthy of considerable reflection.

What about the spiritual life of the Timor Church?
Has it been nourished and deepened by the movement? Is
there any evidence of the renewal of the Church?

Some facets of this complex question have been
dealt with and need not be repeated. There is only one
presbytery, on the island of Rote, where there is any
noticeable renewal attributable to the revival. And
the moderator of this presbytery had at least a year's
training in the Institute at Batu and maintains close
ties with the Batu people. In the heartland of the
movement, the region around SoE, there seemed to me
little evidence of renewed church life. This not to
say that the spiritual life of individual Christians
has not been deepened. Perhaps the lack of influence
of the movement on church life is due to the basically

negative attitude and indifference of the Batu people,
and their Timorese admirers, towards the Church. The
work of the Holy Spirit at Pentecost created, or at
least launched, the Church. It established communities
of believers all over Asia Minor. This has not
happened in the region served by the Timor Church. If
it be said that the work of Christ and the Holy Spirit
instead of bringing renewal to Israel, created a new
community of faith outside Israel (the Christian
Church), and thus the renewal of the Church should not
be expected from such a movement of the Spirit as has
been claimed for Timor, we are left with no alternative
to the conclusion that Christ has no concern for the
renewal of the Church. Thus it seems to me a legitimate
criteria of the genuineness of the work of the Spirit,
whether or not it results in Church renewal. Of course
it may be said that seven years is too brief a span in
which to expect much widespread renewal. But I am
reluctantly forced to conclude that except for Thie
presbytery on Rote, there are as yet few signs of
renewal in church life that can be attributed to the
revival movement. At the same time, there are other
presbyteries where renewal is beginning to make itself
felt (Alor-Pantar, Belu) due to factors or sources
other than the movement of the Spirit we have been
considering.

While the **liturgical** practice of the church has not
been affected as a whole, it should be noted that the
movement has had a salutary effect on the practice of
prayer and singing in the congregations active in it.

As for the theological life and activity of the
Timor Church, except for the new emphases referred to
above, introduced primarily by the Batu organization,
there are as yet no discernable effects of the movement of the Spirit. No new, creative theologizing is
being done, despite the considerable poverty of
theological life in the Timor Church.

If increasing economic strength results from an
improvement in the spiritual condition of a church,
then, with one or two exceptions, it must be concluded
that there has been little change in the spiritual
condition of the Timor Church. Those presbyteries
most intensively involved in the movement, both as
regards sending out and supporting the teams as well as

receiving the ministry of the teams, have, if anything,
performed more poorly than the others in the matter of
financial support for the Timor Church. If it be said
that the local congregations have withheld support from
presbytery and synod programs and agencies but that this
does not mean there has not been an increase in
financial support of the church (which cannot be demonstrated from available data), then this would also
reflect negatively the spiritual condition of those
areas most deeply involved in the movement.

These questions we have been raising and answering
deal with visible effects of the movement on the life
of the church. Turning to a second dimension, what can
be said of the influence of the movement of the Spirit
on individual Christians and everyday Christian life?
Many aspects of this question have been touched on
related to those on the receiving end of the efforts of
the teams. Koch, Tari and others speak of 30,000
people having been healed of all manner of physical and
mental ills between 1965 and 1970. It is impossible to
check this out in any scientific fashion. There is no
doubt in my mind that a great many people did experience
what they considered to be healing through the ministry
of the teams. Many of these healings took place in
people burdened by emotional, guilt problems related to
the general spiritual atmosphere of Timorese society.
Liberating people by the power of the Gospel from the
burden of guilt and fear believing they are under a
curse, undoubtedly carries with it liberation from
physical and emotional symptons. A large percentage of
the healings reported to me were of this nature.
Perhaps it is an open question whether these should be
called miracles.

What was said above about the spiritual blessing
experienced as a result of destroying the power of
fetishes and amulets as a result of confession of sin
and repentance and of reconciliation with God and with
one's fellowmen need not be repeated here. Surely
many, many people experienced such blessings and were
enabled to grow in Christian experience and maturity.

What was the effect of active participation in the
movement of the Spirit on the team leaders and members
themselves? Here too I can only make a couple of
observations based on impressions gained from many
conversations and from the books referred to repeatedly.

My general impression is that for a large portion
of those active as team members the experience was a
most memorable one bringing them deepened faith and
maturity of Christian life. They remained humble in
the awareness that the power was not theirs but God's
working through them for a limited time and for
specific purposes. By it they were further trained in
prayer, in obedience and in relying solely on God's
guidance and power. After they returned to their
normal round of life they could look back on this as
the richest, most satisfying and interesting period of
their lives.

However, over and over again, both from the movement's supporters and its detractors, I heard reports
of team leaders and members succumbing to the spiritual
and moral dangers inherent in this sort of ministry.
The team leader, whatever his or her level of education
or status in society, had become such through a sense
of divine appointment usually by means of a vision, a
dream or an audible voice. Thus the leader's authority
was unquestioned and unlimited as far as the work of
the team was concerned. The team members were assistants
some with special gifts for certain kinds of ministries.
The team was composed of older and younger, male and
female members, few or many in number, and constituted
a communal group, sharing everything in common and
living together in intimate contact both spiritually and
physically. Much time was spent in prayer and fasting
seeking the will of the Spirit. Nothing was undertaken
without a direct sense of divine guidance or command.
It was a case of, "The Spirit says do this," or, "The
Spirit says we must go there.", etc. This tended to
create a strong sense of spiritual authority and power
especially in team leaders, even though these might be
people of very huble origin with little formal education
or extensive experience in the world.

Both critics and admirers noted that sometimes team
leaders or members came to manifest a spiritual pride
which was offensive and in the end self-defeating. Many
were the reports of "improper conduct" between male and
female members of the teams. Team leaders at times
affirmed direct guidance for behavior that was self-
serving or opposed to Biblical standards as well as
mores of the community. In some few cases families
were broken up when husband and wife differed sharply

about the movement, when one was away for long periods,
or became involved with someone of the opposite sex.
And finally there were reports of team leaders and
members profiting materially from their spiritual
ministry or coming to expect expressions of appreciation for their services. So it can be said that some
of the people most active in the movement were led
astray and caused to fall. But my impression is that
this was a small minority.

After looking at the effects of the movement on the
Timor Church and then on the individual involved, what
can be concluded about the effect on Timorese society?
Not very much that is either specific or conclusive.
It has been reported in a few places where the movement
was extraordinary influential that gambling, drinking
the local hard liquor, smoking, wasting both time and
money in large feasts, etc. --generally destructive and
harmful practices--disappeared. There are stories of
messages of criticism or advice to public officials or
influential persons brought by messengers designated by
the Spirit who were illiterate persons, often women.
There seems little doubt that the movement did have, for
a time and in certain places, a positive influence in
society. People of all classes became more open to the
Gospel and responded by cleaning up their lives.
However, there is little evidence that the movement had
the kind of widespread, permanent impact on Timorese
society that the Wesleyan movement, for instance, had
on eighteenth century English society. The spiritual
and moral range and the power of the latter sees to have
been much greater.

Finally, what about the miracles that have been so
widely and spectacularly reported? Did they actually
occur? Were the dead raised? Did water become
communion wine? Did the team members walk on water?
Were the blind made to see, the deaf to hear, the dumb
to speak? Or has there been fertile imagination and
great exaggeration in the repeated telling? I find
these very difficult questions.

There tend to be two general diametrically opposed
answers. People with a conservative evangelical theological orientation, a pentacostal or generally emotional
approach to Christian faith, wholly accept the reports
and defend them uncritically. For them these things

did occur giving proof positive of God's power and
mercy and of his direct, personal concern for men and
women in particular places and times. Some even see it
as the sign of a world-wide revival. Koch can write,
"God has therefore seen fit to begin anew and to
light his lamp afresh in one of the most contemptible
(sic,) corners of the earth today." (pg. 163). By
some the movement was seen as a sign of the Second
Coming of Christ (Acts 2:17-20). Again Koch, "He is
the Coming One and his are the footprints that can be
seen more clearly on Timor than anywhere else in the
world today." (pg. 163).

    The opposite response comes from those holding an
orthodox faith. Such people believe in the Holy Spirit,
in Christ's power over all things, and in radical
changes in circumstances worked by faith. They do not
question whether the reported miracles are possible,
"for all things are possible for God." They find it
difficult to believe that some of them, did in fact
occur. Many of the reported miracles present no
problem except that they would prefer not to call them
miracles because they can understand the spiritual laws
and processes by which they occur.

    These contrasting positions are largely determined
by basic theological presuppositions, one uncritical
the other critical, and neither position is likely to
be substantially influenced by the other.

    It is almost impossible for an investigator to
draw a clear distinction between the objective and
subjective dimensions of a particular case. Details of
place, time and persons involved were obviously not
important to the actors or the reporters. What was
important was the "miracle" itself as a sign of the
power and mercy of God. There seem to have been no
neutral observers on the scene when the events
occurred, only believers who were the sole source of
information.

    I attempted to check on some of the "miracles"
reported in Mel Tari's book, Like a Mighty Wind. I
found it impossible to confirm many of the healings
reported especially of the sort described previously.
Information given me regarding certain specific
cases he mentions makes it impossible for me to

believe they actually took place as reported. For
example, the account of burning the images in a Roman
Catholic church in Portugese Timor, and the case of
hesitation to take action suggested by the Holy Spirit
to bring back to life a woman who had just died. I
met this woman's husband and people told me that the
team had actually tried but had failed. One can only
guess how such a disappointing experience could be
reported as it was. Nor did I find in SoE, amongst
the people I talked with who were intimately associated
with the revival, any who had actually witnessed the
water being turned into wine though many reported
having heard about it. That something occurred once
that might have been understood or believed to have been
a miracle I have no trouble accepting, despite the
many voices affirming that it was pure deception. But
it strains my credulity to accept the report of
Mel Tari that this happened more than 60 times. "Since
October 1967, every time we have communion in our
church we just take water, pray over it, and the Lord
turns it into wine." (pg. 72). In Timor Church general
practice, communion is practiced four times a year.

It is understandable how in the excitment of a new
and astonishing spiritual atmosphere, enthusiastic
participants could produce reports that finally emerge
as miracles but which, with detachment might appear
otherwise. It is also understandable how, in the
immediacy of such unusual experiences, accounts of
events could change and develop to become more astound-
ing than the event itself. It is unfortunate that what
appear to them gross exaggeration in regard to events
claimed to be miracles, has led many people to a negative judgment and a basic rejection of much that has
happened in Timor. Such books as Mel Tari's and
Kurt Koch's give this impression, despite their
affirmations to the contrary. Perhaps for those
touched by God truly there is a unique apprehension of
reality invisible to those who remain bound by the rules
of "natural" observation.

To put the matter in biblical and historical
perspective, I will conclude with a quotation from the
Translator's Preface to the English addition of Koch's
book:

"We must remember that man looks on the
outward appearance, and that the human
race is more impressed by the tinsel of
sight, than by the imperishable jewel of
faith and love. We forget so easily
that the priceless miracle of conversion,
which continues to occur in both
Manchester and Morocco, and in the East
and in the West, is incomparably greater
than the mere raising of a body from the
dead.

Yes, the God of the Bible is still alive
today; the current events in Indonesia
testify to this fact. Let us therefore
rejoice with our brethren and sisters in
this distant land, but having rejoiced,
let us remember that it is not miracles
that God requires of us, but obedience
and that we "do justice and love kindness,
and walk humbly with the Lord our God."
(pp. 5-6)

Well, Dr. Shortess, when I began this report to
you I did not evisage it would turn out to be so
lengthy! But you will agree that it is a complex and
fascinating subject. I hope what I have written
helps to illuminate its multi-faceted character. I
will be glad to receive any comments you care to send.

                    Very truly yours,

                    Frank L. Cooley
                    Institute for Study and Research
                    Indonesia Council of Churches
                    October, 1972

Section D

A REGIONAL SURVEY

FRONTIER SITUATIONS FOR EVANGELISM IN AFRICA, 1972, A SURVEY REPORT

David B. Barrett, Mary Linda Hronek,
George K. Mambo, John S. Mbiti, Malcolm J. McVeigh

15

TABLE OF CONTENTS

I. INTRODUCTION

    This report describes the extent to which the Christian faith
has penetrated across Africa, by means of an overall investigation
concerning the situation in nearly half of the 860 peoples and
tribes on the continent, together with more detailed case studies
of 51 tribes representative of the whole range of peoples in
Africa. It is based on field investigations and other inquiries
over the period 1965-1972, which began with a 3-month field survey
from Senegal to Central African Republic, leading up to the report
'The evangelisation of West Africa today' for the Yaoundé (Cameroon)
consultation in June, 1965. Since then the project has evolved to
cover the entire continent under the title "The evangelisation of
Africa today', sponsored by the All Africa Conference of Churches.
From 1968-1970, questionnaires on the situation in specific tribes
were returned by co-operating missionaries, pastors, sociologists
and several kinds of research worker in all parts of the continent.
Subsequently, the assistance of specialists has been sought in
order to arrive at an accurate analysis of the situation. This
report attempts to give an overall analysis only, and does not go
into details of unevangelised areas in each tribe, or current
mission programs there. The number of unreached areas in each
tribe is given in coded form in Table 4, column 13; persons wanting the actual location of such areas should approach existing
agencies there. Likewise, this report does not go into details
concerning current programs of individual churches and missions at
work in frontier situations today, since the number of these bodies
is legion (207 are listed in the appendix); persons wanting such
information can approach direct any agencies working in the area
they are interested in. In the same way, persons needing to trace
any expert knowledgeable on a particular tribe and its situation
will find that in most cases the only such experts are actually
working there at present, and so can be contacted through the
agencies at work. Neither does this report describe new forms of
Western involvement in mission (assistance to African independent
churches, radio and television ministry, literature, theological
training, urban mission, etc.). Instead, the focus here is not on
what foreign agencies are going, but on what response to Christianity African peoples have made, are making, or could make if they
were to be given the opportunity.

    To be properly understood, a survey of this type should be
interprated as in the main a comparative and cross-cultural study,
setting out the general order of magnitude of the situation -- i.e.
as a survey giving a general idea of the number of unevangelised
peoples, their approximate populations and religious followings,
and their relative position with respect to religious profession
and evangelisation. Detailed local data may be given at numerous

points, but the main objective of the study is to present a con-
spectus or overview of the overall situation. It follows therefore
that neither total accuracy nor total inclusiveness can be claimed
for this type of survey -- neither accuracy to the last diget in
the statistics, nor any assertion that all existing unevangelised
tribes in Africa have been located and included. From this point
of view, the data can be divided into three categories of accuracy.
In a number of cases here, a particular statistic -- number, percentage, or year -- is based on exact data and can therefore be
regarded as accurate (the clearest examples are the dates of
Scripture publication in each tribe). In a number of other cases,
a statistic may be given here to several digits (e.g. '107,092'),
which indicates that it is based on some kind of head count or
other aggregate and therefore lays claim to a certain accuracy.
Such statistics are also reproduced in full to facilitate their
identification by observers familiar with the local situation, who
will therefore know the accuracy or otherwise of the particular
statistic and will know whether more up-to-date figures have
become available. Then thirdly, there is the majority of statistics
produced by this survey, namely those given as rounded estimates
with several zeros (e.g. '100,000'); this is meant to indicate that
they claim only to represent the general order of magnitude at that
point. This is particularly the case with tribal population figures.
The same is also true with percentage figures given in tens (10%,
20%, 50%, 80%, 90%), which are clearly intended to supply only a
rough idea of relative size, in contrast to more exact percentages
(e.g. 'Kenya is 6.4% Muslim') which are based on more detailed data
and calculations. The only exceptions to this are the percentage
figures for traditionalists, which are derived in most cases by
subtracting Muslims and Christians from 100%, and so are usually
given to the last digit. Lastly, it should be stressed that the
data presented here are only the best estimates that were available
at the time of enquiry; but although more detailed or accurate data
may later become available at numerous points, it is not likely to
alter the main conclusions of this survey nor the general order of
magnitude of the situation as it is portrayed here.

II. DEFINITIONS: FRONTIER SITUATIONS AND EVANGELISATION

     There are many kinds of religious frontier in contemporary
Africa, and this survey does not attempt to describe them all.
Rather, it attempts to delineate the basic demographic frontier
or frontiers between Christianity and the other religions -- the
frontier between faith and non-faith, from the Christian point of
view. In particular, it describes the approximate numerical
strength of Africa's *traditionalists*, i.e. those who follow the
religious systems evolved in Africa before the arrival of the

immigrant religions, Islam and Christianity (in this report we
describe them as traditionalists and reject the older terminology
-- pagans, animists, fetishists, etc.). *Frontier situations*,
therefore, are defined here as demographic situations in which
the bulk of the population of a people or tribe are non-Christians
but are relatively open to the Christian faith were it to be adequately presented. *Frontier missions*, similarly, are any projects
of pioneer or primary evangelism and church-gathering directed
towards peoples still largely traditionalist in religion and
culture. Such missions have often in the past been initiated by
foreign missionary societies from the Western world, but are now
increasingly being sponsored under African leadership by the
autonomous Protestant and Catholic churches in Africa.

It is essential throughout this survey to make a clear distinction between (a) *evangelisation*, and (b) *christianisation or
conversion*. Non-Christian peoples can be evangelised without
necessarily becoming Christians or professing conversion. Individuals of another religion, or a family, or a tribe, or a nation,
can be said to have been *evangelised* when they have come into
contact with Christianity sufficiently for them to have heard the
good news about Jesus Christ and to have had an opportunity of
responding to it by faith; i.e. people have been evangelised when
they have been exposed in one way or another to the gospel. If
they then reject Christianity or do nothing further about it, they
are still evangelised but remain as non-Christians. If, on the
other hand, they respond to the gospel and profess to accept it,
they are *christianised*, which means they become professing Christians, and we can speak of them as professing conversion to
Christianity. The number of people in a tribe who have been
evangelised must therefore always be somewhat larger than the
number who have been christianised and profess conversion.

The next point is that the concept of evangelisation goes
deeper than the merely numerical penetration of the population to
proclaim the gospel, i.e. the bringing of numbers of individuals,
families or communities into contact with Christianity and the
confronting of them with the challenge and the offer of Christ.
Evangelisation goes beyond them as individuals or groups to
encompass also the penetration of their tribal philosophy and
world-view by the Christian ethic and world-view. It is for this
reason that the translation of the Scriptures into a tribe's own
vernacular language ('the soul of a people') is of such importance
in the total process of evangelisation, since as a result the culture and tradition of the tribe become gradually permeated with
Christian ideals and values, and traditional words and ideas are
given Christian meaning and become 'baptised into Christ'. In
this survey, therefore, evangelisation has this two-fold connotation

of (a) numerical penetration of tribal populations through proclamation and the hearing of the gospel, and (b) cultural penetration
of tribal philosophies through Scripture translations and christianisation of traditional religion.

It can be seen that data are set out in the tables here in
such a way that they facilitate differing ways of definition or
analysis. Thus if a reader thinks that the dividing line between
our definitions of evangelised and unevalgelised tribes (50%) is
too high, and wishes to define unevangelised at 20%, 10%, or 5%
or less, he can immediately go through Table 4 (column 13) seeing
which tribes remain unevangelised on his new definition. The map
assists in this by showing unevangelised tribes in four colours:
dark red for little-evangelised peoples (10% or less), medium red
for partially evangelised peoples (15-45%), light red for half-
evangelised peoples (50%), and yellow for evangelised (over 50%)
peoples resistant to Christianity (i.e. still 60% or more traditionalist).

Lastly, it should be noted that with the sole exception of
literacy percentages (which are always given for only the adult
population aged 15 and over), all population figures or percentages
in this survey include young children and infants, who are assumed
to have the characteristics of their parents. Thus the children
of Protestants are counted as Protestants, and the children of
Catholics are counted as Catholics; likewise with Muslims and
traditionalists. In the same way, the percentages and numbers of
evangelised and unevangelised include, together with their parents,
infants and young children not yet able to hear or respond to the
Christian faith for themselves. Thus a statement that a tribe is
95% evangelised means that the Christian faith has reached 95% of
all persons capable of hearing and responding, together with their
infants.

III. THE PRESENT EXTENT OF CHRISTIANITY IN AFRICA

The first of the four tables in this report, Table 1, summarises the present situation with regard to the penetration of
Christianity across Africa. Its layout and contents must first be
explained.

Table 1 sets forth, for every nation and territory in Africa
and its surrounding islands, a panoramic view of the progress and
penetration of Catholic and Protestant Christianity, together with
three different kinds of percentage index by which the present
state of evangelisation in Africa may be assessed (cols. e, m, and
w, shown underlined below). Columns n and o give the years when

Catholic and Protestant missionary work was first begun; columns
g and h give the present percentages of professing Christians,
Catholic and Protestant; columns j-l show the total number of
Scripture translations available in the nation's languages, and
columns p-r give the number of Catholic dioceses, Protestant and
other Western denominations, and African independent churches;
columns s and t then contrast the present national totals for
Christians and followers of traditional religion (traditionalists).
Lastly, columns u and y estimate the number of unevangelised persons in each nation: in peoples in frontier situations, and in
the whole nation; and column x summarises the number of peoples
in frontier situations that this report describes.

KEY TO COLUMNS IN TABLE 1

a. Population in mid-1972 (based on United Nations Population
    Division tables).
b. Number of distinct African tribes-in-nations indigenous to
    the nation (Murdock's classification: see explanation at
    beginning of section IV, and map in appendix). In about 185
    cases, a tribe is split by national frontiers (because of
    former arbitrary colonial boundaries) into sufficiently large
    segments to be counted here as being present in each of the
    two or more nations. This explains why the total for the
    continent (1,045) is greater than the total of 860 district
    tribes or ethnic units used in this survey and shown (with
    the exception of pygmy groups) on the map.
c. Size of urbanised opulation (usually, in towns over 2,000
    in size) as percentage of whole population.
d. Literacy in the nation; percentage of literates among adults
    over 15 years of age.
e-h. Religious profession, i.e. percentage of population professing
    (in censuses) to follow the various religions, in mid-1972.
    Professing Christians are often 50% larger in number than
    affiliated Christians (on the churches' rolls or records);
    and affiliated Christians may be from two to five times larger
    than practising Christians who regularly attend church. As a
    very approximate guide, therefore, affiliated Christians may
    be estimated from this table by multiplying professing Chris-
    tians by 0.7; and practising Christians may be estimated by
    dividing professing Christians by 4. Note that although the
    four figures in these columns (and in columns 2-5 of Tables 2,
    3 and 4) usually add up to 100% because of large populations
    of additional religions (e.g. Mauritius, 48.7% Hindu; Falasha
    tribe of Ethiopia, 93% Jewish).
e. *Traditionalists* (followers of traditional tribal religion,
    formerly called pagans or animists), %.

f.   Muslims, %.

g.   Catholics (baptised, catechumens, and all other professing adherents), %.

h.   Protestants, Anglicans, Orthodox, and African independent, %.

i.   Number of distinct African languages indigenous to the nation.

j-1. Number of indigenous African languages in which scriptures (of the three following types) have been translated and published.

j.   Gospels (portions).

k.   New Testaments.

l.   Complete Bibles.

m.   *Existing scripture translations progress* expressed as a percentage of all possible translations into indigenous languages; = cols. j + k + l, divided by 3 times col. i, x 100%.

n.   Year when permanent Catholic missionary work began (excluding 15th-18th century missions in tropical Africa which were later abandoned).

o.   Year when first Protestant, Anglican or independent missionary work began (Nil = no organised missionary work).

p-r. Total number of distinct Christian bodies at work in the nation, of the three types following.

p.   Catholic dioceses or other jurisdictions.

q.   Protestant, Anglican, and Orthodox denominations (excluding dioceses or other sub-divisions).

r.   African independent (indigenous) churches (distinct denominations).

s.   Total number of professing Christians in the nation (derived by multiplying col. a by col. g + col. h).

t.   Total number of traditionalists (derived by multiplying col. a by col. e).

u-x. Present state of evangelisation in the nation.

u.   Number of unevangelised persons in tribes in frontier situations (derived in Table 4, column 14).

v.   Total number of unevangelised persons in nation (rough rounded estimates based on column u, also Table 3, and other data). Note that here as elsewhere in this report, infants and young children of evangelised or unevangelised adults are counted together with their parents. The totals in this column are only intended to give very approximately the general order of magnitude of the unevangelised in each nation. In the Muslim north African nations, the estimates take into consideration such factors as the growing ubiquity of transistor radios and Christian broadcasting, the constant migration of Christians in nations' labour forces, Christian literature programmes and correspondence courses, the presence of numerous foreign chaplaincy churches, and (in the case of Egypt) the widely dispersed Coptic Orthodox Church throughout the land.

Hence it is assumed here that something like 40% of Egyptians have been exposed to Christianity in some form, with the figure reduced to 30% for the rest of the Muslim nations. Since these totals contain millions of Muslims, whose evangelisation presents its own special difficulties and is often virtually impossible to attempt, this column should not be regarded as a measure of evangelistic opportunity; for a measure of the latter sort, it is better to use the preceding column, u, which enumerates peoples as yet unexposed to evangelisation but relatively open to it.

w. *Status of evangelisation* index (SE), indicating the extent to which the total primary evangelistic task in a nation (viewed as the twofold one of evangelising the individuals making up the nation, and of providing the scriptures in all its languages, i.e. numerical and cultural evangelisation) has been completed. This index is defined as follows: SE = (1 - col. v/col. a, x col. m), per cent. The maximum value of this index, 100%, indicates a fully-evangelised nation with the complete Bible available in all its languages.

x. Number of unevangelised or frontier situation tribes-within-nations in this nation (total derived from listing in Table 4). A tribe with its sub-tribes is counted as only one unit in this survey.

IV. THREE CATEGORIES OF REACTION TO CHRISTIANITY

To assist clarity in enumeration, this survey speaks about both *tribes* and *tribes-within-nations*. A tribe is usually defined as a cluster or group of people sharing a common name, language, culture and territory; one usually speaks of there being a total of 860 tribes in Africa, and these are shown with their names on the map appended to this report. Long after the tribes and their boundaries came into existence, however, a whole network of colonial frontiers was superimposed on the continent, which have evolved into the national boundaries of today, also shown on the map; these largely ignored, and still ignore, tribal boundaries. As a result, about 185 tribes are today seriously split by national frontiers into large or otherwise significant units, which then become for their members the basic social units within which people have to live. This unit is referred to in this report as the 'tribe-within-nation'. Thus the single Yao tribe, who live in Malawi, Mozambique and Tanzania, formerly under differing colonial regimes and now under equally differing types of national government, are counted in Table 2 as three distinct units or 'tribes-within-nations'.

For the purposes of analysis, this survey divides the 860 tribes of Africa (1,045 tribes-within-nations) into three categories as follows:

TABLE 1: THE EXTENT OF CHRISTIAN PENETRATION ACROSS AFRICA, MID-1972

Nation	Population mid-1972 (a)	Trt (b)	Urb % (c)	Lit % (d)	Tr (e)	Mu (f)	RC (g)	PAOI (h)	Lang (i)	G (j)	NT (k)	Bi (l)	Z (m)	Origin RC (n)	Proc (o)	RCdio (p)	PrAO (q)	AICs (r)	Christians (s)	Tradits (t)	Frontier (u)	Total (v)	SEZ (w)	Tribes unev (x)
Algeria	15,052,000	24	40	25	0	99.4	0.5	0.1	10	5	4	2	37	1838	1881	4	16	0	90,300	0	84,500	10,000,000	12	0
Angola	5,957,000	30	14	10	17	0	62	21	25	14	8	2	35	1873	1878	8	13	7	4,944,300	1,012,700	48,500	600,000	31	5
Botswana	654,000	13	7	33	38	0	4	58	12	9	6	4	25	1880	1833	1	16	25	405,500	248,500	24,000	100,000	21	5
Burundi	3,788,000	2	3	5	23.4	0.6	58	18	3	21	16	1	67	1879	1911	5	9	2	2,878,900	886,400	1,062,500	660,000	56	1
Cameroon	6,065,000	54	22	70	29	19	38	18	134	21	16	6	10	1406	1947	11	14	11	3,153,800	1,758,900		2,000,000	7	23
Canary Is (Spain)	945,000	1		70	0	0	99	1	1	1		0	100	1456	Nil	1	1	0	935,000	0	0	50,000	95	0
Cape Verde Islands	256,000	1		70	0	0	98	2	1	0		0	100	1894	Nil	1	1	0	253,400	0	2,800	12,000	31	0
Central African Rep	1,598,000	17	29	18	7	7	36	54	24	9	6	1	22	1894	1918	5	10	3	1,438,200	111,900	323,000	80,000	21	4
Chad	3,901,000	38	9	13	42	42	30	15	73	13	1	1	10	1929	1920	5	10	4	1,716,400	546,100		1,500,000	6	4
Comoro Islands	269,000	1			0	99.5	0.5	0.1	2	0		0	50	1845	Nil	0	1	0	1,300	0		250,000	3	0
Congo (Brazzaville)	984,000	15	36	35	0.9	0	59	39.8	16	8	6	1	29	1883	1900	3	5	5	972,200	8,900	6,900	50,000	28	2
Dahomey	2,842,000	9	11	35	66	14	16.5	3.5	17	9	6	2	37	1864	1815	6	28	7	568,400	1,875,700	1,059,500	1,700,000	15	6
Egypt	35,996,000	9	43	25	0	87.7	0.7	12	4	3	1	1	30	1839	1841	11	30	2	4,300,000	0		21,000,000	13	0
Equatorial Guinea	294,000	47	8	73	8.5	0.5	87.5	3.5	10	9	3	0	27	1841	1818	2	1	0	267,500	25,000		15,000	26	0
Ethiopia	26,225,000	2	76	7	14	35	0.8	50	49	14	4	2	21	1839	Nil	8	30	2	13,300,000	3,671,500	1,669,300	5,000,000	17	15
FT Afars and Issas	85,000	10	34	13	0	90.3	3	0.9	2	1		0	35	1883	1821	1	1	3	8,200	0		70,000	2	0
Gabon	491,000	10	10	13	3.4	0.6	68	28	19	4	4	2	33	1844	1842	3	1	3	471,400	16,700		25,000	33	0
Gambia	380,000	5	10	10	12	85	3	2	6	2	1	0	18	1445	1821	1	9	0	19,000	38,000		190,000	5	0
Ghana	9,662,000	33	29	35	25	12	20	43	52	18	5	5	18	1879	1855	8	19	300	6,087,100	2,415,500	906,500	1,900,000	14	10
Guinea	4,120,000	14	10	10	51	87	1	0	11	11		1	45	1849	1928	3	11	0	41,200	1,194,800	1,492,000	2,500,000	18	13
Ivory Coast	4,540,000	31	20	40	24	23	15	5.8	41	18	4	1	17	1895	1833	11	48	40	1,135,000	2,315,400	1,473,600	2,000,000	10	13
Kenya	12,091,000	27	10	20	13	6.4	28.1	38.1	40	28	10	10	48	1862	1844	13	19	160	8,004,200	3,182,000	740,400	2,000,000	40	9
Lesotho	1,086,000	1	2	35	0	0	41	46	2	1	1	2	50	1862	1820	3	9	100	944,800	141,200		50,000	47	0
Liberia	1,222,000	14	15	9	50	8	2.1	42	20	11	1	1	25	1856	1882	2	19	50	513,200	611,000	327,700	370,000	17	7
Libyan Arab Rep	2,009,000	11	25	35	0	97.8	2	0.1	1	1		0	20	1642	1882	4	9	0	48,200	0		1,400,000	6	0
Madagascar	7,356,000	10	14	30	37.2	20.8	25	18	5	1	1	1	100	1642	1820	5	9	20	3,089,500	2,736,400	113,200	2,000,000	73	2
Malawi	4,693,000	11	6	30	32	15	25	28	8	8	7	1	75	1879	1882	9	6	40	2,487,300	1,501,800		800,000	62	8
Mali	5,358,000	18	12	3	77	23	1	0.5	29	7		1	19	1950	1919	6	7	0	85,700	1,146,600	1,689,900	3,000,000	8	7
Mauritania	1,231,000	9	8	3	21.4	99.4	0.6	0	4	1		0	25	1722	1962	1	7	0	7,400	0		1,000,000	5	0
Mauritius	907,000	1	46	62	0	15.8	33.8	1.7	1	1	1	1	33	1859	1880	1	13	0	322,000	0		200,000	26	0
Morocco	16,904,000	14	34	15	0	97.2	1.4	0	21	16		0	51	1867	1862	9	17	0	236,700	0		11,800,000	15	0
Mozambique	8,076,000	18			54	11	27	7	14	6	6	1	36	1870	1842	13	17	80	2,745,800	4,361,600	2,427,000	3,500,000	29	14
Namibia (SW Africa)	660,000	8	26	40	16	0	15	69	7	4	3	1	33	1931	1842	2	4	10	554,400	105,600	26,800	33,000	34	3
Niger	4,103,000	16	6	5	13.6	86	0.4	0	4	4	2	0	33	1931	1927	1	24	1	16,400	558,000	142,500	3,500,000	5	2
Nigeria	58,253,000	106	21	25	58	44	11	34	161	62	17	6	100	1862	1842	25	59	600	26,796,400	5,825,300	1,678,900	15,000,000	13	27
Portuguese Guinea	572,000	8	10	10	46	32	8.9	0.1	24	2		0	3	1849	1940	1	0	0	51,500	331,800	253,000	350,000	95	6
Réunion	495,000	1	22	70	0	0	94.9	0.5	2	0		0	100	1665	Nil	1	34	0	472,200	0		25,000	29	2
Rhodesia	5,433,000	10	22	35	46	0.6	17	37	19	9	7	4	35	1879	1859	5	6	100	2,933,800	2,499,200	81,100	1,000,000	41	1
Rwanda	3,819,000	2	4	10	0	0	52	17	4	0		2	50	1889	1907	5	6	0	2,635,100	1,161,000	24,000	700,000	95	0
St. Helena	6,000	1	33	70	0	0	0	99.9	1	0		0	100	Nil	1859	0	1	0	6,000	0		300	2	0
São Tomé and Príncipe	61,000	1	25		4.3	0.7	94	6	1	0		0		1445	Nil	1	1	0	58,000	2,600		3,000	95	0
Senegal	4,136,000	7	28	5	4.5	89	6.4	0.1	13	2	2	0		1445	1955	6	19	1	264,700	186,800	320,000	2,500,000	16	8
Seychelles	57,000	1	28	10	0	0	90.7	8.1	1	0		0		1770	1843	1	18	0	56,300	0		3,000	3	0
Sierra Leone	2,779,000	11	14	10	51	38	6.7	4.3	15	10	4	1		1858	1804	3	14	3	305,700	1,417,300	1,370,500	1,400,000	95	1
Somalia	2,942,000	10	19	2	0	99.8	0.2	0	2	1		0		1881	1889	1	7	0	6,000	0		2,700,000	15	0
South Africa	21,185,000	24	51	65	12.5	1.3	8	75.4	24	20	11	10		1804	1792	26	59	3200	17,668,300	2,648,100	39,000	1,000,000	44	13
Spanish N. Africa	168,000	1	95	95	0	10	87	0	1	0		0		1631	Nil	1	0	0	147,800	0		8,000	8	0
Spanish Sahara	54,000	4	33		0	80	20	0	1	0		0		1580	Nil	1	0	0	9,600	0		30,000	8	18
Sudan	16,885,000	72	10	20	24	60	10	6	102	26	15	3		1842	1899	7	11	30	2,701,600	4,052,400	3,586,000	10,000,000	20	10
Swaziland	449,000	1	8	25	17	0	9	74	1	2	4	1		1913	1838	1	18	25	372,700	76,300		50,000	43	0
Tanzania	14,002,000	66	8	25	28.6	26	31	14	181	34	9	4		1860	1844	24	24	3	6,314,900	4,004,600	2,854,900	4,000,000	10	21
Togo	1,969,000	18	15	7	61	31	22	8	36	9	2	1		1886	1843	4	7	4	590,700	1,201,100	462,000	800,000	35	12
Tunisia	5,431,000	9	43	85	0	98	0.6	0	3	1		0		1878	1877	4	12	0	54,300	0		3,800,000	40	3
Uganda	10,332,000	23	6	25	22.4	6	40	31	24	20	11	10		1900	1877	12	5	10	7,336,000	2,314,400	142,700	3,800,000	43	4
Upper Volta	5,629,000	26	6	6	56	26	6	1.4	21	11	7	1		1900	1921	4	9	1	506,600	3,152,200	3,609,700	3,800,000	10	21
Zaïre	18,339,000	98	22	22	11.8	0.3	51	35.5	111	69	38	20		1865	1878	48	36	500	15,863,200	2,164,000	987,000	1,500,000	35	12
Zambia	4,584,000	32	23	18	17.4	0.3	22	15.5	34	20	10	2		1889	1882	9	36	49	2,085,700	2,484,500	12,300	1,000,000	40	3
AFRICA TOTALS	367,380,000	1045	23	23	17.4	41.7	16.2	24.4	1439	561	310	138				356	648	5400	149,280,000	63,994,200	29,041,200	130,000,000		263

247

(a) MUSLIM AND ISLAMISED PEOPLES AND TRIBES (Section V, and
     Table 2)

In 1972, a total of 213 tribes in Africa (270 tribes-within-
nations) are Muslim, either completley or solidly (100%) or so
heavily islamised (defined here as 75% or over) that there has
been, and still is, little or no welcome or opportunity for Christian evangelism. These peoples stretch in a solid bloc from the
North African coast down through the Sahara to what we may call
'the Muslim line', running across Africa approximately 100 miles
south of the Sahara Desert, as shown in green on the map. This
religious frontier divides tribes which are 75% Muslim or over
from those to the south with smaller Muslim percentages. A selection of these peoples are described in section V and in Table 2.

(b) RESPONSIVE EVANGELISED PEOPLES AND TRIBES (Section VI, and
     Table 3)

Over the last two hundred years, some 411 tribes of Africa
(512 tribes-within-nations) have come into contact with the
Christian faith to a sufficient degree for them to be called
evangelised peoples, both numerically and also culturally. These
peoples have observed and studied the Christian faith and its
proclaimants for an 'incubatory' period of from one to 50 years
and have then responded to it with varying degrees of enthusiasm,
by forming Christian communities of varying sizes, by absorbing
Christian values and the Christian world-view, and by interpreting
Christianity as the fulfilment of their own traditional religion.
The definition here of a responsive tribe is one in which traditionalists have been converted to Christianity in such numbers
that remaining traditionalists number less than 60% of the tribe.
Clearly, most of these peoples still contain thousands of unevangelised individuals, families, villages and even areas or regions.
However, where these persons in percentage terms are small relative
to the rest of their tribe -- by definition here, a minority, or
less than 50% -- the tribe is defined in this survey as 'evangelised
in the sense that the gospel has penetrated the majority and has
therefore attained sufficient momentum to complete the tribe's self-
evangelisation in the years ahead. These responsive evangelised
tribes are shown on the map as white areas; and a selection are
described in VI and in Table 3.

(c) UNEVANGELISED, PARTIALLY EVANGELISED, AND RESISTANT PEOPLES
     AND TRIBES (Section VII, and Table 4)

The remainder of Africa's peoples, some 236 tribes (263
tribes-within-nations), form the object of this survey as frontier
situations in that they are still largely traditionalists (60% or

over) who are not yet islamised and who have not yet come into
contact with Christianity to the same extent, and who can therefore be described in various degrees as unevangelised or not yet
fully evangelised, either numerically or culturally, but which
are (unlike the islamised tribes) relatively open to evangelisation.
A listing of these 263 peoples is given in Table 4, and they are
shown on the map coloured in red and yellow. The listing was compiled by including, for each nation, all known cases of non-
islamised peoples in which traditionalists numbered 60% or over,
and also all known cases of non-islamised peoples in which the
percentage of persons evangelised was 50% or less (i.e. 50% or
more unevangelised). These criteria mean that the listing contains the following two kinds of tribe, corresponding to the two-
fold definition of evangelisation (in section II) as both the numerical evangelisation of persons and also the evangelisation of
their culture:

     (i)   Tribes with a majority of their population unevangelised,
in which the large number of traditionalists (in almost all cases
60% or over) present what this report is terming a frontier mission
situation (tribes of this kind [218 tribes-within-nations] are
listed in Table 4, and are shown on the map in three shades of red);
and

     (ii)   Tribes which have already been numerically evangelised
(over 50%), leaving only a minority still unevangelised, but which
are resisting Christianity in that the number of traditionalists
still remains high at 60% or over, and which can therefore be
termed culturally unevangelised (42 tribes of this kind [45 tribes-
within-nations] are listed in Table 4, and are shown on the map in
yellow).

In a number of these cases traditional religion was found to
be extremely strong, often even reviving in strength. Since in
almost all cases no attempt has yet been made to initiate Christian
encounter and theological dialogue with these tribal philosophies
and religions, such cases are regarded here as frontier situations
offering great opportunities for dialogue and the eventual evangelisation of these tribal world-views and philosophies.

The main collection of survey data in this report is that
given in the three tables 2-4, with their visual presentation on
the map. These data, and identical layout of the three tables,
will now be described.

On the left of each table are listed peoples and tribes
together with the nations they are found in. For ease of location,
these tribes are named and spelt according to the best classification

available, namely that of the anthropologist G. P. Murdock
(*Africa: Its peoples and their culture history*, 1959), corresponding to the names on the tribal map of Africa appended to this
report. Local spelling often varies considerably, and in many
cases tribes are commonly referred to locally by one or more quite
different names; where these are essential for identification, they
are given in brackets immediately after the Murdock name.   It
should also be noted that often tribes speak a language whose name
is quite different to that of the tribe (such linguistic names are
not given in this survey). Further, certain tribes are followed by
(s.   ), which indicates that the tribe is classified by
Murdock as a sub-tribe of a larger people whose name is given in
the parentheses. Such sub-tribes are not indicated on the tribal
map, but can be located approximately by locating the larger people.
In the enumerations, a tribe with its sub-tribes is counted only
once.

KEY TO COLUMNS IN TABLES 2, 3 AND 4

1.   *Population.* Tribal populations given here are estimates for
     mid-1972 based in most cases on the latest government censuses.
     The method used is to determine the percentage size of a tribe
     in relation to total population at the last census, and then
     to multiply this percentage by the mid-1972 national popula-
     tion.   Rounded figures such as '10,000' are very approximate
     estimates only. The figures for nations in this column are of
     total population.
2-5. *Religious profession.* These estimates of the percentage of a
     tribe professing to follow each religion come from either
     government censuses, or (in most cases) were made by local
     observers familiar with the tribe's religious composition.
     Figures are only given here when known to a reasonable degree
     of accuracy. Note that percentages ending in digits other
     than zero (e.g. '73') claim greater accuracy than round num-
     bers (e.g. '70', '50', '10') which are more likely to be rough
     estimates only.
2.   *Traditionalists* (formerly called pagans or animists), %.
3.   *Muslims*, %. Where this figure is small, it indicates the
     extent of islamisation; e.g. 20% indicates 'slight islamisa-
     tion', and 50% 'extensive islamisation'; those of 75% or over
     are called completely Muslim or islamised tribes.
4.   *Catholics* (baptised, catechumens, and all other professing
     adherents), %.
5.   *Protestants*, Anglicans, Orthodox, and Independents, %.
6.   *Traditionalists.* The number of followers of traditional
     religion in each tribe, obtained by multiplying columns 1 and
     2.
7-10.*Scripture Translations.*

7. Total types of scripture translation which have been pub-
    lished in the tribe's own language (or, if it does not have
    its own unique language, in the major vernacular used by the
    tribe). G = gospel (portion), N= New Testament, B = complete
    Bible; - = no translations. This column is important in
    indicating the extent to which a tribe's language (which is
    the 'soul of the people', the repository of its cultural her-
    itage, traditions and tribal religions) has been 'evangelised'
    or 'christianised' or 'baptised into Christ'. Where the three
    letters GNB occur in this column, therefore, it indicates that
    this primary translation task is 3/3 complete, i.e. 100%.
8. Date of publication of *first gospel (portion)*. Blank spaces
    indicate that no scriptures have yet been published (except,
    in a handful of cases, brief preliminary selections).
9. Date of publication of *New Testament*.
10. Date of publication of *complete Bible*.
11. *Year of origin of permanent Catholic work* (excluding 15th-
    18th century missions in tropical Africa which were later
    abandoned) (c = circa, approximately; i.e. exact date not
    known. Nil = no organised missionary work yet begun).
12. *Year of origin of Protestant work*. The year in which contin-
    uous Protestant or Anglican (or, very occasionally, indepen-
    dent) missionary activity was first begun.
13. *Evangelisation, %*. The figures in this column are observers'
    estimates of the percentage of the tribe who can be said to
    have been evangelised (i.e. to have come into contact with
    Christianity sufficiently for them to have heard the gospel,
    by one means or another (including radio and literature evan-
    gelism), whether or not they have subsequently accepted it.
    Note also that infants and young children of evangelised
    adults are themselves counted as evangelised). In many cases
    observers gave a % figure; but when they gave impressionistic
    non-numerical answers, as shown below, these have been quali-
    fied using the following code, and then entered in column 13.
    Note that the maximum figure given (for 'fully evangelised')
    is 95%, because in practice it is impossible to reach 100%
    since there are always numbers of unevangelised individuals
    however completely the society has been evangelised. The
    figures for nations in this column are averages (for each
    nation, = evangelised in frontier situations + population of
    tribes in frontier situations).
    Descriptive phrases used: *% evangelised*
    'Fully evangelised'; 'all areas evangelised';
        'all have heard the gospel'; 'probably no-
        one has not heard the gospel at least once' . . . 95
    'Mostly evangelised'; 'pretty well evangelised';
        'very few have not heard something of the
        gospel' 90

Descriptive phrases used: *% evangelised*

'No region completely unevangelised'; 'one
    relatively small unevangelised area'; 'only
    small marginal unevangelised areas'; 'only
    isolated villages unevangelised'.   85
'Several areas unevangelised'; 'many people are
    still unevangelised'; 'evangelised, in gen-
    eral'   80
'Fair coverage of evangelisation'; 'well evan-
    gelised', 'extensively evangelised'   70
'A majority has been evangelised'; 'most vil-
    lages (but not individuals) have been touched' . .   60
'About half have been evangelised'   50
'Partially evangelised'; 'evangelisation is
    under way'.   30
'Still largely unevangelised'; 'still virtually
    pioneer work'; 'large areas quite unreached'. . .   20
'Very little evangelised'; 'only slightly evan-
    gelised'; 'mostly unevangelised'; 'very few
    have heard the Gospel at all'; 'most areas
    unreached'.   10
'A very small percentage'; 'scarcely evangel-
    ised'; 'very sparsely evangelised'; 'hardly
    touched by the gospel'; '95% of the territory
    has no Christian contact of any sort'; 'evan-
    gelisation has scarcely begun', or 'its just
    beginning'.   5
'Unevangelised'; 'unreached'; 'under 1% reached
    so far'   0

14.   *Unevangelised.* The approximate number of unevangelised persons
       in each tribe (the unevangelised community, including young
       children and infants), estimated by multiplying column 1 by
       (1-col. 13/100). The figure given in this column for each
       nation is then the total of the figures for each tribe listed
       below it, i.e. the total unevangelised persons in frontier
       situations in the nation.

15.   *Status of evangelisation* index (SE), indicating the extent to
       which the total primary evangelistic task in a tribe (viewed
       as the twofold one of evangelising the individuals and families
       composing the tribe, and of providing the scriptures in a
       tribe's language, i.e. numerical and cultural evangelisation)
       has been completed. This index is defined similarly to Table
       1 column w, as follows: SE = col. 13 x (number of letters in
       col. 7,plus 1 (representing scriptures available in some other
       language or lingua franca such as Hausa, Swahili, English),
       divided by 4), per cent. The maximum value of this index,
       100%, indicates a fully-evangelised tribe with the complete
       Bible available in its own language; the minimum value (zero)

indicates a tribe in which evangelisation of people or language or culture has barely begun.

16.   *Major missions at work*. The major Protestant or Anglican
      missionary body or bodies (or Protestant, Anglican, or indig-
      enous churches) engaged in evangelistic work in the tribe,
      either at present, or recently, or bearing major responsibility
      in the past for evangelisation and translation. Except in a
      handful of cases, Catholic missions are not listed here because
      they are working in virtually all the tribes listed unless
      otherwise stated, with the exception of 0% evangelised peoples.
      In many tribes under 30% evangelised, reports in fact describe
      many new initiatives and kinds of Catholic evangelistic work.
      Lastly, with regard to the work of the African independent
      (indigenous) churches, in a number of cases evangelisation is
      being pursued among a tribe by an independent church from
      another tribe, in which case the name of the body is given;
      whilst the symbol 'AIC' or "AICs' indicates that evangelisation
      is being undertaken in the tribe by an independent church
      formed from within the tribe by its own members (details of 270
      such tribes and their churches, with addresses, are given in
      Schism and renewal in Africa (1968) - see Bibliography).

V.   CASE STUDIES OF MUSLIM AND ISLAMISED PEOPLES (Table 2)

     To the north and east of the Muslim line across Africa (see
map) there are 205 peoples and tribes that are either solidly
Muslim, or over 75% Muslim, or over 75% islamised. A handful of
other Muslim peoples can also be seen to exist just south of the
line. This line, which has been moving steadily southwards in
Africa since the 6th century AD, advanced considerably under British,
French and German colonial rule after 1885, slowed down around 1930,
came to a standstill around 1950, and has remained virtually unchanged since independence in the new Black African states of the
1960s.

     In many of these Muslim tribes Christian evangelism is diffi-
cult, unwelcome, unwanted, even impossible or legally proscribed.
Nevertheless, partial numerical evangelisation (30%) has taken
place in a few tribes here and there, and attempts at cultural
evangelisation have produced scriptures in a number of their languages. Basic comparative data on a selection of 22 such tribes
is given in Table 2. The situation in 5 of these Muslim tribes will
now be described in brief case studies, listed in alphabetical order;
later, case studies will be given of 4 tribes in various stages of
islamisation but well below 75% Muslim (see Yoruba in VI following;
Koranko and Serer in VII, and Mossi in VIII).

1.   The *Kabyle* (1 million) are a Berber tribe in eastern Algeria,
      the most important village-dwelling people in north Africa.
      Before the Muslim conquest in the 8th century they were Chris-
      tians, but after considerable opposition they finally aposta-
      tised and received their name, Kabyle, which is Arabic for
      'those who after lengthy resistance accepted Islam'. They
      are also the only tribe in the once-Christian Maghreb to have
      in any way responded to the Christian faith in the present
      century. Before the Franco-Algerian war and Algeria's subse-
      quent independence in 1962, there were about 200 Kabyle
      Protestants (mainly Methodists), 3,000 Catholics, and the
      rest of the nearly one million Kabyle were Muslim. The accep-
      tance of Christianity by Kabyles was often coupled with
      acceptance of French culture and civilisation, and so with the
      replacement of the French by an unsympathetic Muslim govern-
      ment in 1962, most Christian Kabyles left to live and work in
      France.

      The Berber mentality, especially that of the Kabyle, has
      always been noted for its secessionist and independent char-
      acter; hence it has been observed that over the past two
      hundred years, the Kabyle have experienced waves of Muslim
      religious movements called zawiyas (confraternity, prayer
      house, mutual aid society), which have many similarities to
      the independent churches of Black Africa. The Kabyle have no
      Koran in their own language but have had Christian scriptures
      for a long time: a gospel in 1885, and the New Testament in
      1901; but of the 3,000 copies of the latter printed in 1956,
      only 1,000 were sold in ten years. Two small Christian revival
      movements broke out around 1920 at Methodist mission stations,
      which however failed to take root and spread.

2.   The *Makonde* of southern Tanzania number 550,000 across the
      border in Mozambique. Anglican missions (UMCA) began in 1878
      at Newala, Catholics (Benedictine Fathers of St. Ottilien)
      opened their first mission station at Kitangali in 1932, and
      more recently the Plymouth Brethren (CMML) have begun work in
      Mtwara town. The expulsion or interment of German missionaries
      during the two World Wars was a major handicap to Catholic work
      About 90% of the Makonde have called themselves Muslims since
      1910-1920, adopting Muslim names, not eating pork, keeping of
      feast days (by 30% of the population), and Friday prayers
      (attended by 10%). They have made little change, however, in
      traditional beliefs and customs (spirit dances, rites, sacri-
      fices, taboos, medicine, charms), and in this respect are still
      at least 80% animist who have adopted a bare minimum of Muslim
      customs. There are few educated leaders, and even most teacher
      are unable to read the Koran and often refuse to teach Islam in

the schools. Strong moral, and sometimes physical, pressure
is exerted against Christian conversions, and every year about
20 Catholics apostatise to Islam, usually because of marriage
problems and clan pressures. These usually tend to return to
Christianity when the problems are removed.

Evangelisation has been aided by the migration into Tanzania
of Mozambique Makonde, who are stronger animists fond of
travelling who respond more readily to Christianity than to
Islam. When they settle in an area they have been industrious,
asking for schools and religious instruction for themselves
and their children. This has resulted in numerous small Christian congregations in Tanzania which are slowly influencing the
Tanzanian Makonde. The latter tend to become Christians only
as individuals because of clan pressure demanding written permission before baptism; whereas Mozambique Makonde converts
result in both Christian clans and Christian villages, readily
accepted by other Makonde. Because of their better educational
facilities, Christians are attaining more professional and
government positions, achieving the social status formerly held
by Muslims only. They maintain high moral standards and activity within their churches.

Both Anglican and Catholic missions have attempted to chris-
tianise traditional Makonde customs and clan structures, and
special rites have been developed for blessing houses, new seed,
the new harvest, etc. Burial ceremonies are conducted with
special solemnity. Catholic missions have large staff and
carry on extensive social work and building activities. Makonde
Catholics show a very high level of Christian practice, 60%
attending Sunday mass each week and 85% receiving Easter communion. Anglican work is now fully africanised, with some
slowing down of external expansion; church leaders lack higher
education but congregations are self-reliant and sound, and
recently the practice of church discipline has been abolished.

3.   In northern Nigeria, the *Nupe* (587,000) form a large Muslim
empire which has been described as a 'Black Byzantium'. In
1857, the CMS ship Dayspring penetrated up the Niger River as
far as the Nupe tribe before striking rocks and sinking. The
Yoruba missionary Adjai Crowther then remained in the area
visiting villages and studying the Nupe languages. Early
missionaries found the Nupe friendly, in part the result of
their identifying missions with the British government which
had stopped the Fulani slave raids among the Nupe and surrounding tribes. The administration, however, with the local emirs,
advised the people not to become Christians. Organised CMS
work began in 1890. The initial toll of missionary lives was

high. In 1901 the Sudan Interior Mission succeeded in establishing a Nupe mission station at its third attempt. A third
mission, the United Missionary Society (Mennonite) entered
three or four years later. The lone survivor of the SIM's
first four missionaries translated the gospels and ultimately
the entire Bible. With no Nupe reading public, it remained
unused for years. The Nupe have long been highly islamised
(now 88%), and despite very extensive work by the CMS, particularly in education, very few Christians have resulted;
Anglican Nupe communicants number only 1,000, and total professing Christians 2%. The SIM in 1961 had a membership of
only 185 among the Nupe in its ECWA churches. There is no
Catholic missionary work, their only two town churches in Nupe
country being mainly for Yoruba and Ibo Catholics; indigenous
churches likewise are for immigrant tribesmen only. Extensive
tracts remain unevangelised.

4.   The northwest corner of Mozambique is inhabited by the *Yao*
      (220,000) who are the only predominatly Muslim tribe in the
      country. At the end of the 19th century the Yao became traders
      between Kilwa and the Lake Malawi region, and their contacts
      with the Arab and Swahili culture of the coast had a decisive
      effect on their religious orientation. They became, and remain
      today, the sole example below the equator of the mass conversio
      to Islam of an interior tribe. Christian pioneers in Yao coun-
      try were Anglican missionaries of the UMCA. Bishop Steere
      visited them in 1875, but it was not until 1893 that a permanen
      mission station was established at Unango. Right up to the pre
      sent day Yao Christians are mostly Anglicans. The Catholic
      Church was much slower to begin work among the Yao, opening its
      first station in 1930, also at Unango. In the Catholic diocese
      of Vila Cabral, which is about equally divided between Anglican
      and Catholics, the Catholics have their greatest numbers among
      the southern Makua while Anglicans are strongest among the
      northern Yao. Traditional animism as a separate religion
      among the Yao has virtually disappeared.

5.   The *Zaramo* (296,000) occupy the coast of Tanzania in the vicin-
      ity of Dar es Salaam. About 95% are Muslim in name, but all
      are still strong animists in practice. Catholics (HGM) began
      at Bagamoyo in 1867, initially developing Christian communities
      among freed slaves, and Lutherans (Berlin III Mission) began in
      1887. Little impact was made on the Zaramo themselves until
      the Lutherans began moving inland. The toll of missionary
      deaths on the tropical coast, and the removal of German mis-
      sionaries during the two World Wars, also contributed to the
      ineffectiveness of mission work. A Lutheran effort was made
      to overcome the mwali custom of enclosing girls from puberty

to marriage, strongly followed among the Zaramo, by providing a school to teach childcare and homecraft. This was eventually closed by the Zaramo because the pupils had become entirely from upcountry tribes. Wazaramo now comprise 30% of the population of Dar es Salaam, but they are less than 1% of its Christian population. In rural areas there are almost no Christian churches or Christian contacts. A few Lutheran Zaramo congregations have a fair number of adult baptisms of converts from Islam every year, but hardly any Zaramo at all have become Catholics in the last hundred years. A high loss rate among the few Wazaramo who do become Christians takes place (perhaps as high as 75%) because of the inability of the congregations to shephard newly baptised converts.

VI.   CASE STUDIES OF RESPONSIVE EVANGELISED PEOPLES (Table 3)

In order to understand what is meant by an unevangelised people, it is necessary first to study the concepts of evangelisation and of an evangelised tribe. This section undertakes this by giving in Table 3 comparative basic data on a selection of 45 out of the 411 or so evangelised tribes in Africa, and by describing certain aspects of the evolution of evangelisation in 21 of these 45 tribes. These 21 brief tribal case studies are intended to investigate further various concerns of the overall enquiry in the context of one particular tribe. They now follow in alphabetical order; each should be read in conjunction with its line of related data in Table 3.

1.   The *Ambo* or Obambo number 352,000 in Namibia (South West Africa) with a large number also across the border in Angola. Their evangelisation began in the 1870s under the Rhenish Mission (German Lutheran), who later turned the work over to Finnish Lutherans to become Finland's biggest mission field, now known as the Evangelical Lutheran Ovambokavango Church (180,000 baptised). Anglicans and Catholics arrived much later, both in 1924. These three are the only missions permitted in the area, and all grew rapidly in the 1960s; 60% are now Christian. Missions ran all hospitals and schools, though now all the latter have been turned over to government. In recent years the ELOC has been hampered by its close enforced association with the Dutch Reformed Church, which pays its pastors' and catechists' salaries when they serve elsewhere in the territory outside Ovamboland. Ninety per cent of the people have been evangelised, i.e. exposed to Christianity; traditional animism, though gradually dying, still remains strong.

TABLE 2: A SELECTION OF MUSLIM AND ISLAMISED TRIBES IN AFRICA, 1972

This table gives basic data on a selection of 22 of the 213 peoples and tribes defined in this survey as Muslim (100%) or islamised (75% Muslim or over).
The five tribes marked below with an asterisk, *, are further described in brief case studies in the text preceding this table. A detailed explanation of this table and its columns is given in the text, section IV; and a visual presentation of its data is given in the map at the end. For ease of reference, the meaning of the 16 columns below is given again here, as follows:
Col.1: Total population of tribe in mid-1972. 2-5: Percentage of tribe professing to be respectively, traditionalists, Muslims, Catholics, Protestants (with all other types of Christian). 6: Total professing traditionalists in tribe. 7: Scripture translation published in tribe's own language:
G = gospel, N = New Testament, B = complete Bible; - = none. 8-10: years when G, N, B, respectively, were published. 11,12: years when, respectively,
Catholic and Protestant missionary work began (c = circa, approximately). 13: % of tribe evangelised. 14: Total unevangelised in tribe. 15: SE (status of
evangelisation) index, i.e. extent to which tribe, and its culture, is evangelised. 16: Miscellaneous notes on each tribe and nation; initials = major
Protestant or Anglican churches or missions now or recently at work, with one Catholic order (see Directory in appendix).

Tribe (and NATION)	Population mid-1972	Religious profession,% Tr	Mu	RC	Pr	Tradits	Total	Scriptures Dates Gosp	NT	Bible	Origin RC	Prot	%E	Unevanged	SE %	Main missions at work, etc.
	1	2	3	4	5	6	7	8	9	10	11	12	13	14	15	16
Afar (Danakil)(ETHIO)	420,000	0	100	0	0	0	G	c1967			Nil	1952	1	416,000	0	CBML and 5 other missions. No Danakil Christians at all.
Afar (Danakil)(FTAI)	34,000	0	100	0	0	0	G	c1967			c1955	Nil	1	33,700	0	No Protestant missions.
Abaggaren (ALGERIA)	10,000	0	99	0	0	0	G	1948						9,900	0	Sahara Desert Mission.
Boran (KENYA)	37,700	5	90	2	3	1,900	-		1934	1973			30	26,400	22	BCMS, MCK. Islamised but strong traditionalists.
Fali (CAMEROON)	50,000	20	80	0	0	10,000	-					1875	20	40,000	5	Rapid islamisation since 1955. CBM,NBM,LBM,WBT.
Gosha (SOMALIA)	6,000	0	99	0	0	0	G	1935			1872		1	5,900	0	Barely any contact with missions.
*Kabyle (ALGERIA)	1,000,000	4	99	0	0	0	GN	1885	1901		c1880	1878	5	950,000	4	1% were Catholic,Methodist; 1960s, most left for France.
Kasonke (MALI)	100,000	4	95	0	0	4,000	-				c1880	1878	5	95,000	1	United World Mission.
*Makonde (TANZANIA)	550,000	2	90	5	3	11,000	-				1932	1857	30	385,000	7	USPG, Benedictines. CBML.
*Nupe (NIGERIA)	587,000	10	88	0	2	58,700	GNB	1877	1915	1953	Nil		30	410,900	30	CMS,SIM,UMS; no Catholics or independent churches.
Oasis Berbers (LIBYA)	116,000	0	100	0	0	0	GNB	1905	1932	1963			30	116,000	0	Oases: Gadames, Jalo Jofra, Siwa, etc. No missions.
Pokomo (KENYA)	38,900	1	85	0	14	400	GN	1894	1902			1875	30	27,200	22	Methodist Church in Kenya, AICMS, AIC.
Sanye (KENYA)	2,000	10	90	0	0	200	-						30	1,900	5	Forest hunters, islamised traditionalists.
Schluh (MOROCCO)	1,900,000	0	100	0	0	0	G	1887			c1900	1880	10	1,710,000	5	GMU, BCMS, North Africa Mission.
Segeju (KENYA)	30,000	0	99	0	0	0	GNB	1878	1909	1914	c1890		30	21,000	30	CMS and other missions over the last hundred years.
Yao (MALAWI)	380,000	1	90	4	5	3,800	GNB	1880	1898	1920	1924	1901	10	342,000	10	USPG (also in Mozambique and Tanzania).
*Yao (MOZAMBIQUE)	220,000	1	80	6	13	2,200	GNB	1880	1898	1920	1930	1893	30	154,000	30	UMCA (now USPG).
Yao (TANZANIA)	190,000	1	85	4	10	1,900	GNB	1880	1898	1920	1938	1876	30	133,000	30	UPSG, CBML.
Zaghawa (SUDAN)	60,000	25	75	0	0	15,000	G	1967					1	59,400	0	SUM (in Chad only). Translation work begun.
*Zaremo (TANZANIA)	296,000	3	95	0	2	9,000	G	1967			1867	1887	5	281,200	2	ELCT Coastal Synod.
Zenaga (MAURITANIA)	16,000	0	100	0	0	0	-						5	15,200	1	Arabised Bedouin Berbers. Slight contact with HGM.
Zerma (NIGER)	500,000	25	75	0	0	125,000	GN	1934	1954				2	490,000	1	Africa Christian Mission; 100 Zerma Catholics only.

2.   Another case study brings out again several of the concerns
      of this survey. The *Bamileke* of the Cameroon highlands are
      a virile and progressive people found all over the country as
      wealthy merchants and entrepreneurs. They number around
      866,000 in 1972, and are expanding rapidly in population at a
      rate measured at 2.5% per year (21,600 a year). One of their
      five capitals, Bafoussam, has grown from almost nothing to
      around 30,000 in just a few years. In 1903, the first Pro-
      testant missionary of the Basel Mission visited Bamileke
      country, and a Protestant mission was founded in 1911; Cath-
      olics arrived a year or two earlier. A profusion of 19 or so
      Bamileke dialects has produced considerable rivalry in regard
      to scripture translation; gospels exist in Bandjoun and
      Bangangte, and in 1967 the New Testament was published in the
      latter, a choice that produced considerable ill-feeling and
      nearly provoked a church schism. During the civil war and
      terrorist activities of the 1960s, the Eglise Evangélique du
      Cameroun mounted regular large-scale evangelistic campaigns
      (because the Bamileke lay in their comity area), including
      one for a year and a half from 1961-1962 which resulted in
      many conversions, although several interested chiefs later
      decided to embrace Islam after being confronted with the
      church's inflexible position on polygamy. On the whole,
      however, the Bamileke have not shown much interest in Islam.
      A survey around 1962 in the five Bamileke regions found only
      2,711 Muslins (0.6%), as opposed to 327,683 animists (70%).
      The EEC has in fact grown so rapidly that Bamileke now forms
      one-third of its entire membership; they numbered 28,312 com-
      municant members in 1964-1965, with 37,664 attending church on
      Sundays (8% of the population); by 1972 about 15% are profess-
      ing Protestants. Catholics in 1965 numbered 73,713 (16%), or
      20% including catechumens, increasing to about 29% professing
      to be Catholics in 1972. Despite these extensive Christian
      activities, some 40% remain unevangelised.

3.   The *Duala* (100,000) are a Bantu coastal tribe around the large
      port city of Douala in Cameroon, whose language has now become
      the lingua franca over a large part of the country. British
      Baptists began work among them in 1845, the Basel Mission in
      1884, and Catholics in 1890; and the whole Bible has been
      translated since 1872. Early missionaries, especially the
      German Pallotine fathers, made an all-out effort to destroy
      Duala traditional religion and culture, condemning them as
      diabolical, burning the ritual masks, banning the traditional
      dances, and so on. As a result, although the Duala today are
      numerically all evangelised and all Christians (63% Protestant
      and independent, 37% Catholic), the culture remains unevangel-
      ised; there remains a noticeable cultural void, and an

animistic revival of sorts is occurring. The Duala have also
experienced a series of secession movements, beginning with
the Native Baptist Church in 1888 which has now become the
Eglise Baptiste Camerounaise with 100,000 adherents.

4.   The *Egba* are a Yoruba-speaking people found near the densely-
      populated coast in Nigeria, Dahomey, and Togo, numbering about
      627,000 in Nigeria. The Church Missionary Society first
      arrived among the Nigerian Egba in 1842, and the first Catholic
      station was opened in 1857. Under one-tenth remain strong
      traditionalists, one-half are Muslims, under a tenth Catholics
      and about 33% belong to Anglican, Protestant, or a large
      variety of independent churches. The case of the Egba is
      interesting in that the early Egba converts proved to be
      strongly evangelistic and used their complex social, economic
      and political structures to spread the gospel of Christ. As
      a result, the evangelisation of the 10 million Yoruba-speaking
      peoples can be ascribed in a large measure to them. In this
      the Egba are similar to a number of other influential tribes
      throughout the continent (such as the Ewe of Ghana, Luo of
      Kenya, and Nyasa of Malawi) who became the principal carriers
      of evangelisation and christianisation along existing networks
      of relationships across Africa.

5.   The *Haya* of northern Tanzania (526,000) occupy the area just
      west of Lake Victoria. Catholics (White Fathers) arrived in
      1892 and the Lutheran Bethel Mission in 1910. Christianity
      has grown steadily, this area being now one of the most heavily
      Catholic and Lutheran areas in Tanzania. The number of Luther-
      ans doubled between 1956 and 1965, and a congregational struc-
      ture close to local clan structure has been evolved. The strong
      East African Revival movement since 1940 has resulted in ex-
      tremely rapid church growth and also in two separatist churches
      half the members of one, the Church of the Holy Spirit, returned
      to the Lutheran Church (Diocese of Bukoba) in 1962-1964. The
      strain of excessively rapid growth continues to be felt, with
      an inadequate number of trained leaders and committed Christian
      The Haya have now been completely evangelised (95%), though the
      few immigrant Sukuma and Ruanda settlers are mostly unevangel-
      ised. About 7% are Muslims, this number decreasing slowly.

6.   Possibly the most densely evangelised, and christianised, areas
      in rural and urban Africa are found among the *Ibibio* (1,640,000
      in south-eastern Nigeria near the town of Ikot Ekpene, which was
      devastated and changed hands several times during the 1967-1970
      civil war. Shortly before the war, a survey found that the
      rural triangle stretching from the town to twenty miles east,
      then twenty miles south, had in it 230 churches and missions,

of which 78 were independent churches (indigenous, separatist,
AICs). Further, on the 53 miles of road from the town through
the rain-forest to Opobo on the coast, there were 113 church
buildings, 57 being separatist. Similarly, in the urbanised
area within a five-mile radius of the centre of Abak town,
there were 251 congregations from 50 different denominations
of which 33 were separatist. Church activity of all kinds
continued throughout the fighting, and today many destroyed
churches have been rebuilt.

7.   Although the CMS pioneer missionary in East Africa, J. L. Krapf,
visited Ukambani, the homeland of the *Kamba* (population
1,323,400 in 1972), in 1849 and 1851, translated two gospels
into the Kamba language, and planned to have the first link
of his 'Equatorial Missionchain' established there, no evangelisation actually took place until nearly fifty years later
with the arrival of the Leipzig Evangelical Lutheran Mission
Society in 1892 (shortlived) and the Africa Inland Mission in
1895. The interment of German missionaries in the first World
War severely interrupted the growth of the church since they
had established good contact with the Akama in Kitui district.
The limiting of the main responsibility for the evangelisation
of this large people to a single Protestant group (the AIM)
had an unfortunate effect and has been a factor in the relatively slow growth of Christianity. Seven Protestant groups
and about a dozen strong indigenous churches (AICs) now work
there, in addition to Catholics who arrived relatively late
in 1912 but have since grown rapidly. The East African Revival
movement has large numbers of followers. Whilst about 70% of
the people have now been evangelised and can be described as
under the direct influence of Christian evangelism, there are
still residual areas only slightly evangelised (in Kitui district and south of Machakos). Traditional beliefs remain
strong, particularly those connected with magic and life
crises, and 39% still profess to be traditionalists. Islam
(under 1%) is making very little progress, and only in towns.

8.   The *Kikuyu* (2,433,000) are the largest tribe in Kenya, a Bantu
highlands people forming 20% of the nation's population. They
may now be said to be fully evangelised (95%); geographically,
there is hardly a single unevangelised area in the entire
Kikuyu land. In 1898, the first Protestants reached the
Kikuyu (Church of Scotland Mission), followed by Catholics in
1902 (Consolata Mission). The first serious crisis to face
the churches came in 1929 when many mission adherents broke
away and formed independent churches and schools due to missionary opposition to the Kikuyu practices of female circumcision and polygamy. A second major crisis emerged during the

1952-1960 state of emergency. By 1972 there are over a dozen
Protestant missions and about 700,000 followers of 40 independent churches (AICs), numbering altogether 47% of the Kikuyu;
Catholics number 26%. Since 1937 the East African Revival
movement has had great influence on the Kikuyu, especially
among the Anglican and Presbyterian churches. Traditional
religious beliefs, still adhered to by 27%, are fast disappearing, although many traditional social and cultural values have
reappeared in the churches as Christian values.

9.   The *Kimbu* (50,000) are one of the southern branches of the
     Nyamwezi in Tanzania south of Lake Victoria. The German
     Brudergemeine (Moravians) began working here in 1901, and
     Catholics (White Fathers) opened a mission station in 1933.
     Evangelisation has reached most Kimbu (70%), and there is a
     general feeling that people should have a *dini* (the imported
     Swahili/Arabic word for religion), that is, belong to an or-
     ganised religious group. Christianity continues to grow at
     a moderate rate, with about 25% traditionalists regarding
     themselves as not members of organised religions. There are
     members of the Salvation Army, Watch Tower, and the Anglican
     Church, but with no church workers. No scripture or liturgical
     translations have been made into the Kimbu language; Moravians
     use Nyamwezi (regarded as a foreign language), Catholics use
     Swahili.

     Work among the Kimbu has had to face the major problem of their
     semi-nomadic existence, with hunting and collecting preferred
     to agriculture which is difficult in forest conditions. Thus
     villages move about every six years. A second problem was the
     staffing of early missions by Germans, with their subsequent
     removal or interment during the two World Wars. After World
     War I, some Moravian missions were not staffed until 1932. It
     was during these years that Islam advanced among the Kimbu.
     Islam spread in Ukimbu with the building of the central railway
     line prior to the 1914-1918 war, and made great progress after
     1918 up to about 1930; Muslims now change little at 19%.

10. The first Catholic missionaries began work among the Bakongo
     (*Kongo*) of northern Angola in 1491, and by the 16th century an
     impressive church of a million baptised Kongo with a Kongo
     bishop, Henry, had been established. This early success was
     followed by a period of decline in which all Catholic activity
     was finally eclipsed. The modern era of Catholic missions
     dates from the creation of a new station at San Salvador in
     1881. Italian Capuchins are the principal missionary force
     at the present time. Three Protestant missionary societies
     were at work with the Bakongo previous to the rebellion of

1961: the British Baptists (BMS) who arrived in 1879, the North
Angola Mission after 1925, and the Canadian Baptists (CBMS) who
took up in the mid-1950s work which had been started earlier by
the Angola Evangelical Mission.

The extraordinary success of these various efforts is reflected
in the government census statistics of 1940, 1950 and 1960 for
the districts of Cabinda, Zaire and Uige, which are almost
exclusively Bakongo in ethnic composition. In 1940 the population of these three districts was 47.7% traditionalist, 29.3%
Catholic and 23.0% Protestant. By 1950 the traditionalist
percentage had dropped to 23.9%, with Catholics 41.3% and
Protestants 34.8%. The tendency already apparent in 1950 continued through the next decade, with the 1960 census identifying the Bakongo as 98% Christian (55.8% Catholic; 42.7%
Protestant and 1.5% traditionalist).

The civil war which broke out in 1961 and continues today
caused the migration of 400,000 Bakongo to neighbouring Zaire,
where they have greatly strengthened the local churches, and
also the exodus of all Protestant missionaries from the
northern part of Angola. Despite these upheavals, the Bakongo
(1.4 million of whom originate in Angola) remain one of the
half dozen or so most evangelised and christianised peoples on
the continent.

11. The *Mayogo* of Zaire are a small Sudanic ethnic group of about
25,000 who are located primarily in the region southwest of
Isiro town. Their neighbours include the Azande to the west,
Mangbetu to the north, Medje to the southwest and the Bantu
Budu to the southeast. Protestant missionary work was first
begun in the Isiro area by pioneers of the Heart of Africa
Mission who opened missions among the mangbetu in 1915 and the
Budu in 1921. Although the Mayogo were visited by HAM missionaries, no station was established among them which became an
increasing source of unrest. The eventual result of this feeling of neglect was the schism of the entire Mayogo section of
the church in 1960. During the past twelve years this independent Church of Gamba, as it is called, has been character-
ised by vitality and growth. According to a detailed analysis
of the church carried out in 1969 by staff from the Free
University at Kisangani, the total size of this Christian
community was 5,717 adults 15 years of age and older almost
all of whom were Mayogo. The figure includes baptised members,
catechumens and interested but unregistered Christians. Allowing for growth since 1969 and including children and youth
under age 15, the total Christian community of the Church of
Gamba in 1972 can be estimated at 10,000 or 40% of the population.

Catholic work with the Mayogo is carried on through the Diocese
of Wamba. The first station was opened among the Budu at
Avakubi, northeast of Bafwasende, in 1904. Bafwabaka, in Medje
country, was established in 1914 followed by Maboma among the
Mayogo in 1936. Although we lack for Catholics comparable
statistics to the detailed survey for the Church of Gamba, some
conclusions are possible. In 1967 the Wamba diocese was 28%
Catholic. This includes both adults and children, baptised and
catechumens, but it does not include interested but unregistere
Catholics who whould profess to be Catholics in a government
census. Together with church growth over the past five years,
this means that approximately 40% of the Mayogo are Catholics
in 1972. Our overall conclusion then is that the Mayogo are
about 80% Christian, with the remaining 20% still traditionalists; they are thus yet another fully-evangelised tribe which
has also become nearly all Christian.

12.   The Ovimbundu or *Mbundu*, noted in earlier days as the greatest
      traders of Bantu Africa, are the largest single ethnic group
      in Angola, numbering in 1972 approximately 1,870,000 people.
      The first Catholic church was established in the coastal city
      of Benguela in 1617, but continuous work was not begun inland
      until 1896 at Bailundo. Protestant work dates from 1880 with
      the arrival of the first missionaries of the American Board
      (ABCFM). Today there are four groups at work: the United
      Church of Christ (USA), the United Church of Canada, the Ply-
      mouth Brethren (CMML), and the Swiss Mission Philafricaine.
      Protestant activity was severely restricted after the Angolan
      rebellion of 1961.

      Since two-thirds of the Mbundu live in the exclusively Mbundu
      administrative districts of Benguela and Huambo, the detailed
      government census statistics of 1940, 1950 and 1960 provide a
      reliable indication of Mbundu acceptance of Christianity. In
      1940 the population professed to be 60.1% traditionalist, 29.9%
      Catholic and 10.0% Protestant. A decade later Catholics and
      Protestants had increased to 52.3% and 15.8% respectively,
      while traditionalists were down to 31.9%. After another
      decade, statistics for 1960 showed that Catholic growth had
      maintained its momentum, Catholics increasing to 65.6%, while
      Protestant growth had slackened considerably to reach 16.5%
      of the population, with 17.9% traditionalists. The period
      between 1960 and 1972 has witnessed a considerable reduction
      in Catholic growth (there being fewer and fewer remaining
      traditionalists to convert) and no appreciable change in the
      Protestant situation. The Mbundu today, at 90% Christian,
      are therefore one of the large number of African peoples which
      are not only completely evangelised but also almost completely
      christianised.

13. The *Ngumba* (30,000) are a small forest tribe near the coast
     in southern Cameroon. Evangelised and christianised by the
     American Presbyterian Mission, in 1934 almost the whole tribe
     broke with the mission on being denied services and scriptures
     in the Ngumba language, and formed their own separatist church
     Eglise Protestante Africaine, which has subsequently remained
     a purely tribal church. From 1934-1940 they attempted unsuc-
     cessfully to obtain French missionaries; and in 1943 a large
     section rejoined the Presbyterian mission. The goal of having
     their own scriptures began to be realised in 1957 with their
     translation of the first gospel in Ngumba. In 1962 the EPA
     joined the ecumenical Fédération des Eglises et Missions Evan-
     géliques du Cameroun, and in 1969 they were admitted an asso-
     ciate member of the World Council of Churches. By 1965 the
     tribe was fully evangelised, with 11,000 members in the EPA
     or about 17,000 (69%) professing (out of 25,000 tribal popula-
     tion then), 4,000 adherents of the mission body (or 30% pro-
     fessing), a very few Catholics, no Muslims, and hardly any
     traditionalists at all.

14. The northwestern Bantu tribes known collectively as the *Puku*
     of Equatorial Guinea number about 20,000. Missionaries from
     the Presbyterian Church in the USA first came to the Benga on
     Corisco Island in 1850, and to the Kombe on the mainland of
     Rio Muni in 1865. Catholics followed among the Benga in 1856,
     and the Kombe in 1885. This area was under French rule from
     1875 and shifted to Spanish rule after the Treaty of Paris in
     1900. While these coastal tribes have had the longest contact
     with Christianity, are more stable and less emotional than
     tribes of the interior, the missions have for some time felt
     that there is less church growth among them than among the
     Okak and Ntumu (sub-tribes of the Fang) in the interior, where
     church growth is still rapid. Thus Presbyterian growth has
     averaged only 15 new Puku adherents a year for 115 years; the
     Puku work is described as static, barely holding its own, even
     declining in places; and in 1937 one Kombe Presbyterian chapel
     seceded over personality and linguistic conflicts. Added to
     this unfavourable picture is the fact that for the first 50
     years, the coastal tribes were fearful of the interior peoples
     and opposed evangelising them, though eventually the first
     Protestant missionary to the Ntumu was a Benga pastor in the
     1920s.

     This case is an example of the need for care in comparing
     tribes and their relative church growth. The reason numerical
     growth is miniscule among the Puku is that they are small in
     number and 99% of them are already Christians; it is therefore
     impossible for further growth from conversions to occur. The

Fang tribes, on the other hand, are ten times bigger and still have over 20,000 professing animists from whom conversions come.

15.   The *Sandawe* (35,000) are an isolated non-Bantu tribe in north central Tanzania. Until recently they lived by hunting and gathering, but now they practise intensive agriculture and animal husbandry adopted from their Bantu neighbours. Descendants of early Bushmen who lived in the area in Paleolithic times, they speak a language of the Khoisan stock. Traditionally, they are monogamists. In recent years they have intermarried with the neighbouring Gogo, Turu and Maasai, and now only about 60% are 'pure' Sandawe.

The history of missions here is unusual in that only one mission has entered, namely the Catholic (WF and Passionist). Protestant missions have attempted to enter but have found the click language too formidable to learn. The Catholics founded stations at Kurio (1910), Farkwa (1928) and Ovada (1938), and 80% of the tribe have become Catholic. The area is entirely covered by mission activities.

16.   The *Senga* (10,000) are a central Bantu people in northeast Zambia who speak CiTumbuka and are strongly acculturated to the Tumbuka. Missions date from 1904 when the United Free Church of Scotland (Livingstonia Mission) established a station among the Senga. Though abandoned soon after, its influence remained paramount. The tribe was largely evangelised through the efforts of Tonga and Ngoni teacher-volunteers who worked in co-operation with the Scottish missionaries. No mission station has remained among the Senga because of the unhealthy nature of the country and its isolation; instead, regular visits were made by missionaries from the Tumbuka plateau. The Senga were aided in associating Christianity with traditional religion by the practice of the pioneer missionary Donald Fraser, who preached the gospel under trees previously used for traditional worship and established schools near them. The first evangelistic impact was very great, and the tribe felt a close link with the Livingstonia Mission; but the subsequent neglect of the Senga by the mission left it open to the witchcraft eradication movement of Alice Lenshina, which swept practically all Christians out of the Presbyterian church (CCAP) between 1955 and 1960; as a tribe, the Senga became for a time solidly Lumpa Church adherents. While many have returned, polygamy remains a stumbling block for numerous others. Catholics have never been numerous because most Senga chiefs do not allow Catholic missionary work; consequently a Catholic mission responsible for the Senga had to be opened in 1939 outside the tribal boundaries.

17. The *Tetela* are a people numbering about 300,000 found in cen-
     tral Zaire north of Lusambo and east of Lodja. Catholic work
     among them began about 1910 and is now carried on by the
     Passionist Fathers, Brothers of the Passion, and four orders
     of sisters. The Diocese of Tshumbe is composed almost entirely
     of Tetela people although some tribesmen reside outside the
     diocese's boundaries. Protestant work began in 1914 with the
     arrival of American Methodists. Except for a few Tetela on
     the northern fringe of the tribe who have been evangelised by
     the Plymouth Brethren of the North Sankuru Mission, Protestants
     are mainly of Methodist background.

     The Catholic Church has not been as successful among the Tetela
     as it has in most parts of Zaire (now 51% Catholic). Out of
     247,000 inhabitants in the Diocese of Tshumbe in 1969, 54,200
     were baptised Catholics with 3,000 catechumens (23% of the
     population). Allowing for church growth since 1969 and Tetela
     residing outside the diocese, Tetela Catholics in 1972 are
     estimated at 75,000 or 25%.

     Methodist work has progressed more rapidly, especially since
     national independence in 1960. In 1932 a large people move-
     ment was recorded in the Wembo Nyama area among the eastern
     Tetela; and from 1960-1972 church membership has tripled, most
     of the growth taking place in the Lodja area of the western
     Tetela, with most conversions following family, clan or sub-
     tribal groupings. The 1971 statistics for the Methodist Central
     Zaire Annual Conference, which is almost exclusively Tetela,
     list 34,924 full members and 36,690 preparatory members. In-
     cluding children and youth under membership age, the total
     Methodist community numbers at least 95,000. Including Brethren
     adherents to the north, Protestant Tetela now number about 33%,
     therefore, making Christians 58% of the tribe. The Tetela thus
     are typical of a very large number of African peoples which are
     now in general evangelised, and which have responded by the
     majority joining Christian communities.

18. The *Tumbuka* (350,000) who live in northern Malawi are about 70%
     Christian. The arrival of the Livingstonia Mission of the Free
     Church of Scotland among the Lakeside Tonga (a sub-tribe) in
     1881 probably saved the tribe from extermination by the Ngoni.
     It was from among the Tonga that the mission moved out among
     the Naoni and Ngonde, and among other Tumbuka people. The
     Tonga responded to Christianity in vast numbers, large revivals
     and mass movements into the mission taking place in 1899 and
     1903, and in 1908 the most important of all separatist move-
     ments in Central Africa (Church of the Watch Tower) began with
     Elliott Kamwana baptising 10,000 Tonga at Bandawe. The Tonga

have always been a politically conscious tribe; it was a Mutonga
who in 1928 suggested taking over the church from missionaries
and who subsequently in 1933 withdrew to establish the Black-
man's Church. Other independent churches include the National
Church, Cipangano (Church of the Covenant), Last Church of God.
Anglicans also had a work from early days, now in the Diocese
of Lake Malawi; and Catholics, whose first station was opened
as late as 1938, in the Diocese of Mzuzu. Contributing factors
to past receptivity to Christianity among the Tonga include the
stronger individualism among them compared with other local
tribes, which permitted individual response to the gospel; and
also the complete absence of secret societies exerting control
over them. While traditional religion is dying out among the
Tumbuka, Christianity in both Protestant and Catholic forms is
growing only slowly at present. Presbyterianism remains the
dominant Christian group, with Assemblies of God, Seventh-day
Adventists, Jehovah's Witnesses and others also at work. The
Tumbuka have been fully evangelised in the sense that translated
scriptures have been available for half a century, and the
gospel has for some time now been preached everywhere.

19. The name *Yoruba* can be applied either to the 10 million Yoruba-
     speaking peoples of western Nigeria, or (as in Murdock's
     classification used in this survey and on the map) to the 5
     million Yoruba proper (Ibadan, or Oyo). In 1842, repatriated
     slaves with the Church Missionary Society were the first people
     to bring Christianity to the Yoruba. In 1885 the first Catho-
     lic mission (White Fathers) arrived, but had relatively little
     influence, only 5% being Catholics today. The whole Bible was
     translated into Yoruba in 1884, mainly through Adjai Crowther
     the first African Anglican bishop, Islam is widespread through-
     out the Yoruba and some 43% are Muslims; they are assisted by
     foreign Muslim missionaries, but are not expanding noticeably
     by conversions. There are few unevangelised areas where
     Christian teaching has not reached, and about 47% of the Yoruba
     are Anglicans, Protestants or followers of the scores of
     indigenous churches (prayer groups, Cherubim and Seraphim,
     etc.). Many Yoruba customs, and music, are incorporated in
     church life.

20. The best-documented case of exceptionally rapid response to
     evangelisation concerns the *Tiv* (1,200,000) in the non-
     islamised pagan belt of northern Nigeria. For political
     reasons the Tiv are opposed to Islam, and their extra-
     ordinary response to Christianity appears to be in part due
     to this as well as due to the labours of the Christian
     Reformed Church Mission (Sudan United Mission), virtually
     the only Protestant mission among this tribe. Work began in

1911, initiated by the Dutch Reformed Church of South Africa: there was practically no response for the first thirty years, but rapid growth began around 1940 with the indigenous Bible School movement; by 1965 this had grown into some 900 CRIs (Classes for Religious Instruction). The numbers attending church on Sundays have long been growing phenomenally: in 1955, the total was 21,485; in 1960, 46,888; in 1964, 109,837; in 1968, 199,014. This rapid growth, about ten times as great as the West Africa average, is explained partly by the great emphasis laid by the SUM on church schools, and partly by sophisticated methods such as the Sevav plan for clan evangelisation. By 1967 the Tiv Church (NKST) was served by a large force of 28 missionaries (8 ordained), 31 African ministers and 2,000 lay workers. Catholics began work in 1931 and by 1967 had an equally massive work force of 18 missionary priests (but no Tiv priests), and 1,500 African lay workers.

The speed of christianisation among the Tiv can be clearly seen from the attached graph based on the three government censuses of 1931, 1952 and 1963 (the latter with corrected figures), supplemented by Protestant and Catholic church statistics. In brief, it suggests that the Tiv progressed from unevangelised to fully evangelised in the short space of twenty years, from 1940-1960, and it shows that Tiv response rose from practically nothing (under 0.3% Christian) in 1940 to 95% Christian thirty-two years later in 1972. This is probably the most rapid mass conversion of a major African people in history.

21. The *Zulu* nation is one of the largest Vantu peoples in Africa, with a total population of 3,900,000 inhabiting a large area in eastern South Africa. Zululand is a collection of tribal areas, where a few missionaries and other whites are allowed to work with government permission. The eventual Zulu homeland or Bantustan will be a fragmented mass of pieces fitting in and around white areas. The first mission to work among the Zulu was the American Board (ABCFM), which arrived in 1835 and penetrated into the interior. Anglicans and Catholics followed in 1850-1870. Subsequently a large number of other missions have begun work. In 1890 began the Zulu Nbiyana Church, the first of a thousand or so distinct indigenous Zulu churches to separate from the missions; in the 1960 census, these AIC adherents numbered 19% of the Zulu, increasing to about 25% in 1972 (total 980,000). The Zulu are, in general, evangelised (80%); about 60% are Christians of all types, and about 40% still profess to be traditionalists (50% in the 1960 census). Catholic influence is small, 9%, except for one diocese, Mariannhill, where about 25% of the Zulu are Catholics.

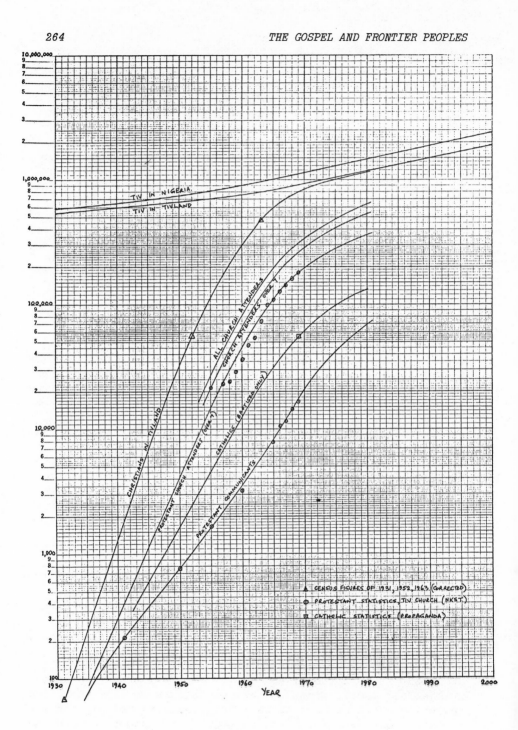

TABLE 3: A SELECTION OF RESPONSIVE & EVANGELISED TRIBES IN AFRICA, 1972

In order to clarify the meaning of evangelisation, and of evangelised peoples, this table gives basic data concerning a selection of 45 tribes out of the 411 peoples and tribes of Africa defined in this survey as evangelised (i.e. peoples in which over 50% of the population has come into contact with Christianity and so has heard the gospel, and which have responded in that traditionalists (animists) are now reduced to under 60% in number). The 21 tribes marked below with an asterisk, are further described in brief case studies in the text preceding this table. A detailed explanation of this table and its columns is given in the text, section IV; and a visual presentation of its data is given in the map at the end (all peoples shown in white = responsive evangelised tribes). For ease of reference, the meaning of the 16 columns below is given again here, as follows:

Col.1: Total population of tribe in mid-1972. 2-5: Percentage of tribe professing to be respectively, traditionalists, Muslims, Catholics, Protestants (with all other types of Christian). 6: Total professing traditionalists in tribe. 7: Scripture translations published in tribe's own language: G = gospel, N = New Testament, B = complete Bible; - = none. 8-10: years when G, N, B, respectively, were published. 11,12: years when, respectively, Catholic and Protestant missionary work began (c = circa, approximately). 13: % of tribe evangelised (note: 95% = fully evangelised', in this survey). 14: Total unevangelised in tribe. 15: SE (status of evangelisation) index, i.e. extent to which tribe and its culture is evangelised. 16: Miscellaneous notes on each tribe; initials = major Protestant, Anglican or AIC churches or missions now or recently at work, with Catholic orders mentioned occasionally (see Directory in appendix); AIC, AICs = one, or more, African independent churches from within the tribe are undertaking evangelisation.

Tribe (and NATION)	Population mid-1972	Religious profession,%				Tradits	Total	Scriptures Dates			Origin		TE	Unevanged	SE %	Main missions at work, etc.
		Tr	Mu	RC	Pr			Gosp	NT	Bible	RC	Prot				
1	1	2	3	4	5	6	7	8	9	10	11	12	13	14	15	16
*Ambo (NAMIBIA)	352,000	40		10	50	141,000	GNB	1891	1903	1954	1924	c1870	90	35,200	90	ELOC, Anglicans. In Angola, mainly Catholics.
Bamileke (CAMEROON)	866,000	55	1	29	15	476,000	GN	1948	1967		c1910	1911	60	346,400	45	EEC, PCMC; 1961, 18 months; evangelistic campaign.
Baya (CENTRAL AFR REP)	436,000	15		25	58	65,400	GN	1933	1951		1923	1923	80	87,200	60	Swedish Baptist, CBM, Assemblies of God.
*Duala (CAMEROON)	100,000			37	63		GNB	1848	1861	1845	1890	1845	95	5,000	95	100% Christian (AICs, etc.) but traditionalism reviving.
*Egba (NIGERIA)	627,000	5	55	7	33	31,300	GNB	1850	1862	1884	1857	1842	95	31,400	95	CMS and numerous others; AICs.
Ewe (TOGO)	500,000	10		60	25	75,000	GNB	1858	1877	1913	1892	1847	95	25,000	95	EET, Eglise Methodiste, Eglise Apostolique, SVD, AICs.
Fang (EQUAT GUINEA)	214,000	10		87	3	21,400	G	1896	1926	1940	c1919	1929	95	10,700	95	EPC, WEC, AICs.
Ha (TANZANIA)	470,000	53	21	20	6	249,000	G	1960			1914	1934	60	188,000	30	CMS, Neukirchner Mission, SPM, SDA, AIC.
*Haya (TANZANIA)	526,000	27	7	50	16	142,000	GN	1920	1930		c1892	1910	90	52,600	67	ELCT (Church of Sweden Mission), WF, SPM, AIC.
*Ibibio (NIGERIA)	1,640,000	3		10	87	49,200	GN	1850	1862	1868	c1890	c1890	95	82,000	95	Most densely evangelised areas in Africa. Many AICs.
Ibo (NIGERIA)	8,000,000	10		30	60	1,200,000	GNB	1893	1900	1906	1885	1857	95	400,000	95	Anglicans, many Protestant and AIC bodies.
*Kamba (KENYA)	1,323,400	39		14	47	516,000	GNB	1850	1920	1956	1912	1892	70	397,000	70	AIM, AICMS, CMS, SPS. Many AICs since 1945.
*Kikuyu (KENYA)	2,433,000	27		26	47	657,000	GNB	1903	1926	1951	1902	1898	95	121,600	95	CSM, CMS, CCM, etc. Many AICs from 1921.
*Kimbu (TANZANIA)	50,000	25	19	26	30	12,500		1933			1933	1901	70	15,000	17	Moravian Church, WF.
*Kongo (ANGOLA)	1,400,000	0		57	43	0	GNB	1888	1893	1916	1881	1879	95	70,000	95	BMS, CBMS, AICs. Many in Zaire as refugees.
Kongo (CONGO-BRAZZ)	520,000	0		53	47	0	GNB	1885	1891	1905	1887	1900	95	26,000	95	SMF (EEC), SA, etc., and AICs.
Korana (SOUTH AFRICA)	10,000	10		10	80	1,000	GNB	1893		1933	1893	1801	95	500	95	LMS, Griquas, a slowly dying race of Hottentot nomads.
Kwena (BOTSWANA)	80,000	40		5	55	32,000	GNB	1942	1957	1970	c1950	1842	95	4,000	95	LMS, UFCSM, USPG, A of God, SDA, AICs.
Labwor (UGANDA)	8,700	20		5	75	1,700					1948	1945	90	900	22	BCMS. Almost all Catholics now.
Lokele (ZAIRE)	30,000	40		15	45	12,000	GNB	1903	1918		1900	1895	90	3,000	67	BMS, Salvation Army, Sacre Coeur, EJCSK, AICs.
Luchazi (ANGOLA)	70,000	50		30	20	35,000	GNB	1935	1963		c1934	c1918	95	3,500	95	AEF, CBML, SDA.
Luvale (ANGOLA)	55,000	50		30	20	27,500	GNB	1902	1928	1955	c1934	c1891	95	2,750	95	CBML, AICs.
Mandja (CENT AFR REP)	136,000	7		25	65	9,500	-				c1943		95	6,800	24	BMM, Brethren Mission, AIC.
*Mayogo (ZAIRE)	25,000	20		40	40	5,000	-				1904	1917	95	1,200	24	HAM (WEC); all members in separatist AIC from 1960.
Mbae (ZAIRE)	15,000	40		25	35	6,000	-				1920	1900	80	3,000	20	BMS, banding over in 1950 to UFM; AIC.
*Mbundu (ANGOLA)	1,870,000	10		23	67	187,000	GNB	1889	1897	1963	1880	1880	95	93,500	95	ABCFM (now UCBWM), UCC, CBML, MF, AICs.
*Ngumba (CAMEROON)	30,000	10		1	89	0	G	1957			1955	Nil	95	1,500	47	All Christians, either EPA (indigenous AIC) or EPC.
*Puku (EQUAT GUINEA)	20,000	1		10	89	200	GNB	1858	1871	1911	1856	1850	95	1,000	95	Ev Presb Church in Rio Muni, AIC.
Ruanda (RWANDA)	3,800,000	30	1	52	17	1,140,000	GNB	1914	1931	1954	1900	1907	90	380,000	90	Bethel Mission, CMS Ruanda Mission.
Rundi (BURUNDI)	3,700,000	23	1	58	18	851,000	GNB	1920	1951	1967	1899	1911	90	370,000	24	CMS Ruanda Mission, WGM, SDA, AICs, and 10 others.
*Sandawe (TANZANIA)	35,000	10	10		80	3,500	-				Nil	Nil	95	1,700	24	WF only; language too difficult for other entrants.
*Senga (ZAMBIA)	10,000	50			50	5,000	GNB	1904	1911	1957	1939	1904	90	1,000	90	UFCSM, AICs. 1955 all Christians swept into Lumpa AIC.
Sotho (LESOTHO)	1,000,000	13		41	46	130,000	GNB	1839	1855	1878	1863	1833	85	50,000	85	Lesotho Ev Ch, other missions, and many AICs.
Swazi (SWAZILAND)	400,000	17		9	74	68,000	GNB	1848	1865	1883	1914	1838	85	60,000	80	19 Protestant and 30 AIC denominations.
*Tetela (ZAIRE)	300,000	41	1	25	33	123,000	GNB	1919	1938	1966	1914	1914	80	60,000	80	Eglise Methodiste, North Sankuru Mission, AICs.
Teuso (UGANDA)	5,000	20			80	1,000	-				1955	Nil	90	500	22	Rapid Catholic conversion of nomadic hunting tribe.
*Tiv (NIGERIA)	1,200,000	5		35	60	60,000	GNB	1916	1936	1964	1931	1911	95	60,000	95	DRC Mission (now CRCN).
Topoke (ZAIRE)	40,000	30		20	50	20,000	G	1923			c1920	1895	85	6,000	42	BMS, Sacre Coeur, DC, AICs.
Toro (UGANDA)	300,000	15		50	30	45,000	GNB	1900	1905	1912	1897	1896	85	45,000	85	CMS, East African Revival Fellowship, SDA, AICs.
*Tsonga (MOZAMBIQUE)	1,500,000	45		1	36	675,000	GNB	1892	1894	1907	1887	1887	55	675,000	55	Swiss Mission, SDA, 5 other missions, AICs.
Tsonga (SOUTH AFRICA)	750,000	30		3	67	225,000	GNB	1892	1894	1907		1875	55	225,000	55	Swiss Mission, several others, and many AICs.
*Tumbuka (MALAWI)	350,000	30		35	35	105,000	GNB	1904	1911	1957	1938	1881	80	17,500	95	Also in Zambia. UPCSM (Livingstonia Mission), AICs.
*Yoruba (NIGERIA)	5,000,000	5	43	5	47	250,000	GNB	1850	1862	1884	1852	1842	80	1,000,000	80	Anglicans, many Protestant and AIC bodies.
*Zulu (SOUTH AFRICA)	3,900,000	40		9	51	1,560,000	GNB	1848	1865	1883	1852	1835	80	780,000	80	ABCFM, many others. About 25% (980,000) are in AICs.
Zumper (Kutev)(NIGERIA)	30,000	30		0	70	9,000	-				1925	1925	80	6,000	20	SUM. Large response to gospel.

VII.   CASE STUDIES OF UNEVANGELISED PEOPLES IN FRONTIER SITUATIONS
       (Table 4)

       The concept of a people being numerically or culturally unevan-
gelised is explained and elaborated on in this section, by giving in
Table 4 comparative basic data on all known cases in Africa of
unevangelised, partially evangelised and resistant tribes (numbering
in all 236), and by describing in more detail the situation in 25 of
these tribes by means of brief tribal case studies. Twenty-three of
these studies now follow in alphabetical order, and two other case
studies of unevangelised tribes (Fon, Mossi) are given in the following section, VIII. Each case study should be read in conjunction
with its line of related data in Table 4.

1.   The *Arusha* or agricultural Maasai are a Bantu nomadic tribe of
       110,000 in northern Tanzania, closely resembling the Nilotic
       Maasai among whom they live and whose culture and language they
       share. The Leipzig Mission began among them in 1904, and
       Catholics since about 1921. More recently, Assemblies of God,
       Adventists and Southern Baptists (USA) have opened work. About
       12% are professing Christians; there are no Muslims, and the
       rest follow relatively strong animistic religion. In 1954 a
       syncretistic Old Testament religion disowning the New Testament
       was begun on Mount Meru by a carpenter named Festo Lekariro;
       and an animistic revival among women under a prophetess Mama
       Karani began in 1960. The Lutheran Church grew very rapidly
       from 3,000 to 7,000 members over the decade 1950-1960, but
       growth has subsequently slowed down. Arusha culture continues
       to impart a sense of superiority to its members, aided by its
       relative isolation from Western influences. Ownership of cat-
       tle still determines social prestige, and the difficulty in
       acquiring cattle if one attends school or takes a job, continue
       to militate against the desirability of education and Christian-
       ity. The people as a whole are still largely unevangelised
       (20% only).

2.   The Batswa or *Central Twa* (100,000 in Zaire) are a pygmy group
       who live interspersed among the various sub-tribes of the
       Bantu-speaking Mongo in the dense equatorial forests east of
       Mbandaka. Although there has been some intermarriage and
       borrowing of culture from their Mongo neighbours, they have
       generally maintained their traditional customs as hunting,
       fishing and gathering peoples. Their semi-nomadic mode of
       life has made Christian evangelisation among them extremely
       difficult. The Catholic Church began work at Bamanya in 1895
       and three Protestant churches (Congo Balolo Mission in 1889,
       British Baptists in 1890, and Disciples of Christ in 1899)
       have been active in the region. All have attempted work among

the Twa but with indifferent success, although the Disciples in 1967 had 4,500 communicant members among them in 40 congregations, with 200 catechumens. The Twa are undoubtedly the most resistant to change of any tribe in western Zaire.

3.   The *Chokwe* and *Lunda* of Angola (population 400,000) can be considered here as a single unit. Although they exist in small numbers in eastern Bié, western Moxico and central Cuando Cubango, they have their greatest concentration in, and are almost the sole inhabitants of, the Lunda District of northeastern Angola. This fact allows us to use the very comprehensive government census statistics of 1940, 1950 and 1960 to analyse the results of evangelistic activities among them. Catholic activity in Lunda District began in 1900 when the Holy Ghost fathers crossed the Cuango River and established a mission station at Mussuco. Progress to the east was slow as evidenced by the fact that no mission station was established at the district capital of Henrique de Carvalho until 1930. Today there are Catholic mission stations in all parts of the district.

Protestant work among the Chokwe-Lunda dates from 1908 with the building of the Luma-Cassai mission by the Plymouth Brethren (CMML). This was followed by the Biula mission in 1917 and still later the Nhama mission at the district capital. There are no Protestant missions north of this city. In 1925 the Seventh-day Adventists began work at Luz, and in the Cuando Cubango district the Africa Evangelical Fellowship has some contact with Chokwe peoples.

On first examination the Chokwe and Lunda seem to represent a unique case from the standpoint of evangelisation, i.e. a case of a people who after a promising beginning have shown a reversion to traditional religion. In the 1940 census the Lunda District reported 96.2% traditionalists, 2.7% Catholics and 1.1% Protestants. By 1950 both Catholics (9.8%) and Protestants (4.9%) had made significant progress, reducing the percentage of traditionalists to 85.3%. This pattern of Christian expansion was in general conformity with what was taking place in other parts of the country. However, the 1960 census showed a startling drop to only 8.5% Catholics and 3.4% Protestants, with the non-Christian population increasing again to 88.1%.

The explanation for this phenomenon seems to lie in what was happening in the Lunda District in the decade 1950-1960. The census reveals not only a decrease in the number of Christians but also an overall reduction of nearly 20,000 in population.

The population figures are as follows: 1940 - 243,400, 1950 - 266,087, and 1960 - 247,273. Whereas one might have expected the population to increase to around 290,000 by 1960, it actually decreased to 247,000. The government explanation is that this is due to the migratory movement of about 40,000 people from the relatively undeveloped Lunda District to greater opportunities mostly in Bié District to the southwest. Of these migrants Christians probably formed a large majority.

The conclusion then is that Christianity has continued to grow among the Lunda and Chokwe but that the conversion rate in their home district has not been sufficient to counter the exodus of labourers. The Lunda-Chokwe taken as a whole are still predominantly traditionalist (about 75%) and the challenge of work among them in Lunda District is especially acute.

4.   The *Dogon* (or Habbe, or Kado) of Mali (312,000) are one of a number of still largely pagan tribes living on the southern fringes of the Sahara Desert and only partially islamised (30%) The Dogon are well-known for their houses built high on the sides of steep cliffs. In the late 1920s a famine swept over their land and thousands died. Because the traditional sacrifices had failed to bring rain, on the arrival of the first workers of the Christian and Missionary Alliance in 1931 men came to their station to enquire if prayer would bring rain. Two hours were spent in prayer to God in Jesus' name, and rain fell. Subsequently the Dogon have responded to the gospel and a large church has evolved, with 40 ordained pastors (Bible School graduates), 100 Dogon catechists, churches throughout the district, and about 7,000 baptised adults across the countryside and in 85 towns.

5.   The Wandorobo or *Dorobo* of Kenya (22,000) are a secretive people who live in small dispersed groups in mountainous forest areas among the Nandi and Maasai. Another 3,000 are scattered in northern Tanzania. Until recently their economy was based solely on hunting and gathering. With the government's continued development of forest areas, the Dorobo are gradually being resettled on farmland. Mission work among them has been very spasmodic. In the 1960s a Kenyan evangelist of the Church Army (Anglican) attempted to reach Dorobo in the dense forests south of Kericho, but they proved too bellicose. In 1969, a Samburu evangelist was sent by the Diocese of Mount Kenya's DMA (Diocesan Missionary Association) to Doldol, northwest of Mount Kenya, the headquarters of 12,000 Dorobo on a 400 square mile tract of country. In 1970 the diocese posted a CMS missionary there. Many local chiefs and elders have welcomed the preaching of the gospel and the adult literacy classes being

run, and a Dorobo church has been built up recording many
baptisms each year. In 1971 a PCEA (Presbyterian) couple
began working among two Dorobo villages northeast of Nakuru,
but found the people illiterate, apathetic and listless. Two
youths had been sent some years before to receive primary
education. One Dorobo had become a Christian as a result of
a stay in hospital, and is now the Presbyterian evangelist,
taking Sunday services in each village; the two youths are
now teachers for the village children.

The Dorobo speak only the languages of the tribes they live
among (Kalenjin or Maasai). Monogamous marriage is the norm;
and villages are held together through well-structured social
systems of authority and moral standards. Christianity can
thus be related to the traditional culture. While a number
of Dorobo families have been evangelised and have responded,
missionaries' policy is not to conduct baptisms until certain
that the new Christians can remain integrated in village life.

6. The Eggon (80,000) are a sub-tribe of the *Mada*, one of the
    numerous plateau peoples of the central belt in northern
    Nigeria. The Sudan United Mission (South African branch)
    entered the area in 1926, and Catholics began with a teacher
    training college in 1953 and a hospital in 1962. Prior to
    1924, missionaries were forbidden by the administration to
    enter the area unescorted because of the warlike nature of
    the tribe. Some time previously, one of the most powerful
    Eggon witchdoctors had prophesied that a man with a white face
    would arrive to teach the way of God; consequently, the
    appearance of the first missionary was taken as a fulfilment
    of that prophecy and he was readily accepted. Subsequently
    the area was thoroughly evangelised (90%), but the Mada have
    remained conservative and resistant to change, with 75% con-
    tinuing to adhere strongly to traditional beliefs. About 5%
    have become Muslims. The only scriptures translated are one
    of the gospels (1935), but the Hausa Bible is used by those
    who are literate. This then is an example of a tribe which,
    although virtually fully evangelised, has remained resistant
    to the gospel.

7. The *Falasha* or 'Black Jews' (30,000) are classified as a sub-
    tribe of the Kemant of 100,000, who are entirely Ethiopian
    Orthodox except for the Falasha. They are descendants of the
    Agau, portions of whom became converted to Judaism during the
    Diaspora when many Jews fled to Ethiopia. They subsist pri-
    marily by agriculture, with ox-drawn ploughs and occasionally
    irrigation. The Church's Ministry among the Jews (Anglican,
    formerly Church Missions to Jews) have worked among them since

1860, and estimate that since then 2,000 baptisms among the Falasha have taken place due to their efforts, with perhaps another 10,000 baptised, indirectly related to their work. CMJ work is based on their two mission stations at Dabat and Jenda. As a result of social and economic pressures, practically all Falasha want to become baptised Christians; however, possibly 80% have still not heard the gospel. The CMJ has helped to organise an Orthodox indigenous missionary society or fellowship of converts to assist with evangelisation.

Attempts to convert the Falasha to Orthodox Judaism have met with little success. They base their faith directly on the Old Testament, without knowing the Talmud. This heritage has prepared them for the teaching of the New Testament. The most effective work among the Falasha by the CMJ has been the establishment of a residential Families' School, where parents live for two years and study the Bible while their children follow the normal government curriculum. After two years, families return to their former villages and witness to the love of Christ, receiving mission support for the first year after they return.

A consistent CMJ policy has been to refer all converted Falasha to the Ethiopian Orthodox Church to be baptised. A drawback has been the lack of training of Ethiopian clergy to build up these new converts in the faith. To assist in this problem, former CMJ personnel among the Falasha have recently joined with BCMS as the teaching staff of an elementary theological school offering Bible preparation for young men wanting to become Orthodox priests.

8.   The *Gbari* (500,000) are a large people widely scattered throughout an area of over 40,000 square miles in the central belt of northern Nigeria. Numerous small tribes are found among them, but the missions and churches working among them have had only limited contact with the Gbari themselves. When the Sudan Interior Mission began work here about 1910, they found the tribe composed of two groups, Gbari Yamma and Gbari Mattai. The former have shown scant response to the gospel, churches established among them proving to be very unstable; but work among the Gbari Mattai has been fruitful from the very beginning. An early contributing factor was the help given by medical missionaries during an epidemic of the disease yaws. The area is now evangelised in general, and the evangelism-in-depth campaign New Life for All has had considerable success here. So far no Catholic mission has been opened.

9.   The *Gio* (92,000) in Liberia are an example of a tribe split
      by arbitrary colonial frontiers. They are part of the large
      Ngere/Dan tribe, now divided up into three by the borders
      between Guinea, Liberia and the Ivory Coast. This confusion
      is mirrored in their nomenclature: the Gio call themselves
      Dan in the Ivory Coast, San in Liberia; in the former terri-
      tory the French called them Yakuba; in Liberia, their kindred
      tribe, the Mano, call them Ngere (country devils); and there
      are at least 25 other names in use. The Liberian Gio have
      two paramount chiefs, one of whom rules over 53 villages and
      50,000 people from his seat in Bahn.

      Missions began in 1938 with the opening of the Liberia Inland
      Mission (WEC) station at Bahn. By an early date the mission
      had trekked throughout Gio territory, and churches had been
      planted. Solid linguistic work was fostered, resulting in
      missionaries learning Gio and translating gospels in 1943,
      and most of the New Testament subsequently. By 1965, the
      LIM had 12 church buildings, about 25 congregations, and some
      2,000 Gio believers; and the Mid-Liberia Baptist Mission also
      had about 1,000 adherents. Both with LIM and Methodist mis-
      sions in Liberia and with the CMA mission in Guinea, the Gio
      have been more responsive than their sister-tribe the Mano.
      In the Ivory Coast, however, the Gio (Dan) response has been
      even greater than in Liberia. Based on their big station at
      Man, begun in 1938, the Mission Biblique there has experienced
      revival, and has numerous African workers. Despite the fron-
      tier, the two Gio churches freely intermingle for meetings and
      conventions.

      The question arises as to why the Gio have responded more than
      their neighbours, and why the frontiers have not impeded the
      vigorous growth of Gio Protestants. The LIM at Bahn have given
      the problem close study, and conclude that response to the gos-
      pel is linked with the initiation ceremony in traditional
      tribal religion. The Mano (as also the Kpelle, Loma and Mende
      of Liberia) have a deeply entrenched ceremony, hence resist the
      change implicit in the gospel, while the Gio have a ceremony so
      weak that they often bring youths to the mission clinic for
      circumcision. The implications of this are that variations of
      response to the gospel may often be due to factors in tradi-
      tional society, or even to missionary knowledge or ignorance
      of such factors.

10.   The *Gogo* (480,000) are a large tribe living in the dry Rift
      Valley area of central Tanzania, who in 1970 were chosen to
      be the first tribal people amongst whom the ugamaa village
      programme (a Tanzanian socialist experiment) was introduced,

meeting with considerable resistance. The Gogo have a long
history of conservatism and resistance to change, and their
strong animism (still 70%) has enabled them to resist Islam
also. The history of missions goes back nearly a hundred
years. The Church Missionary Society came in 1878; early
growth was very slow, attributed to large losses by death,
the relatively short life span of people at that time, and
the shifting cultivation practice which meant that converts
constantly moved elsewhere particularly in times of famine.
In recent years, Christianity has exhibited exceptionally
rapid growth, membership in the Anglican diocese of Central
Tanganyika showing an annual increase of 12% in communicants
and 6% in total adherents during 1960-1970 (respectively,
four and two times larger than the general population increase)
This growth has several causes: the impact of education,
social changes, the East African Revival movement, and the
presence of church structures serving a wide variety of
social, educational, literacy and health needs. The church
was therefore structurally ready to assist the Gogo as they
encountered rapid social change. Other contributing factors
have been the use of the vernacular (rather than the lingua
franca, Swahili) in liturgical services, African leadership,
and dependence on local support rather than on funds from
abroad. About 60% of the Gogo have been evangelised, with
25% of these accepting Christianity. In addition to the
Anglican and Catholic dioceses, there are also several Pentecostal groups.

11. In 1936, the Eglise Evangélique du Togo began missionary work
among the *Kabre* tribe (now 273,000) in the north of the
country. This initiative on the part of a whole church has
produced fruit in the form of, by 1965, 37 Kabre congregations
with approximately 1,500 members, growing by 1972 to a Protestant community of 2% of the tribe. In 1952 the Sudan Interior
Mission opened a station among the Dompago sub-tribe just
across the border in Dahomey. In 1955 the first gospel in
Kabre was published. The Catholic mission by 1972 has reached
practically all Kabre villages, and their adherents number 12%.
This then is an example of a highly-evangelised tribe with
well-organised and long-standing Protestant and Catholic numerical evangelisation, but which still remains 85% traditionalist and whose culture has been evangelised only superficially
so far.

12. The *Kindiga* are a small tribe of about 2,000, living an independent life of hunting and gathering near Lake Eyasi in
northern Tanzania. They speak a Khoisan (click) language,
Hadzapi, in which there are as yet no scripture translations

but several hymns translated from English. There has been a
ready and rapid response to Christianity since the first
visits were made by the Augustana Lutheran Mission of ELCT
Central Synod in 1959 and the first baptisms of 30 persons
in 1965. There has been no Catholic work, and only one other
body, Mbulu Pentecostal Church, has attempted evangelisation.
Virtually all have now been evangelised (95%), with about 60%
still following the somewhat weak traditional animism. The
traditional practice of monogamy has favoured the spread of
the gospel, and the Kindiga, who live in the bush without huts,
are being encouraged to settle in villages as an aid to establishing relationships with them.

13.   The *Kono* tribe (133,000) occupy the Kono administrative district in the Sierra Leone mountains near the northeastern
border with Guinea. They are a vigorous and progressive
people, traditionally governed under some twenty independent
paramount chiefdoms. The discovery of immense diamond-bearing
areas around 1940 made a tremendous impact on the Kono. Before
the mass expulsion of non-Sierra Leonians from the district
around 1964, there were 100,000 Africans engaged in illegal
digging in the area.

Islam is considered a foreign religion, and the Kono are
virtually all animists (95%). The only Protestant mission
(the Evangelical United Brethren) arrived in 1910, but has
only been able tu supply an average of three missionaries over
the years. In 1911, a Sherbro pastor, the Rev. David M.
Caulker, arrived, and laboured for six decades. He translated
the Gospel of Matthew in 1919, but indecision about the value
of vernacular scriptures has prevented further effort to
publish any Kono New Testament.

With these small resources, it is not surprising that Protestants by 1965 numbered only 600 members, or 1,000 baptised,
spread over 21 congregations, with one ordained missionary
and an ordained Sherbro superintendent, with only slight numerical increase over the last seven years; similarly, the
Catholic mission, begun in 1949, now has about 2,000 adherents.
The Seventh-day Adventists also have one small congregation.
The only other Christian work present is in fact the largest--
that of the African independent churches. The Church of the
Lord (Aladura), with around ten Kono centres, may be regarded
as a Nigerian mission, but the God is Our Light Church is a
genuinely Kono movement with Kono membership. Beginning in
1952 on initiatives from independents from Ghana (then the
Gold Coast), by 1965 it had 25 town and country congregations,
and is now making a genuine evangelistic impact on animistic
society.

Here then is a dynamic tribe potentially highly responsive to
the gospel, but for whom to date quite inadequate missionary
resources have been made available by churches beyond its
borders.

14.   A concern of this survey has been the extent to which Islam
      is becoming accepted by hitherto pagan tribes. In this sec-
      tion, we give brief notes of three such tribes, the Koranko,
      Mossi and Serer. The *Koranko* are a tribe of 103,000 in Sierra
      Leone and a somewhat smaller number in Guinea. Only one
      mission is at work -- the (American) Missionary Church Asso-
      ciation, which has 300 baptised members in 20 congregations.
      Islam has progressed to the extent that the northern half of
      the tribe is Muslim or under Muslim influence, while the
      southern half remains more or less unevangelised.

15.   The *Lotuka* (258,000) are an agricultural-pastoral tribe of
      the southern Sudan on the border with Uganda. Catholics began
      working here about 1920, and the Africa Inland Mission in 1951.
      The latter translated the New Testament into the Lotuka lan-
      guage, but achieved little success in evangelisation (7%) prior
      to the expulsion of Western missionaries in 1963. Resistance
      to mission activities on the part of government and the out-
      break of civil war in 1956 prevented the work from ever getting
      properly under way. The Lotuka are friendly and open, willing
      to talk and listen, but hesitant to accept new ideas. Their
      living together in large villages makes them eminently access-
      ible to evangelisation; meanwhile in the absence of outside
      Christian workers, 90% remain strong traditionalists.

16.   The *Maasai* are a Nilotic-speaking pastoral and nomadic people
      who occupy a large part of the Rift Valley in Kenya (numbering
      171,200) and northern Tanzania (numbering 100,000) and who
      have resisted Western education, civilisation and christianisa-
      tion more than most East African peoples. The first to begin
      work among the Maasai was the Africa Inland Mission in 1904 at
      Rumuruti. Other churches working among the Maasai today are
      the Anglican diocese of Nairobi, PCEA, WGM, EAYM (Freidns, PEFA
      and since 1955 the Catholic prefecture apostolic of Ngong (Mill
      Hill Mission).

      Although the Maasai are now about 50% exposed to Christianity,
      only about 22% of them are Christians, and this number is
      largely pupils and past pupils of mission schools. Traditional
      beliefs and religion remain very strong. The Maasai have long
      had a form of military organisation which requires all the male
      population between the ages of 16 and 30 to submit to a special
      discipline and to constitute a warrior class. This system,

coupled with their nomadic way of life and incessant itineration, has been the biggest obstacle to evangelisation and the
building up of church life. Converts so far have been mostly
reached in alienated situations -- in jail, hospital, or among
Maasai living with Christian families of other tribes. A small
number of Maasai are now gradually beginning to settle due to
the recent government introduction of ranching schemes, communal bore holes, wheat growing schemes, and communal cattle
dips. This development is making the establishment of churches
much easier than in the past.

17. The *Maguzawa* or 'pagan Hausa' of northern Nigeria are a small
compact minority of the Hausa people who have consistently
resisted Islam up to the present day, and who live in quite
separate compounds from the Muslim Hausa. Their name (singular,
Bamaguje) means 'Those who fled from the sala (Muslim daily
prayers)'. The main reason for this resistance has been major
tribal functions incompatible with Islam, such as beer-drinking
periods, beer to the Maguzawa being a substance rich in spiritual force. In 1900, about 50% of Hausa-speakers were pagans,
but the proportion is small today. The first Christian mission
to arrive was the Church Missionary Society about 1920, although
real contact with the Maguzawa did not begin until 1955 nor the
first sizeable response until 1965. The first Catholic resident
priest came in 1929, and in 1936 the Sudan Interior Mission
began based on three mission stations. By 1961 a CMS Team
approach was well under way based on the Pauline church-planting
methods advocated by the Anglican missiologist Roland Allen,
including family baptism, local initiative, self-led congregations, seven-day Bible schools, and compound visiting. The
result was a sudden rise in church membership from nothing in
1960 to 220 baptised by 1965, attributed to desire for literacy,
the policy of sending no evangelist to a village until he is
invited, a house provided, and a church farm set up to support
him, and then insisting that no separate 'mission' compound
apart from the village be built, but that workers identify
themselves with the life of the people. The Maguzawa are still
only slightly evangelised (10%) with vast areas west of Zaria
untouched by primary evangelism. Meanwhile Hausa pressure to
islamise the Maguzawa continues, with several large campaigns
under the Sardauna of Sokoto in the 1960s.

18. The *Nen* or Banen (35,000) are a Bantu animistic tribe resistant
to Islam, found in the western Cameroon highlands in the departments of Nkam and Mbam in relatively inaccessible areas. The
Berlin Baptist Mission began stations around 1924, as did the
Catholics. Especially in the southern forest areas, the Nen
were dispersed during the civil uprisings of 1959 onwards. In

new churches among regrouped villages, a youth movement has
emerged attempting to translate the Bible into their own language, Tunen, and seeking in other ways to make the Christian
faith relevant to the Nen.

19. The *Serer* (420,000) are the last remaining sizeable pagan
    tribe in Senegal. They were entirely pagan up to 1870, when
    two brutal jihads (holy wars) were waged against them from
    Gambia and the Sudan ('The Koran or the sword'). The Serer
    resisted Islam until the French protectorate began in 1905,
    and resistance thereafter was still strong (due to the power-
    ful Serer monarchy, and tenacious fetishism and sacrificial
    religion) until around 1950 when the traditional chieftain-
    ships disappeared. Islamisation, which had begun around 1900
    and remained weak until 1945, now developed rapidly, and by
    1972 Muslims had increased to 40%, with 25% Catholics, a few
    Jehovah's Witnesses, and a handful of Protestants, leaving
    34% still traditionalists. New Muslim converts are mostly
    older people, and new Catholics mainly young people.

20. The *Sihanaka* (164,000) are a Malagasy escarpment tribe living
    in northeast Madagascar. After the widespread persecution of
    Merina Christians under Queen Ranavalona II, in 1861 the first
    regular Protestant congregation among the Sihanaka was estab-
    lished; in 1867 the first full-time worker (a Malagasy) settled
    in the area, and in 1875 the first European missionary (London
    Missionary Society), later joined by the Malagasy Home Mission-
    ary Society. Catholics did not open a station until about
    1910. The Sihanaka's belief in the existence of a great God
    and the unseen world should have favoured the spread of the
    gospel; language also favoured this, since Sihanaka is a dia-
    lect not too different from standard Malagasy (in which the
    whole Bible was available from 1835); so their subsequent
    resistance to conversion is somewhat surprising. Virtually
    all the Sihanaka have now been evangelised (95%), in the sense
    that the name of Jesus is universally known and understood,
    even if rejected. But only 23% profess to be Protestants and
    17% Catholics; no Muslim influence from the coast has reached
    the area. The remainder (60%) are strong animists. Among the
    Protestant community, separatist churches have emerged; in
    1960 Eglise du Réveil, in 1964 Eglise Protestante Malgache,
    also Eglise Réformée Indépendante de Madagascar, and others.

21. The *Sonjo* (7,400) are a nomadic Bantu people living among the
    nomadic Nilotic Maasai in northern Tanzania. Almost all (95%)
    follow traditional animism, which is a very strong and complex
    system involving a theocratic social structure, myths of a god-
    man, and an eschatological belief in the return of a messiah.

Lutheran missionaries (ECLT Northern Diocese) began working
among them from 1946, and a Catholic priest from 1952, opening a station (Holy Ghost Mission) in 1966. The subsequent
slow response to Christianity is the result in part of their
inaccessibility, with a general absence of roads, and the
area is very sparsely evangelised. Missions have been able
to assist during the frequent famines that result from their
limited methods of cultivation. In two recent successive
years, two Catholic Sonjo catechists have died suddenly and
mysteriously after speaking publicly against the tribal
religion and the local deity.

22. The *Sukuma* ('Northerners') of Tanzania, with a present popu-
    lation of about 1,770,000 live in widely scattered homesteads
    south of Lake Victoria. Catholics began work among them in
    1883 (Bukumbi), also Anglicans (CMS) shortly after. The
    Africa Inland Mission replaced CMS in 1909. With an apparent
    distrust of anything new, not more than 17% have become Chris-
    tians. One unusual obstacle to evangelisation has been that
    the Sukuma traditionally practised as high moral standards and
    moral code as the Christian ones, leading many to feel Chris-
    tianity brought nothing new. The whole Bible has been avail-
    able in KiSukuma since 1960, but it is an extremely difficult
    Bantu language for missionary work. In 1924 a Baganda inde-
    pendent church, the Malakites or KOAB, created a small Sukuma
    schism from CMS and AIM. A few Sukuma are Muslims, less than
    3% in rural areas. Traditionalism, professed by 80%, is dying
    only where it is expensive to practise traditional rites, and
    elsewhere it remains strong. Evangelisation (30%) has pro-
    gressed unevenly, primarily near schools and churches. Efforts
    to relate Christian worship to Sukuma culture and social struc-
    ture have been made through music, dance societies, architecture,
    Christian action cells, and so on, but all with scant success.

23. The *Turkana* (224,500) of the semi-desert in northern Kenya are
    Nilotic-speaking nomadic pastoralists, owning large herds of
    cattle, camels, sheep, goats and donkeys. They live to the
    west of Lake Rudolf in one of the driest and most inhospitable
    parts of Kenya with temperatures ranging up to 100 degrees F.
    The first mission was opened by the Africa Inland Mission in
    1960. Other recent arrivals include the EAYM (Friends),
    Salvation Army, Reformed Church of East Africa, Full Gospel
    Churches of Kenya, and the Catholic prefecture apostolic of
    Lodwar, whose first station was opened in 1962. Co-ordinated
    by the National Christian Council of Kenya, these bodies have
    initiated an impressive number of secular development projects
    including a fisheries co-operative. Even so the area is only
    slightly evangelised (10%), and less than 5% are Christians.

Traditional beliefs and the traditional way of life adhered
to by the remaining 96% have hardly been affected by Christianity, and the main obstacles remain tenacious animism,
hostile climatic conditions, poor communications and the
whole nomadic way of life.

VIII. JOINT ACTION FOR MISSION IN FRONTIER SITUATIONS

It will be noticed from Table 4 that in quite a number of unevangelised tribes there is a multiplicity of Protestant missions
and churches at work. In some cases the tribe's area and population are so vast that there is room for this number of different
bosies, if they are co-operating fully; but in many other cases,
African hostility or indifference towards such a multiplicity of
foreign bodies from overseas is so great that such bodies have been
forced to work more closely together. In general it may be stated
that a proliferation of missions of different traditions working in
a single tribe is a major obstacle to the tribe's effective evangelisation. For this reason, many missions and churches today are
convinced that any new evangelistic initiatives in the independent
nations of Black Africa can only be undertaken by all interested
outside agencies working together within one single new evangelistic or missionary organisation specially created for the particular
task. To illustrate this, case studies will now be given of two
large traditionalist peoples, the first being the only case in
Africa of a major new evangelistic initiative being undertaken
through joint action for mission, and the second the only known
case at present of any other similar initiative being seriously
considered, both cases being unique in that they involve international groups of Christian organisations.

1.   The failure of over a hundred years of missions to evangelise
      the large *Fon* tribe (1,185,000) of Dahomey is a startling
      illustration of the gaps in evangelisation that this survey
      attempts to uncover. For well over a century, a single Pro-
      testant mission (the Methodist Missionary Society) was respon-
      sible for work among the Fon, who live within its comity area.
      The first Methodist missionary, Freeman, visited the royal
      court at Abomey in 1842; yet 120 years later there were still
      only one hundred Fon Protestants, because the mission had con-
      centrated its resources on the more responsive Gun people on
      the coast. Since around 1945, the Methodist Church had been
      intending to start direct evangelism, but although the matter
      was regularly raised at conferences, there was little action
      taken. By 1972, the Catholic mission begun in 1902 had grown
      to encompass 10% of the tribe; and a small Assemblies of God
      work was also under way. Meanwhile the Fon, a dynamic and

progressive people with highly developed traditional religion,
and with so far little inclination towards Islam, have been
increasing in animistic population at a rate of over 25,000 a
year.

In 1965 the Yaoundé consultation on unevangelised areas drew
attention to the unsatisfactory state of Protestant evangelisation, and within a year or two a number of French-speaking
Protestant churches from ten nations in Africa, Madagascar,
the Pacific, France and Switzerland, together with the Paris
Evangelical Missionary Society and the Swiss Mission, had
agreed to form Action Apostolique Commune (joint action for
mission), an interdenominational missionary team under African
leadership, which would attempt to avoid previous mistakes of
western missions in Africa. With Catholic assistance, the
team translated and in 1967 published in duplicated form the
first scriptures in Fon, St. Mark's Gospel; the translators
then moved on to St. Matthew. Organised team work then began
at Bohicon, 15 kms from Abomey, in mid-1968. By 1972, this
Protestant team, which was originally expected to number nine,
numbered five: two European nurses, and three Africans -- a
pastor, an evangelist, and a youth worker. The search was
still continuing for two additional African team members, an
agriculturalist and a theologian, the latter to enter into
dialogue with Fon traditional religion in the name of Christ,
and to deal with questions of Fon culture and the most suitable type of liturgy to create. From nothing in 1966 the team
has now built up Protestant communities in six villages total-
ling nearly 1,000 Fon adherents, which for practical purposes
form part of the Methodist Church in Dahomey.

Although this experiment in joint action for mission and inter-
denominational collaboration has attracted widespread attention,
the Fon project is unfortunately still the only case of its
kind in Africa today; no other teams of this type have yet been
formed elsewhere. So far as is known, only one other similar
project is even under consideration, in the people next to be
described.

2.   The second case is that of the *Mossi* of Upper Volta, the largest pagan tribe in West Africa (2.81 million), who are today
in process of slowly becoming islamised. For eight centuries
this powerful kingdom has resisted Islam, but now significant
numbers are becoming Muslims, particularly since national independence in 1959; by 1972 about 23% of the Mossi are Muslim.
Catholics number over three hundred thousand, but Protestant
work (confined to the French, American and Swiss Assemblies
of God) is relatively small. By 1965, the Assemblies had 200

congregations with 16,000 believers (30,000 total community) served by 12 mission stations, 25 American and 9 French missionaries. The only other Protestants are a separatist Temple Apostolique, which broke from the mission in 1958, and a group of Yoruba Baptist immigrants in Ouagadougou. By 1972 Protestants had increased to 2% of the tribe. Since the evangelisation of the Mossi is progressing at a rate markedly slower than the average for all West Africa, this people represents a major missionary challenge to churches in other territories. For at least five years now, the idea of a joint action for mission project supported by various outside churches has been discussed, for so far no concrete proposals nor personnel have been forthcoming.

In addition to these two potentially major projects sponsored by international groups of churches and agencies, there is a handful of smaller national joint projects each sponsored by agencies already at work within a single nation. Two cases from Mozambique should be briefly recorded. Under the auspices of the Christian Council of Mozambique (CCM), an interdenominational project was begun in 1967 in the north at Nampula, in the area where the South Africa General Mission had worked until its eviction ten years previously. The resulting Igreja de Cristo em Mozambique (Church of Christ in Mozambique) has been supported by both the CCM and the SAGM, and consists mainly of converts from the *Lomwe* tribe. Secondly on the border with Rhodesia, two missions working with the *Manyika* and *Ndau* (Swiss Mission and Methodist Episcopal Mission) began around 1960 a joint intermissionary church, Igreja de Cristo em Manica e Sofala, supervised by the Intermissionary Committee of Beira based in Rhodesia. By 1966 it had 21 congregations and 3,000 members. Significant though these cases are, however, national projects such as these remain the exception rather than the rule across the continent today.

The present survey demonstrates that there are still at least 234 other tribes in Africa similar to the Fon and the Mossi in that they still have a strong majority of traditionalists (60% or more), remain numerically or culturally unevangelised, are relatively open to Christianity, yet remain without adequate or fully effective missionary work. In total these 236 unevangelised traditionalist tribes have a combined population of 47,200,000. If the churches in Africa and overseas are to meet this evangelistic obligation to peoples who have not heard the good news of Christ, some sort of organised joint action for mission seems essential. This might involve the assembling, training and placing of small interdenominational and international teams under African supervision and leadership, each given a mandate to work for only 10 (or a maximum of 20) years before handing the resulting new Christian communities

over to the existing local churches, denominations or Christian
councils.

IX. SUMMARY FINDINGS AND ANALYSIS

From the data presented in this report, a number of overall
findings and new trends emerge, which we will now summarise under
nine heads.

1. *The population explosion in Africa*
   The population of Africa and its surrounding islands in mid-
   1972 is 367,380,000. The demographic explosion due to natural
   causes (births minus deaths) is causing this to increase at a
   rate of 2.8% per year, i.e. 10,286,640 each year (28,200 a
   day, or 1 every 3 seconds). These masses belong to 44 nations
   and 13 non-sovereign territories, and also belong to a grand
   total of 860 African peoples (or tribes, or distinct ethnic
   units), which are split by national boundaries into 1,045
   tribes-within-nations. Most of these tribes are growing in
   size each year at the average of 2.8%; only a handful are decreasing in size.

2. *The persistence of traditional religion*
   In 1972, Africa's traditional tribal religions are still professed by 64 millions (17.4% of the continent). In many
   tribes these religions are still a very strong force, and are
   even reviving in strength in a number of areas. In at least
   220 tribes (250 tribes-within-nations) traditionalists number
   60% or more, and in 90 of these tribes they are 90% or more.
   Demographic increase (at 2.8% per year) among the total traditionalist community is 1.8 million each year; but more than
   this number are being converted to Christianity, so that the
   total number of traditionalists is gradually decreasing each
   year.

3. *Demographic increase in Islam*
   The total of Muslims in Africa in mid-1972 is estimated at
   41.7%, or 153.2 million. As with all other populations, this
   is increasing due to natural causes at about 2.8% per year,
   i.e. 4.3 million a year. Increase due to conversions to Islam
   is however relatively small, estimated at 250,000 a year,
   mostly taking place in parts of Senegal, Mali, Guinea, Ivory
   Coast, Upper Volta, northern Nigeria and northern Cameroon.
   Since 1950 the earlier expansion of Islam southwards in Africa
   has virtually halted at the line shown on the map, and now
   about 213 peoples and tribes are Muslim or islamised to 75%
   or more.

4.   *The growth of Christianity*
     The total of professing Christians in mid-1972 is 149,300,000
     (40.6%), of which 59.6 million are Catholics (16.2%), 45.2
     million Protestants (12.3%), 16.5 million Orthodox (4.5%), 15
     million adherents of African independent churches (4.1%), and
     13.0 million Anglicans (3.5%). The Christian community is
     growing by demographic increase at about 2.8% per year, and by
     conversion at about 2.2% per year, a total of 5.0% per year or
     7.5 million persons a year. Affiliated Christians on the
     churches' rolls or records number about 104 million, and regu-
     larly practising Christians about 40 million; these are found
     in 356 Catholic dioceses, 648 Protestant, Anglican and Orthodox
     denominations, and in 5,400 African independent churches. Over
     the last eighty years there has been a rapid and remarkable
     christianisation of a large number of African peoples; over
     400 tribes today have responded markedly to Christianity, and
     of these at least 50 are composed of members who are virtually
     100% professing Christians.

5.   *Penetration of the gospel across Africa*
     Evangelisation has progressed at extremely uneven rates across
     the continent over the last hundred years. Because of comity
     arrangements, linguistic difficulties, and arbitrary assign-
     ment of areas to missions by colonial governments, highly-evan-
     gelised tribes exist today next door to virtually unevangelised
     tribes. The general state of evangelisation in 1972 can best
     be shown in tabular form as follows, after which the main fig-
     ures will be elaborated on.

STATE OF EVANGELISATION IN AFRICA, 1972

Types of tribe	Tribes	Tribes-within-nations	Populations (in millions)		
			Total	Evangelised	Unevangelised
Muslim and islamised	213	270	140	57	83
Responsive evangelised	411	512	180	162	18
Unevangelised	236	263	47	18	29
TOTALS	860	1,045	367	237 (65%)	130 (35%)

Types of tribe	Opportunity for evangelisation from outside
Muslim and islamised	Limited or nil; radio and literature approaches only.
Responsive evangelised	Unnecessary; self-perpetuating internal evangelistic momen
Unevangelised	Outside aid necessary, often essential, and welcomed.

The table shows that, of the 860 distinct tribes (1,045 tribes-within-nations) in Africa, 213 (270) are Muslim or mostly islamised tribes with a population of 140 million (the other 13 million Muslims in Africa belonging to non-islamised tribes), 411 (512) with a population of 180 million are evangelised (over 50%) tribes and have responded to Christianity (of which about 150 tribes can be described as now fully evangelised), while 236 (263) with a population of 47 million remain as un-evangelised tribes. With regard to population totals, the fourth column of figures above (based on Table 1, column v) shows that around 65% of Africa can be regarded as evangelised, which is not surprising since many of the largest peoples of Black Africa are not only fully evangelised but are also vir-tually all christianised. Some 35% of Africa (130 million) remain unevangelised. Of these latter, 18 million belong to already evangelised tribes whose present evangelistic momentum ensures the continuation of evangelisation; and some 83 million belong to Muslim and islamised tribes in which no evangelisa-tion is feasible except for radio and literature approaches. This leaves 29 million unevangelised persons in unevangelised or frontier situation tribes.

In addition to numerical evangelisation, cultural evangelisa-tion continues with translations of the scriptures and other attempts at presenting the gospel in intelligible indigenous garb. This task of translating gospels, New Testaments and Bibles into Africa's 1,050 indigenous languages (1,439 lan-guages-within-nations) is now 23% completed. Multiplying these two percentages (23% and 65%), as representing the ex-tent of cultural and numerical evangelisation, respectively, we arrive at a figure of 15% for the status of evangelisation as a whole in Africa today.

6.   *Frontier situations*
Of the 263 tribes-within-nations in frontier situations, 45 are evangelised (over 50%) but resistant to Christianity, 44 are half-evangelised (50%), 106 are partially evangelised (15-45%), and 68 are unevangelised or sparsely evangelised (0-10%). Of the total population of 47 million in these tribes, 31.7 million (67%) are traditionalists. Under present restrictions on immigration and travel, a number of these people have little chance of coming into contact with the gos-pel. The clearest example of this predicament is that of the *Ingassana* of Sudan, a primitive Prenilotic tribe numbering 35,000, who form a totally traditionalist island, with no Muslims nor Christian converts, on the southern edge of the Muslim line. Only one European pioneer, unattached to any mission, is known to have visited them, and he only managed

to produce a primer on the language before being evicted by
the government; subsequently the authorities have refused permission for further visitors from outside.

7. *Agencies of frontier mission*
The great majority of unevangelised peoples have at least one
Protestant missionary agency at work among them, as Table 4
describes; each usually has also at least one Catholic order.
The directory in the appendix lists 207 such agencies or
groups engaged on organised work in frontier evangelistic situations. Of these, 103 are what have traditionally been known
from the African point of view, as foreign missionary societie
orders and agencies, in that they are operated and controlled
from headquarters overseas in Europe, North American and Australasia. In addition, all Catholic orders and missions in
Africa (with the exception of North Africa, Portuguese Africa,
Ethiopia and some islands) operate under the centralised control of the Sacred Congregation for the Evangelisation of
Peoples, in Rome, Italy (also known as Propaganda). But at
least 104 of the agencies listed (together with the large number of independent churches engaged on such work, enumerated
here as a single group) have their headquarters in African
nations, which in this report indicates that they operate mission and evangelistic programmes under African initiative,
leadership and control. If we include the indigenous churches
this means that a large majority of all agencies for frontier
mission are under African control.

In addition to the missionary societies and denominational
agencies for mission, there are several inter-denominational
and inter-church evangelistic enterprises each at work in
numerous African countries operating not de novo but through
existing churches and missions; of these perhaps the most
relevant to this survey is New Life for All, an organisation
in 20 African countries, based in Nigeria, which specialises
in training for total evangelisation through total mobilisa-
tion of all church members. There are also the 24 national
Bible societies and half a dozen other national Bible agencies
under African management in most African nations, which are
responsible with the United Bible Societies for initiating new
translations of the scriptures among unevangelised peoples.
The existence of so many overseas agencies in this listing,
most of which operate independently and autonomously, raises
the question of co-operation between evangelistic agencies.
So far, only one major internationally-supported joint action
for mission project, Action Apostolique Commune in Dahomey,
has been begun, together with a tiny handful of nationally-
supported joint projects; elsewhere throughout the continent,

there is fellowship and mutual recognition between agencies but little or no joint strategical or tactical consultation or planning. The need for organisation and joint planning in evangelisation, if African peoples are to be properly served, is highlighted by the sad fate of peoples inadequately evangelised and followed up, and two examples of this will now be given.

8. *The tragedy of forgotten churches*
Modern historical interpretation of the planting of Christianity in Africa lays stress on the enormous part played by unknown or forgotten African evangelists and congregations. Apart from those whose labours, though unrecorded, are known in local oral church tradition, there are numerous tragic cases of the apparent abandonment of such groups to oblivion, left to their own devices without outside help of any kind.

This survey uncovered several such cases. In 1963, the American Episcopal bishop in Liberia passed through a town new to him, Plibo among the well-evangelised *Grebo* tribe, and was approached by a deputation headed by an old man. He was then startled to receive a piece of paper stating that there had once been an Episcopal mission there with several American missionaries, but which had long since been closed down (later research revealed it was considered 'dead' and closed in 1910). The paper contained a list of the faithful communicants who were still alive after all these years, conducting Sunday worship as best as they knew, and patiently awaiting the return of the mission.

A second example is from the Ivory Coast, where Methodist missionaries have a small work among the 70% traditionalist *Anyi*, one of the evangelised but resistant peoples listed in this report. The Methodists told the survey team about a small indigenous 'episcopal four-square elim type' group near Akoupe (38 kms north of Adzope), which, although in French-speaking territory, followed the Anglican liturgy in English each Sunday. Further enquiries established that this was probably one of the churches founded around 1913 by the African evangelist from the Gold Coast, Philip Swanson, a disciple of Prophet W. W. Harris. Swanson founded 'Church of England' congregations at random, but many were not followed up by the later Anglican missionaries from Accra and had to struggle on as best as they could over the decades without any outside help.

9. *The missionary spread of the independent churches*
The historical (Western) missions and churches may thus have

often failed to follow up their professional type of evangelisation, but a more organic and continuous type of evangelisation based on labour migration and the movements of traders
comes from the African independent churches. During the surv
it was often noted that in all parts of Black Africa indigenou
churches had migrated to and were working in unevangelised
areas, both within their own tribes and language groups, and
also farther afield. Thus the Kimbanguists (EJCSK) of Zaire
have adherents in Namibia, the Church of the Lord (Aladura)
from Nigeria has frontier work among the Kono of Sierra Leone
and the Vapostori (Apostolic Church of Johane Masowe) of
Rhodesia have driven north in convoys of lorries to Nairobi
(Kenya), then to Kampala (Uganda), to purchase large city
properties for a year at a time to serve as the bases for
mobile religious communities concerned to evangelise surrounding areas. The present report does not give further details
of such work by others of the 5,400 distinct indigenous denominations in Africa, because it is largely spontaneous,
unorganised, temporary, unheralded and unrecorded. But it
clearly has been and still is exceptionally effective, and in
aggregate is making a major contribution to the evangelisatior
of the continent.

No people in history has been able to evangelise itself completely ab initio; outside agents of the gospel have usually
assisted as initiators and catalysts until the numbers of
local Christians have become large enough to enable evangelisation to proceed under local momentum. This report attempts
to identify those peoples in Africa who still need and want
such assistance from outside.

X. CONCLUSION: EVANGELISATION AND AFRICAN TRADITIONALISTS:
    A Comment by John S. Mbiti

    The tables in this survey reveal a great deal about the state
of evangelisation in African societies. They also raise many questions yet to be answered. Within a short period of less than two
hundred years (and in many cases less than one hundred), a very
remarkable degree of evangelisation has been reached. Yet, it is
said that Africa generally received 'second-rate' missionaries and
financial backing compared to India, China and Indochina. In
spite of that (whether it is true or not), Africa has reaped far
greater success from the missionary enterprise than any of these
other areas of the so-called 'mission field'. Credit for this
success must be given both to the foreign missionaries with their
home churches, and also to African converts, evangelists, catechists and teachers. The African contribution to Christian

evangelisation has rarely received the credit and publicity it rightly deserves. The story of modern Christianity or the church in Africa has almost exclusively been told as a story of missions and missionaries. That story must be balanced with a history of Christianity or the church spreading through African undertaking.

The physical facilitation of the spread of the Christian faith through missionaries and African converts, though highly desirable, necessary and indispensable, cannot alone account for the high speed with which African peoples are embracing Christianity. Nor would it explain the apparent rejection of Western Christianity by a small number of African peoples (42 tribes in Table 4 who have been evangelised but not converted, with 60% or more still traditionalists; these are shown coloured yellow on the map). While this is not the place to argue out the case or to document it, one is of the opinion that African religion has had a lot to do with the types and degrees of response to Christianity by African peoples.

Another factor applicable only to those who apparently reject Christianity after being fully evangelised is probably the apparent confusion between Christianity and Western culture and values. This means that the rejection is directed principally at Western culture which the societies concerned regard as an intrusion into their own cultures. It is doubtful that traditional African societies (apart from those that have become islamised) are rejecting Christianity as a religious system per se. But it would be unrealistic to expect such societies to distinguish between (Western) culture and the essence of the faith; and it is equally, if not more, unrealistic to imagine that the Christian faith could spread without some form of cultural wrappings.

For African Christianity two urgent problems seem to emerge from this survey. The first concerns the inner life of the church itself, among tribes and peoples that have become evangelised peoples (according to the categories of this survey). Having been evangelised, what then is next for them in the realm of the Christian faith? How does the church move to maturity beyond the point of evangelised peoples? Growth by evangelisation has reached its peak; now comes the opportunity for growth by maturation, thus bringing to full fruition the redeemed people of God, for them to form a solid point of reference and a living home for its members. The church has to search and examine its own reality, its own being, its own role, and its opportunities for service and witness.

The second problem is the question of evangelising those African peoples who are less evangelised and re-evangelising those who have so far rejected Christianity. Who will do this task and

how? This double question provides the church in Africa with a
noble opportunity to join in the missionary enterprise. The
initiative for this must come from within the church and be not
dictated from overseas, if it is to become a genuine African participation in the missionary enterprise. These societies are the
'Samaria' region of missionary outreach for the church in Africa.
If the church responds to the challenge, a new rearrangement with
overseas missionary bodies would have to be worked out concerning
what part, if any, they might play in an African-directed missionary enterprise, in terms of personnel, finance, ideas and the practical implementation of the enterprise. It is to be hoped, too,
that the undertaking will be carried out ecumenically, and with an
openness for innovations, experiements and even avoidance of mistakes for which foreign missionaries have often been criticised.
In planning for this undertaking, the church will no doubt draw
freely from its own experiences and, hopefully, in the process of
evangelising fellow African peoples will contribute new insights
to the theology and practice of missions.

Whether this entry of the church in Africa into the stream
of providing missionary agents will mean putting an end to direct
missionary intervention by overseas agents, it is not for one to
say. But the day may come when some African countries will refuse
to permit foreign missionary bodies to function within their
boundaries. Furthermore a true measure of the maturity of the
church will be for it to stand on its own, among other things, in
the missionary enterprise. This would make it possible to hire
and dismiss or discipline its own missionaries from both Africa
and overseas, in the name and by the authority of its Lord Jesus
Christ, and in the power of the Holy Spirit.

TABLE 4: FRONTIER SITUATIONS IN AFRICA, 1972: UNEVANGELISED, PARTIALLY-EVANGELISED, AND RESISTANT TRIBES

This table lists all known cases of tribes numerically unevangelised (50% evangelised or under, with substantial traditionalist populations remaining), and/or culturally unevangelised (60% traditionalist, or over), which altogether total 236 tribes (with 11 additional sub-tribes), or 263 tribes-within-nations.

A detailed explanation of this table and its columns (which are identical to those in Tables 2 and 3) is given in the text, section IV; and a visual presentation of its data is given in the map following. The 25 tribes marked below with an asterisk, *, are further described in brief case studies in section VII (with two in VIII). For ease of reference, the meaning of the 16 columns below is given again here, as follows:

Col.1: Total population of tribe (or nation) in mid-1972. 2-5: Percentage of tribe professing to be respectively, traditionalists, Muslims, Catholics, Protestants (with all other types of Christian). 6: Total professing traditionalists in tribe (note: the totals for nations in this column are the totals for the tribes shown only; as Table 1 shows, there are many other traditionalists in islamised and evangelised tribes). 7: Scripture translations published in tribe's own language: G = gospel, N = New Testament, B = complete Bible; -- = none. 8-10: years when G, N, B, respectively, were published. 11,12: years when Protestant missionary work began (c = circa, approximately). 13: % of tribe evangelised (note: 0-10% = unevangelised, coloured dark red on map; 15-45% = partially evangelised, coloured medium red on map; 50% = half-evangelised, coloured light red; and over 50% in this table = evangelised but resistant, coloured yellow on map). 14: Total unevangelised in tribe (the totals for nations in this column are simple totals of the figures below them, i.e. totals of the unevangelised in frontier situations). 15: SE (status of evangelisation) index, i.e. extent to which tribe and its culture is evangelised. 16: Miscellaneous notes on each tribe and nation; initials = major Protestant and Anglican churches or missions now or recently at work (see Directory after this table); AIC, AICs = one, or more, African independent churches from within the tribe are undertaking evangelisation.

NATION / Tribes	Population mid-1972 (1)	Tr (2)	Mu (3)	RC (4)	Pr (5)	Tradits (6)	Total (7)	Gosp (8)	NT (9)	Bible (10)	Origin RC (11)	Prot (12)	%E (13)	Unevanged (14)	SE % (15)	Main missions at work, etc. (16)
ALGERIA	15,052,000															
ANGOLA	5,957,000					391,400								84,500		
* Chokwe (Lunda)	400,000	75	0	17	8	300,000	GN	1916	1927		c1900	1908	95	20,000	71	CMML, AEF, MP, UCBWM, SDA, AICs.
Hukwe	9,000	95	0	0	0	8,500	G	1960			c1940	Nil	20	7,200	5	Bushmen. No Protestant missions, though AEF area.
Kwangere	25,000	70	0	30	0	17,500	-				1940	Nil	50	12,500	25	No Protestant mission stations (AEF area).
Mbukushu (Kusso)	6,000	90	0	10	5	5,400	-				c1939	Nil	20	4,800	5	No Protestant mission stations (AEF area).
Mbwela	100,000	60	0	35	5	60,000	-				c1912	1931	60	40,000	15	AEF.
BOTSWANA	654,000					54,000								48,000		
Bushmen (5 tribes)	60,000	90	0	1	9	54,000	-						20	48,000	5	Tribes: Hiechware, Naron, Nusan, Ohekwe, Tannekwe. SDA.
BURUNDI	3,788,000					27,000								24,000		
Twa (Geseru, Pygmies)	30,000	90	0	5	5	27,000	-						20	24,000	5	Very few have joined the churches. CMS.
CAMEROON	6,065,000					1,091,800							31	1,062,500		
Adamawa (Fulani)	380,000	60	40	0	0	228,000	GN	1919	1963			1903	10	342,000	7	Lutherans (Sudan Mission), Norwegian Mission.
Budugum (s.Masa)	10,000	90	0	0	0	9,000	-						20	8,000	5	Norwegian Mission.
Duru	20,000	90	0	0	0	18,000	-						20	16,000	5	Sudan Mission.
Fungom	90,000	60	0	20	20	54,000	-						60	36,000	15	Presbyterian Church in West Cameroon.
Gisei (s.Masa)	10,000	90	0	0	0	9,000	-						20	8,000	5	Norwegian Mission.
Gisiga	30,000	99	0	1	0	29,700	-					1960	10	27,000	2	SMBE among Mofou sub-tribe since 1960. SDA.
Gude	100,000	99	0	0	0	99,000	-					1958	30	70,000	7	NBM; SMBE among Kola sub-tribe since 1958; LBM.
Kapsiki	40,000	80	0	0	0	32,000	-						40	24,000	10	Lutheran Brethren Mission.
Kotopo	10,000	90	0	0	0	9,000	-						20	8,000	5	Lutheran Brethren Mission.
Kundu	70,000	60	0	20	20	42,000	-						60	28,000	15	Presbyterian Church in West Cameroon.
Laka	10,000	99	0	0	0	9,900	GNB	1929	1933	1961			0	10,000	0	Sudan Mission.
Li (Bali)	40,000	80	0	4	16	32,000	-				c1910	c1900	50	20,000	50	Basel Mission (PCWC).
Mambila	40,000	70	20	0	0	28,000	-					1950	30	28,000	7	Cameroon Baptist Convention; WBT (in Nigeria).
Matakam	140,000	98	0	0	2	137,200	GN	1958	1965				10	126,000	7	Swiss and Norwegian SUM, SDA, AIC. Rapid SUM growth.
Mbum	20,000	30	60	0	0	18,000	GN	1936	1965				10	18,000	7	Norwegian Mission, SUM. Heavily islamised.
Mundang	80,000	60	0	25	15	48,000	GN	1933	1948			c1920	50	40,000	37	Also in Chad. Lutheran Brethren Mission, AIC.
Musei (s.Masa)	10,000	90	0	0	0	9,000	-						10	9,000	5	Mainly in Chad (Lutheran Brethren Mission).
Mugu	50,000	80	0	5	0	40,000	GN		1964				50	25,000	37	Also in Chad. Lutheran Brethren Mission, AIC.
Namshi	30,000	60	0	40	0	18,000	-				1938	1924	20	24,000	17	Lutherans (Sudan Mission).
* Nen	35,000	60	0	20	20	21,000	-				c1924		70	10,500	17	German Baptists (Union des Eglises Baptistes), PEMS.
Podokwo	25,000	90	0	0	0	22,500	-						10	22,500	12	Unevangelised sub-tribes: Mada, More, Muktale.
Tigon	25,000	90	0	0	0	22,500	-					c1940	10	22,500	12	Also in Nigeria. CRC Mission (SUM).
Tuburi	120,000	60	0	20	20	72,000	-					1950	50	60,000	50	Also in Chad. Lutheran Brethren Mission.
Utange (s.fiv)	100,000	60	0	20	20	60,000	GNB	1916	1936	1964			50	50,000	50	CRC (Nigeria), Presbyterian Church in West Cameroon.
Wute	60,000	60	0	20	20	36,000	-						50	30,000	12	EPC.

Statistical table of peoples by country (columns headed ①–⑮). Values as read:

Country / People	① (Pop)	②	⑦ (Pop)	⑧	Scripture yrs	⑫	⑬ (Pop)	⑭	⑮ Remarks
CANARY ISLANDS	945,000		0				0	0	
CAPE VERDE ISLANDS	256,000		0				0	0	Gospels published in Brava Island Creole in 1936.
CENTRAL AFRICAN REP.	1,598,000		5,000				2,800		
Binga (Pygmies)	2,000	99	2,000				1,800	2	Scattered groups in southwest of nation. Little contact.
Mbimou (s.Sanga)	5,000	60	3,000	GN			1,000	20	Swedish Baptists.
CHAD	3,901,000		522,000				323,000		
Bua	20,000	80	16,000	G	1938	64	16,000	10	SUM (among Nanjere and Lele sub-tribes).
Gaberi	30,000	60	18,000	G	1934 1950	20	15,000	12	Lutheran Brethren Mission, CMML, SUM, AIC.
Masa (Banana)	80,000	85	68,000	GN	1932 1943	50	64,000	15	CMML, SUM, SJ (Jesuits), Capuchins.
Mbai (s.Sara)	60,000	68	40,800	GN		20	18,000	52	BMM (among Sara Madjingai), CMML, SUM, AICs.
Sara	700,000	60	420,000	G	1950	70	210,000	35	
COMORO ISLANDS	269,000		0				0	0	
CONGO (BRAZZAVILLE)	984,000		8,100				6,900		
Bakwili (s.Dzem)	10,000	60	6,000			45	5,500	10	Swedish Baptists.
Ngwili (s.Sanga)	3,500	60	2,100	GN	1930 1947	60	1,400	45	Swedish Baptists. Revival in 1939.
DAHOMEY	2,842,000		1,609,000				1,059,500		
Bariba (s.Bargu)	330,000	70	231,000	G	1953	48	297,000	5	ECHA (SIM), Southern Baptists, Assemblies of God.
Boko (s.Busa)	20,000	80	16,000			10	19,000	1	Also in Nigeria. ECHA (SIM).
Dompago (s.Kabre)	30,000	85	25,500	G	1955	5	15,000	25	WF, ECHA (SIM).
Egba (Nagot)	393,000	60	236,000	GNB	1850 1862 1884	10	59,500	85	Eglise Methodiste, ECHA (SIM).
* Fon	1,185,000	90	1,066,500	G	1967	85	592,500	25	MMS, Action Apostolique Commune.
Somba	85,000	40	34,000			50	76,500	2	Assemblées de Dieu.
EGYPT	35,996,000		0				0	0	
EQUATORIAL GUINEA	294,000		0				0	0	
ETHIOPIA	26,225,000		2,112,600				1,669,300		
Anuak	52,000	95	49,400	GN	1956 1962	41	46,800	7	Bethel Evangelical Church.
Bako	50,000	90	45,000			10	45,000	2	SIM. Very rapid growth.
Berta (Shankilla)	20,000	90	12,000			10	14,000	7	Nomads, also in Sudan. SIM, Chrischona Mission.
Darasa	500,000	80	400,000			20	150,000	17	SIM, SPM, SDA, AIC. Evangelised by Kambatta tribe (SIM).
* Falasha (s.Kemant)	30,000	0		GNB	1840	70	24,000	20	The 'Black Jews', 7% Ethiopian Orthodox; SDA, CMJ.
Gimira	30,000	98	29,400	G		50	21,000	7	Bethel Evangelical Church.
Kafa	500,000	70	350,000			40	300,000	20	Big SIM work.
Konso	10,000	80	8,000			30	7,000	7	SIM.
Masongo	10,000	99	9,900		1935 1968	5	9,500	1	RCA. In forest inaccessible except by plane.
Nuer	70,000	90	63,000	GN	1943	20	56,000	15	Bethel Evangelical Church.
Ometo	500,000	80	400,000	G		30	350,000	15	SIM, SPM, SDA, AIC.
Reshiat	10,000	99	9,900			5	9,500	1	UPUSA.
Suri	30,000	90	27,000			5	28,500	1	Also in Sudan. UPUSA. The few Christians are Orthodox.
Wallaga (Galla)	1,000,000	70	700,000	GNB	1893 1899	40	600,000	40	Christians mainly Orthodox. HM, UPUSA, SDA. 1937 revival.
FrT OF AFARS AND ISSAS	85,000		0				0	0	
GABON	491,000		0				0	0	
GAMBIA	380,000		0				0	0	
GHANA	9,662,000		814,000				906,500		
Builsa	80,000	60	48,000	G	1962	25	56,000	15	CSM (Presbyterian Church of Ghana).
Chakossi (Chokosi)	22,000	60	13,200			30	15,400	15	Assemblies of God, Evangelical Presbyterian Church.
Dagari (LoDagaa)	200,000	70	140,000		1935	30	180,000	7	Also in Ivory Coast. WBT, BMM.
Dagomba	220,000	40	88,000	G	1912	10	198,000	2	Preab Church of Ghana, AoG, Ghana Baptist Convention, SDA.
Grunshi	200,000	75	150,000			10	120,000	10	Assemblies of God, BMM.
Gurensi	250,000	90	225,000	G	1962	40	175,000	15	Assemblies of God among Kusasi sub-tribe.
Konkomba	80,000	60	48,000	G	1943	30	48,000	15	Also in Togo. WEC, AoG, Apostolic Church, WBT, AIC.
Mamprusi	80,000	60	48,000	G	1941	30	56,000	15	Methodist, AoG, Ghana Baptist Convention.
Moba	80,000	65	52,000	G	1940	30	56,000	15	AoG, WBT. Moba hymnbook has 100 indigenous hymns.
Vagala	3,000	60	1,800			30	2,100	7	

Table with columns headed by circled numbers ① through ⑬ (plus an unnumbered "Cat." name column at left and a notes column at right).

Cat.	①	②	③	④	⑤	⑥	⑦	⑧	⑨	⑩	⑪	⑫	⑬	Notes
GUINEA	4,120,000							1,122,800					1,492,000	
Gbande	66,000	80	15	0	0	5	G	52,800	1954			10	52,800	CMA.
Kissi	266,000	95	3	1	1	1	GN	252,700	1935	1966		10	239,400	
Kpelle	200,000	60	15	24	0	1	GN	120,000	1922	1967		10	140,000	CMA.
Loma (Toma)	66,000	91	6	3	0	0	G	60,100	1961			20	52,800	CMA.
Malinke	1,060,000	60	40	0	0	0	GN	637,200	1931	1932		5	1,007,000	CMA.
IVORY COAST	4,540,000							1,961,300					1,473,600	
Anyi	210,000	70	1	20	20	9	G	147,000	1927		1927	60	84,000	Wesleyan Methodist, AICs.
Baule	868,000	75	1	12	12	1	GN	651,000	1946 1953	1922	1927	60	347,200	CMA, WEC, SDA, UPM, AICs.
Bete	369,000	60	10	10	10	10	GN	221,400				60	184,500	Mission Biblique, UPM, SDA, WBT, AICs.
Brong	57,000	60	10	30	0	0	G	34,200	1959			60	22,800	Also in Ghana. AICs.
Dan (Yakuba)	278,000	70	10	10	0	10	GN	194,600	1970	Nil		60	139,000	Mission Biblique, UPM, WBT.
Gagu (Pygmies)	25,000	99	0	0	0	1	G	24,700				5	23,700	WBC.
Guro	100,000	75	4	10	0	15	GN	75,000	1951 1960	c1955	1963	10	50,000	WBC, Mission Biblique, UPM.
Kuiango	50,000	92	4	4	0	0	G	46,000	1967	c1955		10	45,000	Free Will Baptist Mission.
Ligbi	20,000	50	50	0	0	0	-	10,000		1933		10	16,000	Free Will Baptist Mission.
Lobi	40,000	99	1	0	0	0	G	39,600	1940 1965	c1930		10	36,000	Also in Upper Volta. WEC, Free Will Baptist Mission.
Ngere	150,000	90	10	0	0	0	G	135,000		c1930		20	75,000	Mission Biblique, SDA.
Semufo	528,000	65	30	0	4	1	G	343,200	1960	c1950		20	422,400	CEMS.
Wobe	40,000	79	1	10	10	0	G	39,600		c1930		10	28,000	Mission Biblique, UPM.
KENYA	12,091,000							921,300					740,400	
* Dorobo	22,000	99	0	0	1	0	-	21,800		Nil	c1965	36	19,800	DMA Diocese of Mount Kenya, CA, CMS, PCEA.
Duruma	112,700	42	25	9	4	1	-	47,300		1905	1885	10	67,600	MMS, Elim MA.
El Molo (s.Samburu)	1,000	97	0	2	1	24	-	1,000				40	800	BCMS.
Giryama	335,900	82	4	1	21	1	GN	275,400	1892 1908 1908	1902	1846	50	168,000	CMS, HGM, SA, AICHS, AICs. 1959 large Pentecostal revival.
* Maasai	171,200	78	0	1	20	1	GN	133,500	1905 1922	1955	1904	50	85,500	AIM, CMS, MHH, PEFA, PCEA, CA. Mobile population, resistant.
Mbere (s.Meru)	54,400	66	0	14	0	20	G	35,900	1903 1926	1951		40	32,600	Methodists, AICs.
Sagala (s.Taita)	8,000	60	0	25	25	0	G	4,800	1892		1891	20	4,800	CMS, HGM, AIC.
Samburu	60,500	96	0	0	3	2	G	58,200	1961	c1950	1883	20	48,000	BCHS, CCH, CA.
Suk (Pokot)	103,200	90	0	1	0	7	GN	92,900	1936 1967	1952	1934	50	82,600	BCHS, CA, PGCK, AIC.
Tharaka (s.Meru)	57,300	61	0	0	14	25	G	35,000	1934		1931	50	28,600	AIM, AICHS, Methodists, AICs.
* Turkana	224,500	96	0	0	3	1	G	215,500	1972	1962	1960	10	202,000	AIM, AICHS, PGCK, SPS; many secular development projects.
LESOTHO	1,086,000							0					0	
LIBERIA	1,222,000							461,000					327,700	
Gbande (Bandi)	32,000	80	10	10	0	10	G	25,600	1954		1922	37	25,600	Order of Holy Cross (Anglican), SPM, AIC.
* Gio (s.Dan)	92,000	95	0	5	0	5	G	87,400	1943	1938	1926	20	73,600	Liberia Inland Mission (WEC), AIC.
Kpelle	200,000	80	0	0	20	20	GN	160,000	1922 1967	1908	1931	50	100,000	Also in Guinea. Lutheran Church, Methodists, MLM, SDA, AIC.
Kran (Tchien)	25,000	80	0	20	0	20	G	20,000	1953		1924	37	12,500	Also in Ivory Coast. PAOC, MLM (GABB), AICs.
Loma (Toma)	60,000	80	0	0	0	5	G	48,000	1961			20	36,000	Liberia Inland Mission, Methodists, Free Pentecostal Church.
Mano (s.Ngere)	80,000	95	0	0	0	20	GN	76,000	1946	1933	1924 1926	20	56,000	Liberia Inland Mission (WEC), Methodists, AIC.
Sapo	30,000	80	0	0	0	0	G	24,000	1956			15	24,000	Baptists, Pentecostals, several AICs.
LIBYAN ARAB REP	2,009,000							0					0	
MADAGASCAR	7,356,000													
Antanosy (s.Antandroy)	210,000	50	5	35	0	10	GNB	213,900	1828 1830 1835	1900	1888	70	113,200	ELM. Slight islamisation on coast.
* Sihanaka	164,000	60	0	17	0	23	GNB	115,500	1828 1830 1835	c1910	1861	50	105,000	PEMS, LMS (now Eglise de J-C à Madagascar), AICs.
MALAWI	4,693,000							0					0	
MALI	5,358,000							1,123,600					1,689,900	
Bambara	1,660,000	30	68	0	1	0	GNB	498,000	1923 1933 1961	1895	1919	40	830,000	GMU, CMA. Over 10,000 Protestants, 10,000 Catholics.
Bobo	100,000	70	30	0	0	0	GN	70,000	1939 1954	1926		50	80,000	CMA.
* Dogon (Habbe)	312,000	60	30	5	5	5	GN	187,200	1933 1957	1931		50	156,000	Cliff-dwellers. CMA.
Kagoro	30,000	95	5	0	0	0	-	28,500				50	27,000	Catholics only.
Kita	150,000	43	55	2	0	0	GN	64,500	1931 1932	c1880	1954	5	142,500	Catholics only.
Malinke	268,000	30	69	1	0	0	GN	80,400			1923	20	214,400	United World Mission, CMA.
Minianka	300,000	65	35	0	0	0	-	195,000				20	240,000	CMA.

Name	(a)	(c)	(d)	(e)	(f)	(g)	(h)	Mission years	Translation years	(n)	(o)	(p)	Notes
MAURITANIA	1,231,000										0		
MAURITIUS	907,000										0		
MOROCCO	16,904,000										0		
MOZAMBIQUE	8,076,000					2,898,300					2,427,000		
Chewa	40,000	73	0	24	3	29,200	GNB	1891 1898 1905	c1885 c1921	41	16,000	60	Also in Malawi. IHM (now Church of the Nazarene).
Chuabo	250,000	73	7	12	3	197,500	GNB	1891 1898 1905	c1892 c1933	60	150,000	10	SDA.
Gomani	80,000	73	0	24	3	58,400	GNB		c1885 c1921	40	32,000	60	Also in Malawi. IHM.
Kunda	50,000	79	7	24	2	36,500	GN	1917 1930	c1885 c1921	60	25,000	12	IHM.
Lomwe	1,000,000	73	0	12	2	790,000	GNB	1891 1898 1905	c1885 c1922	30	700,000	60	SDA, AEF, Igreja de Cristo em Moçambique (CCM).
Majenga (s.Nyanja)	80,000	73	43	21	1	58,400	GNB		c1885 c1893	30	32,000	22	USPG, IHM.
Makonde	300,000	36			0	108,000	G	1919 Nil	1919	50	150,000	60	Catholic missions only.
Makua	1,200,000	66	18	15	1	792,000	GNB	1927	c1909 c1922	50	840,000	12	USPG, AEF.
Manyika	100,000	75	1	22	2	75,000	GNB	1903 1908 1949	c1892 c1893	60	40,000	15	Wesleyan Missionary Society, WF (withdrew 1970), ICMS.
Ndau	500,000	75	1	22	2	375,000	GNB	1910 1919 1957	c1892 c1900	60	200,000	60	Episcopal and Free Methodist, AICs from Rhodesia, ICMS.
Nsenga	80,000	73	0	24	3	58,400	GN	1919 1923	c1885 c1921	60	32,000	60	USPG, IHM.
Sena	300,000	75	1	22	2	225,000	G	1897	c1892	60	150,000	45	Zambezi Industrial Mission; WF (withdrew 1970).
Tavara	80,000	73	0	24	3	58,400		1891 1898 1905	c1885 c1921	50	40,000	25	IHM.
Zimba	50,000	73	0	24	3	36,500	GNB	1891 1898 1905	c1885 c1921	60	20,000	12	IHM.
NAMIBIA	660,000					30,100					26,800		Bushmen. Mainly Lutheran work as with !Kung bushmen below.
Heikum	16,000	90	0	0	-	14,400	-			26	12,800	5	ELOC; ELC (RM) has 2,000 among !Kung and Heikum; NGK.
Kung	10,000	90	0	0	-	9,000	-	1875 1879	Nil	20	8,000	5	NGK in SWA; main church is Herero Church (AIC).
Ovahimba (s.Herero)	10,000	67	0	0	33	6,700	GN		1955	40	6,000	30	
NIGER	4,103,000					140,000					142,500		
Kurfei	50,000	90	10	0	0	45,000	-			5	47,500	1	SIM.
Mauri	100,000	95	5	0	0	95,000	-			5	95,000	1	SIM.
NIGERIA	58,253,000					1,896,000					1,678,900		
Afawa (s.Warjawa)	10,000	90	10	0	0	9,000	-		1953	38	9,000	2	SIM, Baptists; handful of AC (CMS) converts.
Afo	25,000	99	0	0	0	24,700	-			10	10,000	0	CMS, Qua Iboe Mission.
Ankwe (s.Angas)	10,000	99	10	0	0	9,900	-			10	9,900	1	SIM (especially in Yagba sub-tribe), AIC (Aladura).
Basakomo (s.Basa)	60,000	70	10	10	0	42,000	-	1897	1928	30	42,000	15	Partially islamised.
Butawa	150,000	90	0	0	0	135,000	-			0	150,000	0	
Chawai	20,000	50	50	0	0	10,000	-	1923	1913	0	20,000	0	SIM (together with AMS), CMS.
Daka	30,000	90	0	0	0	27,000	-			1	29,700	0	
	7,000	90	0	0	0	6,300	-			0	7,000	0	
Dibo (s.Nupe)	10,000	90	10	0	0	9,000	G	1935	1953 1926	90	9,900	2	CMS efforts from 1961 effective but not followed up.
* Eggon (s.Mada)	80,000	75	10	5	15	60,000	-			1	8,000	0	SUM (South African branch).
* Gade (s.Gwandara)	5,000	75	5			4,500	-			80	5,000	45	SIM, Southern Baptist Convention.
* Gbari	500,000					375,000	GN	1913 1956	Nil c1910		100,000	60	CMS, QIM.
Ibaji (s.Igala)	20,000					18,000				0	20,000	0	QIM.
Igala	500,000	60	20			300,000	GNB	1924 1935 1970	1932	50	250,000	50	QIM.
Igbira	400,000	46	50			184,000	G	1891	1953	30	280,000	15	SIM, WBT, AICs.
Jaba (s.Katab)	60,000	90	20			54,000	G	1921	1910	10	59,400	5	CMS, Southern Baptist Convention.
Jarawa	150,000	90				105,000	G	1940	1933	10	135,000	5	SIM, SUM.
Jerawa	70,000	90				63,000	G	1924	1915	0	70,000	35	SIM (began in Rukuba sub-tribe), SDA.
Jukun	20,000	90				18,000	G	1914	1910	70	6,000	5	SUM (CRC, EUB). Tribe slowly declining in numbers.
Kadara	40,000	90				36,000			1934	1	40,000	0	SIM.
Kamantan (s.Katab)	10,000	90				9,000				0	10,000	0	CMS.
Kamuku	40,000	90	20			36,000		1913 1956	1954	10	36,000	2	SIM (ECWA).
Koro	35,000	70				24,500	GN		1958	20	28,000	15	SIM (ECWA).
Lungu (s.Katab)	10,000	90				9,000				20	10,000	0	CMS.
Mada	100,000	70	10		19	90,000		1857 1880 1932	1953 1926	70	30,000	17	SUM, Southern Baptists, SDA, CMS, SIM.
* Maguzawa	100,000	90	10	40		15,000			1929	10	90,000	10	CMS, SIM. The 'pagan Hausa', resistant to Islam.
Mbula	25,000	60	0	0		118,800		1938	1929	60	10,000	15	SUM (Danish Lutheran).
Mumuye	120,000	99	0			9,500	G		1923	0	114,000	2	SUM (EUB), WBT. Resistant.
Ngmo (a.Karekare)	10,000	95	10	0	4	18,600				0	5,000	0	Also in Dahomey and Niger.
Shanga (s.Fienga)	5,000	93	3	0		63,000			Nil 1960	5	19,000	1	SUM (Danish Mission).
Vere	20,000	90	0	0						20	56,000	5	SIM.
War-jawa	70,000												

	(1)	(2)	(3)	(4)	(5)	(6)	(7)	(8)	(9)	(10)	(11)	(12)	(13)	(14)	(15)
PORTUGUESE GUINEA	572,000					243,600							253,000		
Balante	200,000	79	10		1	158,000	-				c1954	28	160,000	5	NTM, WEC. Also in Senegal (60% evangelised there).
Banyun	15,000	92	0		0	13,800	-					20	12,000	5	
Biafada	15,000	60	33	8	0	11,000	-					20	10,500	7	
Bijogo	15,000	88	0	10	1	22,000	-					40	15,000	7	
Diola	25,000	35	60	2	2	5,200	G					50	7,500	10	WEC: responsive.
Manjaco (s.Pepel)	80,000	84	5	10	1	33,600	-	1961			1953	40	48,000	25	WEC: 50% have been islamised since 1940. WEC: responsive.
REUNION	495,000					0							0		
RHODESIA	5,433,000					151,400							81,100		
Hlechware	1,600	90	0	5	5	1,400	-					60	1,100	7	Bushmen. Scattered groups of Christians.
Ndau	200,000	75	0	12	12	150,000	GNB	1910 1919 1957			1895	60	80,000	60	AEF, United Church; strong AICs.
RWANDA	3,819,000					27,000							24,000		
Twa (Gesera, Pygmies)	30,000	90	0	5	5	27,000	-					20	24,000	5	Very few have joined churches. CMS, EPR, EdP.
ST. HELENA	6,000					0							0		
SAO TOME E PRINCIPE	61,000					0							0		
SENEGAL	4,136,000					186,800							320,000		
Diola	220,000	20	70	0		44,000	G	1961		c1875		50	110,000	25	HGM, WEC. 50% have been islamised since 1940.
* Serer	420,000	34	40	25	1	142,800	-			c1850		50	210,000	12	Last pagan tribe in Senegal; rapid islamisation. HGM.
SEYCHELLES	57,000					0				1953			0		
SIERRA LEONE	2,779,000					911,700							1,370,500		
Kissi	64,000	80	7		3	51,200	GN	1935 1966		1949		41	44,800	22	AoG, Methodists.
* Kono	131,000	95	0	0		126,300	G	1919				30	66,500	25	EUB, AICs.
* Koranko	103,000	69	30	1		71,000	G	1899		c1960	1945	50	92,900	25	MCA. Southern half unreached; north being islamised.
Limba	233,000	69	35	4	1	140,000	G	1911 1966		c1960		10	93,200	45	AIM ('the Limba Church'), AoG, NBM, UPC.
Loko	80,000	60	39	1		48,000	G				1889	60	40,000	25	AoG.
Mende	859,000	60	40		17	343,600	GNB	1867 1956 1959				50	601,300	30	UBC, CMS, SDA, United Methodists, AICs (Aladura).
Temne	828,000	15	60			124,000	G	1865 1868			1842	30	414,000	37	CMS, MCA, EUB, AIM, UPC, AoG, SDA.
Yalunka	19,000	40	60			7,600	G	1907			1952	5	18,000	2	MCA.
SOMALIA	2,942,000					0							0		
SOUTH AFRICA	21,185,000					179,400							39,000		
Venda	260,000	69	0	30		179,400	GNB	1920 1923 1936		1966	1872	85	39,000	85	Berlin Mission, CRC, DRC, PAOC, SA, SABNS, etc; and AICs.
SPANISH N. AFRICA	168,000					0							0		
SPANISH SAHARA	54,000					0							0		
SUDAN	16,885,000					3,696,000							3,586,000		
Anuak	30,000	95	1	4		28,500	GN	1956 1962		N11	1937	10	27,000	7	Also in Ethiopia. Church of Christ in the Upper Nile.
Didinga	30,000	95	1	0		29,700	-					10	24,000	5	Presbyterians, Anglicans.
Dinka	1,940,000	99	0	0	1	1,843,000	GN	1905 1940		N11	1905	20	1,746,000	7	Entirely unreached; no entry allowed.
Ingessana	35,000	99	0	0	0	34,600	-					0	35,000	0	Formerly SIM. Muslim Brotherhood (Egyptians).
Koalib	320,000	70	20	10	0	224,000	GN	1934 1963		c1920	1920	30	224,000	7	Percent Muslim gradually rising. Formerly SIM.
Krongo (s.Tumtum)	121,000	70	29	0	1	84,700	G	1954 1969			1930	10	108,900	7	Formerly SIM.
* Lotuka	258,000	90	4		0	232,200	GN	1947		N11	1951	7	239,900	10	Formerly AIM; Episcopal Ch in the Sudan; many Catholics.
Meban	130,000	99	0		0	128,700	G	1969		N11	1938	2	104,000	10	Formerly SIM. No Muslims.
Murle	121,000	99	0		0	119,800	G	1935 1968		c1930	1952	1	119,800	1	Church of Christ in the Upper Nile.
Nuer	844,000	99	0		0	835,600	G	1911		1902	1913	1	835,600	1	Church of Christ in the Upper Nile.
Shilluk	93,000	75	0	15	10	69,700	Q	1947 1963		1902	1902	30	65,100	15	CCUN. Enforced islamisation in 1960s failed.
Topotha	60,000	99	0	10		59,400	-					10	54,000	2	In former AIM area.
Uduk (s.Koma)	7,000	85	0	0	15	6,000	GN	1947 1963		N11	1938	60	2,800	45	Formerly SIM. Revival 1967. Now 500 baptised.
SWAZILAND	449,000					0							0		
TANZANIA	14,002,000					3,312,000							2,854,900		
* Aruaha	110,000	88	2		10	96,800	GN	1905 1922		c1921	1904	39	88,000	15	Ev Lutheran Church in Tanzania, HGM, Assemblies of God.
Barabaig (s.Tatoga)	49,000	98	0	1	1	48,000	-			N11	1958	20	47,000	1	ELCT, Pallotine Fathers, Elim Pentecostal Church.

Group	Pop.	(a)	(b)	(c)	(d)	Christians	Scr	Dates	(i)	(j)	(k)	No.	(n)	Notes
Burungi	20,000	80	10	2	8	16,000	-		1957	Nil	50	10,000	12	CMS (Diocese of Central Tanganyika), Elim Pentecostals.
Dorobo	3,000	99	0	0	2	3,000	-		Nil		0	3,000	0	Several small bands of hunters in Masai District.
* Gogo	480,000	70	5	11	13	336,000	GNB	1886 1899 1962		1878	60	192,000	60	CMS (Diocese of Central Tanganyika), AIC.
Iraqw	218,000	83	5	12	13	181,000	G	1957	Nil	1939	60	87,200	30	CMS, GFF, Church of God, Elim Pentecostal Church.
* Kindiga (Hadza)	2,000	60	0	1	40	1,200	-		Nil	1959	95	100	24	ELCT, Mbulu Pente Church. Now completely evangelised.
Kwere	63,000	50	33	17	0	32,000	GN	1905 1922	1911	1960	30	44,100	7	Elim Pentecostal Church, HGM, SDA.
Maasai	100,000	95	50	15	3	95,000	GN		1957	1933	30	80,000	15	ELCT, HGM, Elim Pentecostal Church.
Matumbi	72,000	35	0	15	0	25,200	GN		1905	Nil	30	80,400	7	Catholic missions only (Capuchins).
Nyakyusa	355,000	69	25	10	25	245,000	GN	1895 1908	Nil		60	142,000	45	ELCT, Moravians, BMEA, AICs.
Nyamwezi	590,000	60	25	10	5	354,000	GN	1897 1909	1879	c1880	30	413,000	22	Moravian Church, SPM, WF, Salvation Army, AIC.
Safwa	102,000	97	0	1	2	99,000	GN	1904 1913			30	71,400	22	Moravian Church, Anglican Church.
Shambala	310,000	95	1	65	20	40,000	GN	1896 1908	1868	1867	50	155,000	37	ELCT, Anglicans, AIC.
* Sonjo	7,400	80	3	3	1	7,000	GNB	1895 1925 1960	1966	1946	10	6,700	2	ELCT, HGM, Bantu tribe living among Maasai.
* Sukuma	1,770,000	19	11	11	6	1,416,000	G		1883	1887	10	1,239,000	30	CMS, AIM, SDA, WF, Maryknoll, AIC.
Turu	316,000	79	8	10	3	250,000	G		1909	1935	40	190,000	30	American Lutheran Mission, WF.
Zinza	89,000	75	1	20	4	67,000	G	1930	1890	1940	30	36,000	30	AIM, SPM, CMS. Dying tribe being absorbed into Sukuma.
TOGO	1,969,000					769,900						462,000		
Adele	4,000	79	7	20	1	3,200	-			c1955	55	1,200	17	Strong Catholic work; EET recently.
Ana	49,000	55	0	22	16	27,000	-				70	24,500	50	EET (Bremen Mission), AICs; unreached area by Atakpame.
Basari	100,000	80	5	10	5	80,000	GNB	1850 1862 1884			30	70,000	7	EPC; church growth methods used.
Chakossi (Chokosi)	29,000	49	48	3	2	14,200	-				30	17,400	10	EET; Catholic mission has reached nearly all villages.
* Kabre	273,000	85	1	1	2	232,000	G	1955		1937	40	109,200	30	EET; very active Protestant and Catholic work.
Kabu	22,000	75	0	20	5	16,500	-				60	11,000	30	AoG, WBT. Strong Catholic evangelisation.
Moba	94,000	88	0	0	2	82,700	G	1941		c1945	50	47,000	25	Catholic mission has reached nearly all villages.
Naudeba (Losso)	118,000	75	0	10	1	88,500	-				40	47,200	15	Resistant, highly islamised;
Tem (Kotokoli)	100,000	19	74	0	6	19,000	-				20	80,000	5	Eglise Ev du Togo, Eglise Methodiste.
Wachi (e.Fon)	235,000	88	0	11	1	206,800	G	1967	c1950	1958	50	117,500	25	
TUNISIA	5,431,000					0	0					0		
UGANDA	10,332,000					189,100						142,700		
Jie	34,000	80	0	20	5	27,200	-		1957		51	27,200	5	Also Dodoth (a.Jie) unevangelised.
Karamojong	227,000	60	0	15		136,300	-	1932	1933	c1920	20	90,800	20	BCMS, Baptists, Verona Fathers.
Niporen (a.Nyangiya)	1,000	80	35			800	-				60	700	7	
Suk (Pokot)	30,000	83	0	2		24,200	GN	1936 1967	1962	1958	20	24,000	15	BCMS, Verona Fathers, AIC.
UPPER VOLTA	5,629,000					3,080,300						3,609,700		
Birifor	100,000	89	1	0	0	89,000	-		1930		26	90,000	2	Upper Volta Mission, WEC.
Bobo	300,000	65	25	8	2	195,000	GN	1939 1954	1957	1924	10	240,000	15	CMA, WF.
Busansi	280,000	62	25	12	1	173,600	-				40	168,000	5	Many Catholics (WF).
Dafi	50,000	60	28	10	2	30,000	-				40	35,000	4	Assemblies of God, CMA.
Dagari	50,000	65	15	20	0	32,500	-		1930	1950	40	30,000	10	Upper Volta Mission.
Deforo	15,000	70	26	3	1	10,500	-				20	12,000	2	
Dian	15,000	75	20	10	0	11,200	G	1948	1942	1941	10	13,500	2	Upper Volta Mission (from WEC).
Dorosie	15,000	85	10	0	0	12,700	-				20	12,000	2	Catholics.
Grunshi	250,000	50	50	5	0	125,000	G	1947 1958	1960	1947	5	237,500	1	Also in Ghana. Upper Volta Mission.
Guin	80,000	80	20	0	0	64,000	-				5	76,000	7	CMA.
Gurma	300,000	53	40	6	1	159,000	GN	1940 1965	1930		30	240,000	1	SIM.
Karaboro	50,000	73	18	8	1	36,500	-				30	35,000	7	
Komono	15,000	90	10	0	0	13,500	-				5	14,200	7	
Lilse	80,000	81	8	1	1	64,800	-				5	56,000	7	Catholics (WF).
Lobi	100,000	98	1	0	0	98,000	GN	1930 1939	1939		10	90,000	4	WEC, Upper Volta Mission.
Minianka	100,000	93	5	1	0	93,000	-				5	90,000	2	CMA (also in Mali).
* Mossi	2,815,000	60	23	15	2	1,689,000	-		1900	1924	30	1,970,500	22	AoG (French, US), CMA, Apostolic Church, AIC.
Nunuma	50,000	81	8	10	0	40,500	G	1930 1939			10	35,000	10	Catholics (WF), Upper Volta Mission.
Samo (Samogo)	150,000	70	30	0	0	105,000	G	c1960	Nil	1947	30	120,000	10	CMA, WF.
Sissala (e.Grunshi)	100,000	75	25	0	0	75,000	G	1948		1956	2	98,000	5	Also in Ghana. Upper Volta Mission, WBT.
Tusyan	40,000	75	20	5	0	30,000	-				20	32,000	5	
Wara	10,000	75	24	1	0	7,500	-				20	8,000	5	
ZAIRE	18,339,000					1,468,500					56	987,000		
Azande	200,000	64	0	28	8	128,000	GN	1918 1938			60	80,000	45	Norwegian Baptist Mission, AIC.
Bembe (s.Rega)	300,000	73	2	16	9	219,000	G	1936			50	150,000	25	UPMGBI.

	(1)	(2)	(3)	(4)	(5)	(6)	(7)	(8)	(9)	(10)	(11)	(12)	(13)	
Bira	70,000	77	2	13	8	53,900	G	1930			50	35,000	25	Emmanuel Mission, ACM.
Budu	80,000	63	0	29	8	50,400	-		c1917	c1914	90	8,000	22	WEC (HAM), ACM.
* Central Twa (Pygmies)	100,000	60	0	10	30	60,000	-		1895	1889	50	50,000	12	ECZ (Disciples of Christ, BMS, Congo Balolo Mission).
Hunde	300,000	66	0	26	8	198,000	G	1940		c1921	40	180,000	20	SFM, Mission Baptiste du Kivu.
Kela	180,000	66	0	17	17	118,800	G	1940		1929	40	36,000	40	North Sankuru Mission, DC, AIC.
Kuba	130,000	62	0	26	12	80,600	GRB	1905 1911 1927	c1940	1891	80	52,000	60	APCM, Westcott Mission, AICs.
Mbuti (Pygmies)	35,000	90	0	7	3	31,500	-				60	28,000	5	CMS (begun by Apolo Kivebulaya), SDA, AIM, EM.
Rega	400,000	66	0	25	9	264,000	GN	1934 1957		c1900	20	200,000	37	AIC (Bapostolo). Resistant.
Shila	120,000	64	0	28	8	76,800	-				50	48,000	15	CMML (Luanza Mission).
Songomeno	50,000	75	0	16	9	37,500	-				60	20,000	15	CMML (Luanza Mission).
Tabwa	250,000	60	1	36	3	150,000	-				60	100,000	15	North Sankuru Mission, AICs.
ZAMBIA	4,584,000													
Luvale	50,000	65	0	5	30	32,500	GRB	1902 1928 1955	1954	c1900	81	12,300	95	CMML, AMEC, AICs.
Mashi	4,500	99	0	0	0	4,500	-		Nil	Nil	95	2,500	1	Nomadic bushmen with no Christians at all.
Subia	11,000	70	0	20	10	7,700	-			c1944	50	5,500	12	Capuchins, Holy Cross Sisters (Catholic).

AFRICA TOTALS 367,380,000 31,663,600 39 29,041,200

Population of the 236 tribes 31,663,600

Population of the 263 tribes-within-nations:- 47,207,000

METHODOLOGY OF THE SURVEY

The statistics presented here are based on three main sources: (1) government census figures of total population in nations, as standardised and published by the United Nations ('World population prospects, 1965-85, as assessed in 1968', UN Population Division, New York, December 1969); (2) figures for tribal populations from the same censuses, updated to mid-1972 by computing the size of the tribe as a percentage of the nation at the last census, then multiplying this by the mid-1972 national population; and (3) figures for religious profession, published in government censuses over the last seventy years for about half the nations of Africa, updated graphically to mid-1972. The justification for defining 'Christians' as those who profess to be such (irrespective of their affiliation or practice) is the Universal Declaration of Human Rights (United Nations, 1948), Article 18: 'Everyone has the right to freedom of thought, conscience and religion; this right includes freedom to change his religion or belief, and freedom, either alone or in community with others and in public or private, to manifest his religion or belief in teaching, practice, worship and observance.' This fundamental right also includes the right to be called a follower of any religion.

These basic demographic statistics were then supplemented by official church statistics, church documentation, missionary atlases and maps, questionnaires each describing the situation in a single tribe filled out by persons familiar with the tribe concerned, field investigations by the authors, and, in cases where hard statistical data were not available, by the best observers' estimates available.

DIRECTORY OF CHURCHES AND MISSIONS ENGAGED ON ORGANISED WORK IN
FRONTIER SITUATIONS IN AFRICA

The listing below gives the initials (if commonly used, and used
in Table 4) and full names, together with the nation in which
each's headquarters are situated, of 207 churches, missions, agencies, and groups engaged on organised work in frontier evangelistic
situations in Africa. In Table 4, initials are usually given for
reasons of space, but in a few cases where there is space available
and the initials may not be widely used or known, the full name has
been given. Where the headquarters is in an African nation (shown
preceded by asterisk, *), the mission has been initiated by and is
being operated by African leadership; where headquarters are in
Western nations, the missions are usually referred to (from the
African standpoint) as foreign missionary societies, orders and
boards, and are usually under foreign control although in most
cases co-operating with African denominations. It has to be remembered also that virtually all churches in Africa -- the 648
Protestant, Anglican and Orthodox churches, the 356 Catholic dioceses, and in particular the 5,400 African independent churches --
are engaged in outreach, evangelism and evangelisation though their
individual members, families and congregations; and very many
churches organise short-term evangelistic campaigns and other large-
scale evangelistic enterprises. From this point of view every
church in Africa is working on the frontier between faith and non-
faith. However, for purposes of clarity, we restrict this list to
those churches and missionary agencies which sponsor and are engaged on organised or permanent evangelistic work, i.e. in some
sense centrally organised, or operated on a permanent or semi-per-
manent basis. Note again that although the listing contains a
number of Catholic agencies no attempt has been made to list com-
prehensively all Catholic missionary orders at work; the names and
addresses of these may usually be obtained from the Catholic directory of the nation concerned.

INITIALS	NAME	HEADQUARTERS
	Action Apostolique Commune	*Togo
ACM	Africa Christian Mission	USA
AEF	Africa Evangelical Fellowship (formerly SAGM)	*South Africa
AICMS	Africa Inland Church Missionary Society	*Kenya
AIM	Africa Inland Mission	UK, USA
AIC	African ndependent hurch (single group)	*HQs in 37 African nations
AICs	African independent churches (details in *Schism*: see bibliography)	*HQs in 37 African nations
AMEC	African Methodist Episcopal Church	USA
AMS	African Missionary Society	*Nigeria
ABCFM	American Board of Commissioners for Foreign Missions, now UCBWM	USA
APCM	American Lutheran Mission	USA
	American Presbyterian Congo Mission	USA
AWM	American Wesleyan Mission	USA
	Assemblées de Dieu	France, Switzerland
AoG	Assemblies of God	USA
BMM	Baptist Mid-Missions	USA
BMS	Baptist Missionary Society	UK
BMEA	Baptist Mission of East Africa (SBC)	USA
	Basel Mission	Switzerland
	Benedictine Fathers of St. Ottilien	Germany
	Berlin Mission, now Evangelical Lutheran Church in South Africa	Germany (GDR), South Africa
	Bethel Evangelical Church	*Ethiopia
	Bethel Mission	Germany (FRG)
BCMS	Bible Churchmen's Missionary Society	UK
BS	B ble societies and agencies	*Bible Houses in 24 African nations, plus half a dozen agencies in others
CBC	Cameroon Baptist Convention	*Cameroon

297

CBMS	Canadian Baptist Missionary Society	Canada
	Chrischona Mission	Germany (FRG)
CMA	Christian and Missionary Alliance	USA
CMML	Christian Missions in Many Lands	UK
CRCM	Christian Reformed Church Mission	USA
CA	Church Army in Kenya	*Kenya
CMS	Church Missionary Society	UK
CMS (Ruanda)	Church Missionary Society (Ruanda Mission)	UK
CCUN	Church of Christ in the Upper Nile	*Sudan
CSM	Church of Scotland Mission	UK
CBM	Church of the Brethren Mission	USA
CMJ	Church's Ministry among the Jews (formerly Church Missions to Jews)	UK
CBM	Congo Balolo Mission (Regions Beyond Missionary Union)	UK
CCM	Conselho Cristão de Moçambique	*Mozambique
CBFMS	Conservative Baptist Foreign Missionary Society	USA
CCM	Consolata Catholic Mission	Italy
DLM	Danish Lutheran Mission, see SUM	Denmark
DMA	Diocesan Missionary Associationa (6 Anglican dioceses in East Africa)	*Kenya, Tanzania
DCT	Diocese of Central Tanganyika	*Tanzania
DC	Disciples of Christ	*Zaire
DRC	Dutch Reformed Church Mission	*South Africa
	East African Revival Fellowship (no organised structure or addresses)	*Kenya, Uganda, Tanzania
	Eglise Apostolique au Togo	*Togo
	Eglise de Jésus-Christ à Madagascar	*Madagascar
EJCSK	Eglise de Jésus-Christ sur la terre par le prophète Simon Kimbangu	*Zaire
ECZ	Eglise du Christ au Zaire	*Zaire
EEC	Eglise Evangélique du Cameroun	*Cameroon
EEC	Eglise Evangélique du Congo	*Congo-Brazzaville

EET	Eglise Evangélique du Togo	*Togo
ELM	Eglise Lutherienne Malgache	*Madagascar
	Eglise Méthodiste au Togo	*Togo
	Eglise Méthodiste au Zaire	*Zaire
EPC	Eglise Presbytérienne Camerounaise	*Cameroon
EPR	Eglise Presbytérienne du Rwanda	*Rwanda
EPA	Eglise Protestante Africaine	*Cameroon
EdP	Eglises de Pentecôte	*Rwanda
EMA	Elim Missionary Assemblies (Pentecostal Church)	UK, USA
EM	Emmanuel Mission	UK, USA
ECWA	Evangelical Churches of West Africa	*Nigeria
ELCT	Evangelical Lutheran Church in Tanzania	*Tanzania
ELOC	Evangelical Lutheran Ovambokavango Church	*Namibia (Wouth West Africa)
EPC	Evangelical Presbyterian Church	*Ghana
EUB	Evangelical United Brethren	USA
	Free Methodist Church	USA
	Free Pentecostal Church	*Liberia
	Free Will Baptist Mission	USA
FGCK	Full Gospel Churches of Kenya	*Kenya
GBC	Ghana Baptist Convention	*Ghana
GFF	Gospel Furthering Fellowship	USA
GMU	Gospel Missionary Union	USA
HAM	Heart of Africa Mission, now WEC	UK
	Herero Church (Oruuano)	*Namibia (South West Africa)
HM	Hermannsburger Mission	Germany
HCC	Holiness Church of Canada	Canada
	Holy Cross Sisters	USA
HGM	Holy Ghost Mission (CSSp)	France, USA
ICM	Igreja de Cristo em Mocambique	*Mozambique
ICMS	Igreja de Cristo em Manica e Sofala	*Mozambique
	Intermissionary Committee of Beira	*Rhodesia
IHM	International Holiness Mission (Pilgrim Holiness Church)	USA

LIM	Liberia Inland Mission (Worldwide Evangelization Crusade)	UK
LMS	Livingstonia Mission	UK
LBM	London Missionary Society	UK
	Lutheran Brethren Mission	USA
	Lutheran Church in Liberia	*Ligeria
MM	Maryknoll Mission	USA
	Methodist Church of Liberia	*Liberia
MMS	Methodist Missionary Society	UK
MHM	Mill Hill Mission	UK
MCA	Missionary Church Association	USA
	Mission Baptiste du Kivu (CBFMS)	USA
	Mission Biblique	France
MP	Mission Philafricaine	Switzerland
NGK	Nederduitse Gereformeerde Kerk in SWA	*South Africa
NM	Neukirchner Mission	Germany
NLFA	New Life For All	*Nigeria (and offices in 20 other African nations)
NTM	New Tribes Mission	USA
NBM	Nigerian Baptist Mission	*Nigeria
	North Angola Mission	UK
	North Sankuru Mission	UK
	Norwegian Baptist Mission	Norway
NLM	Norwegian Lutheran Mission	Norway
OFMCap	Order of Friars Minor (Francisans,Capuchins)	Italy
OHC	Order of the Holy Cross (Episcopal)	USA
	Pallotine Fathers	Germany
PEMS	Paris Evangelical Missionary Society	France
PAOC	Pentecostal Assemblies of Canada	Canada
PEFA	Pentecostal Evangelistic Fellowship of Africa	*Kenya
PCWC	Presbyterian Church in West Cameroon	*Cameroon
	Presbyterian Church of Wast Africa	*Kenya
PCEA	Presbyterian Church of Ghana	*Ghana

RCA	Reformed Church of America	USA
QIM	Qua Iboe Mission	UK (Northern Ireland)
RM	Rhenish Mission (RMG)	Germany (FRG)
	Sacred Congregation for the Evangelisation of Peoples (Propaganda)	Vatican City
SA	Salvation Army	UK
SDA	Seventh-day Adventist Mission	USA
SMBE	Société Missionaire Baptiste Européenne (EBMS)	Switzerland
SJ	Society of Jesus	Italy
SPS	Society of St. Patrick	Ireland
SVD	Society of the Divine Word	Italy
SAGM	South Africa General Mission, now AEF	*South Africa
SABMS	South African Baptist Missionary Society	*South Africa
SBC	Southern Baptist Convention	USA
SIM	Sudan Interior Mission	USA
	Sudan Mission	USA
SUM	Sudan United Mission	UK, Australia, New Zealand
SMF	Svenska Missionsforbundet	Sweden
	Swedish Baptist Mission	Sweden
SFM	Swedish Free Mission	Sweden
	Swiss Mission	Switzerland
UFM	Unevangelized Fields Mission	UK
	Union des Eglises Baptistes	*Cameroon
UBC	United Brethren in Christ	USA
UBS	United Bible Societies	*UK (Africa office in Kenya)
UCBWM	United Church Board for World Ministries	USA
UCC	United Church of Christ	USA
UFCSM	United Free Church of Scotland Mission	UK (Scotland)
UPC	United Pentecostal Church	USA
UPMGBI	United Pentecostal Mission of GB and Ireland	UK
UPUSA	United Presbyterian Church (USA)	USA
USPG	United Society for the Propagation of the Gospel	UK
UWM	United World Mission	USA

UMCA	Universities Mission to Central Africa, now USPG	UK
	Upper Volta Mission	Canada
	Verona Fathers	Italy
	Wesleyan Methodists	UK
	Westcott Mission	UK
WF	White Fathers	Italy
WGM	World Gospel Mission	USA
WEC	Worldwide Evangelization Crusade	UK
WBT	Wycliffe Bible Translators	USA
ZIM	Zambezi Industrial Mission	UK

BIBLIOGRAPHY OF TRIBAL STUDIES OF EVANGELISATION IN AFRICA

Literature describing most of the peoples and tribes of Africa is voluminous; for the Kabyle of Algeria, for example, one published bibliography lists 732 descriptive books, articles and reports. For many African tribes, there are one or more published anthropological studies describing their traditional culture and, often, religion; and for several tribes, there are books or booklets describing the coming of missions or (more usually) of one particular mission. However, for very few tribes are there any accounts of their numerical and cultural evangelisation by the entire range of missions and churches at work in them. The bibliography below lists items approximating to this latter sort, i.e. items in which cultural, historical, missionary and evangelisation data are given in terms of one or more specific tribes (the names of which then follow in parentheses). Items below marked with an asterisk, *, mainly describe unevangelised peoples in frontier situations; the rest describe for the most part peoples defined in this survey as already evangelised.

Andersson, E., *Churches at the grass-roots: a study in Congo-Brazzaville*. London: Lutterworth, 1968. (Kongo, and others).

*Ayivi, E., "Joint apostolic action in Dahomey", *International Review of Mission*, LXI, 242 (April, 1972), p.145-149. (Fon).

Barrett, D. B., *Schism and renewal in Africa: an analysis of six thousand contemporary religious movements*. Nairobi: Oxford, 1968. (Appendix with notes on African independent churches in 270 tribes, 46 of which are unevangelised and shown in Table 4 of the present report).

Biebuyck, M. O., "La société Kumu face au Kitawala", *Zaïre*, XI, 1 (1957), p.7-40. (Kumu).

Bureau, R., *Ethno-sociologie religieuse des Duala et apparentés*. Yaoundé: Recherches et études camerounaises (IRCAM), 1962, p.1-372. (Duala).

Debrunner, H. W., *A church between colonial powers: a study of the church in Togo*. London: Lutterworth, 1965. (Ewe, and others).

Du Plessis, J., *The evangelisation of pagan Africa: a history of Christian missions to the pagan tribes of central Africa*. Cape Town: Juta, 1929. (The standard history up to 1925; massively documented).

*Flatt, D. C., "A contrast in evangelistic approach", *Church Growth Bulletin* (Pasadena), III, 5 (1967), p. 218-9. (Notes on the Arusha; longer work forthcoming).

*Forsberg, M., *Land beyond the Nile*. New York: Harper, 1958. (Ethiopia: Uduk. An autobiographical narrative only).

*Grimley, J. B. and G. E. Robinson., *Church growth in central and southern Nigeria*. Grand Rapids: Eerdmans, 1966. (Data on almost all Nigeria's 100 tribes).

Hellberg, C. J., *Missions on a colonial frontier west of Lake Victoria*. Lund: Gleerups, 1965. (Haya).

*Krass, A. C., "A case study in effective evangelism in West Africa", *Church Growth Bulletin*, IV, 1 (1967), p.244-250. (Chakossi).

Kuper, H., "The Swazi reaction to missions", *African studies*, V, 3 (1946), p.177-189. (Swazi).

*Lawson, J. S., Ayam, B. B., and D. B. Barrett., "The evangelisation of West Africa today: a survey across 21 nations and 150 tribes". Unpublished provisional report (duplicated) for Yaoundé Consultation, Cameroon, June 1965.

Mbiti, J. S., *New Testament eschatology in an African background*. London: Oxford, 1971. (Kamba).

*Olson, G. W., *Church growth in Sierra Leone*. Grand Rapids: Eerdmans, 1969. (Mende, Kono, and others).

Pauw, B. A., *Religion in a Tswana chiefdom*. London: Oxford, 1960. (Tlhaping).

*Payne, F. G., (The Church's Ministry among the Jews in Ethiopia). London, 1972. (Falasha).

Reid, A. J., *Congo drumbeat: the Methodist Church among the Atetela of central Congo*. New York: World Outlook, 1964. (Tetela).

*Roux, A., (Action A postolique Commune au Dahomey), Journal of the Paris Mission, January 1968. (Fon).

Rubingh, E., *Sons of Tiv: a study of the rise of the church among the Tiv of central Nigeria*. Grand Rapids: Baker, 1969. (Tiv).

Sangree, W. H., *Age, prayer and politics in Tiriki, Kenya*. London: Oxford, 1966. (Tiriki, s.Wanga).

Swantz, L. C., *The Zaramo of Tanzania*. Dar es Salaam: Nordic Tanganyika Project, 1965. (Zaramo).

Taylor, J. V., *The growth of the church in Buganda*. London: SCM, 1958. (Ganda).

Van der Poort, C., "Unification et separatisme religieux: un exemple congolais", *Revue congolaise des sciences humaines* (Kisangani, 3 (1971). (Mayogo).

Webster, J. B., *The African Churches among the Yoruba, 1888-1922*. Oxford: Clarendon, 1964. (Yoruba).

Whisson, M., *Change and challenge; a study of the social and economic changes among the Kenya Luo*. Nairobi: Christian Council of Kenya, 1964. (Luo).

Williamson, S. G., *Akan religion and the Christian faith: a comparative study of the impact of two religions*. Accra: Ghana Universities Press, 1965. (Ashanti, Fanti, and others).

EVANGELISATION AND RESPONSE
TO CHRISTIANITY IN AFRICA, 1972

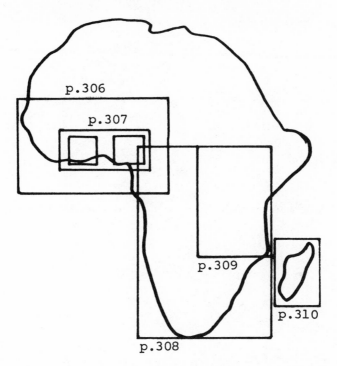

I. Breakdown by TRIBAL Groupings, pp.306-310

		TOTALS
MUSLIM AND ISLAMISED TRIBES (75% or over)		270
RESPONSIVE EVANGELISED TRIBES		512
UNEVANGELISED AND RESISTANT TRIBES		263

Evangelised (over 50%) but resistant	45
Half-evangelised (50%)	44
Partially evangelised (15—45%)	106
Sparsely evangelised (0—10%)	68

Total tribes within nations 1,045

KEY ——— tribal boundaries

------- national boundaries © D. B. Barrett 1972

See Key p.310 for tribal names of coded areas,
e.g. A2,K13 etc.

II. Breakdown by POLITICAL Groupings, p.310

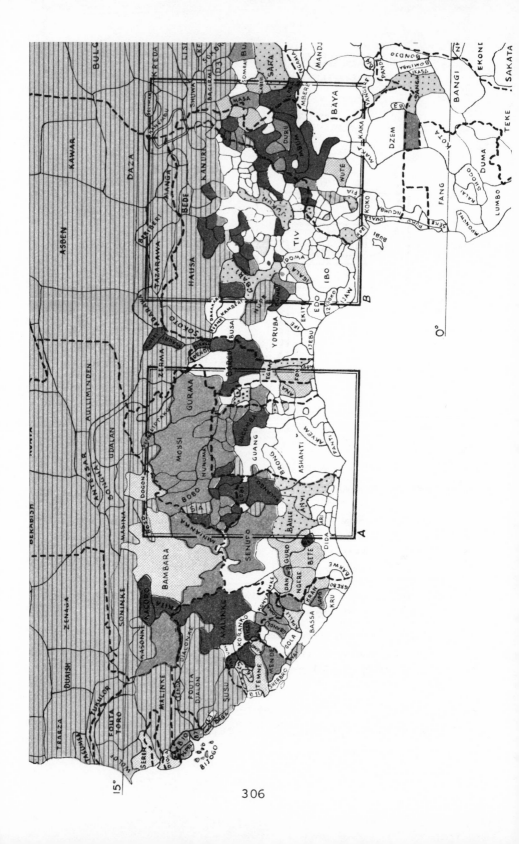

306

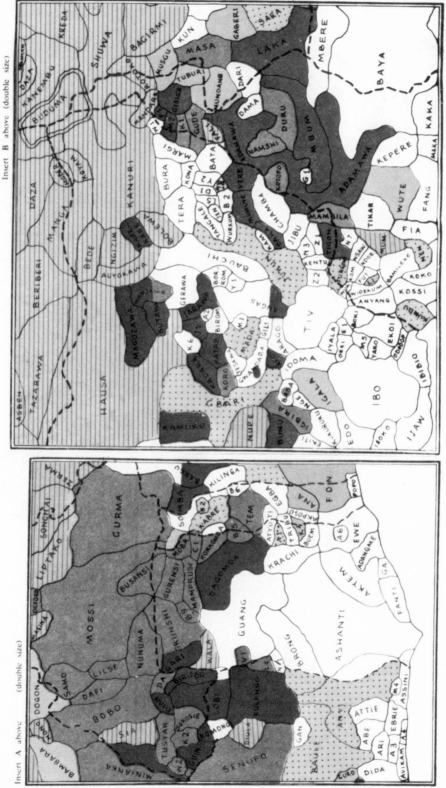

Insert B above (double size)

Insert A above (double size)

307

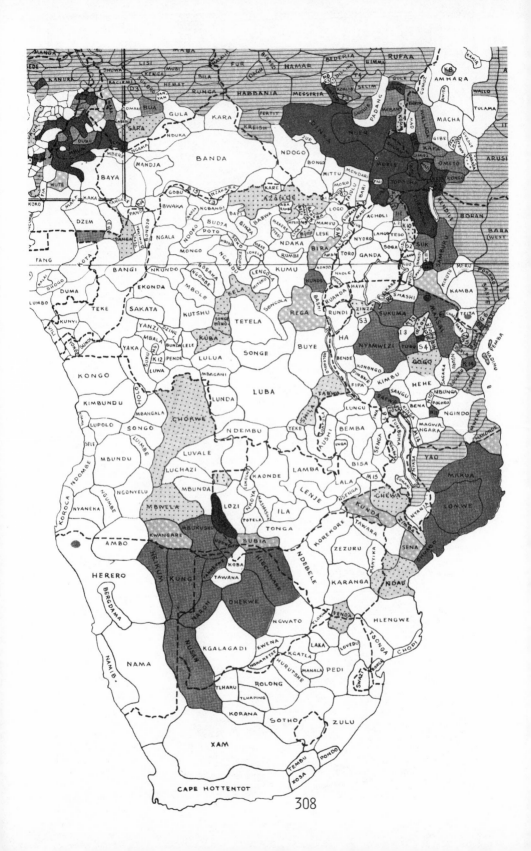
308

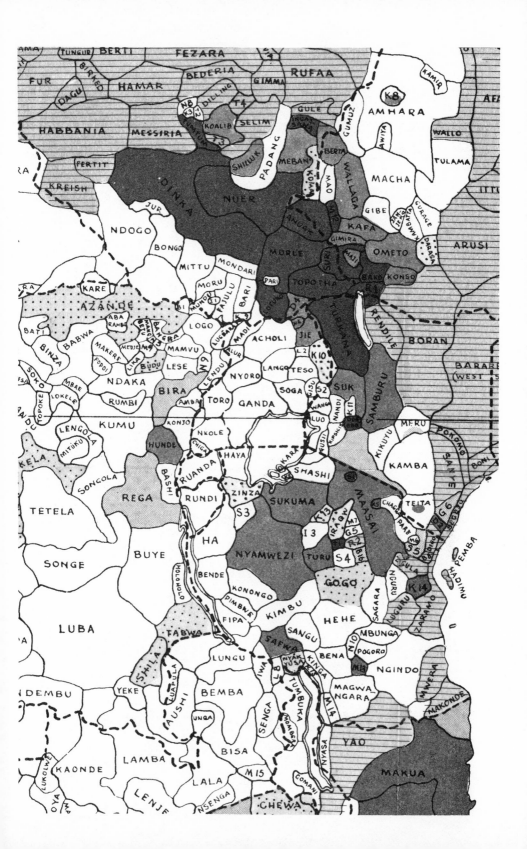

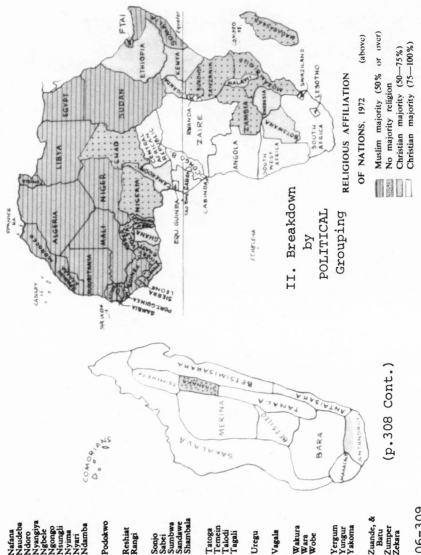

II. Breakdown
by
POLITICAL
Grouping

RELIGIOUS AFFILIATION
OF NATIONS, 1972   (above)

Muslim majority (50% or over)
No majority religion
Christian majority (50—75%)
Christian majority (75—100%)

(p.308 Cont.)

Key to names of tribes too small to be shown

A1	Adele	J1	Jerawa, & Chawai	
A2	Afusare			
A3	Adjukru	K1	Kapsiki	N1 Nafana
A4	Alagya	K2	Karaboro	N2 Naudeba
A5	Arusha	K3	Katla	N3 Ndoro
A6	Avatime	K4	Kebu	N4 Nyangiya
		K5	Kerewe	N5 Ngbele
B1	Babukur	K6	Kurama, & Gure	N6 Ngongo
B2	Bachama	K7	Kunama	N7 Nsungli
B3	Bangandu	K8	Kermant	N8 Nyima
B4	Banyun	K9	Kuku	N9 Nyari
B5	Basari	K10	Karamojong	N10 Ndamba
B6	Basila	K11	Keyu	
B7	Biafada	K12	Kwese	P1 Podokwo
B8	Bondei	K13	Kindiga	
B9	Builsa	K14	Kwere	R1 Reshiat
B10	Balante	K15	Kisi	R2 Rangi
B11	Bulom			
B12	Barea	L1	Li	S1 Sonjo
B13	Bogo	L2	Labwor	S2 Sabei
B14	Bofi	L3	Landuma	S3 Sumbwa
B15	Banziri	L4	Ligbi, & Degha	S4 Sandawe
B16	Burungi	L5	Longuda	S5 Shambala
		L6	Loko	
C1	Chakossi	L7	Limba	T1 Tatoga
		L8	Lambya	T2 Temein
D1	Dera			T3 Talodi
D2	Duruma	M1	Mama	T4 Tagali
D3	Dekakiri	M2	Matakam	
D4	Didinga	M3	Marmata	U1 Uregu
		M4	Mekyibo	
E1	Egede	M5	Mbembe	V1 Vagala
		M6	Mbugu	
G1	Galim	M7	Mbugwe	W1 Wakura
G2	Gafsa	M8	Mbula	W2 Wara
G3	Gadames	M9	Mayogo, & Badjo	W3 Wobe
G4	Gagu	M10	Menasser	
G5	Goroa	M11	Merari	Y1 Yergum
G6	Giryama	M12	Masongo	Y2 Yungur
		M13	Marunbi	Y3 Yakoma
H1	Harari	M14	Matcngo	
		M15	Mpezeni	Z1 Zuande, & Baru
I1	Idio			Z2 Zumper
I2	Itsekiri			Z3 Zekara
I3	Iramba			

This KEY applies to pp306-309

PART II

The Consultation

THE REPORT OF THE FINDINGS COMMITTEE

16

INTRODUCTION

In the providence of God we have been brought together in this Consultation, coming from the cultural background of fourteen countries and the ecclesiastical conditioning of 60 missionary agencies both Roman Catholic and Protestant. Among us are university administrators, professors, and graduate students; pastors, missionaries, and mission agency executives; linguists, researchers, translators; educators, theologians, editors; church executives, Bible distributors, and aviation administrators. Numbering more than 90 men and women, lay and ordained, over half having had overseas missionary experience in one or more of 36 countries, we have united in a common quest to learn "how to effect responsible action toward unevangelized peoples by national churches and missionary agencies."

These have been days of rich fellowship, of new and renewed acquaintance and deepening friendship. We have grown in mutual understanding, respect and love, recognizing both the large areas of common belief and commitment and those areas in which understanding and convictions differ. We have been conscious of the gracious ministry of the Holy Spirit among us and we give thanks for His presence and blessing.

Together we have sought information on existing frontier mission situations. We have shared experience on initial contact as well as on the continuing communication of the Gospel. We have made an earnest effort to understand the implications for freedom of indigenous churches under the Holy Spirit in tension with the need for responsible transmission of the essentials of the Gospel. We have sought to update our knowledge of current governmental policies and relations with church and missions. And, finally, we have labored to develop a statement of principles and suggested guidelines for future engagement in frontier missions.

In this search for understanding and guidance regarding the evangelization of frontier missions in our time, we have followed three main themes: (I) Indigenous Culture in Relation to Evangelism;

(II) The Indigenous Church Under the Holy Spirit; and, (III) Guidelines and Practical Measures. In addition to general discussion of these principle themes, we have met in small groups to narrow the focus of each general theme by relating the theme to six specific sub-topics: (I) Initial Contact; (II) Total Effect of Christianization on Culture; (III) Church/Mission and Government Relations; (IV) The Catechumenate; (V) Bible Translation; and, (VI) Development of Leadership and Leadership Resources for the National Church.

Out of these general discussions and from the small group exchanges have come the following summaries and suggested guidelines which we would recommend for prayerful consideration by all of us concerned with the problems and challenges of evangelizing the frontier areas of our world.

SUMMARIES OF DISCUSSION

In the discussion, both in the general session and in small groups, based on Dr. Mbiti's paper, there were the following points of general agreement:

1. The world-wide diversity of cultures is part of the total human reality. It is only in the terms of his own cultural experience that any person is intelligible to himself or to others. Even God's historical self-communication, through Jesus Christ, is in the limited terms of one particular region. But Christian faith, far from being bound exclusively to this or to any other particular culture, can be lived and expressed in the terms of any culture. Each culture is, therefore, an appropriate vehicle for living the Christian faith, just as each language is an appropriate instrument for communicating God's word to men.

2. Each culture has its elements of sin and aberration and its good elements. It is not, however, within the competence of the missionary as a foreigner to pass judgment on the cultures of the peoples to whom he is sent, just as it is not his place -- but God's -- to pass judgment on the sinfulness or holiness of persons. Rather, he should let the Gospel, inserted as a leaven in each culture, bring about a gradual transformation within the culture.

3. It is regrettable that, due to an ethnocentrism (which is not an exclusively Western form of blindness), missionaries have not always recognized the real significance of cultural diversity. But this recognition today, if it is accompanied by a constant

struggle against the blinding influences of ethnocentrism, should make a notable difference in the attitudes and methods of missionaries in frontier situations.

In the discussion on Dr. Minz's papers, the following points found general acceptance:

1. In recognizing the need to affirm the freedom of the indigenous church under the Holy Spirit, a certain tension was also asserted: a tension between the freedom and obedience of the indigenous church leaders and of the missionary witnesses. Both have their freedom under the Spirit and both are called to obedience; neither should be restricted. Hence the need for a continuing dialogue--with emphasis on listening.

2. The difficulties of such dialogue should not be minimized, since we are all caught up in certain types of "bondages"--institutional, cultural and personal--which hinder our openness to the Spirit and to the dialoguing partner. Such dialogue will help us to avoid repeating the mistakes of the past. At the same time, too much emphasis on past mistakes and present cultural differences can also become a barrier and impede the dialogue.

RECOMMENDATIONS OF SMALL GROUPS

Group I: Initial Contact

We rejoice that the Spirit of God is already at work through his Church in all continents, moving across ethnic and other barriers. We recognize that the church in the respective continents has primary responsibility of initiating the witness by word and life in each unevangelized region or community.

We believe also that the Christian Mission as mandated by our Lord is to all people and for all time, and that this Mission is conditioned by particular circumstances. We, therefore, recommend for prayerful consideration by all churches and missionary agencies the following points:

1. There is urgent need in the church everywhere for re-education as to the opportunity and nature of Christian mission, particularly in frontier situations still without the Gospel.

2. There are at least three types of situations open for cooperation of Western and Third World churches in Christian mission:

a.   Situations within the country of the missionary body, both
ethnic communities and new kinds of frontiers.

b.   Situations in other areas where there is already a Christian
community, but where missionary activity is undertaken by
invitation of, and in cooperation with the local church.

c.   Situations in other areas where there is no Christian
community and where Christians of one or more countries may
engage in partnership in mission.

3.   Freedom under the Holy Spirit requires Christian responsibility
and this responsibility requires repentance with regard to mistakes
of the past and great sensitivity as to the methods of today and
tomorrow.

4.   Preaching the Gospel in frontier situations should be careful
and non-threatening and should seek to secure the participation of
all converts, so that the church may be the people of God witnessing through ministry and mission in the world situations where
they are; denominational divisions should be avoided wherever
possible.

5.   It is very important that frontier mission be undertaken wherever possible on a cooperative basis that manifests love, understanding, forebearance and mutual trust under the guidance of the
Holy Spirit.   Even as under pressure of extreme persecution such a
spirit often prevails, should it not also prevail under the
extreme urgency of the frontier mission task?

6.   There are valid ways for cooperation between Christians of one
country and another in terms of servanthood and co-workership, but
there is also a need for mutual adjustment in basic attitudes and
agreement in terminology so as to avoid centering initiative
exclusively in either party; Christ is to be the center at all
times and in all ways.

Group II: Total Effect of Christianization on Culture

1.   Whenever or wherever the free and open presentation of the
Gospel becomes subject to arbitrary limitation or continuing opposition by governments around the world, we affirm our faith and
hope in the power and direction of the Holy Spirit, who, when one
door is closed can cause new doors to open, leading to even more
effective mission than before.

2. Relating to the obligations and opportunities for individual Christians and missionaries as agents of social change,

> a. We affirm the right and obligation of the individual Christian in any country to involve himself in political action to further the cause of social justice to the degree compatible with his conscience as a part of his Christian witness.

> b. We suggest that foreign missionaries or agencies witnessing to Christ in countries negatively influenced by power structures in their homelands may find their most effective role in changing such policies or attitudes by communicating directly to their own governments.

> c. We affirm the obligation and right of any church to give a responsible Christian witness to its government and society, but we advise against any official or formal alignment by church or mission agency with any specific political power structure, recognizing at the same time that a decision such as this against a formal alignment is in itself a political decision.

Group IV: The Catechumenate

From our discussions on the catechumenate in the light of the main themes of the Conference, we recommend:

1. That the first priority in teaching the message of Christ be to listen to the people, to respect and recognize the integrity of what they hold about reality, truth and value.

2. That the methodology of instruction be determined by the mode of thought and pattern of gaining information of the individual catechumens.

3. That the catechumenate be understood as a process of socialization into Christian life within a specific cultural context.

Group V: Bible Translation

1. The written Word of God is one of the main and indispensable tools to convey God's message of salvation to man. Therefore, we consider it imperative to accelerate the translation of the Scriptures into the mother tongues of all peoples. All agencies that are evangelizing frontier groups should include as a part of their

task the work of Bible translation, since the availability of the
Scriptures in any culture's language is basic to the freedom of
the local church to respond to the leading of the Holy Spirit.

2.   We are concerned about many areas where some evangelism has
already taken place (in many cases, years ago) where the Bible has
not yet been translated. We feel it is imperative that Bible
translation be pursued in all these areas as well as in new frontier situations, being convinced that hearing or reading something
in another language does not convey the same depth understanding
as hearing it in the mother tongue.

Group VI: Development of Leadership

We agree with those investigating other aspects of frontier mission situations that no one pattern (in this case of categories or
types of leadership) can be prescribed for frontier situations
world wide. Rather, we recommend that the development of leadership in each local situation should follow guidelines such as the
following:

1.   The form of leadership should be determined by, and not determine, the needs of the church in the given situations; form
follows function rather than being an *a priori* determinant of
function.

2.   Forms of leadership should be responsive to the socio-cultural-
economic situations in which the church finds itself and should
utilize the insights of that society and culture in serving God's
people in a way that that society can economically support.

3.   Leadership is for the common life, ministry, and witness of
the congregation; God's purpose in giving gifts for ministry is to
build up the congregation as his people in a given society.

4.   The biblical concept of leadership is that of an enabling type
of leadership, leadership which enables God's people to be that to
which they are called, leadership which regards its function as
being that of equipping the saints for ministry (Dph. 4) rather
than doing tasks for or ruling over the layity.

There are six things for which, we believe, God's people need to
be equipped; these are not in any necessary sequential order:

   1.   Growth in grace, maturity, sanctification.

2. Life as a community in ministry to one another, a community which isn't exclusive of other denominations than their own but inclusive and open, based on mutual respect, a diakonia within the family and to people generally, satisfying religious needs and meeting all kinds of personal and social needs.

3. The use of the Scriptures, that they may speak to people in the culture; familiarity with the Christian tradition and faithfulness to it, both requiring literacy.

4. Ability to articulate the faith and to apply the Gospel to moral and ethical questions.

5. Ability to teach and nurture the faithful within the community.

6. Evangelistic outreach to others, both in the ethnic group and beyond tribal boundaries.

Types of leadership which would equip God's people to do these things would include the following, several of which might be found in one person or persons:

1. The counselor/pastor/confidant type--those to whom people should look up and to whom they go when burdened, lost, and uncertain.

2. The teacher/catechist type--those who, by virtue of their gifts and special training, have a fuller knowledge of Scripture, a deeper understanding fo the Church's doctrine and tradition than the congregation at large, and are equipped to teach and communicate this knowledge and ways of utilizing it to people at all levels of development.

3. Liturgical leader.

4. Preacher and exhorter.

5. Animaters of group action.

The church should distinguish between that type of leader who appears spontaneously and whose role needs to be recognized and developed, and that type of leader who requires additional training in order to be specially equipped. The latter type of leader should work together with and not be imposed upon or dominate the former. The church should regard the forms of leadership in a society as part of God's gift to his church for ministry and not

impose foreign forms. To take the responsibility for the life and
growth of the church away from the church's natural or charismatic
leaders may be indicative of a failure to trust the Holy Spirit
and a reliance upon merely human resources and strategies.

We are confident that that mission which trusts the Lord to do
through the new church the work He is seeking to do will not be
disappointed. We call upon workers in frontier missions to be as
sensitive as possible to the givens of the local situations and
to the leadership of the Holy Spirit.

GENERAL RECOMMENDATIONS

1. The Consultation on Frontier Missions recommends that, for the
furtherance of mission to unevangelized peoples on the frontiers
of Christian mission, a central, independent or semi-independent
research agency be established somewhere in the Third World with
the following tasks and characteristics:

   a. Its central role will be to discover (both directly and by
   proxy, by stimulating others to dig) in the library and in the
   field, all relevant information, and to coordinate, focus and
   test it, in order to make practical procedural recommendations
   solidly founded in facts and on relevant concepts for the
   social sciences. Its research would be both basic and applied,
   both long-term and short-term, both broadly and narrowly
   focused, and it would explore all the ramifications of the
   applications of the social sciences to evangelism in today's
   world.

   b. Its permanent staff would be (1) very few in number, (2)
   highly competent in both training and experience in the social
   sciences including demography and in missions, and (3) international in composition.

   c. It would give technical counsel and guidance to field
   research projects and pilot projects undertaken by others also
   involved in the total effort.

   d. It would bring together in active participation on a temporary and rotating basis other qualified people not on the
   permanent staff for continual cross-fertilization of ideas.

   e. It would call upon existing information and research agencies to assist in the areas of their special competencies.

f. It would formulate recommendations to planning agencies at
all levels.

g. It would ensure a regular flow of information from all
sources to all points of need.

h. It would coordinate the continuing monitoring and evaluating of studies of the program.

All participants of this Consultation are encouraged to go back to
their churches and/or agencies to raise the question of the establishment of such an agency and to also do so with whatever larger
fellowships they belong to.

2. This Consultation recommends that national churches and agencies on all continents be encouraged to engage in making surveys
similar to that presented to this Consultation by Dr. David
Barrett for the African continent, at the same time to seek to
improve and enlarge the same by including additional data thay may
be useful in carrying on the program of evangelization.

3. This Consultation authorizes its Steering Committee to meet at
least once more to determine the feasibility of establishing a Continuing Committee to serve the following purposes:

a. As a consultative group to assist Dr. Pierce Beaver with
the editing, publication and distribution of the report of this
Consultation.

b. To forward the Report of this Consultation to mission agencies or groups (e.g. E.F.M.A., I.F.M.A., Catholic Mission
Council, D.O.M./N.C.C. USA, etc.) for their information and as
a basis for inviting their support and participation in the
purposes of this Consultation.

c. To take required steps toward the establishment or designation of a research agency for the furtherance of mission to
unevangelized peoples.

d. To take required steps toward the achievement of completing
a comprehensive survey to ascertain clearly the nature and location of the unevangelized people of the world and the distribution of such data to all interested mission agencies.

e. To plan, as feasible, for the scheduling of a follow-up
Consultation on Frontier Missions at a time to be determined
by the Committee after canvasing the agencies here represented
and other interested groups; the location of this Consultation

should preferably be in an overseas area in contact with frontier situations.

RESOLUTION OF APPRECIATION

This Consultation expresses its hearty appreciation to the Steering Committee of this Consultation and particularly to its Chairman and Executive Secretary, Dr. R. Pierce Beaver; and to the Chicago Cluster of Theological Schools, and especially Fr. Robert J. Flinn, S.V.D., for the gracious hospitality and management of all necessary details to make this Consultation possible.

STATEMENTS BY OVERSEAS CHURCHMEN **17**

STATEMENT
Theodore Manaen

These four days of consultation on Frontiers have been a wonderful experience for me. I had feared that the conference would just be a clash of mind and an intellectual exercise. I praise God! My fear has turned to be unfounded and these four days of meeting was a time of warm fellowship of men and women, deeply concerned about the evangelization of unevangelized areas of the globe. I'm confident its findings and reports will open up new horizons and give a realistic sense of direction to mission boards and missionaries.

The papers prepared for the conference were of great value. The statistical paper by Dr. Barrett on Africa I thought was of immense value. I would urge on the continuing committee to request Dr. Barrett to make his expertise and the technical know-how available to Asian and Latin American churches so that similar reports could be prepared. I understand a world-wide conference on evangelism is scheduled some two years later in Switzerland. A report on the pattern of Dr. Barrett's paper could be prepared on Asian and Latin American countries and made available to such a conference to a great advantage.

Coming from India as I do, I would like to make a few observations about the Christian Church in my country. Although we form only about 2.6% in a vast population of 550 million people in India, the church in India is no more defensive and apologetic. The church in India has become a reality now. I agreed with Dr. Peter Wagner when he made an observation yesterday that churches in the world are in the sunrise. The churches in northeast India are growing in a wonderful way and by and large the Gospel is being preached effectively in the country. After several centuries, the doors of Nepal have been opened to the Gospel and the churches have been

established and believers meet and worship. After an effort of
about a hundred years, a church has been established in Bhutan
today and we know what is happening in the far eastern countries
of Korea and Indonesia. We can see real evidence of the movement
of the Spirit across the world today.

In my country, the church groups are increasingly realizing the
value of the three "selfs" -- self-supporting, self-governing and
self-propagating. As far as the self-propagating aspect is concerned, the churches are preaching within the country. Some
missionaries are also going across the national frontiers. Churches
are increasingly becoming evangelical. With regard to the aspect
of self-governing issue, I'm happy to say that with increasing number of trained personnel, most churches are self-governing. The
newly immerged church of North India, of which I am a member, with
its national bishops is self-governing for all intent and purpose.

Most churches are self-supporting. But for such churches who have
not reached a self-supporting stage, financial assistance may have
to be continued for some time. Financial assistance, particularly
in respect to various institutional projects like schools and hospitals in which churches are involved is absolutely necessary. I
take the liberty of saying that the most churches in the third
world will need financial assistance for some time. We have no
reason to be oversensitive on this issue nor overapologetic. My
country has to depend for 20% of resources for development work on
foreign aids and loans. And 80% of this 20% financial aid comes
from the United States of America. Aid and assistance are not bad
things in themselves as long as they are made available without any
strings attached to them. Even missionaries from this country or
from other countries should not fight shy to go and work on unevangelized areas. Time has come when the young churches, mission
boards and missionaries must work in unison under the guidance of
the Holy Spirit.

The question of culture and indigenization of existing churches in
the third world seems to have engaged some attention of the conference. I should think if Paul and Silas had engaged themselves
so much in planning anthropological researches and anxiety for the
preservation of culture, I wonder whether the Christianization of
Europe would have taken place at a time when it did. The anxiety
for indigenization should not be overplayed. In my country, the
whole question is in a process of understanding and should be
allowed to unfold itself. The over much anxiety of anthropology-
orientated missionaries can upset churches.

We were discussing about unevangelized frontiers. Our Lord commanded that we must be His witnesses in our Jerusalem.   Our

Jerusalem is our neighborhood and our Judea and Samaria are our
countries. I would like to draw your attention to a particular
frontier in this country. Thousands of students come from Asian
and African and Latin American countries into the United States
every year and many come to work for a period of time. This
particular community of people can certainly be "a frontier". If
a proper rapport can be established with them by looking after
their interests and helping them and if the Gospel could be
brought to them, this particular frontier can certainly be reached.
I would urge that some thought be given to this frontier and if
possible some missionaries be assigned this work. Many can turn
to the Lord and when they go back to their countries they can bring
others to the Lord. I'm grateful for the privilege given me to
address this learned gathering.

THE PRESSING NEED IN MISSIONS TODAY
Musembe Kasiera

A point has been made at this Consultation by one of our brothers
from Indonesia that, our brothers from the West want to hear from
those of us from overseas, but do they listen? I therefore do
not know whether what I want to say will be received. I am not
even sure whether this is the place or whether this is the proper
group to which I should be making this statement.

I want to speak to you, from an African perspective, on what I see
as the pressing need in missions today: the need to train capable
leadership/ministry *for the times*. I want particularly to highlight what I see as the indifference among the Western churches in
responding to this need. After looking into a number of sources,
including the background from which I come, I have come to the
conclusion that, in certain quarters among the Protestant churches
in the West, there is great indifference towards the need to train
capable leadership/ministry in the African churches. Some have
made deliberate attempts to stifle local initiatives aimed at
alleviating this problem.

The Rev. Daniel N. Wambutda in an article, "An African Christian
Looks at Christian Missions," cites the opposition he received on
the grounds that the London Diploma in Theology was enough. In

the same article, he mentions the case of his friend who had to
struggle for two years to try to overcome the obstacles placed in
his way by missionaries (*Practical Anthropology*, V. 17, pp. 170-1;
the contents of the article will be referred to hereafter by only
citing Wambutda). A short conversation with one of the speakers
at Urbana '70, an African minister, then studhing at Dallas Theological Seminary, revealed that, he too, had received a good amount
of opposition from the missionaries prior to his coming to the
United States. If you were to ask Dr. John Mbiti, who is here with
us, of his experiences along this line, he will at least tell you
that he did not have the blessing of his church all the way.

In the face of what seems to be widespread opposition then, one
is forced to grant that there must be reasons that warrant such a
widespread attitude. There are reasons given and we find them
inadequate to explain this apathy. They simply do not stand the
test, as much as we would like to grant their validity. Wambutda
gives three reasons that underlie this attitude and I have run
into four others. We shall therefore see, on the one hand, why
the Western Church is indifferent towards offering an African educated ministry, and on the other hand, why the African Church calls
for such a ministry.

1. It is argued that if you educate an African he will be proud.
    The same idea was expressed by a retired missionary that, if
    I went for a fourth year of college I would simply be looking
    for prestige. It is true that education is uppermost in
    Africa today. Job opportunities depend on one's educational
    attainment. Sad to say, one's future hinges, to a great
    measure, on one's performance in the final examination. One
    reads statements like, "G.C.E. OR SCHOOL Certificate passes
    are stepping stones to success." It certainly was not the
    African idea to make Western education as the sole criterion
    for measuring one's success. It was the colonial administra-
    tion that made Western education as the status symbol of the
    people. And to assure its high status in society, only a
    priviledged few could attain education. Any argument there-
    fore, that education should be limited to the African so as to
    keep him humble does not hold water. It is rooted in the col-
    onial mentality of elevating the few and suppressing the
    majority. Only the "yes men" have the privilege to advance.
    Wambutda well observes that even if it were true that someone
    becomes proud because of his educational status, it is the
    attitude that should be attacked rather than the education
    he has.

2. It is said that if you give an African higher education, you
    would be creating a gap between him and his people, such that,

when he ministers to his people he would be talking over their heads. Surely, if a minister talks over the heads of his audience, it can hardly be said that he made use of his education. For the educational system he goes through alerts him to the fact that he must communicate with his audience. Common sense indicates that to communicate, the speaker must place himself at the level where his listeners are.

However, it is a false presupposition that an educated African minister will be speaking to those lacking formal schooling only. Taking Kenya for an example, the progress of education there is staggering to the imagination. A DAILY NATION reporter puts it this way, 'EDUCATION is "the mostest" in Kenya. It takes the biggest slice of the budget. Education now has the highest number of Kenyans benefitting from it' (DAILY NATION, December 12, 1972; figures quoted here came from this paper). The reason behind such a big drive in education is the effort to fulfill the government's pledge to the people to provide education for all Kenyans. This priviledge has been denied to them during the colonial administration. The goal has not been realized yet, but they are closer than when they began.

At the time of Uhuru, in 1963, there were only 151 secondary schools. In 1966, the number rose to 400. This year, the figure stands at 800 schools with an overall enrollment of about 200,000 students. In 1963, there was only one university serving the whole of East Africa. Now, after nine years of independence, there are three universities serving the needs of East Africa. Kenya students at university in 1963 were 471; now, there are 4,063. The adult literacy centres being run by the National Literacy Programmes are 850. With the help of the Unesco technical assitance, more literacy centres are planned for those areas where there are no adequate educational facilities. Kenya is only one example of new independent nations all over Africa that have embarked on ambitious programmes in the field of education. It is therefore false to argue that to educate an African minister you would be creating a gap between him and his people. If the argument held any water in the past, it no longer does in "the now" period.

3. It is further argued that Paul did not preach education but the "pure Gospel." It is true that if we were to look for an apostolic sermon on education we would find none. It is equally true that the apostles were not ignoramuses, and at no time did they slight education. There is no doubt that they themselves went through some form of schooling over the three year period

they were with Jesus. From St. John's upper room discourse
account, it is abundantly clear that Jesus wished to teach
them further, but due to the heaviness of their hearts, Jesus
promised to send another teacher to them. Upon graduation,
the apostles went to the peoples "of all nations," among other
things, teaching them to observe all that had been commanded
of them. St. Paul took no exception to the teaching ministry.
I venture to say that it was his educational preparation that
made him to "become all things for all men."

If the disciples are to be taught to observe what Jesus commanded, it is necessary therefore that the teachers be trained.
And this is the point of our present concern. There are *VERY
FEW* Africans equipped to teach their own people. May I illustrate this point. There is a church in Kenya that has national
pastors taking care of all its congregations, with the exception of two city congregations. It has come to the attention
of the executive leadership in this church that, the members
in these congregations need to be grounded in the Word of God.
Scripture places the responsibility of teaching these people
in the hands of the pastors. It happens to be that the training system these pastors went through did not equip them for
this task. Instead, missionaries are employed all year round
conducting regional Bible studies from one place to the next.
One often wonders about the wisdom of refusing to educate an
African for this task, but instead the missionary is preferred
for the task! It seems to be one of the ways in which a position for a missionary is secured from one term to the next.

4. One of the reasons Wambutda gives as underlying this indiffer-
    ence is the fear that if an African is educated "he may take
    off into the world." Considering a Christian minister, there
    are probably two ways in which "taking off into the world" can
    be understood. The one is where a professing Christian disre-
    gards his commitment to Jesus Christ, and loses his desire for
    the things of God. This could happen to any Christian irre-
    spective of colour or race. There is absolutely no ground on
    which to hold that the African is more prone to do this than
    any other Christian in the West. This is not to deny that
    there are people in Africa who have had second thoughts about
    their Christian commitment. They are there, but their "after"
    decisions have been prompted by reasons other than the educa-
    tion they have. We concur with Wambutda that "it is better
    for the African to be allowed to develop his love for God des-
    pite the world, if his faith is to be genuine."

Another sense in which a Christian minister can be seen as
taking off into the world is in the Western's distinction

between the "sacred" and the "secular." A Christian trains
for the ministry with a view to working in a given religious
institution. Later on he finds out that the institution has
not made provision to accommodate him. The alternative left
to him therefore is that of working in the "secular field."
To the Western mind, this person has "taken off into the world."
Dr. George W. Doxsee--President, C.N.E.C. Canada, adequately
addresses himself to this question.

In an article, "Enough Fuel For The Second Stage?" Doxsee
focuses on financial assistance to nationals. He sees it as
"the missing link in missions." He states, "Because of this,
today in several countries we find many nationals in secular
teaching and government jobs who have been thoroughly and
capably educated by various missions in their own colleges,
and even overseas in England, U.S.A. and Canada. Most of
these have a zeal and vision for evangelism or pastorate but
have tried and not had enough to sustain their families. This
is a sad waste of dedicated and capable Christian stewardship
and needs immediate review and attention before we have more
casualties." (THRUST, Vol. 3, March, 1971, p. 11)

Because they do not want to assist the nationals financially
(partly, due to their formula for the indigenous church), and
because they refuse to acknowledge their failure to teach
stewardship to the new churches they helped establish, some
of the Western missionary societies see a solution in suppres-
sing the desire of the nationals to get an education. This may
be their solution, to save face, but it certannly does not
help the nationals who want to be equipped for given situations
in their own countries. They are happy to keep educational
level of the pastors below the eighth grade. In this way they
would not be faced with the need to sustain an educated minister.

5. With respect to training nationals overseas, a number of reasons
    have been advanced. That if you bring nationals to Europe,
    America, or Canada you would be giving them a higher standard
    of living unknown to them. This reasonsing rests on the assump-
    tion that all Africans come from "jungles," away from the so-
    called civilization. One gets the impression that a majority
    of Westerners know nothing about Africa besides the Africa de-
    picted in the adventures of Tarzan. Sad to say, even the
    missionaries help to sustain this image by showing out-of-date
    pictures of Africa. There is definitely no justification what-
    soever for a missionary to show in 1970 pictures which he took
    in 1943 when he first went to Africa. Contemporary history

shows that Africa is changing so fast that the Africa of this year is significantly different from the Africa of last year.

Although a majority of African nations depends on agriculture for its economy, industrialization is increasing at a comparatively high rate. The industries found in Africa are the same as those found in Europe, Canada, and the United States. Qualifications required to fill a position in any one of the industries are the same as those for a position in an industry in the West. If they are any different, the conditions are made tougher for the African. Should any one have gone this route, and decides to come to the West for education, he will certainly not have "just emerged from the bush." Even if it were one of the students just graduated from high school coming to the West, he would by no means be a stranger to Western living. Although Africa is a land of contrast, it also offers a standard of living comparatively higher than one some people in the West know. Some students studying in the West have been known to live in humbler dwellings than the ones they lived in in their own countries. Therefore, one case in a given country can not stand for many cases in many countries.

6. In connection with the foregoing reason, it is said that because foreign students find life in the West so comfortable, they decide to stay in the West rather than go back to their own countries. In support of this argument, cases of people from the Bahamas and other parts of the West Indies are cited. It can not be denied that such cases have occurred. What is questionable is the logic that makes them the universal bases on which other cases must be evaluated. There is no justification in hindering someone's education on the basis of an experience he is not part of.

On the basis of the information available, there is no evidence to the effect that there is a Kenyan who came overseas to train for the ministry and decided to stay. Even if someone stayed, it is unfair to let one case jeopardize the chances of other people. Every case needs to be considered on its own merits, than on the generalized policy that is not inclusive. Looking at the case from a material point of view (as the Westerners do), one gets the impression that the whites want a comfortable life for themselves and a destitute life for the blacks. If they really believe that "the material blessing" they have comes from God, why should they be bothered if a fellow Christian also wants to be blessed of God? This attitude points to a deeper problem. The denial of education to an African has its roots in a deep-seated psychological problem: to suppress the black man educationally, socially, politically, and economically.

7. The final reason we consider is that which holds that nationals, when trained overseas, are not accepted by their own people in their own countries. To give some hearing to this argument, I suggest that we look at two kinds of people the overseas trained African goes back to: those in the leadership bracket, and the general membership in the Church. It is possible that there could be resentment towards the overseas trained personnel from a few among the church leaders. These men were hand-picked by the missionaries after they showed their passive submission to the orders given by the missionaries. In turn, they operate on the basis that anyone who aspires to a position of leadership should likewise show the same kind of submission. Because the overseas trained personnel are more likely to be preferred by the members of the church, these leaders make it unnecessarily difficult for them, so as to find a case against them. This way, they satisfy themselves that they have minimized what would have been a threat to them.

However, I refuse to accept that this is the general attitude adopted by all national leaders towards the overseas trained men. A majority of the leaders recognizes that there is a lot of work to be done. Many leaders keep pointing out that they could use help in their fields of endeavour. They recognize that they have made their contribution, and they need those to whom they can transfer the responsibility as they pass off the scene. They would welcome someone trained overseas with both hands. For they know that such an individual is going to train many more workers for the ministry.

With respect to general membership in the church, it is utterly false to suggest that they would resent overseas trained persons. One does not need to go far for evidence. Many of the people in government services and in executive positions in the industries have at one time or another been educated overseas. These people have been received otherwise. We all know the great confidence and respect the missionaries command among the ordinary citizens they work. Anyone that has been able to go to study in the country from which the missionary came commands the same respect and confidence of the citizens to the same degree, if not greater.

The foregoing are reasons given by missionaries, executive leaders of mission boards, and other leaders in the Western Church for their indifference towards providing an educated ministry in

Africa. We have made an effort to show that the reasons are not
convincing as far as we are concerned. One is tempted to connect
this indifference to colonial practice of holding the African down.
We grant that there will be many in that camp that will not be
convinced by our explanation. The effort here is not to convince
them, for they are the ones that want to do the convincing. Our
effort is to present the other side that has not been listened to.
We proceed to throw more light on it by showing why the African
Church needs an educated ministry. We shall do this by citing
several voices of authority on the African scene.

The Rt. Rev. Bishop Stephen S. Neill, in his book, *A History of
Christian Missions*, states, "The fifth and gravest danger to the
African Churches is the increasing alienation from them of the
intellectual elite, and particularly of the political leadership
in the newly emerging countries" (Penguin Books: Harmondsworth,
1964, p. 502). He sees this alienation as two-fold: a political
gap and a generation gap. The Church (i.e. Western missions)
takes blame politically because it identified with colonialism
(Parenthesis are mine). On this wise, Neill says, "It has to be
admitted that the Church and its leaders have often failed to
discern the signs of the times, partly through sheer conservatism,
and partly through preoccupation with more immediate tasks"
(p. 502).

With respect to the generation gap, Neill says, "Naturally, the
majority of the pastors are simple men, faithful and diligent but
theologically not highly trained, and often unaware of the questions that are surging through the minds of the younger people in
the Church - questions to which they would be unable to offer an
answer, even if they understood the question" (p. 503). This is
the very point I am trying to make. The Church has alienated
itself from its youth. As a result, the young people are "growing
out of the Church." They are really not asking too much of the
Church when you stop to consider the kind of programmes the
churches in the West embark on in an effort to keep their youth
in the Church.

The prevalent thinking among the educated in Africa, especially
those educated in the West, is that the Church or Christianity is
"for those who do not know better." A recent conversation with
three Kenya agricultural students, visiting St. Louis, produced
several thought-provoking statements most of us would not be
anxious to listen to. After they expressed concern that my programme of studies did not include studies of African traditions
and religions, I asked, "At what stage of your development did you
adopt this reactionary attitude towards Christianity?" One of the
answers came out like this, "When I was in high school, the priests

kept telling us that Jomo Kenyatta was the devil's agent, that he was leading people to darkness. After independence, the same priests started praising Mzee Kanyatta for his wise leadership, and praying for him that God would continue to guide him. This change of attitude made me think, and I concluded that there is something hypocritical about Christianity." This is a historical situation African Christian leaders must deal with!

Another question I asked was, "On the basis of what you have told me, do you see anything in Christianity that transcends the African Traditions and Religions?" Without exception, all three said that Christianity does not offer anything more than what the African Traditions and Religions can offer. "If our traditions had been systematically reasoned out and written down, they would parallel Islam, Judaism, and Christianity" they all submitted. Surprisingly, this is not the thinking of only a few. In Bishop Neill's circular letter number 10, of October, 1972, he mentions that there are those who advocate that Christianity should be abandoned. Neill definitely demonstrated his far-sighted insight in his book cited above when he said, "The danger in this is that educated Africans may come to think that Christianity is a stage that can be passed through and left behind" (p. 503). It cannot be denied that we are in that crucial moment of history. How Christianity may go through this stage in Africa is going to depend on how the Western Church is going to respond to the need to train capable African educated ministry/leadership.

In a letter to one of the ecumenical leaders in New York, the General Secretary of the National Christian Council of Kenya said, "...the things he says in his letter about an educated ministry are very true and proper as far as the Kenyan situation is concerned." He was referring to the contents of my letter to one of the missionaries in Kenya, in which I had referred to this need. In reply to my letter, Bishop Neill, in his capacity as the Head of the Department of Philosophy and Religious Studies at the University of Nairobi, said, "We are of course anxious as soon as possible to appoint fully qualified Kenyans to the staff... Until we have Kenyans with a really competent knowledge of Greek and Hebrew, we are bound to go on appointing foreigners; at present I do not know of any Kenyan who could be appointed in the field of biblical studies with the hope of ultimately becoming a professor."

To my present knowledge, Dr. John S. Mbiti is the only one in East Africa that has attained the highest training in Theology and Biblical Studies. When we think of the meaningful work he is presently engaged in, we are filled with a great sense of appreciation for a trained ministry. His published works have caught

the attention of educated Africans all over Africa, who would
otherwise have no room for Christianity. Our prayer is that God
may raise many more men like him all over Africa to meet the present challenge. It is only through such men that Christianity
can be vindicated before the Africans that have been turned off.
What we ask of the Western Church is a change in attitude, from
a state of indifference to a positive state of response to a
realistic situation that exists now in Africa, and train the
Africans that will help Christianity take root in Africa.

18

A BLADE OF GRASS? A RICH MAN? OR A PROPHET?
Holly Arpan

December 10, 1972, was a typically uncomfortable winter day
in the Windy City of Chicago when I arrived at the Shoreland Hotel,
once noted for its luxury both of service and appointments but now
rather definitely in the dowdy dowager class, to attend the Consultation on Frontier Mission as observer-reactor-reporter. A more
cynical observer might have been tempted to draw invidious comparisons between the present condition of the hotel and the character
of the cause for which the Consultation had been called, but such
comparisons would have failed to take into consideration either
the efficiency and cooperation of the admittedly straitened management or the dynamism of the participants.

I had been asked to attend the Consultation "as a committed
Christian who is also discerning, objective, not taken in by
pietistic verbiage or posturing, who also has, or can acquire, a
concern for remote primitive peoples under tremendous pressures
to change their way of life or be destroyed or absorbed into the
dominant culture."

My assignment was to observe and react to a group of a hundred
or so mission "pro's" as they collectively and individually tried
to answer such questions as "How to effect responsible action towards unevangelized peoples by national churches and western mission
agencies?" or, "How to understand the freedom of the indigenous
Church under the Holy Spirit in tension with the transmission of
the essentials of the Gospel -- i.e., the common Christian Faith?"
In addition, I had been asked as an outsider to try to interpret
all that went on at the Consultation, not only to the participants
and their agencies, but to the general public as well.

If, at the outset, I may have felt some degree of confidence
in filling the requirements of being a committed Christiwn with a
concern for spreading the good news of Christ "to the uttermost
ends of the earth", my first reading of the list of Consultation
participants was more than enough to undermine any illusions as to
my ability to interpret with any accuracy or depth the multi-level,
point-counterpoint proceedings and interplay of human reactions
which were to make up the informal and formal agenda of the next
three days.

In the first place I was confronted with a bewildering kalei-
descope of unfamiliar organizations, auxiliary groups, agencies as
well as a whole new kettle of alphabet soup -- MAF, SIM, DWM, FAST,
CMA, LSTC, EFMA, etc., etc., etc. Up until that point I had
thought myself to be reasonably knowledgeable about the scope and
complexity of global missions. After all, I had had an aunt and
uncle for years serving under the American Board as medical missionaries in North China and later under the London Missionary
Society in Southwest China. As they say in the South, I had some
"nearly relatives" supported by the Dutch Reformed Church in what
is now modern-day Iraq, plus a first cousin financed by the London
Missionary Society in China and India. A Maryknoll priest had
once helped me though customs in Bolivia, a doctor from a 7th Day
Adventist hospital had dosed me with penicillin in Ecuador. As a
child attending a Southern Baptist Sunday School I had read about
Adoniram Judson and the beginnings of Baptist missions in Burma.
Then, too, I knew personally, missionaries from both the southern
and northern Presbyterian Churches and had even visited with some
of them in Kenya, Brazil, Ecuador and Egypt. But such previous
contacts offered only minor help in orienting me as I attempted to
identify and sort out the missionary melange that made up the Consultation.

In addition to my general confusion by the more than "57
varieties" of mission related groups and individuals present, I
also discovered I had brought with me, in spite of the best of
intentions, some highly unnecessary mental baggage -- a motley
collection of pre-conceptions, sterotypes, myths and prejudices
(both pro and con) which would have to be discarded and the sooner
the better. Some of these misbegotten ideas I hadn't really realized I had had. To reword the cliche, I didn't think I was
really prejudiced one way or another about missionaries (or even
anthropologists!) -- "some of my best friends were.....!" But, as
the Consultation progressed, I was to be reminded again and again
that missionaries are, first and last, individuals, and, more
importantly, they are human beings who approach and meet their
common calling in ways that frequently are as distinctive and individualistic as they are constrained and conformed by denominational
patterns.

Like many Protestants, I have had to struggle to keep from thinking of the Roman Catholic church as monolithic and ridigly homogeneous. (For that matter, I have the same problem with Islam or Buddhism, etc.) But I was to learn quickly, for example that there were Catholics at the Consultation who were more liberating in their ideas of the church and social justice than I was quite prepared to be. As a Presbyterian, USA, I was reasonably familiar with our Commission on Ecumenical Mission and Relations, but I discovered I knew little about the Fuller Seminary School of World Mission, and even worse, I learned that for years I had been confusing the work of the American Bible Society with that of the Wycliffe Bible Translators!

And as for what I knew about the national churches overseas, while I had attended both Protestant and Catholic church services in Seoul, Sao Paolo, Quito, Nairobi, Delhi, Kuala Lumpur, Cuernavaca, Fiji, etc. and had attended meetings of the World Council of Churches in Evanston, I was to be reminded over and over during the Consultation how little I really knew first-hand of the problems or the vitality and maturity of those churches I had so long "supported".

So, as I sat with the Steering Committee on the first evening of the Consultation, mentally tossing out one pre-conception after another, I found myself thinking about those questions Christ had asked the followers of John the Baptist: "When you went out. . . what did you expect to see? a blade of grass bending in the wind? . . .A man dressed up in fancy clothes?. . .a prophet?"

I was to keep asking myself those questions all during the Consultation as I listened to the plenary sessions, participated in the small group discussions, talked with and questioned individual delegates and worked with the Findings Committee in an attempt to summarize the opinions expressed during the meeting. In fact, I am still asking those questions now as I try to put on paper my reactions to the Consultation both in terms of what I heard and what I did not hear.

WHAT WAS IT ALL ABOUT?

How did it happen? Whose idea had it been? What were its goals, either stated or unstated? Why hold this particular kind of consultation at this moment in history? These were other questions I needed to have answered, not just when I first took on the assignment, but as I listened and talked with the delegates.

It was obvious from the standpoint of the denominational diversity represented that this was no ordinary gathering of the godly, and yet it could not really be considered an official ecumenically-derived event. True, I had learned that various denominational boards had help fund the meeting; that support agencies had contributed study material, personnel and money; that ecumenical organizations such as the National Council of Churches were indirectly represented through persons who had helped in the planning, but the basic nature of the Consultation still defied pigeon-holing.

There were two men, however, who stood out as originators or prime movers for the Consultation. First, there was Bishop Edwin W. Kortz, executive director for the Moravian Church's mission work, and then there was Prof. R. Pierce Beaver, consultant to the Division of Overseas Ministries, National Council of Churches and retired professor of Missions, University of Chicago. Both men had had extensive experience in mission work overseas in addition to administrative and consulting work, factors which had contributed to their awareness of problems and opportunities for global mission. Each man, by virtue of his position, had been on the receiving end of increasing questions and requests for guidance from mission personnel in the field, from leaders of national churches overseas, from mission boards and lay church people.

Certainly, both men, out of their previous and present contacts, were well aware of growing tensions stemming from a proliferation of mission methodologies, from growing insistency of the indigenous churches for authnomy, or from the political realities of the Third World.

But what to do about it? Although neither man would claim full credit for having actually initiated the idea which had been growing through a series of conversations, apparently it was Bishop Kortz who finally suggested "Why don't we try.....?", while it fell to the lot of Pierce Beaver to take on the responsibility of putting the idea into action.

Later, as an ad hoc steering committee was formed, broadly representative of concerned mission workers, several basics were formulated:

1.   The Consultation would be just that -- a chance for people to
     get together in an unofficial relationship to continue and
     deepen the on-going dialog as experienced "on the field" about
     mutual concerns related to mission and its future spread.

2. The meeting should provide opportunities for person-to-person discussion among people representing the widest possible spectrum of Christian mission.

3. Through such contacts, hopefully, the Consultation might serve to broaden the base of mutual understanding among the diversity of participants, thereby contributing to a lessening of the tensions -- or even suspicions -- that historically have hindered the reception and impact of the Gospel around the world.

4. In order that the Consultation should not become, as Prof. Beaver expressed it, "merely one more 19th century model adventure in Western cultural and ecclesiastical imperialism," it was essential to have the strongest representation possible of representatives from the Third World churches.

5. As a means of focusing the discussions toward a central theme of crucial importance to the present and future spread of the Gospel, the Consultation would be directed specifically toward the problems and methods of reaching the unreached, essentially primitive peoples of the world, hence the eventual Consultation title, "Consultation on Frontier Mission."

6. Although the Consultation was to be essentially unofficial and unaligned save as to common purpose, it was hoped that consensus could be reached in significant areas which could lead to the formulation of some guidelines and advice for future consideration and implementation to official boards and agencies as ways which might stem the proliferation and duplication that so often contributes negatively to Christian witness both at home and overseas.

Obviously, these were no small dreams, and full implementation of any one of them could well occupy the creative energies of any group for a period much longer than the three days allotted for the Consultation. But, if the results of the Consultation may have fallen somewhat short of the goals outlined by the steering committee in some areas, I, for one, was deeply impressed, even astonished, by what did come out of the planning.

At this point, I would like especially to commend the decision of the steering committee to request participants to submit study papers *before* the meeting began. Even though, in a few cases, circumstances prevented distribution of all of the papers before the opening of the Consultation, having most of them in hand for pre-meeting reading provided a common base for initial reaction and discussion, thereby cutting down on verbiage, pious or otherwise, and also supplied a common denominator of information which added greatly to the value of the discussions.

WHO CAME?

As indicated earlier, one of the goals of the steering committee was to bring together a group widely representative of the world mission thrust. In fact, the Chicago Cluster of Theological Schools had been asked to host the meeting for just that reason since it in itself provides a neutral meeting ground for ecumenical (conciliar) Protestants, conservative Evangelical Protestants and Roman Catholics, in addition to offering an excellent program of World Missions of its own.

In this regard, it was unquestionably gratifying to the steering committee that the list of registrants so nearly fulfilled their goals.

There were representatives from the auxiliary agencies such as the Wycliffe Bible Translators, the American Bible Society, the United Bible Societies, Final Advance of Scripture Translation, Mission Aviation Fellowship, the William Carey Library, etc., etc. Seminaries, universities and research groups were represented by delegates, both student and professors, from the Fuller School of World Mission, the Evangelical Theological Seminary, the Chicago Cluster (which includes Catholic Theological Union, Bellarmine School of Theology, Chicago Theological Seminary, De Andreis Seminary, Lutheran School of Theology, Meadville/Lombard Theological School and the Northern Baptist Seminary), the Center for Applied Research in the Apostolate, and Concordia Seminary.

Overseas universities or schools represented included Makerere University in Uganda, Scarritt College in the Philippines, Instituto Linguistico in Mexico and Nommensen and Simalungen universities in Indonesia.

Canadian Catholics came from the Scarboro order, the Holy Ghost Fathers, the Entraide Missionaire, the Canadian Catholic Conference, and Catholic Missions, Montreal. American Catholics were represented by missionaries from the Jesuit Missions, Divine Word Missionaries, the Province of St. Augustine of the Capuchin Order, Franciscan Province of the Sacred Heart, Redemptorist Missions and White Fathers of Africa, and by sisters from Maryknoll and Sisters of Mercy.

Mission board representatives came from COEMAR of the Presbyterian Church, USA, the Eastern Mennonite Board, United Methodist Board of Global Ministry, Lutheran Church in America Board of World Mission, Mennonite Board of Mission, Christian Church (Disciples of Christ) Division of Overseas Ministry, Conservative Baptist Foreign Mission Society, Anglican Consultative Council, General Program Council of the Reformed Church in America, Board of World Mission of the Evangelical Covenant Church of America, the Patna-Peru Jesuit Mission Office, Church of the Nazarene Department of World Missions, American Lutheran Church Division of World Mission, Baptist Board of International Ministries, World Mission Prayer League, Inc., US Catholic Mission Council, the Moravian Church, the MARC Division of World Vision, International, the Church of the Brethren's World Ministry Commission, the Oriental Missionary Society, and others.

Among the overseas contingent, which represented more than 20% of the Consultation, were graduate students from Kenya and Indonesia, plus representatives from the United Church of Christ in the Philippines, from the Methodist Church in Bolivia, the Federation of Churches in Colombia, the Christian and Missionary Alliance in Indonesia, the Protestant Christian Church of Indonesia, Mekane Yessus (Lutheran) Church of Ethiopia, Malagasy Lutheran Church, the Burma Baptist Convension, the United Church of North India, the Kenya Christian Council, and others.

While all the board representatives present were genuinely entitled by virtue of former service to be included in the term "missionaries in the field," the other delegates to the Consultation, currently involved in or on furlough from overseas work represented nine American Protestant denominations or mission organizations, including the Christian and Missionary Alliance, United Methodist Church, Church of the Brethren, Oriental Missionary Society, Reformed Church in America, Mennonite Church, United Presbyterian Church, USA, Presbyterian Church, US, and the Evangelical Covenant Church in America.

Taken all together, the Delegates represented Christianity and Christian service in 36 countries by 60 missionary agencies and 14 nationalities. They included professors, university administrators, linguists, students, researchers, theologians, pastors, missionaries and fraternal workers, church executives, editors, authors and more than a few anthropologists.

For some the Consultation meant a fresh opportunity to renew acquaintances with co-workers of former years; for others it would mean rubbing shoulders and sharing worship and ideas with persons formerly regarded with suspicion, even outright animosity. For

the representatives from the indigenous churches, the Consultation
would give them another chance to present their case for autonomy
and freedom under the Holy Spirit and for a lessening of friction
caused by continuing paternalistic attitudes of the founding denominations. For those who felt Christian mission to be inseparable
from the fight for human justice, the Consultation would enable
them to share their views and experiences with equally devoted and
consecrated Christians whose emphasis was directed to the personal
salvation of individuals -- and vice versa!

For many there would be opportunities of personal exchange
outside of the structured sessions where mutual problems could be
discussed on a one-to-one basis.

And then there were the graduate students, both from the
United States and overseas, to whom the Consultation would offer
a rare chance to talk first hand with mission workers in the far
corners of the world and to hear directly of the problems, challenges and aspirations of those with whom they someday would be
co-workers.

These then were the "reeds," the "blades of grass" that made
up the Consultation on Frontier Mission. These were those peculiar
social animals known as missionaries, that sub-culture of humanity
whom some overly glib and self-righteous anthropologists and sociologists deprecate on grounds that they "serve" only to dominate,
who destroy more values than they instill, who "come to do good and
do very well indeed!" These were the "culture-vultures" who col-
lect and value the cultural artifacts of a people but ignore the
value systems they represent. These were the spiritual band-aiders
who tape up the miseries of humanity but fail to act creatively
toward eliminating the causes, -- so we often hear.

Yes, these were the people frequently accused of "crying poor"
in order to maintain their own livelihood, those who might very
well indeed be concerned with promoting the "unwanted and unneeded"
intrusion of Christianity around the world in order to protect
their own vested interests as well as the economic interests of
their home countries.

And yet, what did I hear from these people during the course
of the Consultation? Over and over there was expressed an awakened
realization of how religious and cultural values of any people
could and should be used constructively in presenting the Christian
message; that the good news of Christ is beyond and above any culture; that Christ himself is not the captive of any race or culture;
that the Christian message was to fulfill, not to destroy; that it
is the Holy Spirit, not the alien missionary, who sits in judgment

on all cultures, even our own. There was constant emphasis on the power of the Holy Spirit to move through committed Christians in forms of effective witness against human sins of greed, power and oppression, injustice and violation of human integrity. There was frank admission of "wrong roads taken" or "roads not taken" in the past, but there also was a seemingly genuine and growing willingness to explore new avenues of action based realistically on the actualities to today's world in *cooperation* with the indigenous churches.

Admittedly, the spirtual decibel level was not quite so loud when it came to expressing full readiness to let the indigenous churches work out their own salvation as they try to make the Christian message more relevant to their own cultures. In fact, there still remained more than a few echoes of the old admonition "Papa knows best!" But, there were significant -- and encouraging -- numbers who heard with conviction and understanding the message on the matter as expressed by John Mbiti of Uganda and Nirmal Minz from India.

Most of all, however, I was constantly reminded that these people were human beings, sub-culture or not, who in response to the call of God (define that how you may!) had chosen a vocation and a way of life that placed on them almost impossible burdens of frustration and loneliness -- Who was it who said a missionary's life was a series of one parting after another? They may have been reeds shaken by the peculiar winds of the 20th century; by the standards of the people they try to serve, they may even qualify as "rich men dressed in silk and satin." But, from where I sat, this particular group of latter-day prophets were well aware of the need for change to meet the needs of today and tomorrow. More importantly, moreover, there seemed to be among them a general, if not total, willingness to adapt accordingly, even though such change meant the acceptance of the prophetic imperative of working themselves out of a job!

WHAT THEY DID NOT SAY

In one of the Consultation study papers, the author, A. R. Tippett, organized his material around a series of "givens." Somewhat reversing his approach, I would like to conclude my reactions to the Consultation in terms of what was *not* given, what was omitted or physically absent, or what was unanswered or unspoken. I fully realize that some of these "unspokens" are justifiably beyond the possible range of this particular Consultation given the limitations of time, etc. In fact, some of them might well become the basis for later consultations of a similar nature. As a lay person,

however, in spite of my over-all favorable reactions to the planning, process and results of the Consultation, I left the meeting
feeling that several important -- at least to me -- issues had
never quite broken into the clear.

Let me begin with the "unspoken" which I as a woman might be
most likely to mention, namely, the role and responsibility of
women in Mission. Pierce Beaver, in earlier correspondence, had
mentioned that the Consultation hopefully would include a sizeable
proportion of women on the grounds that "we need their knowledge,
experience, understanding and insight, often so different from
that of men. Women can think with mind and heart in unison as men
seldom do. They have courage to come to a decision and to act in
faith while men temporize and try to find theological foundations
to disguise their timidity. Above all, in the Christian world
mission, women have been far more able and ready to identify with
people of other races and nations then have men." (I trust that
the above quotation will not embroil Dr. Beaver too seriously
with those Consultation delegates who are of a strong Pauline
bias!)

Unfortunately, outside of a handful of Catholic women religious, there turned out to be an almost complete absence of women
at the Consultation -- even including wives. True, there were two
eminently qualified women on the steering committee who contributed
significantly to the planning and implementation of the Consultation. One, Betsey Muldrow, missionary in Ethiopia, through her
personal gifts and experience in the field has also been making
effective contributions in missionary education within her own
denomination (Presbyterian, USA) while she and her husband are on
furlough; just as Louise Paw has been doing through her work with
the Baptist Board of International Ministries while she is on
leave from Burma.

With the above two exceptions gratefully noted, let's recall
what happened at the plenary dinner which opened the Consultation.
It was a truly impressive occasion as, one by one, the delegates
stood to introduce themselves and to identify their denomination
and the area of the world in which they served. And yes, there
were several wives present but they were introduced *by their hus-
bands* (underscoring mine!) with one sole exception, and later, if
I am not mistaken, she also was the only wife to make independent
contributions to the work of the Consultation.

Granted that this foregoing action may on the surface seem of
neglible importance, but since it in itself is highly representative of the dead weight of tradition which acts to limit the

recognition of women as human beings, persons in their own right, the criticism implied still stands.

However, of considerably greater importance was the fact that absolutely nothing was discussed during the Consultation as to women's role, responsibility or positive contribution in all areas of Christian service and witness whether at home or abroad, and that in spite of the fact that women are in the majority as workers in mission and certainly the most dedicated among lay members in the study and support of the global outreach of all churches. I recognize that this particular "unspoken" is deeply involved with a whole host of other "unspokens" such as ordination, denomination- al tradition and other restrictive vises of culture. But even Paul had his Lydia, his Priscilla and his Thecla. At the Consul- tation on Frontier Mission, their contemporary counterparts were noticeably absent. As a result, the Consultation was the poorer for lack of a greater degree of testimony, advice and inspiration from those other human beings who also were created in God's image (Gen. 1:7).

Why?

Before I leave the subject of the "not presents," there was one other inexplicable gap in the registration. With the excep- tions of some American Black graduate students who helped present one of the morning devotional services, there was a complete absence of representation from American Black Christians. It may be that some were invited to attend but declined for various rea- sons, but again one is forced to note the regrettable fact, and to wonder "why?".

My next "unspoken" comes from a deceptively simple question posed very early in the Consultation but which remained both un- answered and not discussed. The question, which was raised by Father Joseph Connors, executive secretary, US Catholic Mission Council, was basically "Why Mission at all?" Perhaps the dele- gates considered the answer to be so obvious that it needed no discussion, or possibly there were those not taken in by its sur- face simplicity who felt, to deal with the "unspokens" behind the question was a task too complicated to be considered by this par- ticular group. For behind that question lay implications related strongly to the career and life purpose of every individual repre- sented at the Consultation. The question also is one that is raised with increasing frequency by every Christian who either supports or withdraws support from mission. And it is never raised more loudly than at budget time or when some area of the world where we are involved with mission has a palace coup or seem- ingly favors whoever is our "enemy-of-the-week."

Those present at the Consultation, including myself, may be convinced of the continuing validity of the mission imperative, but surely no one present could be unaware of the growing number of Christians who increasingly doubt both the present and future relevance of that imperative, especially as it relates to needs beyond the home horizon. Serious doubts as to method as well as need, over-concern or cynicism about past mistakes, frustrations felt by Christians at home over seeming rebuffs from the national churches in terms of help needed or wanted, dissatisfactions, myopic or otherwise, with "results" from the mission dollar -- these are only some of the "unspokens" underlying that base question. As a lay reactor, I was both concerned and disappointed that no attempt was made to answer the question even if only in terms of suggestions which might be helpful in missionary education in the local church.

One other rather curious "unspoken" of the Consultation involved the attitude which should be taken by "career" missionaries, their sponsoring boards, and the leaders and membership of the national churches toward the amateur gospeller, the zealous evangelist who, without knowledge of language, customs, local religion or government, enters a country in an *ad hoc* fashion to "preach the Gospel" and who, through his unguided, untutored zeal unwittingly breaks down lines of communication painstakingly established through years of careful preparation.

The question of what to do with groups or individuals dedicated to the concept of "instant evangelization of the world" certainly is not new as of Explo '72, but during the Consultation it continued to be both unasked and unvoiced. However, even though the question may not have been raised in an explicit fashion much of the Consultation discussion and even some of the Finding Committee's recommendations were addressed, in a peculiarly oblique manner, to the problem.

For example, instead of encouraging the "instant" approach, time and again there were cautions expressed against too hasty initial contact. The value of simple, personal conviction as an adequate base for witnessing for Christ anywhere or to any people was balanced by statements such as "No one attempting to teach the Gospel to people of another culture should begin his work without a working knowledge of anthropology and sociology." Or, "Language training is a 'must' for the effective communication of the Gospel. Or, "We must study the religion, the value systems and the cultural background of peoples so as to insure greater effectiveness and understanding for the message of Christ." "Indigenous cultures and value systems must be treated with respect."

Nor is there any short cut to salvation time-wise in the statement "Painstaking translation of the Bible into the spoken language of a people is necessary to provide a continuing witness that outlasts any other kind of initial contact." (It will be noted that there is another time-consuming element included here, namely the presupposition that the hearer should become a reader.)

It is true, of course, that the above statements or conclusions were really a part of the thinking which the Consultation was formulating in the way of guide-lines to be followed by all mission workers, indigenous or otherwise, in accomplishing the particular root task that was the focus of the Consultation, i.e., how best to reach the unreached, essentially primitive peoples of the world. And yet, as I listened and waited for some open expression of that unspoken question which never quite surfaced, I was also aware of another curious factor. The people or groups for whom the message was intended simply were not there to hear!

The foregoing "unspokens" may vary considerably in importance, and certainly are far from a complete list, but there remains one more, quite possibly the most important "unspoken" of the whole meeting. I will admit that perhaps it was just as well that it remained unvoiced by this particular group at this particular time since it has been the basis of unresolved concern of Christian thinking since the very beginnings of church history. I refer to that base question "What is the essential Gospel?" -- the irreducible "true" Gospel, stripped so far as it is humanly possible of layers of secular or temporal cultural incrustations. Can we really "export" the Gospel, "pure and undefiled", free from contamination of our own culture? If so, then just what is that basic good news and how do we make it real and important to those we try to reach in terms of their needs, not ours? It is all very well to quote, even with honest fervor and belief, "Believe on the Lord Jesus Christ and you shall be saved." (Even Islam has a similarily super-simplified "formula for belief"). But, how do we make our faith meaningful to a pygmy in Africa, or to a highly educated Buddhist priest, or to Stone Age peoples on a Pacific island?

And, if by some miracle of communication, we feel we have gotten some part of our message across, what difference do we feel compelled to expect this to make in their everyday lives? Is it a *sine qua non* of the Christian message to impose on our hearers an essentially foreign and alien set of moral patterns? If so, out of which national culture or out of which period in history? Or, if we expect them in their turn to become evangelists of that basic good news, are we willing to admit that their understandings of "our" Gospel is as valid as our own understanding of it? If so,

would we be willing in our turn to hear out their Gospel preached
to us in *their* terms?

True, the great mystery of the ages of how God through Christ
and the Holy Spirit can and does speak to man in every age and in
every condition may never be solved, but does that excuse us in
this time from a continuing reexamination of the bases of our faith
so as to avoid filtering our good news through our own cultural
biases and pre-judgments?

WHAT WAS ACCOMPLISHED?

Since this report is included as a part of the larger over-all
Consultation report which also includes that of the Findings
Committee, I shall only comment briefly here on my own reactions,
as well as those of others, to a few of the contributions and/or
accomplishments of the Consultation as a whole.

I have mentioned earlier the position and background papers
that contributed so greatly to the preparation for the Consultation
Since they also are included in the over-all Consultation report,
I can only hope that those who receive copies can find time to give
them the study they deserve. As for me, one of my most fervent
wishes as I read through them was for a photographic memory or some
kind of instant reading technique. Only occasionally did I feel I
was being compelled to learn more about Mission than I really cared
to know! And I should say, with due gratitude to the authors, that
most of the papers were admirably free of abstruse theological
jargon which can be in its own way as great a barrier to communication as any other discipline's peculiar argot.

In addition to the study papers, delegates were furnished with
a highly interesting statistical *tour de force* in the form of the
survey on the state of Christianity on the continent of Africa
compiled under the direction of David Barrett, research officer
for the Anglican Consultative Council. Even though some statisti-
cians may take issue with certain technical points relating to
statistical methodology, and even though there are some inaccur-
acies of reportage (which could only be expected in such a continental size task) the work done by Barrett and his associates is a
definite first, and it is no wonder the Consultation urged churches
in other areas of the world to compile similar reports as soon as
possible. Of course, there are probably some of a hyper-critical
or cynical nature who may feel such a study is just another example
of a Western urge for soul-counting. There are others who may
quarrel with definitions set by the report. But as a basis for
mission strategy and planning, whether by mission boards or local

churches, the Barrett report must stand both as a landmark accomplishment, a useful, much needed tool, and a prototype for other similar studies to come.

I also must mention the work-in-progress report, *Scripture Translation Information Bank: Status of Bible Translation -- Western Hemisphere*, prepared and furnished to the Consultation by the Final Advance on Scripture Translation. As the agency itself would be the first to admit, the total work to which it is dedicated is far from complete, but the record of what has been accomplished, even in only one section of the world, is no less impressive because the task is not yet finished. It is not my intention to take sides with or against the policy of certain governments who would limit Bible translation to a "national" language in the interest of reinforcing the spread of that particular language or languages. Actually in some countries with four or more "national languages" one could well argue that there still remains plenty of work for the linguists and translators even with a limited area as permitted. But, certainly as long as we consider the Bible as central to our faith, its translation is indispensable to the spread and continuing support of that faith.

As to the Finding Committee's report, I personally found this both amazing and challenging. Considering the diversity of background and denominational conditioning I had rather doubted that the Consultation could come together in consensus on anything but the time of day, and even that would have been subject to qualifications of time zones or the International Date Line! That such consensus did result I feel was due largely to three factors: 1) the opportunity to read the major study papers beforehand; 2) the openness of the small group discussion sessions where the delegates could express their reactions to the major themes and to the six selected sub-topics freely and informally; and 3) the direction and guidance of the Holy Spirit.

One of the most important contributions to the success of the small group meetings was the presence in each of two or more of the overseas Christians which unquestionably added an extra dimension of interest and vitality to the discussions. Personally, I could only regret not having a six-way personality split so that I could have taken part in all of the discussions! For that reason I was particularly glad to be able to work with the Findings Committee and thereby learn, even at second-hand, of some of the "multi-logues" that took place in each group.

Lack of time precluded the possibility of small group reaction or discussion of the final paper submitted by Charles Taber, editor of *Practical Anthropology*, on the topic "Evangelizing the Unreached

Peoples: What to do and How to do it." Instead, the Consultation
as a whole formed the discussion group and once again, perhaps
even more remarkably so because of the greater number involved,
there was this surprising phenomenon of agreement as the plenary
body unanimously recommended adoption of the major part of his
suggestions.

To be sure, there were individual reservations regarding some
of the points of agreement in any of the consensus areas. Some of
the more socially concerned delegates felt the positions agreed on
did not go far enough. Others felt they went too far. Kinds of
witness, problems related to the imposition of Western moral values
or church organization also provoked varying reactions. Not everyone was fully agreed on the "rights" or even the "responsibility"
of the outsider, *sic*, missionary, to speak to national problems or
to instigate new mission except through the local church, and not
everyone was unanimous in what were the basics needed for the
training of church leadership or even as to requirements for church
membership, etc., etc., etc. But more significant than these var-
iations of opinion, to me at least, was the number of important
areas of agreement that were reached. Surely the Consultation had
good reason to be aware of and thankful for the activating presence
of the Holy Spirit.

While the foregoing has related primarily to reactions expressed directly related to ideas presented formally during the
Consultation, I suspect that many of the delegates found their
deepest satisfaction in face-to-face encounters experienced outside the formal meetings. For my part, my particular extra bonus
came from meal-time or after-meeting personal contacts with missionaries from other denominations and with the overseas Christians

As I talked with Jaime Bravo, the Bolivian Methodist pastor,
who was exiled from his country and twice "psychologically killed"
by firing squads that did everything except pull the trigger, as
a result of his determination to apply his Christian convictions
to the practical needs of his people, I recognized how small had
been the demands on my own witness and how inadequate my own response.

It was exciting to hear Samuel Kim, Korean missionary to
Thailand, tell of the growing momentum of evangelism within the
Korean church, just as it was somewhat discouraging to hear from
Nirmal Minz of the lack of that same missionary impulse among some
of the churches of India. The report from Mrs. Louise Paw from
Burma about how the Burmese church has continued to grow even
though cut off from outside help and/or guidance was perhaps the
most welcome news I heard during the Consultation, matched only

by a similar report from the Indonesian contingent about the regeneration taking place in the nationalized Batak church.

Also, the opportunity I had to become acquainted with some of the Canadian Catholics provided me with a most enlightening and enjoyable experience. Even at the risk of untoward reaction, I can not but express the hope that their bishops enjoy long service and continued grace. Likewise my contacts with their American counterparts reinforced my optimism relative to the continuing yeasty work and power of the Spirit of Vatican II.

And then there was Paul Long from the southern Presbyterian Church, now serving in Brazil, whose accent and theology brought a sudden nostalgia for the church of my childhood, and also perceptibly deepened my own now somewhat vertigial southern accent!

Another high point, among all the other memorable experiences, had to be the occasion when one of the Philippine delegates, himself a fluent speaker of English, complained in effect: "If you people who speak English natively can't understand each other, how do you expect us to understand what you are trying to tell us?"

In a more sober vein, the above complaint was related importantly to Charles Taber's discussion of communication problems as connected with mission work, an area of concern which merited much fuller discussion than its place on the agenda permitted. Certainly, careful research into the question of what happens to the Christian message as it passes from communicator to hearer might shed valuable light which could help explain and eliminate past mistakes, thereby not only helping to avoid repetition, but even more usefully, facilitating future communication.

I believe it is a fair observation that some of the delegates still seemed to cling to a conviction that the power of the Holy Spirit must be arbitrarily confined to an "either/or" choice between soteriology or syncretism. In other instances, there was disagreement in emphasis as to whether people are "saved from sin" or "saved to life." And, there were still times when I detected traces of the attitude, "You do God's work in your way, and I in His." But, on balance, I cannot help but feel that significant beginnings were made through the Consultation toward establishing mutual trust and cooperation among God's committed people which, hopefully, will continue to grow in vitality and power. As the Chinese birthday wish might express it: "May the shadow of the Consultation never grow shorter."

A MILESTONE IN MISSION ADVANCE
C. Peter Wagner

The Consultation on Frontier Missions, I have high hopes, will prove to have been a milestone in the modern missionary movement as far as United States mainline denominations are concerned. As one of my friends aptly commented afterward on the way to O'Hare Airport, "We have just turned a page of church history." In order to be faithful to the Great Commission of our Lord to "make disciples of all nations," the entire force of the Christian church on all continents needs to be mobilized for cross-cultural missions. In a day which is seeing fresh breezes of spiritual awakening sweep not only America but many other parts of the world as well, the recent retreat of many American mainline denominations from classical evangelistic and church planting missions worldwide is anachronous. It desperately needs to be reversed, and quickly. My dream is that the vision projected by the Consultation to move out again to the unreached peoples of the world will so permeate American churches that the next decade will see a full and enthusiastic return to biblical priorities in mission. If it does, we truly will have entered a new chapter of church history.

A NEW CONFRONTATION WITH FRONTIER MISSIONS
John E. Buteyn

A unique feature of this Consultation was the wide range of church and missionary agencies represented. There were numerous Roman Catholic agencies, representatives from such groups as the Christian Missionary Alliance, Fuller School of Missions, Conservative Baptist, Missionary Aviation Fellowship, Wycliffe Bible Translators, the Oriental Missionary Society, as well as from the Conciliar churches, such as United Methodist, United Presbyterian and Presbyterian Church in the U. S., United Church of Christ and the Reformed Church in America, to name a few.

The delegates were almost equally divided into four groups: from Roman Catholic missionary agencies, from overseas churches and mission agencies, from the conciliar churches, and from churches and agencies who identify themselves as non-conciliar conservative evangelicals.

A feeling of close fellowship, rare in the face of such diversity, seemed to pervade the entire consultation.

A strong emphasis was placed on the importance of being sensitive to differing cultures in all phases of mission. At times, it seemed as if all the participants were anthropologists.

The plan for the meeting, which had been under development for more than a year, called for non-USA churches - those in Latin America, Africa and Asia - to be well represented in order to highlight the importance of the indigenous church. Before its conclusion, however, the Consultation was led to see the indigenous church in a new dimension, e.g. not as limited to the churches of the Third World, but existing in all six continents.

An exciting dimension of the consultation was the provision of data about Africa and the many unreached areas. This was the result of a carefully documented study by the Rev. David Barrett and his research team.

The survey indicates that Christianity is spreading in Africa at the rate of over seven million a year. But it also shows that there are some 30 million unevangelized Africans in frontier situations. Of the remaining 100 million unevangelized, about 83 million belong to Muslim and Islamized tribes, among whom there is only limited opportunity for evangelism, such as via radio and literature.

There are many opportunities. In some cases, the most effective way of witness would be for the western churches to assist churches and Christians within a country. In other cases, there will no doubt be opportunities for western churches to join in ventures of partnership with non-western churches. Such efforts will *not* be carried out as western implants which disregard culture and local customs.

In the light of this significant data about Africa, the Consultation underscored the importance of having similar information about Latin America and Asia. This was left as a challenge for overseas churches and western churches to try to gather such information. Also, it was stressed that more opportunities for frontier evangelism exist in North America, including the United States, than we generally acknowledge.

My personal reaction to this consultation was a very positive one. Obviously, many questions remain...how can the strong motivation for mission of certain western churches be channeled, when many Third World churches want little or limited help in evangelism - even though the need may be great? What does it mean that the whole church has the responsibility for bringing the whole Gospel to the ends of the earth to the end of time? How can this be done effectively when so many cultural, language and theological barriers still separate the Christian Church?

These are questions that challenge us all as we look anew at the unmet opporutnities for evangelism and search our fresh ways of confronting them in the light of our Biblical mandate.

REGISTRANTS IN THE CONSULTATION

ANDERSON, Gerald H. United Methodist Church. President of Scarritt College for Christian Workers. Missionary in the Philippines 1960-1970. ADDRESS: Scarritt College, Nashville, Tennessee 37203.

ARPAN, Holly (Mrs. Floyd). United Presbyterian Church in U.S.A. Clerk of Session, First United Presbyterian Church, Bloomington. Department of Journalism, University of Indiana. ADDRESS: 1340 Sheridan, Bloomington, Indiana 47401.

BARNEY, G. Linwood. Christian and Missionary Alliance. Director of Studies and Professor of Anthropology at Jaffray School of Missions. 4-1/2 years in Laos as Missionary Linguist. ADDRESS: Jaffray School of Missions, Nyack, New York 10960.

BARRETT, David B. Church of England. Church Missionary Society. Research Consultant, Church of the Province of Kenya. 16 years Kenya, other parts of Africa, Central America. ADDRESS: P. O. Box 40230, Nairobi, Kenya, Africa. United Kingdom.

BATO, Lamesa. Evangelical Church Mekane Yesus Lutherano (Swedish, German-Hermansburg, American, Norwegian, and Finland Lutheran Missions). Student in School of World Mission, Pasadena. Pastorate, 18 years. ADDRESS: Enttoto Evangelical Church Mekane Yesus, P. O. Box 30438, Tel. 18178 Addis Ababa, Ethiopia. Ethiopia, Addis Ababa.

BEAVER, R. Pierce. United Church of Christ. Consultant to Division of Overseas Ministries, National Council of Churches of Christ. Professor Emeritus of Missions, The Divinity School of The University of Chicago. Missionary to China; Director of Missionary Research Library, 1948-55; Professor of Missions, University of Chicago, 1955-71. ADDRESS: P. O. Box 59, Sherman, Connecticut 06784.

BENNETT, Charles T. Baptist. Mission Aviation Fellowship (also United Presbyterian Center for Mission Studies). Director of Research (for both organizations). Southeast Mexico, 13 years. ADDRESS: Box 2828, Fullerton, California 92633.

BERGSTEDT, Alan. Final Advance of Scripture Translation. Director,
Administration and Research, 6 years. ADDRESS: 1740 Westminster
Drive, Denton, Texas 76201.

BOBERG, John T.   Roman Catholic. Divine Word Missionaries.
Professor of Missions, Catholic Theological Union. ADDRESS: 5401
South Cornell, Chicago, Illinois 60615.

BOLIN, William Gerald. Roman Catholic. Redemptorist Fathers.
Director, Mission Office. 13 years in Thailand, 9 years along
Mekong River in N.E. Thailand, 3 years in Bangkok as Program
Director of Catholic Relief services. ADDRESS: P. O. Box 6,
Glenview, Illinois 60025. TELEPHONE: 312/724-0425.

BRAVO, Jaime. Evangelical Methodist Church in Bolivia. United
Methodist Board of Global Ministries. Student in Southern
Methodist University. 6 years as Pastor and District Superinten-
dent. ADDRESS: 105 Hawk Hall, S.M.U., Dallas, Texas 75222.
Casilla 356, La Paz, Bolivia. Bolivia, South America.

BRIDGES, Alvin. United Presbyterian Church. Mission Program
Agency UPC. Board Member. ADDRESS: 2950 Warren Boulevard,
Chicago, Illinois 60612.

BUTEYN, John E. Reformed Church in America. General Program
Council/World Ministries. Secretary for World Ministries. 15
years experience as staff member. ADDRESS: 475 Riverside Drive,
Room 1818, New York, New York 10027.

CASON, J. Walter. United Methodist. Board of Global Ministries,
United Methodist. Assoc. Prof. of Mission, Evangelical Theolog-
ical Seminary, Naperville, Illinois. 12 years Liberia, 8 years
Theological Education Fund (Africa). ADDRESS: 329 East School
Avenue, Naperville, Illinois 60540.

CERVIN, Russell A. Evangelical Covenant Church of America.
Evangelical Covenant Board of World Mission. Executive Secretary.
ADDRESS: 5101 North Francisco Avenue, Chicago, Illinois 60625.

CONNORS, Joseph M., S.V.D.   Roman Catholic. United States
Catholic Mission Council. Executive Secretary. Homeland Mission
Administration. ADDRESS: 1325 Massachusetts Avenue, N.W.,
Room 500, Washington, D.C. 20005.

COOK, Franklin. Church of the Nazarene. Department of World
Missions. 11 years administrative experience. ADDRESS: 6401
The Paseo, Kansas City, Missouri 64131.

CROUSE, Merle. Church of the Brethren. World Ministries Commission. 2 years in Turkey, 10 years in Ecuador. ADDRESS: 1451 Dundee Avenue, Elgin, Illinois 60120.

DENIS, Sr. Margaret. Roman Catholic. Canadian Catholic Conference. Consultant to the Canadian Bishops on the Religious Education of Indian and Metis People. 7 years teacher in Northern Canada. 6 years as religious education consultant. ADDRESS: 10 Montcrest Boulevard, Toronto 270, Ontario, Canada. Canadian.

DONOVAN, Sr. Nancy. Roman Catholic. Maryknoll Sisters. Mission education and promotion in the mid-west. 15 years in Guatemala and Mexico in pastoral work, teaching and cooperatives. ADDRESS: 1447 West Thome Avenue, Chicago, Illinois 60660. Mission Bachujon, Chilon, Chiapas, Mexico.

DOWEY, Alexander, O.F.M. Roman Catholic. Franciscan Province of the Sacred Heart (Chicago, St. Louis). Associate Pastor in the parish of Monte Alegre, Para, Brazil (Amazon Region) with involvement in Basic Education Movement (Radio School Movement). Theology student, 3 years. Rector of Minor Seminary, 5 years. Hinterland pastor, 5 years. Regional Coordinator of Movimento de Educacao de Base. ADDRESS: 5654 North Rogers Avenue, Chicago, Illinois 60646, (Until 1/10/73). Padres Francisianos, 68.220 - Monte Alegre, Para, Brazil.

DUEWEL, Wesley L. Member of non-denominational Oriental Missionary Society. Personal denominational membership is in Free Methodist Church. President of The Oriental Missionary Society. 25 years service in India, Principal of Allikobed Bible Seminary. 6 years as Vice President at Central office. 2 years as President of Society. ADDRESS: Box A, Greenwood, Indiana 46142.

ELSON, Benjamin F. Wycliffe Bible Translators. Executive Vice President. 30 years with WBT. 20 years in Mexico. ADDRESS: Box 1960, Santa Ana, California.

FAJARDO, Jose D. Cumberland Presbyterian. Missionary in Colombia. Missions in Education and Evangelistic work and in inter-denominational work. ADDRESS: Apt. Aereo 6215, Cali, Colombia. Colombia.

FLATT, Donald C. Lutheran Church in America. Pastor of Austin Messiah Church, Consultant to LSTC and CCTS. 11 years in Tanzania as British Colonial Officer and as missionary of the Augustana Lutheran Church. ADDRESS: 825 North Waller Avenue, Chicago, Illinois 60615.

FLINN, Robert J., SVD. Roman Catholic. Divine Word Missionaries. Coordinator, Chicago Cluster of Theological Schools. 1 year in the Philippines. 3 years working for the Congregation for the Evangelization of Nations, Rome. ADDRESS: 1100 East 55th Street, Chicago, Illinois 60615.

FRIESEN, Delores (Mrs.). Mennonite. Mennonite Board of Missions. Missionary in Accra, Ghana. 1965-67 Nigeria, Theological Education. 1967-68 Ghana, Theological Education and Literature. 1969-71 Nigeria, Islam in Africa Project (Lit. Development). 1971-72 Ghana, Theological Education and Literature Development. ADDRESS: P. O. Box 6484, Accra, Ghana (after Jan. 21). Box 370, Mennonite Board of Missions, Elkhart, Indiana 46514.

FRIESEN, Stanley. Mennonite. Mennonite Board of Missions. Missionary, Accra, Ghana. 3 years in Theological Education, 2 of which were with African Independent Churches in S.E. Nigeria. 2 years with the Islam in Africa project. 1 year in Ghana in literature development. ADDRESS: P. O. Box 6484, Accra (north), Ghana. Mennonite Board of Missions, Box 370, Elkhart, Indiana 46514.

GINTING-SUKA, A. Gereja Batak Karo Protestant, former President of the Church. Short Term Missionary in U.S.A. ADDRESS: 6313 A Ocean Avenue, Ventnor, New Jersey 08406. 16 Samanhudi Medan, Indonesia. Indonesian.

GROSS, Matthew, O.F.M. Roman Catholic. Capuchin Order. Missionary in Papua, New Guinea, 10 years service. ADDRESS: 106 East 23rd Street, Hays, Kansas. Catholic Mission, Pureni via Tari, S.H.D., Papua, New Guinea.

HAGGERTY, Philip J. Roman Catholic. Holy Ghost Fathers. Director of Theology Students, 30 years. ADDRESS: 5401 S. Cornell Avenue, Chicago, Illinois 60615.

HARDON, John, S.J. Roman Catholic. Jesuit Fathers. Professor, Bellarmine School of Theology. ADDRESS: 5430 S. University Ave., Chicago, Illinois 60615.

HESTERMAN, Lowell. American Lutheran Church. Division of World Missions - ALC. Africa Secretary. 2-1/2 years Ethiopia. 9 years ALC/DWM. ADDRESS: 422 South 5th Street, Minneapolis, Minnesota 55415.

HILLMAN, Eugene. Roman Catholic. Holy Ghost Fathers. CARA Overseas Research Director. 18 years in Tanzania, Masai District. ADDRESS: 1615 Manchester Lane, N.W., Washington, D.C.

HINTZE, Otto. Lutheran Church, Missouri Synod. A founder of the LC-MS Mission in Papua/New Guinea. Professor of Missions, Concordia Seminary, Springfield, Illinois. ADDRESS: Concordia Seminary, Concordia Court, Springfield, Illinois 62702.

HOEKSTRA, Harvey T. Reformed Church in America. World Ministries, RCA. Missionary, S.W. Ethiopia. 14-1/2 years the south Sudan, translator, Ahudk, N.T. ADDRESS: Box 301, Jimma, Ethiopia.

HOPKINS, Paul A. United Presbyterian Church. COEMAR. Regional Secretary for Africa, 20 years related to work in Africa. ADDRESS: 475 Riverside Drive, New York, New York 10027. 134 Biddulph Road, Radnor, Pennsylvania 19087.

HUTCHINSON, Warner A. United Bible Societies. Administration, Asia and Latin America. ADDRESS: 1865 Broadway, New York, New York 10023.

JESCHKE, Richard A., S.V.D. Roman Catholic. Divine Word Mission-aries. Student at Catholic Theological Union, Chicago, Illinois. 2 summers of Parish work in Mississippi, U.S.A. ADDRESS: 5404 S. Woodlawn Avenue, Chicago, Illinois 60615. 174 Lawndale, Elmhurst, Illinois 60126.

JONES, Dunstan, O.F.M. Roman Catholic. Capuchin Province of St. Augustine. Director of Cathechist Training Centre Erave, S.H.D., Papua, New Guinea. 10 years in New Guinea. ADDRESS: St. Augustine Monastery, 220-37th Street, Pittsburgh, Pennsylvania 15201. Capuchin Mission, Erave, S.H.D., Papua, New Guinea.

KAMASI, F. Lawrence. Christian and Missionary Alliance, Indonesia. Administrative responsibility. 16 years as professor, president of National Church, Editor, Extension Theological Education. ADDRESS: 135 N. Oakland Avenue, Pasadena, California 91101, (until June, 1973). Jalan Fachruddin No. 9, Jakarta, Indonesia. Indonesia.

KANE, J. Herbert. Professor of Missions, Trinity Evangelical Divinity School. ADDRESS: Trinity Evangelical Divinity School, 2045 Half Day Road, Bannockburn, Deerfield, Illinois 60015.

KASIERA, Musembe E. Pentecostal Assemblies of God (Kenya). Graduate Student at Concordia Seminary, St. Louis, Missouri. Lay minister in Mombasa, Kenya for 8 years. ADDRESS: 6519 San Bonita, 1-W, St. Louis, Missouri 63105. P. O. Box 98653, Mombasa, Kenya. Kenya.

KIM, Samuel I.   Presbyterian Church of Korea.   Field Director of
South East Asia.   17 years missionary in Thailand, teaching in
theological schools for 7 years, student work for 5 years, evan-
gelistic work for 5 years.   ADDRESS: 425 N. El Molino Avenue,
Pasadena, California 91101.   14 Pramuan Road, Bangkok, Thailand.
Korean.

KNITTER, Paul, S.V.D.   Roman Catholic.   Divine Word Missionaries.
Professor, Catholic Theological Union.   ADDRESS: 5401 S. Cornell
Avenue, Chicago, Illinois 60615.

KOPPELMANN, Herman H.   Lutheran Church, Missouri Synod.   Board of
Missions.   Associate Executive Secretary for World Areas. 24 years
with the office.   ADDRESS: 210 North Broadway, St. Louis,
Missouri 63102.

KORTZ, Rt. Rev. Edwin W.   Moravian Church.   Board of Foreign
Missions of the Moravian Church.   Executive Director.   ADDRESS:
69 West Church Street,   Bethlehem, Pennsylvania 18018.

KRASS, Alfred C.   United Church of Christ.   United Church Board
for World Ministry.   Consultant on Evangelism.   6-1/2 years
Frontier Evangelism in Ghana.   ADDRESS: UCBWM, 475 Riverside
Drive, New York, New York 10027.

KRATZ, James D.   Mennonite.   Board of Mennonite Missions. 6 years
Toba Indian Work, Argentina; 5 years Administration.   ADDRESS:
1628 Morton Avenue, Elkhart, Indiana.

LAVALLE, Guy A., O.M.I.   Roman Catholic.   Entr'aide Missionnaire,
Montreal.   Executive Director of main office in Montreal.   4 years
with Canadian Indians in Inner-City Project.   ADDRESS: 1216 Rue
Panet, Montreal, Canada.   Canada.

LEHNHART, Robert E.   United Presbyterian.   Mission Aviation Fellowship.   Director of Operation.   1959-62 Pilot-mechanic, Mato Grosso,
Brazil.   1966-67 Pilot-mechanic, Oriente, Ecuador.   1962-66, 1967-
72, Administration Headquarters, California.   ADDRESS: Box 2828,
Fullerton, California 92633.

LINDBERG, David.   Lutheran Church in America.   Professor, Lutheran
School of Theology at Chicago.   6 years in Japan.   ADDRESS: 1100
East 55th Street, Chicago, Illinois 60615.

LINDELL, Paul J.   Lutheran.   World Mission Prayer League, Inc.
General Director.   Home Staff, with frequent visits to fields
overseas for past 32 years.   ADDRESS: 232 Clifton Avenue, Minneapolis, Minnesota 55403.

LITTLE, Paul E.   Plymouth Brethren.   Associate Professor, School of World Mission, Trinity Evangelical Divinity School; Assistant to the President, Inter-Varsity Christian Fellowship; Associate Director for Program, International Congress on World Evangelization, Switzerland, 1974.   Several short terms in Africa and Latin America. ADDRESS: P. O. Box 130, Prospect Heights, Illinois 60070.   12 No. Parkway Drive, Prospect Heights, Illinois 60070.

LONG, Paul B.   Presbyterian Church in the U.S.   Board of World Missions.   Field Pastor, Evangelist.   19 years, 9 Congo; 10 Brazil. ADDRESS: 110 Kellogg Place, Wheaton, Illinois 60187.

LYNCH, Jack.   Roman Catholic.   Scarboro Missions.   Mission Education Department.   Guyana, less than 1 year.   3 years in Canada. ADDRESS: 2685 Kingston Road, Scarboro, Ontario, Canada   MIM IM4. Canada.

MAC INNIS, Donald.   East Asia Department, National Council of Churches.   15 years in China and Taiwan.   ADDRESS: 475 Riverside Drive, New York, New York 10027.

MALAYANG, Jose A.   United Church of Christ in the Philippines. Invited by Commission on Ecumenical Mission & Relations, United Presbyterian Church-USA, Doctorial Student, Wayne State University, Detroit, Michigan.   Assistant Minister, University United Presbyterian Church, Rochester, Michigan.   ADDRESS: University Presbyterian Church, 1385 South Adams Road, Rochester, Michigan 48063. c/o United Church of Christ, Cagayan De Oro City L-305, Philippines. Philippines.

MANAEN, Theodore.   Church of North India.   World Mission Prayer League-USA.   On home staff of World Mission Prayer League. 2 years working with the church in India.   Formerly Secretary-general of the Congress Party in India.   ADDRESS: 228 Clifton Avenue, Minneapolis, Minnesota 55603.   India.

MANN, Edward F., S.J.   Roman Catholic.   Jesuit Missions.   Director, International Apostolate, Chicago & Detroit Provinces of Jesuits. 31 years in India.   Administration in Education & Mission Government. ADDRESS: 3431 North Ashland Avenue, Chicago, Illinois 60657. 201 Dempster Street, Evanston, Illinois 60201.

MARTIN, Luke S.   Mennonite Church.   Eastern Mennonite Board of Missions and Charities.   Associate Secretary, Overseas Ministries. Evangelism & Service, Saigon, Vietnam since 1962.   ADDRESS: EMBMC, Salunga, Pennsylvania 17538.   Box 991, Saigon, Vietnam.

MBITI, John.   Anglican Church of Uganda.   Professor and Head of
Department of Religious Studies, Makerere University, Kampala, Uganda.
Visiting Professor at Union Theological Seminary, 1972-73, Broadway
at 120th Street, New York, New York 10027.   ADDRESS: Makerere University, P. O. Box 7062, Kampala, Uganda.   Kenya.

MELLIS, Charles.   UPCUSA (Membership only - not a representative).
Mission Aviation Fellowship.   President.   4 years overseas, 3 in
both halves of New Ghinea.   27 years as administrator (including
the above).   ADDRESS: (MAF) Box 2828, Fullerton, California 92633.
524 North Stadford Avenue, Fullerton, California 92631.

MINZ, Nirmal.   Gossner Evangelical Lutheran Church.   Gossner Mis-
sion Society, Berlin, Germany.   Adhyaksha (Bishop).   20 years.
ADDRESS: Gossner Evangelical Lutheran Church, Ranchi, Bihar,
India.   India.

MORONEY, William F.   Roman Catholic.   White Fathers of Africa.
Mission Education & Promotion in U.S.A.   8 years in Tanzania.
ADDRESS: 2020 West Morse, Chicago, Illinois 60645.

MULDROW, Elizabeth S. (Mrs. William F.).   United Presbyterian
Church in the U.S.A.   The Program Agency.   Missionary to Ethiopia.
U.P.C.U.S.A. Board of National Missions in New Mexico, 4 years.
ADDRESS: 701 Tulip Tree House, Bloomington, Indiana 47401.
Box 1111 Addis Ababa, Ethiopia/The Africa Office UPCUSA, 475
Riverside Drive, New York, New York 10027.

NEMER, Lawrence, S.V.D.   Roman Catholic.   Divine Word Missionaries.
Professor of Church History & Missions, Catholic Theological Union.
ADDRESS: 5401 South Cornell, Chicago, Illinois 60615.

NORDBY, Juel.   United Methodist Church.   Board of Global Ministries of United Methodist Church.   Executive Secretary for Central
and South Africa.   1951-60 Angola, District Superintendent, Theo.
Education.   ADDRESS: 475 Riverside Drive, Room 1531, New York,
New York 10027.   Norway.

NUDING, Paul.   Lutheran Church in America.   LCA Board of World
Missions.   Secretary for Missionary Personnel.   Missionary in
Japan.   ADDRESS: 231 Madison Avenue, New York, New York 10016.

PATTEN, Pat.   Roman Catholic.   Congregation of the Holy Ghost.
2nd year Theology Student.   ADDRESS: Catholic Theological Union,
5401 South Cornell, Chicago, Illinois 60615.

PAW, Louise (Mrs.).   Burma Baptist Convention. American Baptist
Board of International Ministries. Overseas Program Associate.
14 years with Burma Baptist Convention. ADDRESS: American Baptist
Churches, Valley Forge, Pennsylvania 19481. 1 Chapel Road, University P.U., Rangoon, Burma. Burma.

PEDERSEN, Ruben. Lutheran Church in America. Board of World
Missions LCA. Secretary for Africa. Missionary in Tanzania.
ADDRESS: 231 Madison Avenue, New York, New York 10016.

PENCE, Alan R.   Wycliffe Bible Translators. Vice President,
Operations. 12 years in Papua, New Guinea as Bible translator and
Director of the Wycliffe program. ADDRESS: Box 1960, Santa Ana,
California 92702.

PETERMEIER, Virgil, O.S.C.   Roman Catholic. Student for Agats
Missions in Irian Barat, Indonesia. ADDRESS: Catholic Theological
Union, 5401 South Cornell, Chicago, Illinois 60615. Crosier House
of Studies, 2620 East Wallen Road, Fort Wayne, Indiana 46825.

PIATT, Dan.   Final Advance of Scripture Translation (FAST). Evangelism and Bible Translator. ADDRESS: 1740 Westminster Drive,
Denton, Texas 76201.

RADJAGUKGUK, Robinson.   Batak Lutheran Church of Indonesia. Student
at Concordia Seminary, St. Louis. ADDRESS: Fac. Theologia, University HKBP Nommensen, Ojalan Asahan 4, Pematang Siantar, North
Sumatra, Indonesia. Indonesia.

RASOLONDRAIBE, Peri. Malagasy Lutheran Church. Division of World
Mission, The American Lutheran Church. Post graduate student at
Luther Seminary, St. Paul, Minnisota. New ministry among young
people from rural area in big cities. Evangelization to rural
people, 5 years. ADDRESS: 1588 B Eustis Street, Apartment 207,
St. Paul, Minnesota 55108. Madagascar.

READ, William R.   United Presbyterian Church USA. MARC Division,
World Vision International. 17 years in Brazil with UP-USA Church.
ADDRESS: 2125 Mar Vista Avenue, Altadena, California 91001.

REKO, H. Karl. Lutheran Church, Missouri Synod. Formerly, New
Guinea Lutheran Mission. Assistant Director of Placement, Concordia
Seminary, St. Louis. 1967-72 Teacher, St. Timothy Seminary, Wabag,
New Guinea. ADDRESS: 6445 San Bonita, St. Louis, Missouri 63105.

REUSCH, Sr. Anne. Roman Catholic. Maryknoll Sisters. Engaged in
Mission Education in USA, 2 years. 15 years in Hong Kong, mainly
pastoral work. ADDRESS: Maryknoll Sisters, Maryknoll, New York
10545.

RIGOS, Cirilo A.   United Church of Christ in the Philippines. United
Church Board for World Ministries, USA. Consultant on Mission to the
UCBWM. ADDRESS: c/o UCBWM, 475 Riverside Drive, New York, New York
10027. c/o Cosmopolitan Church, 1368 Taft Avenue, Manila, Philippine
Philippines.

ROBINSON, Milton H.   United Methodist Church. Board of Global
Ministries U.M.C.   Missionary. 23 years in Latin America, Argentina and Bolivia. ADDRESS: 102 South San Gabriel Boulevard,
Pasadena, California 91107. Route 1, Box 313, Port Lavaca, Texas
77979.

SHENK, Wilbert R.   Mennonite. Mennonite Board of Missions.
Secretary for Overseas Missions. 4 years in Indonesia. 9 years
in administration. ADDRESS: P. O. Box 370, Elkhart, Indiana 46514.

SIHITE, Wilmar. Batak Church. Graduate Student, Concordia Semin-
ary. ADDRESS: Concordia Seminary, Box 39F, 801 DeMun Avenue,
St. Louis, Missouri 63105. Nommensen University, Peniataicz
Siaritai, Sumatra, Indonesia. Indonesian.

SMITH, Joseph M.   Christian Church (Disciples of Christ).
Division of Overseas Ministries (UCMS). Missionary in China and
the Philippines. ADDRESS: P. O. Box 1986, Indianapolis, Indiana
46206.

STREET, T. Watson. Presbyterian Church in the U.S.   Executive
Secretary, Board of Missions PC-US. ADDRESS: Box 330, Nashville,
Tennessee 37202.

SUNDBERG, Rodney A.   United Presbyterian Church, U.S.A. Commission
on Ecumenical Mission & Relations. Secretary for Evangelism and
Church Development. 1940-48, China, Evangelism. 1948-56, Philippines, Evangelism & Administration. ADDRESS: Room 927, Riverside
Drive, New York, New York 10027.

TABER, Charles R.   Baptist General Conference of North America.
United Bible Societies. Translations Consultant for West Africa.
7 years Central African Republic, teacher training and school
supervision. ADDRESS: Bible Society of Ghana, P. O. Box 761,
Accra, Ghana.

TESFAI, Yacob. Evangelical Church of Eritrea, Ethiopia. Student.
ADDRESS: Lutheran School of Theology at Chicago, 1100 East 55th
Street, Chicago, Illinois 60615. P. O. Box 905, Asmara, Ethiopia.
Ethiopian.

TIPPETT, Alan R. Methodist Church of Australasia. School of World Mission, Pasadena, California. Professor of Missionary Anthropology. 20 years in Fiji Islands. 11 years in Missionary research. ADDRESS: 135 North Oakland Avenue, Pasadena, California 91101. Australian.

TRA, John, S.V.D. Roman Catholic. Divine Word Missionaries. Center for Applied Research in the Apostolate (CARA). 14 years in New Guinea. ADDRESS: 1025 Michigan Avenue NE, Washington, D. C. 20017.

VANDEVORT, Eleanor (Miss). Episcopal Church. Formerly United Presbyterian. Residence Hall Director and Reading/Study Skills Tutor at Gordon College, Wenham, Ma. 13 years Linguist/Translator in South Sudan. ADDRESS: Gordon College, Wenham, Ma.

WAGNER, C. Peter. Lake Avenue Congregational. Fuller Seminary School of World Mission. Associate Professor of Latin American Affairs. 16 years in Bolivia/Andes Evangelical Mission. ADDRESS: Box 989, Pasadena, California 91102.

WEBSTER, Warren. Conservative Baptist Church. Conservative Baptist Foreign Mission Society. General Director. 16 years in Pakistan. ADDRESS: P. O. Box 5, Wheaton, Illinois 60187.

WESTBURG, Harry. Evangelical Covenant Church. Mission Board. Missionary in Japan. ADDRESS: 5101 North Francisco Avenue, Chicago, Illinois 60625.

WINTER, Ralph D. United Presbyterian Church in U.S.A. Until recently, missionary under COEMAR. Professor, Fuller School of World Mission. Director, William Carey Library (Publications). 15 years under COEMAR. 10 years in Guatemala. ADDRESS: 135 North Oakland Avenue, Pasadena, California 91101.

PART III

Appendices

THE DECLARATION OF BARBADOS

A

For The Liberation of the Indians

The anthropologists participating in the Symposium on Inter-Ethnic Conflict in South America, meeting in Barbados* January 25-20, 1971, after analysing the formal reports of the tribal populations' situation in several countries, drafted and agreed to make pubic the following statement. In this manner, we hope to define and clarify this critical problem of the American continent and to contribute to the Indian struggle for liberation.

The Indians of America remain dominated by a colonial situation which originated with the conquest and which persists today within many Latin American nations. The result of this colonial structure is that lands inhabited by Indians are judged to be free and unoccupied territory open to conquest and colonisation. Colonial domination of the aboriginal groups, however, is only a reflection of the more generalised system of the Latin American states' external dependence upon the imperialist metropolitan powers. The internal order of our dependent countries leads them to act as colonising powers in their relations with the indigenous peoples. This places the several nations in the dual role of the exploited and the exploiters, and this in turn projects not only a false image of Indian society and its historical development, but also a distorted vision of what constitutes the present national society.

We have seen that this situation manifests itself in repeated acts of agression directed against the aboriginal groups and cultures. There occur both active interventions to "protect" Indian society as well as massacres and forced migrations from the homelands. These acts and policies are not unknown to the armed forces and other governmental agencies in several countries. Even the official "Indian policies" of the Latin American states are explicitly directed towards the destruction of aboriginal culture. These policies are employed to manipulate and control Indian populations in order to consolidate the status of existing social groups and

---

*The Barbados Symposium was sponsored jointly by the Programme to Combat Racism and the Churches Commission on International Affairs of the World Council of Churches, together with the Ethnology Department of the University of Bern (Switzerland). A report of the Symposium is in preparation.
The views expressed are those of the members of the Symposium, and not necessarily those of the co-sponsors of the Symposium.
This Declaration is WCC document PCR 1/71 (E).

classes, and only diminish the possibility that Indian society may free itself from colonial domination and settle its own future.

As a consequence, we feel the several States, the religious missions and social scientists, primarily anthropologists, must assume the unavoidable responsibilities for immediate action to halt this aggression and contribute significantly to the process of Indian liberation.

The Responsibility of the State

Irrelevant are those Indian policy proposals that do not seek a radical break with the existing social situation; namely, the termination of colonial relationships, internal and external; breaking down of the class system of human exploitation and ethnic domination; a displacement of economic and political power from a limited group or an oligarchic minority to the popular majority; the creation of a truly multi-ethnic state in which each ethnic group possesses the right to self-determination and the free selection of available social and cultural alternatives.

Our analysis of the Indian policy of the several Latin American nation states reveals a common failure of this policy by its omissions and by its actions. The several states avoid granting protection to the Indian groups' rights to land and to be left alone, and fail to apply the law strictly with regard to areas of national expansion. Similarly, the states sanction policies which have been and continue to be colonial and class-oriented.

This failure implicates the State in direct responsibility for and connivance with the many crimes of genocide and ethnocide that we have been able to verify. These crimes tend to be repeated and responsibility must rest with the State which remains reluctant to take the following essential measures:-

1)   guaranteeing to all the Indian populations by virtue of their ethnic distinction, the right to be and to remain themselves, living according to their own customs and moral order, free to develop their own culture;

2)   recognition that Indian groups possess rights prior to those of other national constitutencies. The State must recognise and guarantee each Indian society's territory in land, legalising it as perpetual, inalienable collective property, sufficiently extensive to provide for population growth;

3) sanctioning of Indian groups' right to organise and to govern in accordance with their own traditions. Such a policy would not exclude members of Indian society from exercising full citizenship, but would in turn exempt them from compliance with those obligations that jeopardise their cultural integrity;

4) extending to Indian society the same economic, social, educational and health assistance as the rest of the national population receives. Moreover, the State has an obligation to attend to those many defficiencies and needs that stem from Indians' submission to the colonial situation. Above all the State must impede their further exploitation by other sectors of the national society, including the official agents of their protection;

5) establishing contacts with still isolated tribal groups is the States' responsibility, given the dangers - biological, social and ecological - that their first contact with agents of the national society represents;

6) protection from the crimes and outrages, not always the direct responsibility of civil or military personnel, intrinsic to the expansion process of the national frontier;

7) definition of the national public authority responsible for relations with Indian groups inhabiting its territory; this obligation cannot be transferred or delegated at any time or under any circumstances.

Responsibility of the Religious Missions

Evangelisation, the work of the religious missions in Latin America also reflects and complements the reigning colonial situation with the values of which it is imbued. The missionary presence has always implied the imposition of criteria and patterns of thought and behaviour alien to the colonised Indian societies. A religious pretext has too often justified the economic and human exploitation of the aboriginal population.

The inherent ethnocentric aspect of the evangelisation process is also a component of the colonialist ideology and is based on the following characteristics:

1) its essentially discriminatory nature implicit in the hostile relationship to Indian culture conceived as pagan and heretical;

2)   its vicarial aspect, implying the reification of the Indian and
     his consequent submission in exchange for future supernatural
     compensations;

3)   its spurious quality given the common situation of missionaries
     seeking only some form of personal salvation, material or
     spiritual;

4)   the fact that the missions have become a great land and labour
     enterprise, in conjunction with the dominant imperial interests.

As a result of this analysis we conclude that the suspension of all
missionary activity is the most appropriate policy on behalf of both
Indian society as well as the moral integrity of the churches
involved. Until this objective can be realized the missions must
support and contribute to Indian liberation in the following manner:

1)   overcome the intrinsic Herodianism of the evangelical process,
     itself a mechanism of colonialisation, Europeanisation and
     alienation of Indian society;

2)   assume a position of true respect for Indian culture, ending
     the long and shameful history of despotism and intolerance
     characteristic of missionary work, which rarely manifests
     sensitivity to aboriginal religious sentiments and values;

3)   halt both the theft of Indian property by religious missionaries
     who appropriate labour, lands and natural resources as their
     own, and the indifference in the face of Indian expropriation
     by third parties;

4)   extinguish the sumptuous and lavish spirit of the missions
     themselves, expressed in various forms but all too often based
     on exploitation of Indian labour;

5)   stop the competition among religious groups and confessions for
     Indian souls - a common occurence leading to the buying and
     selling of believers and internal strife provoked by conflict-
     ing religious loyalties;

6)   suppress the secular practice of removing Indian children from
     their families for long periods in boarding schools where they
     are imbued with values not their own, converting them in this
     way into marginal individuals, incapable of living either in
     the larger national society or their native communities;

7) break with the pseudo-moralist isolation which imposes a false puritanical ethic, incapacitating the Indian for coping with the national society - an ethic which the churches have been unable to impose on that same national society;

8) abandon those blackmail procedures implicit in the offering of goods and services to Indian society in return for total submission;

9) suspend immediately all practices of population displacement or concentration in order to evangelise and assimilate more effectively, a process that often provokes an increase in morbidity, mortality and family disorganisation among Indian communities;

10) end the criminal practice of serving as intermediaries for the exploitation of Indian labour.

To the degree that the religious missions do not assume these minimal obligations they, too, must be held responsible by default for crimes of ethnocide and connivance with genocide.

Finally, we recognize that, recently, dissident elements within the churches are engaging in a conscious and radical self-evaluation of the evangelical process. The denunciation of the historical failure of the missionary task is now a common conclusion of such critical analyses.

The Responsibility of Anthropology

Anthropology took form within and became an instrument of colonial domination, openly or surreptitiously; it has often rationalised and justified in scientific langauge the domination of some people by others. The discipline has continued to supply information and methods of action useful for maintaining, reaffirming and disguising social relations of a colonial nature. Latin America has been and is no exception, and with growing frequency we note nefarious Indian action programmes and the dissemination of sterotypes and myths distorting and masking the Indian situation - all pretending to have their basis in alleged scientific anthropological research.

A false awareness of this situation has led many anthropologists to adopt equivocal positions. These might be classified in the following types:

1)   a <u>scientism</u> which negates any relationship between academic
     research and the future of those peoples who form the object
     of such investigation, thus eschewing political responsibility
     which the relation contains and implies;

2)   an <u>hypocrisy</u> manifest in the rhetorical protestation based on
     first principles which skillfully avoids any commitment in a
     concrete situation;

3)   an <u>opportunism</u> that although it may recognize the present
     painful situation of the Indian at the same time rejects any
     possibility of transforming action by proposing the need "to do
     something" within the established order. This latter position,
     of course, only reaffirms and continued the system.

The anthropology now required in Latin America is not that which
relates to Indians as objects of study, but rather that which
perceives the colonial situation and commits itself to the struggle
for liberation. In this context we see anthropology providing on
the one hand, the colonised peoples those data and interpretations
both about themselves and their colonisers useful for their own
fight for freedom, and on the other hand, a redefinition of the
distorted image of Indian communities extant in the national
society, thereby unmasking its colonial nature with its supportive
ideology.

In order to realize the above objectives, anthropologists have an
obligation to take advantage of all junctures within the present
order to take action on behalf of the Indian communities. Anthropologists must denounce systematically by any and all means cases
of genocide and those practices conductive to ethnocide. At the
same time, it is imperative to generate new concepts and explanatory
catagories from the local and national social reality in order to
overcome the subordinate situation of the anthropologists regarded
as the mere "verifier" of alien theories.

The Indian as an Agent of his own Destiny

That Indians organise and lead their own liberation movement is
essential, or it ceases to be liberating. When non-Indians pretend
to represent Indians, even on occasion, assuming the leadership of
the latter's groups, a new colonial situation is established. This
is yet another expropriation of the Indian populations'
inalienable right to determine their future.

Within this perspective, it is important to emphasise in all its historical significance, the growing ethnic consciousness observable at present among Indian societies throughout the continent. More peoples are assuming direct control over their defence against the ethnocidal and genocidal policies of the national society. In this conflict, by no means novel, we can perceive the beginnings of a pan-Latin American movement and some cases too, of explicit solidarity with still other oppressed social groups.

We wish to reaffirm here the right of Indian populations to experiment with and adopt their own self-governing, development and defence programmes. These policies should not be forced to correspond with national economic and socio-political exigencies of the moment. Rather, the transformation of national society is not possible if there remain groups, such as Indians, who do not feel free to command their own destiny. Then, too, the maintenance of Indian society's cultural and social integrity, regardless of its relative numerical insignificance, offers alternative approaches to the traditional well-trodden paths of the national society.

Barbados, 30 Janury 1971

Miguel Alberto Bartolome

Guillermo Bonfil Batalla

Victor Daniel Bonilla

Gonzalo Castillo Cardenas

Miguel Chase Sardi

Georg Grünberg

Nelly Arvelo de Jiminez

Esteban Emilio Mosonyi

Darcy Ribeiro

Scott S. Robinson

Stefano Varese

B

A meeting was held in Asunción, Paraguay, 7-10 March 1972, of
representatives of Protestant and Roman Catholic Missions working
among Indians in Latin America. The Conference was called by the
Programme to Combat Racism of the World Council of Churches, and
organized by the Movement for Evangelical Unity in Latin America
(UNELAM). Invitations went principally to member churches and
Christian Councils, but missions working independently were also
invited. The aim of the meeting was to share experiences related to
the situation of the Indian communities in Latin America, as well as
to discuss the question of the responsibility of Christian Churches
towards these people. The discussion was based on the Barbados
Declaration[1] in which a group of anthropologists from Latin America,
meeting at the beginning of 1971, was strongly critical, among other
things, of the missionary work of the Churches and called for its
suspension.

The participants in the Asunción Conference came from Argentina,
Chile, Ecuador, Columbia, Mexico, Panama, Peru and Paraguay, and
represented Anglican, Methodist, Adventist, and Catholic Churches.
In addition, the co-ordinator of the Barbados Symposium was present,
as well as two other signatories of the Declaration, two women
anthropologists from Argentina and leading members of the Paraguayan
Society for Indian Questions. Of special significance was the
active participation of several Indians from Paraguay. The representative from Panama, a Methodist minister, was himself an Indian of
the Cuna tribe. A staff member of the WCC Programme to Combat
Racism was also present.

The background of the Barbados Declaration was introduced by
extracts from documents of that meeting on the situation of the
native peoples of Latin America - documents which unfortunately had
not yet been published[2], and by a presentation by three members of

---

*This introduction was written by Karl Ernst Neisel, on the
staff of UNELAM, and is translated from the German.

[1] See "For the Liberation of the Indians," IRM, April 1971,
pp. 271-84.

[2] The full report of the Symposium is now after long delays being
published. Reviews and comments on it may be published in due
course: The Situation of the Indian in South America, Geneva, W.C.C.
S Fr. 39.50.

the Symposium. These were followed by extensive reports from those present of their experience of the work of the Churches among the Indians. The Barbados Declaration was then critically examined, with full discussion of the section concerned with Missions. The meeting agreed to publish as the Asuncion Document the convictions, demands and proposals which had been worked out in three groups and unanimously agreed. (The representative of the Mennonite Mission in Chaco had to leave the Conference early and could not give his views on the final statement.)

The meeting was given exceptional attention by the Paraguayan press. The statement was published in full by a number of papers on Sunday, 12 March. The astonishing unanimity in the fundamental theological statement is all the more notable since the Roman Catholic participants shared actively in the consultation. Difficulties arose in the discussion when it came to making judgments on particular situations. It was obvious, and was proposed in the final statement, that this All Latin American meeting should be followed by national and regional consultations in which concrete situations of conflict could be discussed in more detail.

Unfortunately a number of missions did not accept the invitation. Two evangelical mission societies working in Paraguay publicly dissociated themselves from the conference. This was all the more regrettable because the discussion took place in a very open atmosphere and because, for the work among the Indian population, the greatest possible common mind among Christian groups is unquestionably needed. It is to be hoped that at future national and regional conferences a broader confessional participation will be achieved. To bring this about, personal contact will be necessary to overcome suspicions. Agreement among Christian confessions and groups should be possible wherever concern for the people entrusted to them is given first place.

ASUNCION STATEMENT

1. Church and Mission

Missionary work is the very raison d'etre of the Church: Church and Mission are synonymous. We recognize that Christ's first command (Mt. 28:19) is to go in his name and preach the Gospel to all nations.

But since "there are so many kinds of voices in the world, and none of them is without signification" (I Cor. 14:10), the first and principal task of the authentic mission of the Church is to discover the presence of God the Savior in every people and every culture,

the place where the Gospel of Christ is incarnate - Gospel which is
at the same time a judgment on everything which dehumanizes and
destroys man.

Through Christ men are enabled to enter into the fulness of life;
for the Gospel is fulfilled when "the good news is announced to the
poor, deliverance is preached to the captives and recovery of sight
to the blind, the oppressed are set at liberty and the year of the
Lord's favor is proclaimed" (Lk. 4:18).

In obedience to Christ we have to become "as Jews to win the Jews,
and as those who are outside the law to win them that are outside
the law" (I Cor. 9:20-21), and thus to become as the natives among
the natives. At times this will lead us to bear a silent witness to
Christ, when Christianity, owing to concrete historical circumstances,
is identified with oppressive social structures causing the name of
Christ to be blasphemed. At other times we shall be compelled to
raise our voices in denunciation and to proclaim by our words and
our lives that Christ is justice and love for all, without discrimination. The Church, the symbol of salvation and the leaven of the
world, is not the refuge of the saved but a community of brethren
serving the world in the love of Christ.

2.   Mission and Colonialism

We acknowledge that there have been times when our Churches have
been inseparable from and instrumental in the enforcement of ideologies and practices of tyranny, so that, as the Scripture says,
"because of you the name of God is dishonoured among the Gentiles"
(Rom. 2:24). Notwithstanding persistent and courageous efforts for
the protection of certain Indian groups, we recognize that
historically speaking, our Churches have not succeeded in impregnat-
ing Latin American societies with a liberating Christian love, free
from discrimination of race, creed or culture.

Nevertheless, this admission of the deficiencies and mistakes of
missionary activity does not lead us to the conclusion that all
missionary activity should be brought to an end, as the Declaration
of Barbados affirms. The Church's task, in its missions to the
Indians, is basically

a) To renounce all ideologies or practices which connive at any
form of oppression, particularly when they claim to be based on
religious motives and to be justified "in the name of the Lord."

b) To denounce, in a spirit of truth, and not merely with words but with actions, every case of exploitation occurring in our national societies and in our Churches themselves, even if this involves denunciation of specific persons and institutions.

c) To proclaim with faith in the Holy Spirit Christ's Gospel, essential for the full liberation of the Indian, and thereby to liberate the Church itself, once again, to bear authentic witness.

We are convinced that in this way many of the divisions separating the Churches and Christians from one another will disappear in the unity of a truly human and profoundly Christian mission of liberation.

3.   Church and Racial Discrimination

Although racial discrimination in Latin America is concealed or denied by various devices, we are forced to admit the existence of racialism, which is demonstrated in innumerable ways, including the following:

a)   The legislation still in force in certain countries is a discriminatory and even overtly racialist legislation. In other countries, although the legislation itself is not racialist, it is a dead letter in actual fact (ownership of land, protection of native rights, civil documentation etc.).

b)   The expropriation of native lands, on the pretext that they belong to nobody, and which are seized by procedures ranging from fraud to force and even genocide.

c)   Indian questions are dealt with in a paternalistic way and even with threats, leading to exploitation, and a state of dependence and fear in the Indian.

In many cases the Church has been involved in these practices, in which racialist criteria have taken the place of those of the Gospel.

4.   The Church's Mission

We believe that now is the time for the Churches to have a frank discussion concerning the cultural situation of the Indians, problems of interracial friction, racial discrimination, spoliation of land, wage discrimination etc.

In this dialogue it is essential that the Indians themselves and
their organizations should take part, as prime agents in their own
destiny.

There should be a critical participation by specialists in the
human sciences. And the Church itself should have recourse to the
help of technical teams to evaluate its programmes and examine the
feasibility of opening up new areas of activity.

The Churches should not shrink from giving definite support to the
formation of specifically Indian organizations, and should use their
moral force, through the mass communications media, to endeavour to
spread the concept that the Indian has rights which are inalienable.

It is for the ecumenical organizations, at national and continental
level, to stimulate national or regional meetings between Latin
American bodies engaged in the struggle against racialism and/or on
behalf of the Indians. They should gather and disseminate information, and study and investigate the actual situations of the Indians,
in particular where interracial friction and indigenous religious
concepts are concerned - though without idealizing them.

It is especially recommended that, using the experience of this
conference, other national and regional conferences should now be
organized among representatives of the different Churches, which
aould carry forward the analysis of the Indian problem and of conflict situations in missionary activity, and prepare the ground for
a responsible programme.

Reprinted from The International Review of Mission, v. LXI, No. 243
(July 1972) by permission.

LANGUAGES IN THE WESTERN HEMISPHERE
Benjamin F. Elson

C

Since this consultation is interested in "frontier" situations
it will be valuable to examine the Indian population of the
Western hemisphere, for many such groups can be defined as
"frontier" from the point of view of this consultation.

The accompanying computer printout of languages in the Western
hemisphere is the result of research carried on principally by
Dr. and Mrs. Joseph Grimes of the Wycliffe Bible Translators
and sponsored by FAST, International. It has been printed
especially for the delegates to the Consultation on Frontier
Missions. The document deserves a few additional comments.

The Ethnologue, of which this document constitutes a part, was
originally conceived by Dr. Richard Pittman of the Wycliffe
Bible Translators and has gone through various editions under
his personal supervision and sponsorship. About three years
ago Dr. Pittman turned the project over to Dr. and Mrs. Grimes.
These three have had primary responsibility for gathering
together the data on languages and Bible Translation.

The purpose of the Ethnologue is to make available to those
interested, information about the languages of the world,
particularly those which do not have the Bible translated into
them.

Like all projects of this sort, this one suffers from a lack
of information in spots where one would desire more. Many
languages are listed without estimates of the number of speakers.
If there is an agency working with a group, the term "progress"
is used. There are many questions one would like to ask about
that "progress." In spite of the lacunae, it is probably the
most comprehensive information available today on extant and
recently extinct languages of this hemisphere.

There are 981 languages listed for the Western hemisphere.
However, 107 may be subtracted from that total leaving 874. The
107 are double listings or obvious errors. For example Chuj is
listed as being both in Mexico and Guatemala, Haida as being
both in Canada and the United States, etc. There is no reason
to think that these are not mutually intelligible because they
happen to fall on two sides of a geo-political border. In addition, for 228 listings the editors tell us that the languages
are either extinct or there is considerable doubt about the
viability of the group that speaks the language. This leaves
the total of 646 language names that represent viable groups
for which a special missionary enterprize might be launched.
Of this 646, 444 are listed as having already a missionary

agency working with them. This leaves 202 groups that could be
genuinely frontier situations.

It should be remembered that the purpose of the Ethnologue
and the aim of the editors is to present a picture of the
current situation and needs relative to Bible translation work.
I feel certain, therefore, that where agencies are listed it
is with this in mind. I also feel certain there are other
agencies that are not listed that may be working with various
groups but which have no interest or intention to engage in
Bible translation.

There is another way to view the situation. The concentration
of Indian groups from the point of view of population density
occurs in two major areas: Mexico-Guatemala and the Quechua-
Aymara area of South America. In Mexico, Indians are concentrated principally south of Mexico City, although there are
sizeable groups to the north and east of the city as well. In
Guatemala they are located throughout the Republic. The second
major concentration is the Quechua-Aymara population running
along the Andean Highlands from Colombia to Chile passing through
Ecuador, Peru and Bolivia. The remaining Indian groups of the
hemisphere are, comparatively small and isolated. There are, of
course, a great many groups in the Amazon basin, but they are
generally small and scattered. For example, in all of Brazil
the Indian population is probably less than one million while
the total population of Brazil is in the neighborhood of eighty
million.

One of the most difficult problems which those of us who have
been involved in a ministry to Indian peoples have encountered
has been our realization, in the past ten to fifteen years
particularly, that many groups having the same name speak divergent languages. This is particularly true of southern Mexico.
Twenty-five years ago the official listing of Indian groups in
Mexico numbered 52. However, the current printout lists 177.
This is because for major groupings like Zapoteco, Mixteco,
Chinanteco, etc. a phenomenal number of mutually unintelligible
dialects have been discovered. For example, for Zapoteco which
was once thought to be a single language, the printout lists
27 different dialects. It should be made clear that these are
not dialects, equivalent, say, of British English as opposed
to American English, but actually mutually unintelligible forms
of speech. I understand from some of the workers in these
languages that some of them are so different that between some
dialects, one recognizes only a few roots as, for example,
between English and German or French and Italian.

In groups where an agency is listed as working, I am sure we
can assume that there is a missionary witness for Jesus Christ.
Therefore, the number of truly "frontier" situations may be
relatively small.

DETERMINING FRONTIER SITUATIONS IN BIBLE TRANSLATION

D

T.P. Kehler, A.W. Bergstedt

The number of minority language groups in the world which do not have scriptures in their language is an unknown figure. The nature of language and translation introduces several dynamic factors which hinder a clear picture of the status of world Bible translation. First, use of a minority language may disappear in time because the speakers have become bilingual in a national or trade language through acculturation. This occurs when a language group is surrounded by and is in contact with the dominant language group. Secondly, language groups are interrelated. The degree of interrelation is dependent on socio-historical and geographical factors. The result is a distribution in the degree of interrelations of languages in a given geographical region. Languages range from being mutually intelligible to being completely distinct.[1,2]

There are several factors in translation which combine with linguistic factors to further complicate a definitive description of Bible translation status. Knowledge of linguistic structure and translation theory are essential factors in producing a good translation.[3] In evaluating Bible translation status on a world basis, inadequacy of translations in language groups must be taken into account. Ancient translations based on old forms of a language are often unreadable. Also, if linguistic analysis is inaccurate, the resulting translation will need revision. A revision requires incorporating current linguistic discoveries in a revised translation. In the case of closely related languages, revision of a translation completed in the related language may be sufficient. For mutually intelligible languages it is assumed the translation is readable in either language. Examples of the problems mentioned are illustrated in many cases of partial translations based on partial linguistic analysis done in the 18th or 19th century. In reality, groups such as these do not have the Bible in their language. There is a range of translation quality from completely unreadable to readable. One must take this into account in determining translation status.

These factors have been briefly discussed to bring out the following point: a set of continuously varying parameters must be dealt with in order to determine the magnitude of the Bible translation task. Therefore, statistical analysis has limited accuracy. One must keep in mind that all results are estimates based on certain presuppositions when assigning discrete values to continuous parameters. The determined number of languages in the world will vary according to definitions of mutual intelligibility and dialect differences. The determined number of translations needed on a world basis will be dependent on the researcher's definition of a readable translation.

Estimates based on a well defined procedure are possible. In the remainder of this paper we describe briefly a procedure for studying translation status. Gathering information for a tabulation of minority group Bible translation needs and activities involves three factors:

1) communication with linguists and Bible translation experts,
2) compilation of data from sources for overall consistency and review,
3) iteration (continuously reporting and correcting data).

The last item involves segmenting the data into categories. At present, a survey of some typical categories in use is given as follows: language name, alternate names and dialects, population figures (including a monolingual and bilingual breakdown), geographic and geopolitical breakdown, missionary agencies and their Bible translation activity, Bible translation publication dates (i.e. New Testament, portions, entire Bible), revision history and translators, and a Bible translation priority code. The Bible translation priority code includes the following possible entries: definite need, work in progress, reachable by another translation, needs revision, scripture available (at least the New Testament), unlikely to survive, extinct, too bilingual or need undetermined. Data is entered into these categories and then sent to experts for corrections and additions. The updated material then becomes the basis for future update. Since contributors will differ on how data is to be categorized, there will be an eventual evolution of the organized tabulation. The overall system must be improved by category changes if they are to be introduced. Eventually it is expected that the categories and the statistics in those segments will converge to a representative picture of the actual distribution of needs. The important point of this procedure is that reports with our best current descriptive data are in continual circulation for discussion and correction.

A computerized data base of the world languages is in the development stage. F.A.S.T. (Final Advance for Scripture Translation) in cooperation with the Summer Institute of Linguistics is collecting data and distributing reports on the results of collected information.[4] An example of a frontier situation in Bible translation is shown in the report on Peru given in Tables 1 and 2.[5] Table 1 illustrates the change in statistics due to updating with the addition of a new category.[6] The first column figures are from available publications as of 8/72.[7] The second column are figures taken from the updated entry (1/73) including recent survey results. The new category

added as a result of studies of the data is "reachable in another translation". It is expected that this new category will remove some statistical problems encountered previously. Consequently, as the studies
proceed, an increasingly accurate representation of the actual situation is expected.

Table 2 is a listings of the language groups of Peru in alphabetical
order according to the following categories: definite need, work in
progress, New Testament available, reachable in another translation,
too bilingual, and need uncertain or extinct.

The magnitude of the world-wide task is illustrated by the list of languages in Table 3.[8] The iterative process for every language in Papua
New Guinea is started. Data will be collected similarly for every area
of the world.

In summary, though there are many implicit difficulties in compiling
data of this nature, it is expected that a procedure of successive
approximations will coordinate the efforts of individual researchers
and organizations to produce a much clearer picture of frontier Bible
translation needs in the future. Currently data is on file for over
5,000 language groups. An updating procedure for this data is currently in progress.

TABLE 1

STATUS OF BIBLE TRANSLATION - PERU, SOUTH AMERICA

	PRE-UPDATE (8/72)	UPDATED FIGURE (1/73)
Number of Languages	60	72
Definitely Need Translation	7	15
Number with New Testament	3	6
Number with Portions (excludes those with NT)	32	30
[1]Work in Progress	34	28
[2]Too Bilingual	5	7
Reachable in Another Translation	1	12
Uncertain	10	5
[3]Extinct	1	

* *

1. Categories such as NT and work in progress over lap in 1 case where
    a modern language version is in preparation.
2. A new category, added since the S.T.I.B. report.
3. Listed under Too Bilingual.

TABLE 2

LANGUAGE GROUPS WITH A DEFINITE NEED FOR TRANSLATION

NAME	POPULATION	REGION AND REMARKS
Campa, Cachumasheri Campa, Ucayali Mayos	500–1,000 5,000	Closely related to Machiguenga Ucayali, Pachitea, and tributaries. Between Tapiche and Blanca. Recent attempt to contact unsuccessful.
Morunahua	150	Headwaters of Embira. Contact not established – hostile.
Another Panoan language		Manu Park, Pamagua River. Area is not open at present.
Quechua, Cerro de Pasco Quechua, Paztaza	10,000	Closely related to Junin Quechua. Northern jungle, SIL plans to begin work March 1973.
Quechua, Ferrenaja Quechua, Huancayo Quechua, Huanuco	10,000	Lambayeque region. Huanuco area. Have portions. Several dialects will need adaptations.
Quechua, Yanyos Remos		At least one edition needed. Between Tapiche and Callaria. Also in Brazil. No contact but some recent leads.
Stone-Axe People	100	Highly nomadic: Parus, Tahuananu, and Piedras Rivers. Contact not esta- blished – fearful.
Taushiro	12	Off Tigre River. Quite monolingual S.I.L. beginning.
Yaminahua=Nishinahua		Huacapistea and Manu. S.I.L. needs to allocate there ASAP. Related to Jaminahua of Brazil where NTM work but separate translation seems necessary.

387

TABLE 2

LANGUAGE GROUPS WITH WORK IN PROGRESS

NAME	POPULATION	AGENCY	REGION AND REMARKS
Achual=Maina	2,000–3,000	SIL	Pastaza and Corrientes. Portions of NT ready to print. Different from Jivaro Ecuador.
Amahuaca	2,000	SIL	Eastern Huacapistea River area. Also in Brazil. Portions printed in 1963.
Amarakaeri=Amarakaire		SIL	
Amuesha=Amuese, Amueixa, Amoishe, Amagues	4,000	SIL	Central and Eastern Pasco Region and Eastern Junin. Portions of Scripture published in 1956.
Andoque	Very few	Independent	Also in Colombia.
Arabela=Chiripuno?, Chiripunu	105	SIL	Tributary of Napo. Portions of Scripture have been published.
Bora=Mirana		SIL	Northeast Yaguas River area. Also in Colombia. Portions published in 1962.
Campa, Pajonal	3,000	SIL	Central Gran Pajonal area. Closely related to other Campa and Machiguenga.
Candoshi=Shapra, Morato	2,000	SIL	Amazonas. Portions 1958.
Capanahua=Kapanawa	400	SIL	Tapiche-Buncuyo Rivers. Portions published in 1968.

LANGUAGE GROUPS WITH WORK IN PROGRESS, CONTINUED

NAME	POPULATION	AGENCY	REGION AND REMARKS
Cashibo=Cacataibo	1,000	SIL	Central and Southwest of Pucallpa. Portions 1964.
Cashinahua=Kaxinawa	500	SIL	Also in Brazil. Portions published.
Chayahuita	2,000	SIL	Northwest and south of Barranca. Portions published in 1965.
Culina=Madija	2,000?	SIL	Purus and also Brazil. Portions published in 1967.
Huitoto, Muinane	1,500?	SIL	Northeastern Ampiyacu River area. Also in Colombia. Portions Mark, Acts 1961.
Huitoto, Murui	200	SIL	Northern Putumayo River region. Portions published in 1963.
Machiguenga	5,000	SIL	East Central Urubamba River area. Portions published in 1962.
Mayoruna	500	SIL	Also in Brazil.
Nomatsiguenga	1,000-2,000	SIL	South Central Junin Region. Portions published in 1969. Closely related to other Campa and Machiguenga.
Quechua, Ancash	125,000	SIL	Ancash. Portions published in 1946. Work in progress. Several dialects included which will need adapted translations.

LANGUAGE GROUPS WITH WORK IN PROGRESS, CONTINUED

NAME	POPULATION	AGENCY	REGION AND REMARKS
Quechua, Ayacucho		SIL	Southwestern Ayacucho region. NT published in 1958. SIL is working in literacy and a popular version.
Quechua, Junin		SIL	Central Junin region. Portions published in 1954. Closely related to Cerro De Pasco Quechua.
Quechua, San Martin		SIL	Portions published.
Sharanahua=Marinahua, Chandinahua, Marinawa, Mastanahua	200	SIL	Also in Brazil.
Shipibo=Conibo= Pisquibo		SIL, SAM	Northeastern Middle Ucayali River area. Portions published in 1954. Three mutually intelligible dialects.
Ticuna=Tikuna, Tukuna	16,000	SIL	Northeastern Amazon River region. Also in Colombia. Portions published in 1964.
Urarina=Shimacus	2,000	SIL	
Yagua	2,000	SIL	Northeastern Amazon River region. Portions published in 1964.

TABLE 2

LANGUAGE GROUPS WITH THE NEW TESTAMENT

NAME	POPULATION	AGENCY	REGION AND REMARKS
Aguaruna	12,000	SIL	Located in Western upper Maranon River area. Had portions in 1942—NT ready to print (1973).
Campa, Ashaninca	15,000	SIL, SAM and MEN.	Tambo and tributaries. Closely related to other Campa, and Machiguenga. NT in 1972.
Huambisa	5,000	SIL	Northwestern Lower Maranon River area. Had portions since 1965—NT is ready to print (1973).
Piro	1,500	SIL	East Central Urubamba River area. NT 1960.
Quechua, Ayacucho		SIL	Southwestern Ayacucho region. NT 1958. SIL is working in literacy and on a popular version.
Quechua, Cuzco		EUSA	Central Cuzco region, NT 1947.

TABLE 2

LANGUAGE GROUPS REACHABLE IN ANOTHER TRANSLATION

NAME	POPULATION	AGENCY	REGION AND REMARKS
Angotero=Enoabellado and Secoya	500?		Northern Peru and Ecuador. Can use Secoya translation in Ecuador.
Aymara		ABS	Puno. Translation being done in Bolivia by ABS.
Campa Pereñe	2,000	SIL	Amazonas. Needs some work in this language.
Huarayo=Esse' ejja	Very few		Work in progress in Bolivia.
Isconahua	17 or more		Callaria River. Most closely related to **Shipibo**.
Manchineri Piro	200?		Acre. Mark published. Work terminated in Peru.
Mastanahua of Sharanahua	150		**Purus. Mutually intelligible with Sharanahua.**
Ocaina	100 or less	SIL	Northeastern Pebas area. Also in Colombia. Portions published in 1966. SIL work terminating.
Orejon=Coto	200	SIL	Northeastern Ampiyuca River area. Portions 1967. SIL work about to terminate.
Quechua, Andahuaylas			Mutually intelligible with Quechua, Ayacucho.
Quechua, Huancavelica			Need to determine the possibility of area revision of exisiting NT. Mutually intelligible with Quechua, Ayacucho.
Quechua, Santa Rosa			Napo River region. Can use translation of Ecuadorian Jungle Quechua.

TABLE 2

LANGUAGES WHICH ARE TOO BILINGUAL TO NEED A TRANSLATION

NAME	POPULATION	AGENCY	REGION AND REMARKS
Andoa	2-3?		2 or 3 in Ecuador (See Zaparo). Bilingual in Spanish and Quechua.
Chamicuro	150		Bilingual in Spanish.
Cocama=Kokama	10,000	SAM, ABWE	Northeastern Lower Ucayali River area. Portions published in 1963. SIL work has terminated because speakers are fairly bilingual.
Iquito			Northern Nanay River area. Portions (Mark) published in 1963. SIL work terminated because of widespread use of Spanish.
Jebero=Xebero, Chebero			Portions published in 1959. SIL work terminated because of widespread use of Spanish.
Omagua			Almost extinct. All are bilingual in Spanish.
Resigaro	4		Bilingual in Ocaina and/or Huitoto.

TABLE 2

LANGUAGE GROUPS WITH UNCERTAIN NEED

NAME	POPULATION	REGION AND REMARKS
Jagara	5,000	Tupe. May all be bilingual.
Masco=Mashco Dialects: Huachipaire, Inopari, Sapiteri, Toyeri, Amarakaeri		Eastern Yacu and Acre River area. Also in Brazil. Portions in 1960. Closely related to Amarakaeri and some are quite bilingual.
Quechua, Chachapayas		
Quechua, Cajamarca		
Quechua, Ica		

TABLE 3

LANGUAGES OF PAPUA NEW GUINEA[8]

ABAGA
ABAU=GREEN RIVER
ABELAM=MAPRIK
ADJORA = ADJORIA
AEKA = AIGA
AGA BEREFO
AGAMA = YERIPA, YAREPA, YERIBA
AGARABI = AGARABE
AIOME
AION = PORAPORA
AKOLET
AKRUKAY
ALAMBLAK
ALATIL = ARUOP ARU, ERU
ALAUGAT
AMAIMON
AMANAB
AMBASI = TAIN-DAWARE
AMELE = FUAZ
AMI
AMPALE = AMPELE, WAJAKES, WOJOKESO
AMTO
ANDARUM
ANEM
ANGAATAHA = LANGIMAR, NANGAMA
ANGAL HENENG,SOUTH
ANGAL HENENG, WEST = AUGU
ANGAL, EAST = MENDI
ANGAUA
ANGGOR = WATAPOR, WATAPU, SENAGI
ANGORAM
ANOR
ARAFUNI
ARAPESH, BUMBITA = MUHIANG
ARAPESH, MOUNTAIN
ARAPESH, SOUTHERN
ARAWE ARAWE = PILILO
ARIGIBI
ARINUA = ARINWA, HEYO
ARONA = AROMA, GALOMA
AROP
ASARO
ASAT
ATA
ATEMBLE = ATEMPLE-APRIS

ATO
AU
AUNALEI = ONELE, ONI, SETA, SETI
AURAMA = TUROHA, URI
AUYANAAUYANA = KOSENA
AWA
AWAR = NUBIA
AWARA
AWIN = AIWIN
AZERA = ADZERA, ATZERA, ACIRA
BAGASIN
BAHINEMO = GAHOM, WOGU
BAIBAI
BAINING
BALI-VITU
BAM
BAMU = IOWA
BANAROBANARO= PORAPORA, BANAR
BANONI
BAO
BARAI
BAREJI = BAREDJI
BARIAI
BARIM
BÁROK   = KOMALU, KANAPIT, KULUBI
BARUGA
BARUYA = BARUA
BAU
BEBELI = BENAULE
BEMBI
BENABENA
BEPOUR
BIAKA
BIANGAI
BIBASA
BIBLING
BIMIN
BINANDERE
BINUMARIEN = BINUMARIAN, BINAMARIR
BISIS
BITARA
BIWAT = MUNDUGUMOR
BIYOM
BOGATI
BOIKIN = BOIKEN, NUCUM, YANGORU

BOLA
BONGU
BONKIMAN
BOSILEWA
BOSMAN = BOSNGUN
BRERI = KUANGA
BUANG BUANG = MAPOS, MAPOS BUANG
BUDIBUD
BUINBUIN = TELEI, RUGARA
BUJI = BOJEBUJI = BOJE, BUGI
BUKAUA = BUKAWA
BULU
BUNA
BUNABUN = BUNUBUN, BUBUBUN
BUGAIN
BURUM = BULUM
BUSA
BWAIDOGA
CHAMBRI
CHENAPIAN
CHUAVE
DAGA
DAHATING
DAIAMUNI = DEAMUNI, DAIOMUNI
DANGAL
DAONDA
DEDUA = DEDUAE
DEGENAN
DIA = ALU
DIBIASU
DIMAR = BOSKIEN, BOSIKEN
DIODIO
DOBU
DOMU = DOM
DOMUNG
DONA
DORIRI
DUAU
DUNA
EDAWAKI
EIVO
ELKEI
EMERUM
EMIRA EMIRA = MUSSAU, MUSAU
ENDANGEN = ENDANGAN
ENGA = ENGA-KYAKA
EREWA
FAIWOL = FAIWOLMIN FAIWOL
FAS
FASU

FINUNGWAN
FOI = KUTUBU, FOE, FOI-I, MUBI RIVER
FORABA
FORAN = MIS-KEMBA, WAGI
FORE
FUYUGEFUYUGE = FUJUGE, FUYUGHE
GABIANO
GADSUP
GAHUKU
GAIKUNTI
GAINA
GAKTAIGAKTAI = MALI
GAL = BAIMAK, WEIM
GAMA = PIRUPIRU
GAMEI = GAMAI, BOROI
GANATIGANATI = KENATHI, AZIANA
GANGLAU
GANIMARUPU
GAREA
GARUH = ARINI, BAWAIPA, BUTELKUD-GU
GARUS = ATE, EM
GASMATA
GAWIGL = KAUIL GAWIGL = KAUIL, TAM
GEDAGED GEDAGED = GRAGED, SIAR, SIA
GENAGANE = GENOGANI
GENDE
GIBAIO
GIMI
GIRA
GIRI = KIRE-PUIRE
GITUA = GITOA, KELANA
GOBASI
GOGODALA = GOGODARA
GOPE = ERA RIVER, PAIA, BAIA
GOROVA
GOROVU
GUHU-SAMANE = PAIAWA, TAHARI, MURI
GUMASI
GUMINE = GOLLUM, GOLIN, MARIGL
GUSAP = YANKO WAN, BIAPIM
GUWOT = GUWET
HAHON = HANON
HALIA = HANAHAN, TULON, TASI
HAMTAI = KAPAU, KUKUKUKU, INAUKINA
HAROI
HAURA = VAILALA, KEURU, BAIBALA, EL
HEWA
HOP
HOTE = HO'TEI, HOTEC, YAMAP
HULA

HULI = HULI-HULIDANA
HUNJARA HUNJARA = HUNTJARA, KOKO
IATMUL = BIG SEPIK
IBUKAIRU
IDIDA
IDNE
IKUNDUN = MINDIVI
IMANDI
INDINOGOSIMA = ME'EK, MEHEK
IPIKOIIPIKOI = IPIKO
IPILI = IPILI-PAIELA
IRUMU
ISEBE = BALAHAIM, PANIM
ITAEM
IWAM, SEPIK = YAWENIAN
IWAMIWAM = MAY RIVER
JABEM = LAULABU, JABIM
KAIAN
KAIBU KAIBU = KAIPU
KAIEP
KAIKOVU
KAIRI = GAIRI
KAIRIRU
KAITAROLEA
KAIWA
KAKOA
KAKUNA = MAMUSI
KALIKU
KALOKALO
KAMANOKAMANO = KAMANO-KATE
KAMASA
KAMASAU
KAMBAIRA
KAMBERATARO
KAMBOT
KAMNUM = AUTU
KANDAS = KING
KANINGRA
KANITE
KAPIN = SAMBIO, TAIAK, TAIEK, KATUM
KAPRIMAN = WASARE
KARA = LEMAKOT, LEMUSMUS
KARAM KARAM = AFORO
KARAMI
KARANGI
KARAUMA
KARE
KAREMA = KAIPI, UARIPI, MILAREPU
KARUA KARUA = GARUA, XARUA
KASEREKASERE = WAILEMI

KASUA = BOSAVI
KATE = KAI, KATEDONG
KATIATI
KAVWOL = KAWOL KAVWOL = KAWOL, KAU
KAWACHA
KELAKELA = GELA
KENEDIBI
KEOPARA = KEAPARA, KEREPUNU
KEREWO = KEREWA, KEREWA-GOARI
KERIAKA
KEWA, EAST
KEWA, SOUTH = POLE
KEWA, WEST = PASUMA
KEWAH = KEWA'
KIARI
KIBULIKIBULI = KIBUDI
KILENGE
KILMERA = KILMERI
KINALAKNA
KIRIWINA
KIS
KIWAI, COAST
KIWAI, DOUMORI
KIWAI, MADUDUWO
KIWAI, WABADA
KIWAIBORA
KOBON
KOIARI
KOIARI, MOUNTAIN
KOITA
KOKILAKOKILA   DORAM
KOL
KOLOM
KOMBA
KOMBIO
KOMISANGA
KOMUTU
KONOMALA = MULIAMA, NOKON
KOPO-MONIA
KORAK
KORAPE = KORAFI, KWARAFE, OKEINA
KORIKI = PURARI, EVORRA, EVORA, KAU
KOSORONG
KOVAI
KRISA
KUANUAKUANUA = TOLAI
KUBE
KUKUYA
KUMAI
KUMAN KUMAN = CHIMBU

KIMDAURON
KUMUKIO
KUNI
KUNIMAIPA
KUNUA = KONUA
KURADA = NUAKATA
KUTO = PANARAS
KWALE
KWANGAKWANGA = GAWANGA
KWARE
KWATO
KWOMA
KWOMTARI
LABU = LABU', LABO
LAEWOMBA = LAEWAMBA, LAIWOMBA
LAMOGAI
LAUISARANGA = LAU'U
LAVATBURA-LAMUSONG
LAVONGAILAVONGAI = DANG
LEMIO
LERON
LIHIR = LIR
LOBODALOBODA = ROBODA
LOS NEGROS
LOTE
LOU-BALUAN-PAM
LUGITAMA = PAHI, WANSUM
LUKEP = SIASI, SIASSI, TOLOKIWA
MADAK
MAI-HEA-RI = MAIHIRI
MAILU
MAIMAI
MAIPUAMAIPUA = VAIMURU, KAIMARI
MAIROIVA
MAISAN = MAISIN
MAKARIM
MALALAMAI
MALAS
MALASANGA = SIGABAC
MALEK
MALEU
MALON = MALOL, MALOLO
MAMAA = MAMA
MANAGALASIMANAGALASI = MANAGULASI
MANAMBU
MANGA = MANGA BUANG, KAIDEMUI
MANGAP
MANUBARA
MANUGORO
MAOP

MAPE
MAR
MARA
MARALANGO
MARALIINAN = MARALINAN, WATUT
MARI
MARING = MARENG, YOADABE-WATOARE
MASEGIMASEGI = MANGSENA, MASEKI, MA
MATARU
MAWAK
MAWAN
MEDLPAMEDLPA = MELPA, HAGEN
MEKEO = MEKEO-KOVIO, KOVIO
MENGEN
MENI
MENYE = MENYAMA, MENYANIYA
MERA MERA = UBILI
METAN
METRU = ALU, GALU
MIANMIN
MIDSIVINDI
MIGABAC = MIGABA'
MIKAREW
MIKARUMIKARU = DARIBI, MIKAURU, ELU
MINANIBAI = MAHIGI
MINDIK
MINDIRI
MINENDON = MENANDON
MINI
MISIMAMISIMA-PANEATI = PANAIETI, PA
MITMIT
MOEWEHAFEN
MOKARENG
MOMARE = MOMALE, MOMOLE
MOMOLILI
MORAFA
MORIGI = MORIGI ISLAND MORIGI = MO
MORIMA = MOLIMA
MOROMIRANGA
MOTU = TRUE MOTU
MOTU, POLICE = MOTU
MUGIL = BUNU, SAKER
MUGUMUGU
MUKAWA
MUMENG
MUNIWARA = MAMBE
MUNKIP
MUP
MURIK
MUSAK

MUSAR = AREGEREK
MUSOM
MUYUW = MUYU MUYUW = MUYU, MUYUA
MWATEBU
NABAK
NAGATMAN
NAGOVIS NAGOVISI = SIBBE
NAHOA NAHOA = TAKU
NAHU
NAKAMA
NAKANAI NAKANAI = OUKA, MAUTUTU, LO
NAKE = ALE
NAKGATAI
NALIK = LUGAGON, FESOA, FESSOA
NAMBIS, SOUTH COAST
NAMBO
NAMUNI
NANKINA
NARAK = KANDAWO, GANJA NARAK = KAN
NASIOI
NAUNA = NAUNE
NEGIRA
NEK
NEKGINI
NEKO
NEMBI
NEMEYAM
NENGAYA
NGAING
NGALA = KARA, SOGAP, SWAGUP
NII
NISSAN
NOMANE
NOMU
NONDIRI
NORTH COAST CENTRAL
NORTH COAST CENTRAL ISLANDS
NOTSI
NOTUNOTU = EWAGE
NUK
NUKU
NUMANGGANG
OBI
OGANIBI
OKSAPMIN
OMIE = AOMIE
OMONK = UNANK
ONO
ORIGANAU
ORIOMOORIOMO = BINE, KUNINI, GIDRA

ORLEI = OLO
OROKAIVA = ORAKAIVA
OROKOLO OROKOLO = ELEMA, KAIRU-KAUR
OSUM
OYANA
PAK-TONG
PALEI
PANARAS
PAPAPANA
PAPITALAI
PARAWEN PARAWEN = PARA
PASISMANUA = KAULONG, KOWLONG
PATPATAR = GELIK, PALA, PATPARI
PAWAIA = PAVAIA, SIRA
PAY = BANARA, DAGOI, HATZ FELDHAFEN
PAYNAMAR
PELIKAWA
PEPEHAPEPEHA = EME-EME, HEI, OBERI
PETATS
PIDGIN = NEO MELANESIAN, NEW GUINEA
PIKIWA
PILA = BONAPUTA-MOPU, SUARU
PIU = SANBIAU, LANZOG, KURUKO
POLOPA
PONDOMA
PORAPORA
POROME = POROMI, KIBIRI, KAI-IRI
PULIE
RAMBUTYO
RAO = ANNABERG, RAO BRERI
RAUTO = ROTO
RAWA = RAUA
REMPI = REMPIN, A'E, EREMPI
ROINJI = GALI, BILIAU
ROMKUN = ROMKUIN
RORO
ROTOKAS
RUGO = ROGO
RURUHI'IP = RURUHIP, YA'UNK, YAHANG
SAEP
SAIPA
SAKAM
SAKE = SAHE
SAKI = TURUTAP, YAKIBA
SALT = SALT-YUI, SALT-IUI
SAMBU = SEIM
SAMOSAMO-KUBO
SANIO SANIO = SANIO-HIOWE
SAPOSA
SARUGA

SASENG
SAU SAU = SAMBERIGI, SANABERIGI
SAUK
SAWOS = TSHWOSH
SELEPET SELEPET = SELEPE
SENE
SENGAM
SENGSENG - ASENGSENG
SEPEN
SEPIK PLAINS
SERKI
SESASESA = MAMISU, SONGU
SETAUI KERIWA
SETIALI
SEWA BAY
SIALUM
SIANE
SIARSIAR = LAMBON, LAMSSA
SIMBARI
SIMOG
SINAGEN = GALU
SINAGORO = SINAUGORO
SINASINA
SINDAMON
SINSAURU
SIO = SIGABAC
SIPOMASIPOMA = SIBOMA
SIRAK
SIRASIRA
SIROI SIROI = SUROI
SIWAI = MOTUNA
SOKOROK
SOLOS
SOM
SOUTH COAST INLAND
SOWANDA
SUA
SUAIN
SUAU
SUENA SUENA = YEMA, YARAWE, YARAWI
SUGANGA
SUI
SUKI
SUKURUM
SULKA
SUMARIUP
SUMAU = KARI
SURSURUNGA = HINSAL, KINSAL
TABAR
TABRIAK

TAGA
TAGULA
TAIRORA
TAKALUBI = TAKARUBI
TAMAN
TAMI
TANGGA = TANCA, ANIR
TANGU = TANGGUM
TANGUAT
TANI = BANARA, WAGIMUDA
TAO-SUAME
TATE = TATI, LORABADA, LOU
TATOTO
TAUADETAUADE = GOILALA
TAULILTAULIL-BUTAM
TAVARA = TAWARA, TAVORA
TAWI-PAU
TEBERA
TELEFOL = TELEFOMIN, TELEFOLMIN
TENIS = TENCH
TEOP
TEREBU = TEREPU, TURUPU
TIANG
TIDITIDI = TEDI
TIFAL = TIFHLMIN
TIGAK = OMO
TIMBE
TINPUTZ = TIMPUTSTINPUTZ = TIMPUTS
TOARIPI = MOTUMOTU
TOBO
TOGO
TONG ISLAND
TORAU TORAU = ROROVANA
TORRICELLITORRICELLI = LOU
TROBRIANDS
TUAMTUAM = TUOM
TUBETUBE
TULU
TUMARA
TUMIE = TUMUIP, TOMOIP, TOMOYP
TUMLEO
TUTAKO
UBIR = UBIRI, KUBIRI
UFIM
ULINGAN = MORO-SAPRA-ULINGAN
UMAIDAI = TURAMARUBI, TURAMA RIVER
UMAIROF = MORUBANMIN, SISIMIN
URAMA KAA, IWAINU, URAMA-IWAINU
URATURAT = URAKIN
URI VEHEES

URIGINA = URIGINAU
URIMO
URIMURIM = KALP
URUAVA
USARUFA = USURUFAUSARUFA = USURUFA
USIAI, NORTH COAST = MANUS, MOANUS
USIAI, SOUTH COAST
USINO = KARI
UTU
UVOL
VANIMO
VEHES = BUASI
VIVIGANI = VIVIGANA, IDUNA
WADAGINAN = WADAGINAMB
WAFFA
WAGUMI
WAHGI
WAIMA
WAISERA = OWENIA, OWENDA, WAIJARA
WAMAS
WAMPUR
WAMSAK = WOMSAK
WANAMBRE = VANAMBERE
WANAP = KAYIK
WANTOAT
WANUMA
WAPIWAPI = WAPE
WARIS
WASHKUK
WASKIA = WOSKIA, VASKIA
WATAKATAUI
WATALUMA
WATAM = MARANGIS
WATIFAWATIFA = WATIWA
WEDAU = WEDAUN WEDAU = WEDAUN
WERI = WELI, WELE

WEST COAST
WIRU = WITU
WOGAMUSIN WOGAMUSIN = WONGAMUSIN
WOM WOM = WAM
WORIN
WOWONGA
YABEN
YABIYUFA
YABONG
YAGARIA YAGARIA = KAMI
YAGAWAK
YAGWOIA
YAKAMUL
YAMALELE = IAMALELE
YAMBES
YAPUNDA = REIWO
YAREBA
YAUAN
YAUGIBA
YEGA, GONA
YEGA, OKEINA = CAPE NELSON
YEKORA
YELE = YELEJONG, ROSSEL ISLAND
YELOGU
YERAKAI
YESSAN-MAYO YESSAN-MAYO = MAYO, MAY
YIL
YIMAS
YOIDIK
YONGGOM = YONGOM
YUBANAKOR
YURI
ZANOFIL
ZIA = LOWER WARIAZIA = LOWER WARIA
ZIMAKANI, BAGWA = BAEGWA, DEA

REFERENCES AND FOOTNOTES

1. Greenberg, Joseph. 1956. The measurement of linguistic
    diversity. Language. 32:109-115.
2. Grimes, Joseph E. 1964. Measures of linguistic divergence.
    Proceeding of the Ninth International Congress of Linguists.
    Hague. Mouton.
3. Nida, Eugene A. 1964. Toward a science of translating.
    Netherlands. E.J. Brill.
4. F.A.S.T. does not make final linguistic decisions regarding
    entries into the data base; this is done at the present
    time by the principle researchers of S.I.L.
5. This data is from G. Elder, Director of S.I.L. Peru.
6. The changes indicate the inaccuracy of the collecting procedure
    along with new available information.
7. Pittman, R.S. Ed. 1969. ETHNOLOGUE. Santa Ana. Wycliffe
    Bible Translators.
8. Prepared from ETHNOLOGUE listings from the computer data
    base (8/72).

ABBREVIATIONS

ABS	American Bible Society
ABWE	Association of Baptists for World Evangelism
EUSA	Evangelical Union of South America
F.A.S.T.	Final Advance of Scripture Translation
MEN	Mennonite
NT	New Testament
SAM	South American Mission
SIL	Summer Institute of Linguistics
STIB	Scripture Translation Information Bank

Dr. Kehler is Research Consultant at F.A.S.T. International,
Denton, Texas and Adjunct Assistant Professor, University of
Texas at Arlington for the Summer Institute of Linguistics.

Alan Bergstedt, a former missionary in the Philippines, is now
Administrative Director of the Final Advance of Scripture
Translation (F.A.S.T.) in Denton, Texas.

REFLECTIONS ON MISSIONS
Elizabeth Elliot Leitch

E

First of all, though the world changes and conditions under which
mission work must be carried on change continously, the mandate of
Christ does not change. It is relevant and inescapable. We have
the good news. It is meant for everyone. It is our business to
see that it gets to them.

As a former missionary to "primitive frontier peoples" I am sure
that the Gospel is meant for them as much as it is meant for me.
They are, perhaps, "closer" to the Kingdom in that they are not so
complicated as highly civilized people, and therefore may be called
more childlike. Childlikeness is a condition for entering that
Kingdom, as Jesus made clear. I have seen some Indian peoples who
seem ready at once to swallow anything told them, including the
Gospel. I am not one to leap to conclusions regarding the degree
of spiritual progress. That, it seems to me, is a thing only God
is qualified to assess. But I am ready to believe that He does,
in His own way, break through and reveal Himself, not only through
but also apart from the conscious witness of the missionary.

Witnessing, I believe, is primarily a matter of knowing something
other people don't know. (If I am standing on a street corner when
there is a smash-up, I am, willy-nilly, a witness. I may not be
called upon to testify in court, but I am nevertheless a witness.)
If God has brought me to a knowledge of Himself, I am His witness.
I must keep on learning to know Him. This is the first task of the
missionary. Through my experience of Him, through the Word which
I have in my hands, and through the unseen work of the Holy Spirit,
God accomplished His mission on earth.

Identification was a very big word in missions when I was young.
I have identified in varying manners and degrees with several different kinds of people who are foreign to me. Through that effort
(made at first because I thought they wanted me to identify) I
learned to appreciate them as people--learned why they do what
they do, why they live as they live. It was an immensely important

experience for me as an individual, but as for the effect it had on
them I can say very little. Nothing--repeat, NOTHING--bridges the
gap between me as a foreigner, (a freak, an oracle, and a liability)
and them. I am forever and incorrigibly a foreigner, and no effort
to live as they live, eat what they eat, dress as they dress, or
hold my fork or my chopsticks properly will ever serve to make them
or me forget that I am <u>not</u> one of them. But the fact that I try
may show them something of my attitude of honest friendliness. It
may, after a while, offend them. They are quick to accept differences, and are sometimes offended by what is so obviously unnatural
or fake. I lived, for example, in an Auca house--a house without
walls or floors or funiture. The Aucas themselves had built it for
me and of course I was grateful for it. But it was not easy for me.
I happen to like privacy, a concept the Aucas did not understand. I
like neatness, organization, and furniture! When the time came for
me to start teaching my little daughter her school work by correspondence course, living without walls made it an impossibility. She
had no place to write, no place to keep her books where the crickets
would not eat them, no way of keeping six Indians from hanging over
her shoulder and asking "What are you doing? Why? Why won't you
come out and swim with us? What is that?" I decided we needed a
house with walls. I got some Quichua Indians to come and build us
one, and the Aucas loved it. It made life much more interesting
for them for they had more things to look through and examine and
ask questions about. It made no difference whatsoever in their
attitude toward <u>me</u>. They had not thought of me as an Auca when I
lived as they live. They thought no less of me when I lived in a
foreign kind of house. And, incidentally, life was made infinitely
easier and happier for me.

I learned that it is not always possible, let alone desirable, for
a missionary to interpret how the Gospel ought to work in a given
culture. We hold in our hands a treasure--the Word of God. We try
to show to others that God has something to say to them. If they
receive it, God Himself will interpret His message. It will take
effect in ways we cannot predict. Many mistakes have been made,
I fear, by missionaries who insist that their job includes the
definition of Christianity in terms of a particular culture. Chris-
tianlty can and must change cultures--of course. But the Missionary
is not Christ. He is only a servant.

And this brings me to the whole question of attitude. We are "your
servants for Jesus' sake." I believe that every problem of foreign-
ness, of cultural shock, of manners and customs can be resolved if
the missionary remembers his position. He lays down his life, first
for Christ, to do with as He wills, then for the people to whom
Christ sends him. He asks for no regard save that of knowing that

he does the will of the Father. "What kind of thanks do I get?" is
a question which may only be answered with "What kind do you expect?"

"Except a corn of wheat fall into the ground and die it abideth
alone. But if it dies, it bringeth forth much fruit."